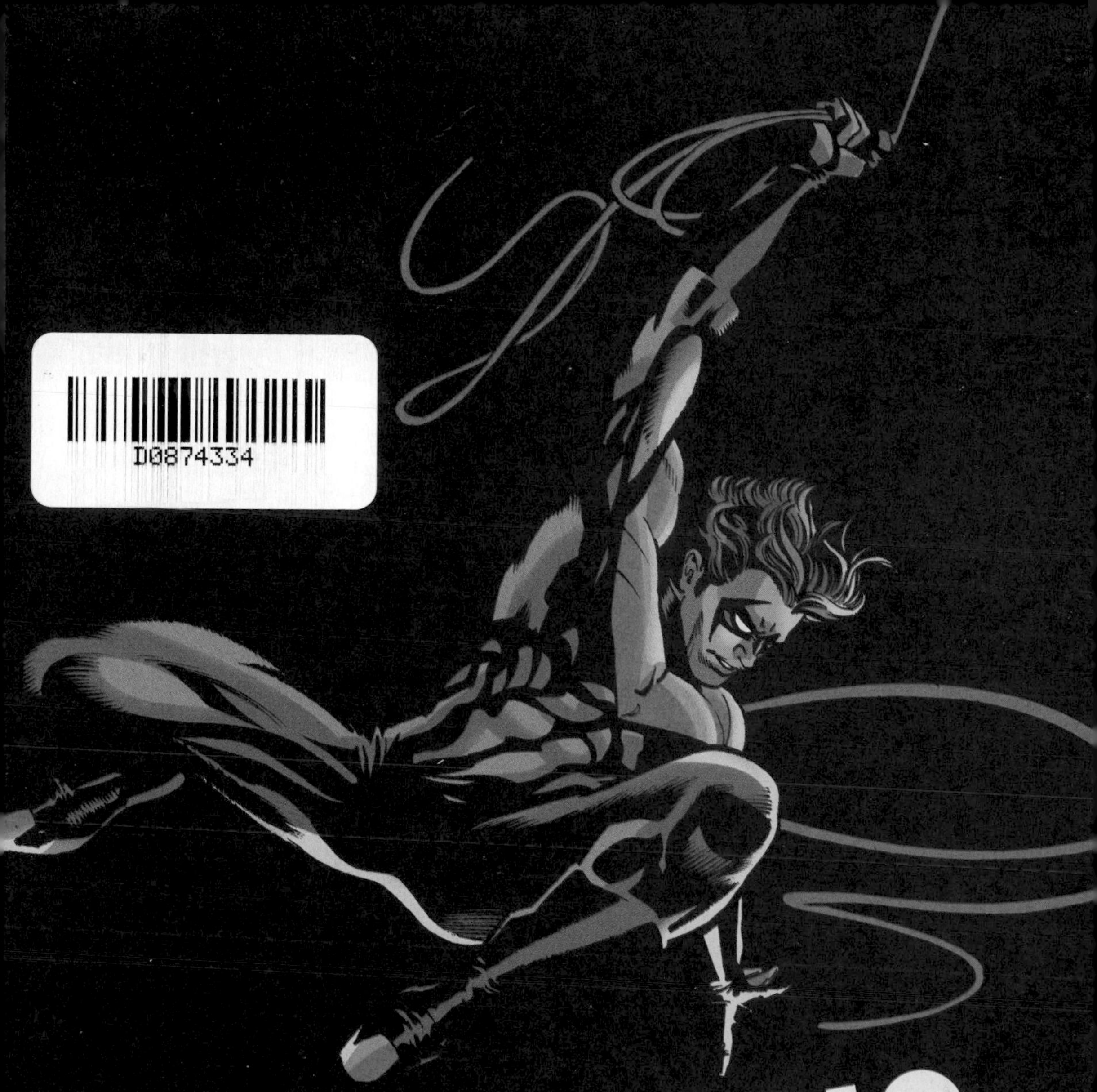

# NIGHTWING BIG GUNS

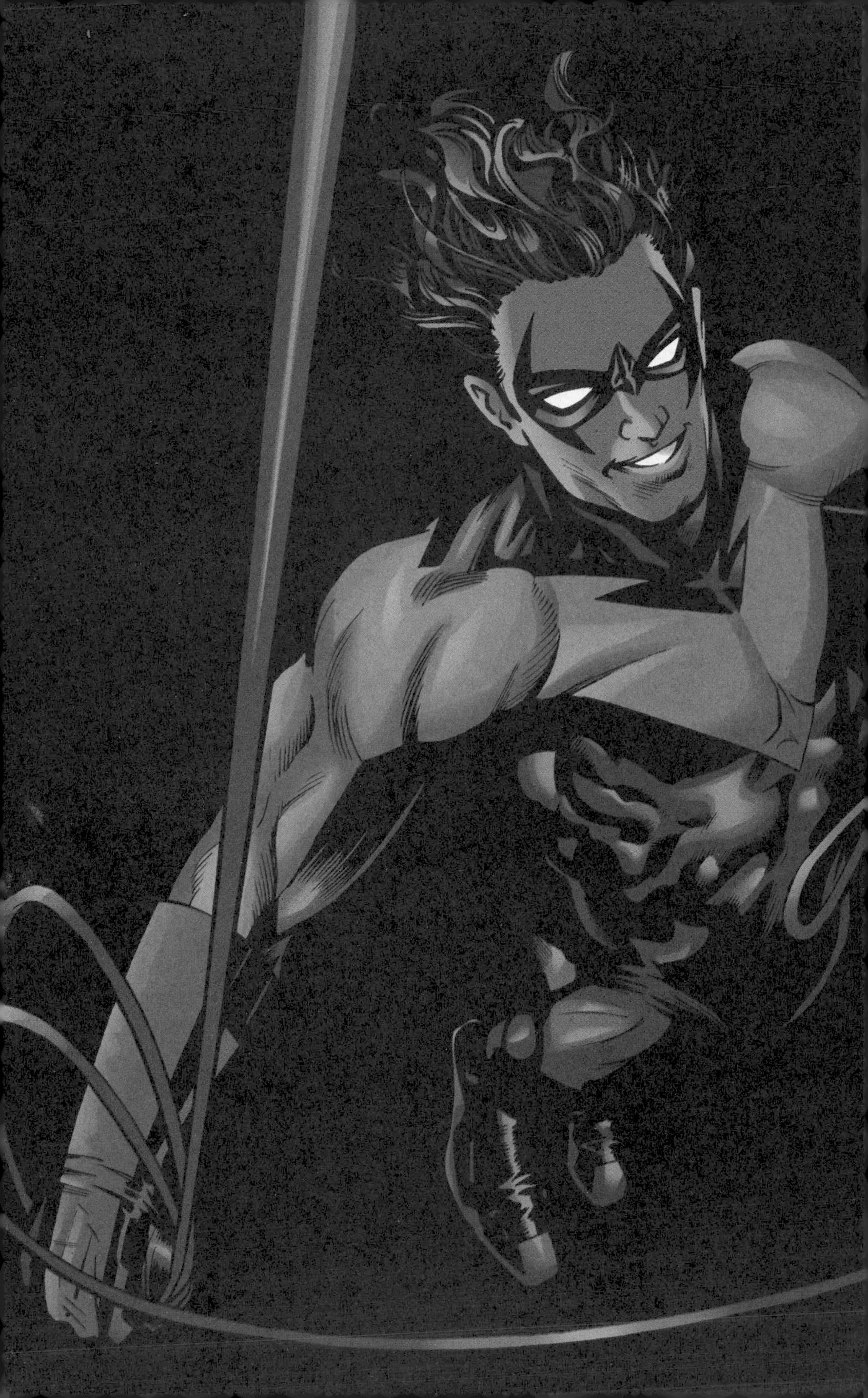

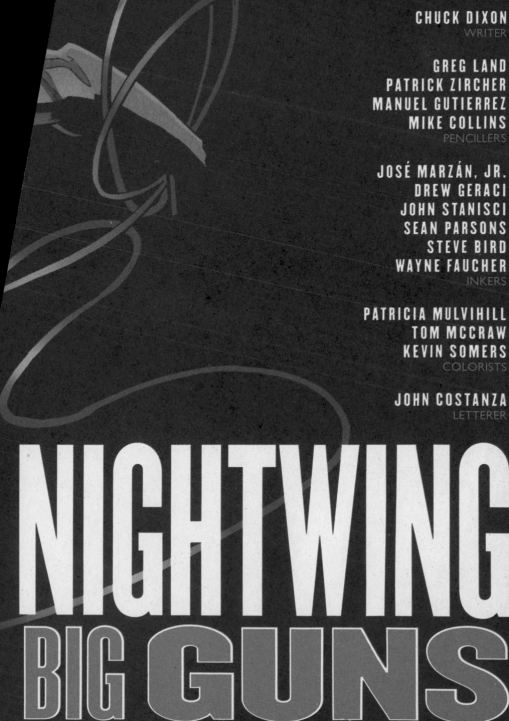

CHUCK DIXON
WRITER

GREG LAND
PATRICK ZIRCHER
MANUEL GUTIERREZ
MIKE COLLINS
PENCILLERS

JOSÉ MARZÁN, JR.
DREW GERACI
JOHN STANISCI
SEAN PARSONS
STEVE BIRD
WAYNE FAUCHER
INKERS

PATRICIA MULVIHILL
TOM McCRAW
KEVIN SOMERS
COLORISTS

JOHN COSTANZA
LETTERER

# NIGHTWING
## BIG GUNS

NIGHTWING: BIG GUNS.
Published by DC Comics. Cover and compilation copyright © 2004 DC Comics.
All Rights Reserved. Originally published in single magazine form in
NIGHTWING SECRET FILES & ORIGINS 1, NIGHTWING 47-50, NIGHTWING
80-PAGE GIANT 1. Copyright © 1999, 2000 DC Comics. All Rights Reserved.
All characters, their distinctive likenesses and related indicia featured in this publication
are trademarks of DC Comics. The stories, characters and incidents featured in this
publication are entirely fictional. DC Comics does not read or
accept unsolicited submissions of ideas, stories or artwork.
DC Comics, 1700 Broadway, New York, NY 10019.
A Warner Bros. Entertainment Company.
Printed in Canada. First Printing.
ISBN: 1-4012-0186-5
Cover illustration by Greg Land and Karl Story.
Publication design by Peter Hamboussi.

# CAST OF CHARACTERS

## NIGHTWING

Dick Grayson's life changed forever when he witnessed his aerialist parents fall to their deaths, the victims of an extortion scheme. Knowing the pain of such a loss, the wealthy Bruce Wayne took in the youth, and in a short time Dick was being trained to work alongside Gotham City's famed crime-fighter, Batman. Befitting his circus heritage, Dick chose a more colorful outfit than that of his new partner, and became Robin, the Boy Wonder. Batman and Robin proved to be a perfect crime-fighting team, but, as he grew to manhood, Dick began to separate himself from his mentor, unwilling to become a doppelgänger of the obsessed Bruce Wayne.

Asserting his independence, he changed his persona from Robin to Nightwing, and then left Gotham for the nearby city of Blüdhaven. Wanting to gain access to places Nightwing could not, Dick Grayson trained to join the city's police, only to discover that he couldn't get a job with the corrupt force.

Nightwing is a master of a half-dozen martial arts disciplines with an emphasis on aikido, as well as being armed with twin escrima sticks made from an unbreakable polymer. He also carries several dozen modified batarangs along with de-cel jumplines and gas capsules.

## TORQUE

In a city full of dirty cops, Dudley Soames was the dirtiest. He played all sides, including feeding information on crime boss Blockbuster to Nightwing. The price he paid for his actions was having his head rotated 180 degrees — permanently. For anyone else that would have meant instant death, but thanks to the radical drug therapy of Dr. Sandra Pavaar, Soames lived. Having mastered his new world-view, Soames took the name Torque and now seeks vengeance on everyone who wronged him. His only agenda is mayhem.

## NITE-WING

The city of Blüdhaven does not function very well, as seen in its daily failures at public services. This is nothing new — just ask Tad Ryerstad, who was raised under the auspices of the Child Services Department. After shuttling through a series of foster homes, Tad ran away at age twelve and the department never noticed. This indifferent upbringing twisted Tad into a sociopath, schooled as much on comic books and television as he was in any educational setting. His view of the world is warped, and he metes out his personal brand of "justice" far more violently than his costumed inspiration. Recently, Nightwing tried to train him, channeling the aggression into something positive. Instead Nite-Wing killed an FBI agent and split from Nightwing, not understanding the consequences of his actions.

# ORACLE

The niece and adopted daughter of Gotham City Police Commissioner James Gordon, Barbara Gordon was entranced by her uncle's clandestine associations with Gotham's mysterious guardian Batman. Inspired by the Dark Knight to create her *own* costumed identity, Barbara began aiding and abetting Batman's war on crime as Batgirl. But a bullet from the psychotic Joker ended all that. Now paralyzed from the waist down, Barbara nevertheless refuses to live a sedentary life in a wheelchair. With a vast computer network and her own photographic memory, Barbara Gordon has become the all-seeing Oracle — information broker to the costumed crimefighters. And no longer content to remain on the sidelines of crime-fighting, Oracle is itching to take a more proactive role in trouble-shooting global crises. She often uses Black Canary as her "arms and legs" to carry out missions.

# BLOCKBUSTER

Roland Desmond is Blüdhaven's undisputed crime boss, amassing enough money and connections to ultimately gain control of Gotham City's underworld. Desmond's key attribute is his mind. He gained his body's bulk as a result of experimental steroids to cure a debilitating heart disease. His vast fortune has been raided time and again by Oracle and he has sworn to bring her down. Blockbuster is not above using costumed vigilantes to do his bidding, including Lady Vic, Brutale, Mouse and Giz. In recent times, his heart could no longer handle the strain of his bulk, making a transplant an absolute necessity. To accomplish this, he sought out the mysterious Oracle, only to find Black Canary posing as the information broker. Blockbuster sent Black Canary, Deathstroke, Lady Vic, and Grimm to Gorilla City on a mission to retrieve a new heart from one of the hidden land's apes. The transplant was a success, and Black Canary was rescued.

# BLÜDHAVEN POLICE DEPT.

Like everything else in the city, the Blüdhaven P.D. is corrupt from top to bottom. A 1971 anti-corruption committee eliminated the post of Police Commissioner when the position's power and influence began to rival that of the mayor. Today, Police Chief Francis Alexander Redhorn is still more powerful than the mayor but at a lower (official) pay grade. A laundry list of federal agencies has been, for decades, investigating Redhorn and his department's connection to organized crime. Most recently, this investigation turned to the operations of Roland Desmond. Stories of secret offshore "retirement" funds, intentionally bungled investigations, and entire precincts on the take lead nowhere as the FBI, DEA and Treasury Department are led on countless wild-goose chases down innumerable blind alleys. The Blüdhaven P.D. continues to have the highest rate of early retirement of any police department in the country. Recently, incriminating records were found by Nightwing, implicating Redhorn, who abandoned his force, leaving things in greater disarray than usual.

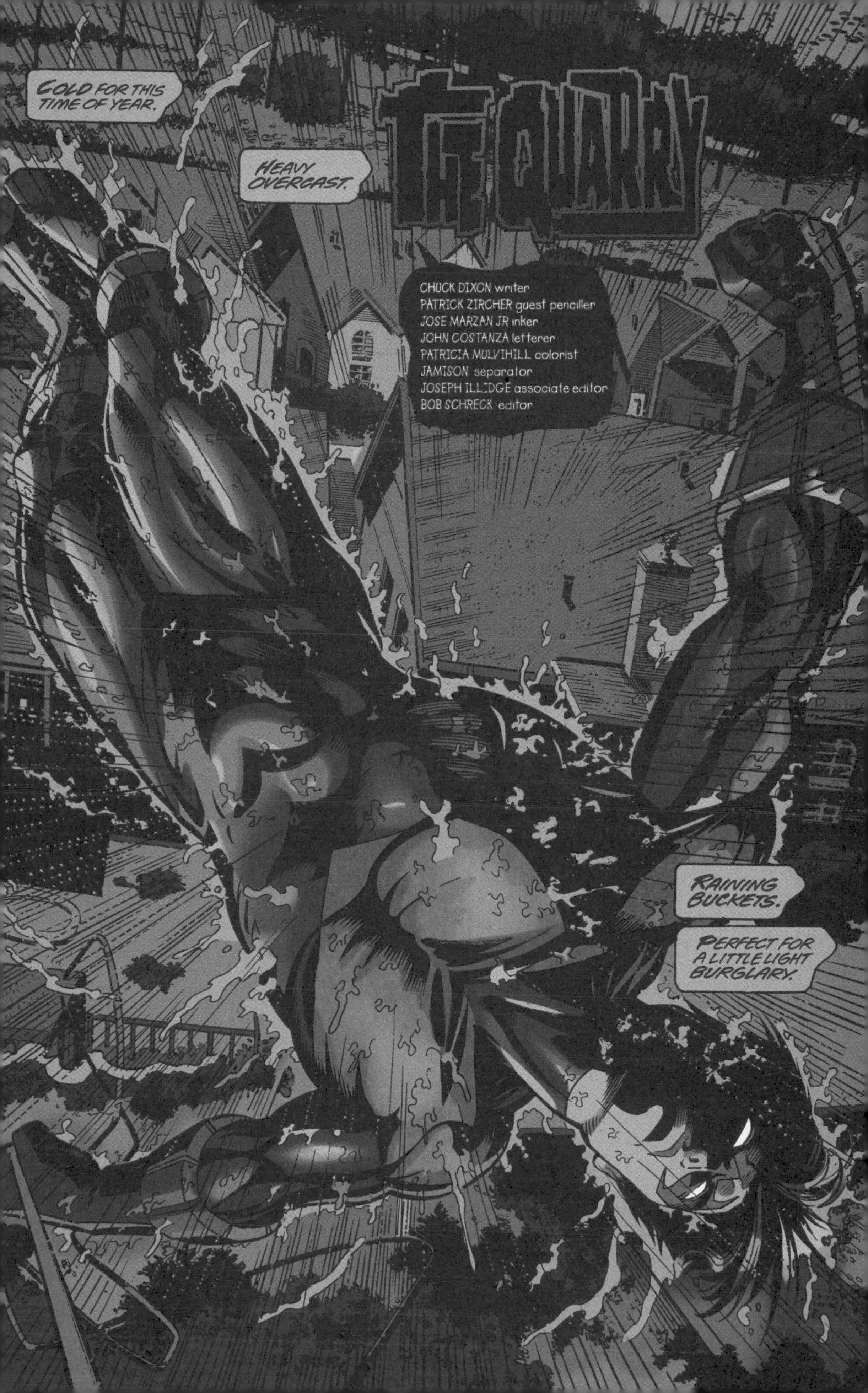
COLD FOR THIS TIME OF YEAR.
HEAVY OVERCAST.
THE QUARRY
CHUCK DIXON writer
PATRICK ZIRCHER guest penciller
JOSE MARZAN JR inker
JOHN COSTANZA letterer
PATRICIA MULVIHILL colorist
JAMISON separator
JOSEPH ILLIDGE associate editor
BOB SCHRECK editor
RAINING BUCKETS.
PERFECT FOR A LITTLE LIGHT BURGLARY.

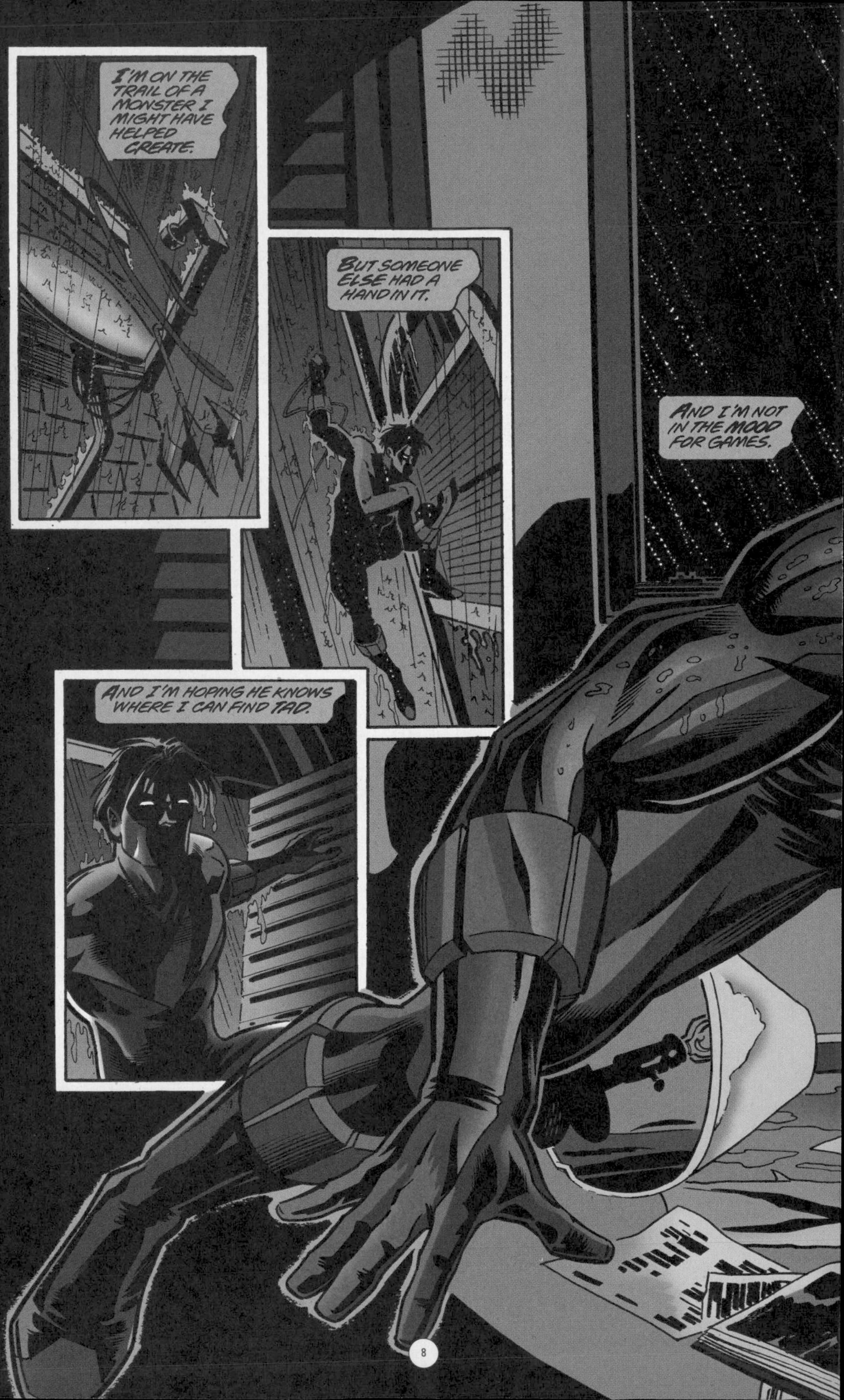
I'M ON THE TRAIL OF A MONSTER I MIGHT HAVE HELPED CREATE.
BUT SOMEONE ELSE HAD A HAND IN IT.
AND I'M HOPING HE KNOWS WHERE I CAN FIND TAD.
AND I'M NOT IN THE MOOD FOR GAMES.

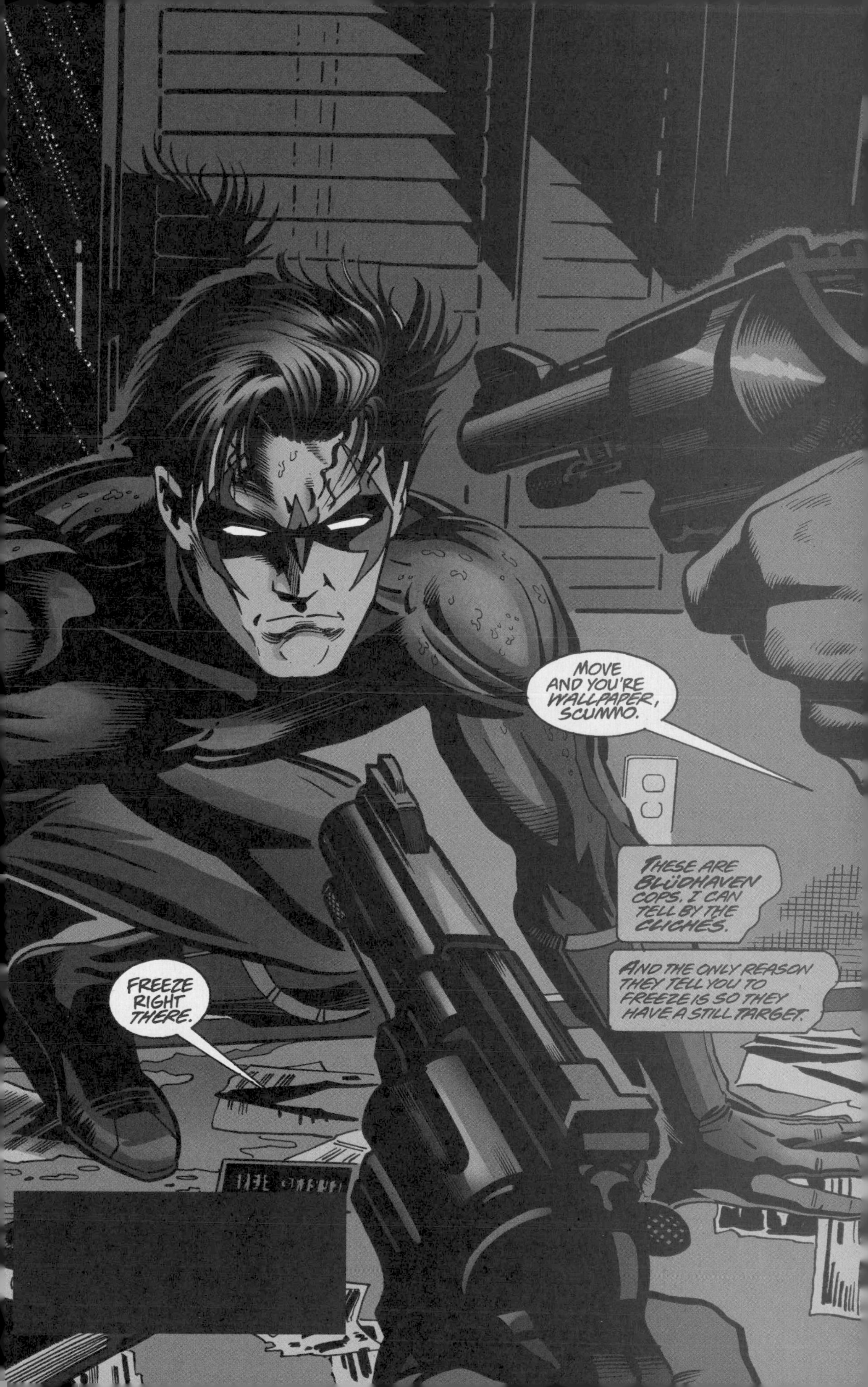
MOVE AND YOU'RE WALLPAPER, SCUMMO.
THESE ARE BLÜDHAVEN COPS. I CAN TELL BY THE CLICHES.
AND THE ONLY REASON THEY TELL YOU TO FREEZE IS SO THEY HAVE A STILL TARGET.
FREEZE RIGHT THERE.
[redacted]

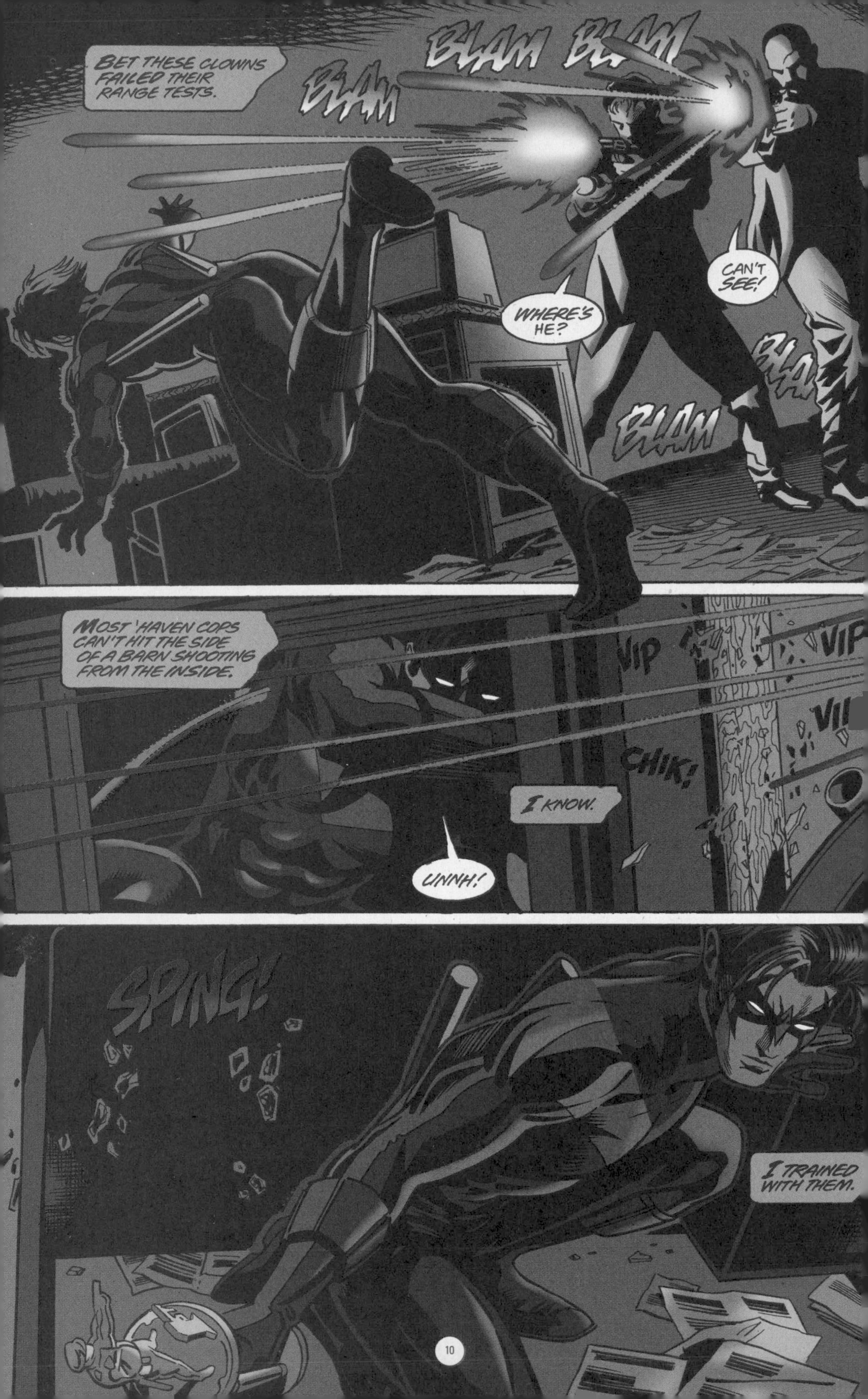
BET THESE CLOWNS FAILED THEIR RANGE TESTS.
BLAM
BLAM BLAM
WHERE'S HE?
CAN'T SEE!
BLAM
BLAM
MOST 'HAVEN COPS CAN'T HIT THE SIDE OF A BARN SHOOTING FROM THE INSIDE.
VIP
VIP
CHIK!
I KNOW.
UNNH!
SPING!
I TRAINED WITH THEM.

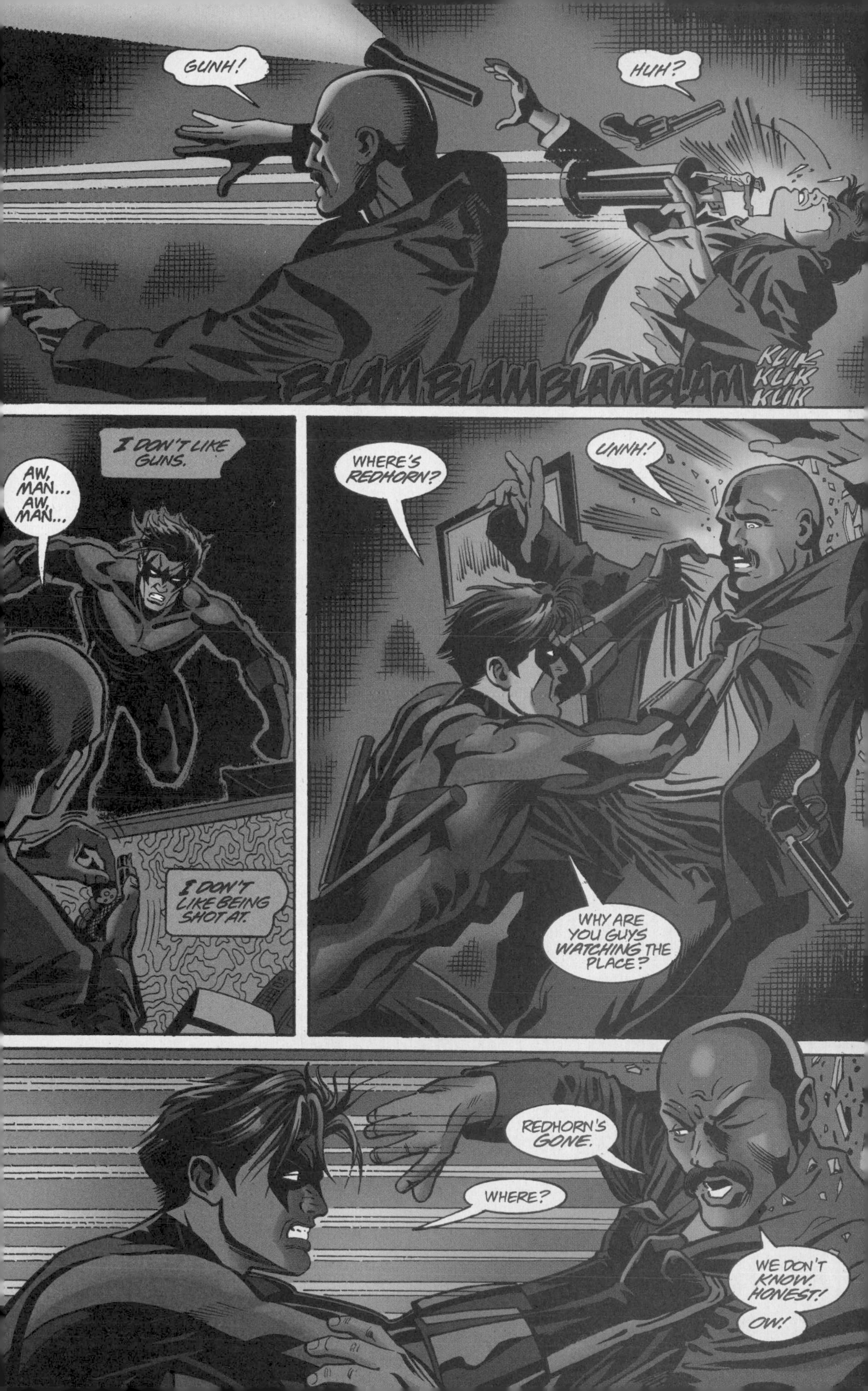
GUNH!
HUH?
BLAM BLAM BLAM BLAM
KLIK KLIK KLIK
I DON'T LIKE GUNS.
AW, MAN... AW, MAN...
I DON'T LIKE BEING SHOT AT.
WHERE'S REDHORN?
UNNH!
WHY ARE YOU GUYS WATCHING THE PLACE?
REDHORN'S GONE.
WHERE?
WE DON'T KNOW. HONEST!
OW!

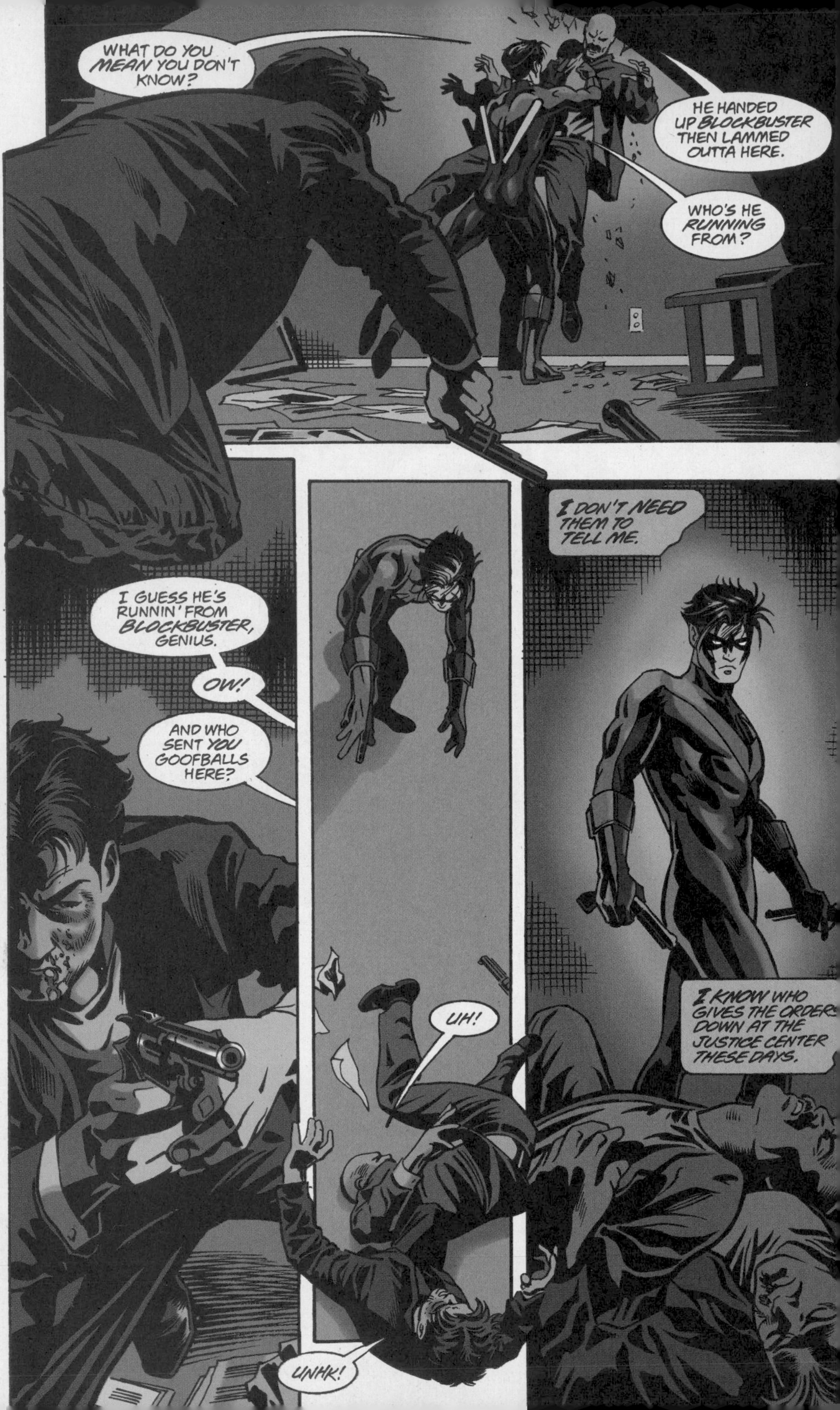
WHAT DO YOU MEAN YOU DON'T KNOW?
HE HANDED UP BLOCKBUSTER THEN LAMMED OUTTA HERE.
WHO'S HE RUNNING FROM?
I GUESS HE'S RUNNIN' FROM BLOCKBUSTER, GENIUS.
OW!
AND WHO SENT YOU GOOFBALLS HERE?
UH!
UNHK!
I DON'T NEED THEM TO TELL ME.
I KNOW WHO GIVES THE ORDERS DOWN AT THE JUSTICE CENTER THESE DAYS.

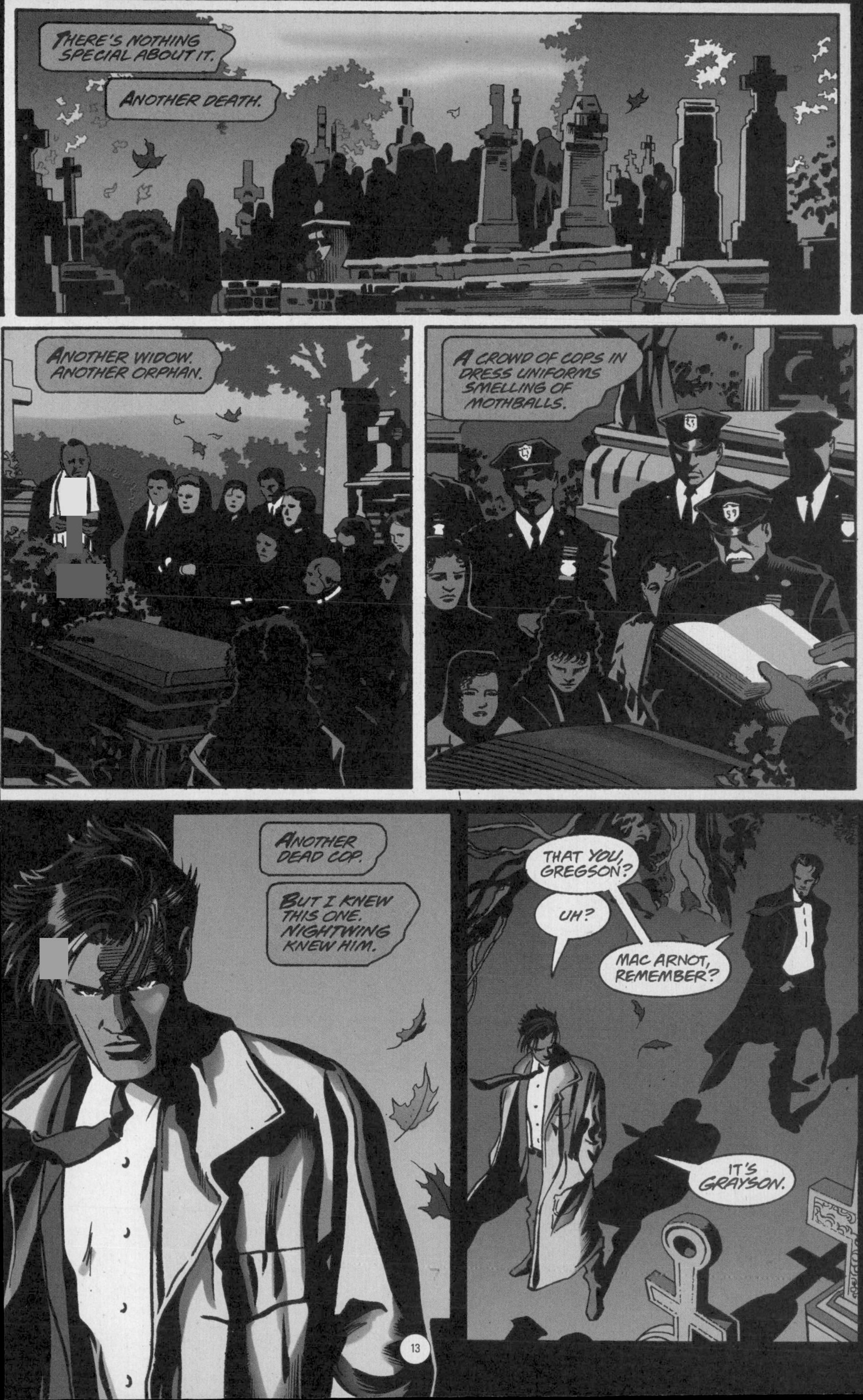
THERE'S NOTHING SPECIAL ABOUT IT.
ANOTHER DEATH.
ANOTHER WIDOW. ANOTHER ORPHAN.
A CROWD OF COPS IN DRESS UNIFORMS SMELLING OF MOTHBALLS.
ANOTHER DEAD COP.
BUT I KNEW THIS ONE. NIGHTWING KNEW HIM.
THAT YOU, GREGSON?
UH?
MAC ARNOT, REMEMBER?
IT'S GRAYSON.

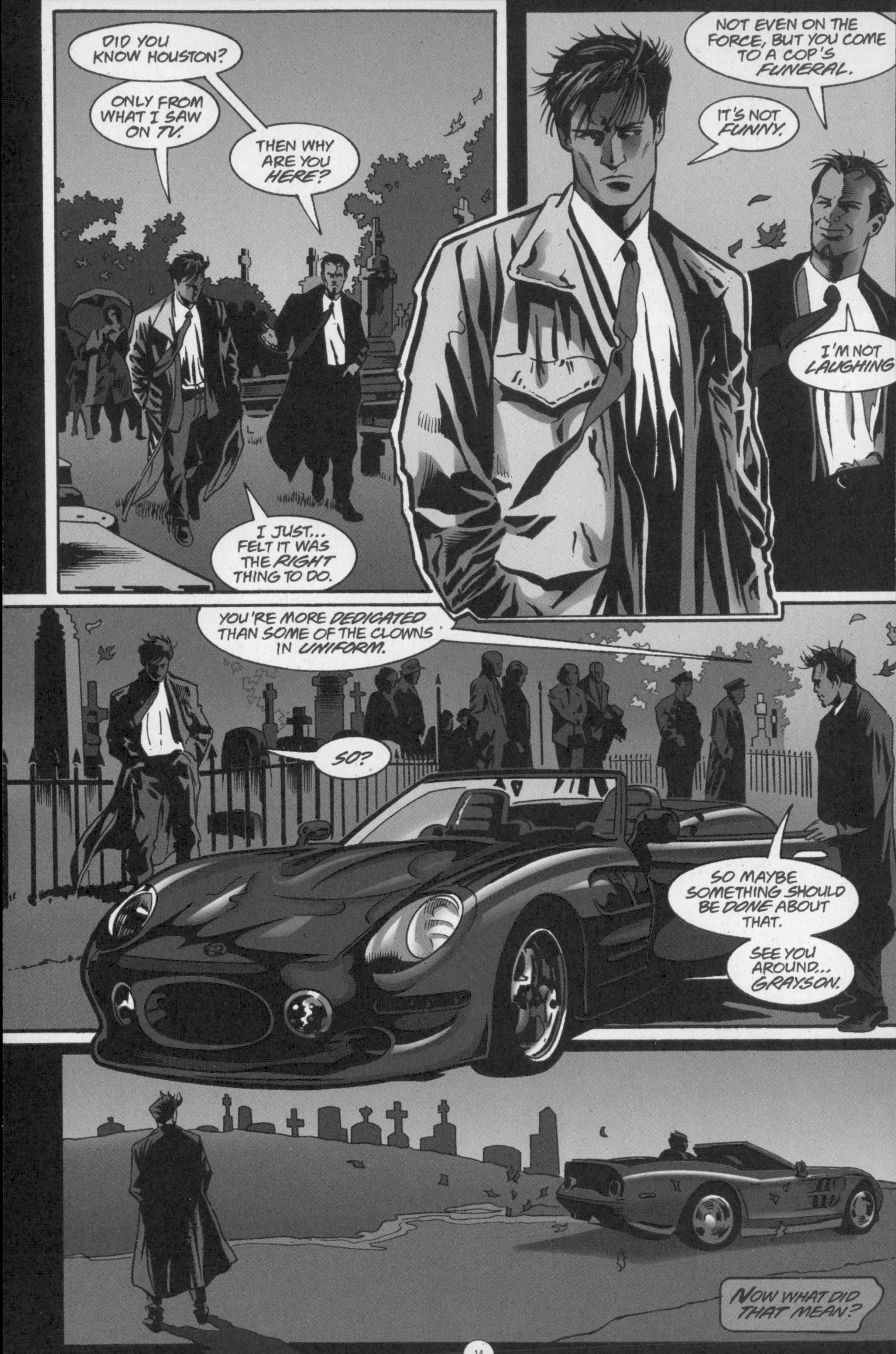
DID YOU KNOW HOUSTON?
ONLY FROM WHAT I SAW ON TV.
THEN WHY ARE YOU HERE?
I JUST... FELT IT WAS THE RIGHT THING TO DO.
NOT EVEN ON THE FORCE, BUT YOU COME TO A COP'S FUNERAL.
IT'S NOT FUNNY.
I'M NOT LAUGHING
YOU'RE MORE DEDICATED THAN SOME OF THE CLOWNS IN UNIFORM.
SO?
SO MAYBE SOMETHING SHOULD BE DONE ABOUT THAT.
SEE YOU AROUND... GRAYSON.
NOW WHAT DID THAT MEAN?

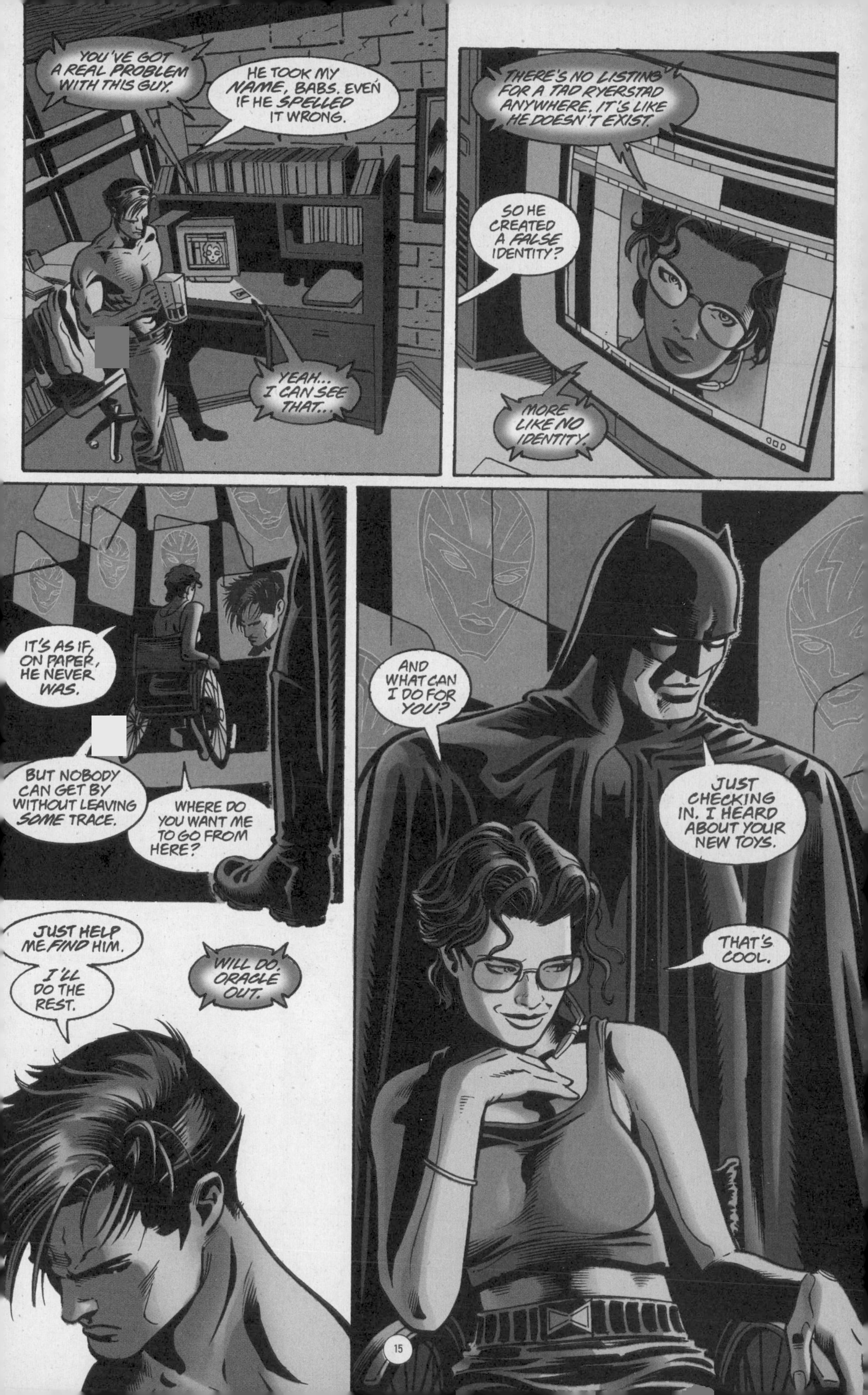
YOU'VE GOT A REAL PROBLEM WITH THIS GUY.
HE TOOK MY NAME, BABS. EVEN IF HE SPELLED IT WRONG.
YEAH... I CAN SEE THAT...
THERE'S NO LISTING FOR A TAD RYERSTAD ANYWHERE. IT'S LIKE HE DOESN'T EXIST.
SO HE CREATED A FALSE IDENTITY?
MORE LIKE NO IDENTITY.
IT'S AS IF, ON PAPER, HE NEVER WAS.
BUT NOBODY CAN GET BY WITHOUT LEAVING SOME TRACE.
WHERE DO YOU WANT ME TO GO FROM HERE?
JUST HELP ME FIND HIM.
I'LL DO THE REST.
WILL DO. ORACLE OUT.
AND WHAT CAN I DO FOR YOU?
JUST CHECKING IN. I HEARD ABOUT YOUR NEW TOYS.
THAT'S COOL.

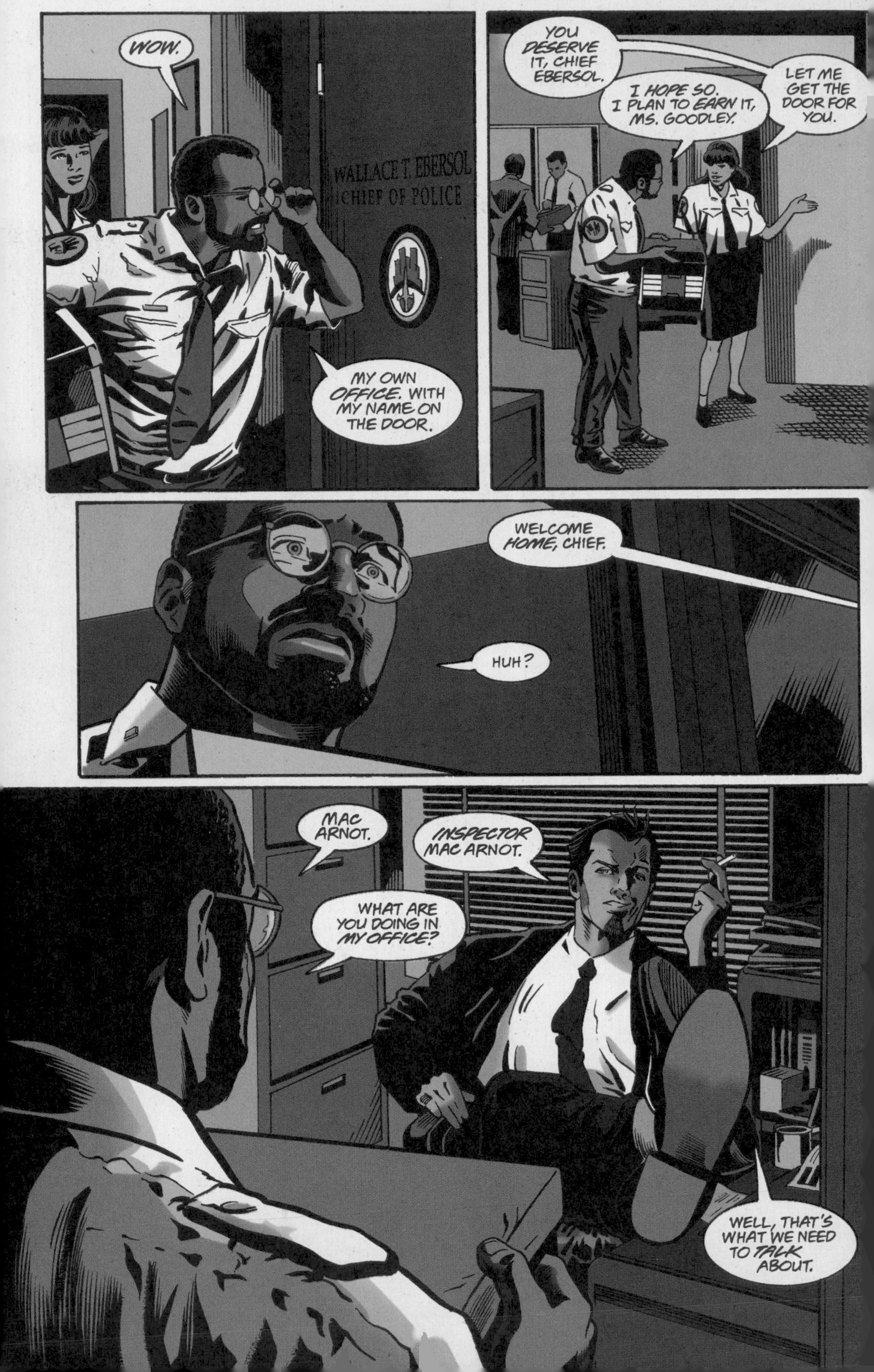
WOW.
WALLACE T. EBERSOL
CHIEF OF POLICE
MY OWN OFFICE. WITH MY NAME ON THE DOOR.
YOU DESERVE IT, CHIEF EBERSOL.
I HOPE SO. I PLAN TO EARN IT, MS. GOODLEY.
LET ME GET THE DOOR FOR YOU.
WELCOME HOME, CHIEF.
HUH?
MAC ARNOT.
INSPECTOR MAC ARNOT.
WHAT ARE YOU DOING IN MY OFFICE?
WELL, THAT'S WHAT WE NEED TO TALK ABOUT.

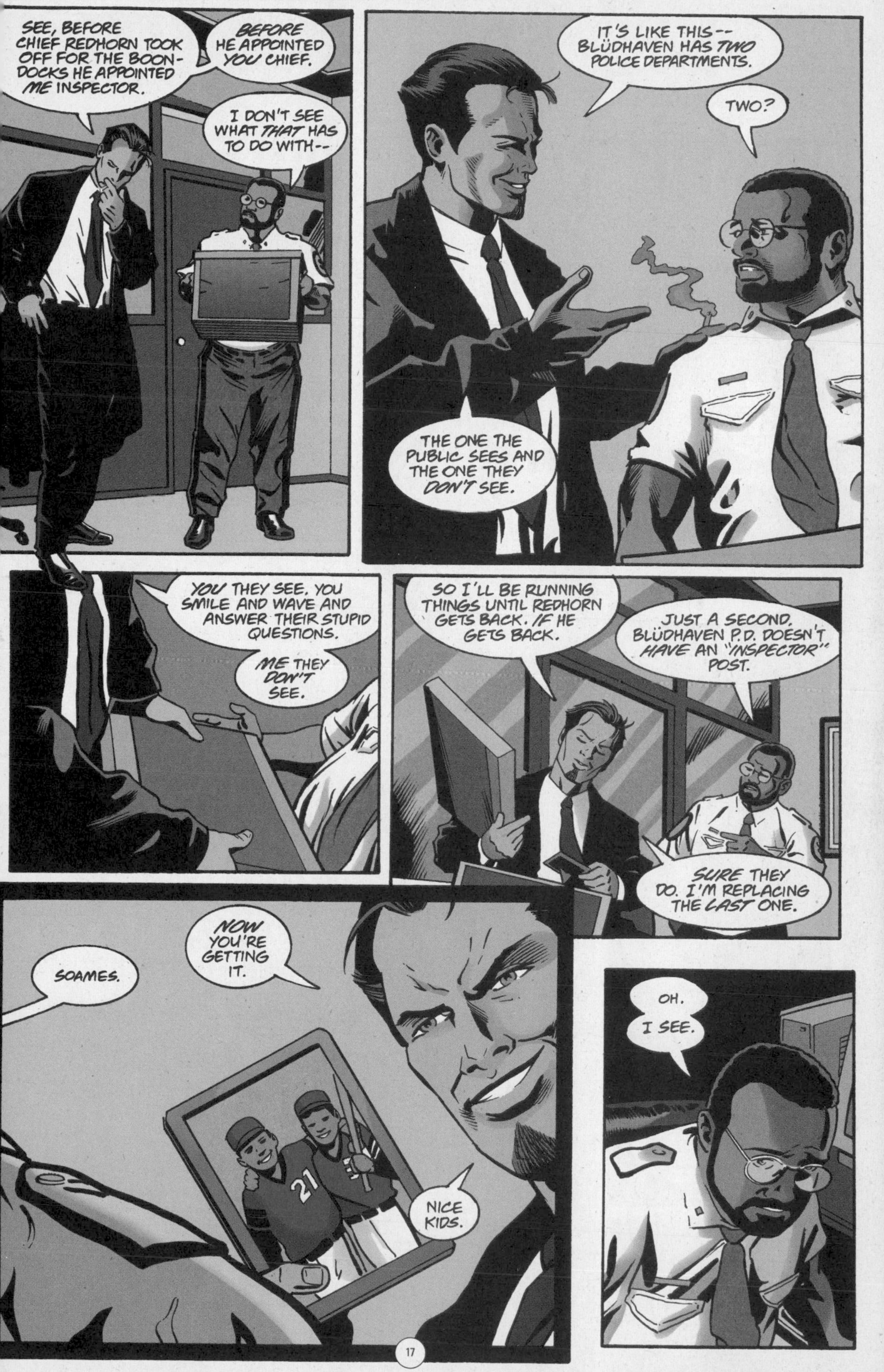
SEE, BEFORE CHIEF REDHORN TOOK OFF FOR THE BOON-DOCKS HE APPOINTED ME INSPECTOR.
BEFORE HE APPOINTED YOU CHIEF.
I DON'T SEE WHAT THAT HAS TO DO WITH--
IT'S LIKE THIS-- BLÜDHAVEN HAS TWO POLICE DEPARTMENTS.
TWO?
THE ONE THE PUBLIC SEES AND THE ONE THEY DON'T SEE.
YOU THEY SEE. YOU SMILE AND WAVE AND ANSWER THEIR STUPID QUESTIONS.
ME THEY DON'T SEE.
SO I'LL BE RUNNING THINGS UNTIL REDHORN GETS BACK. IF HE GETS BACK.
JUST A SECOND. BLÜDHAVEN P.D. DOESN'T HAVE AN "INSPECTOR" POST.
SURE THEY DO. I'M REPLACING THE LAST ONE.
SOAMES.
NOW YOU'RE GETTING IT.
NICE KIDS.
OH.
I SEE.

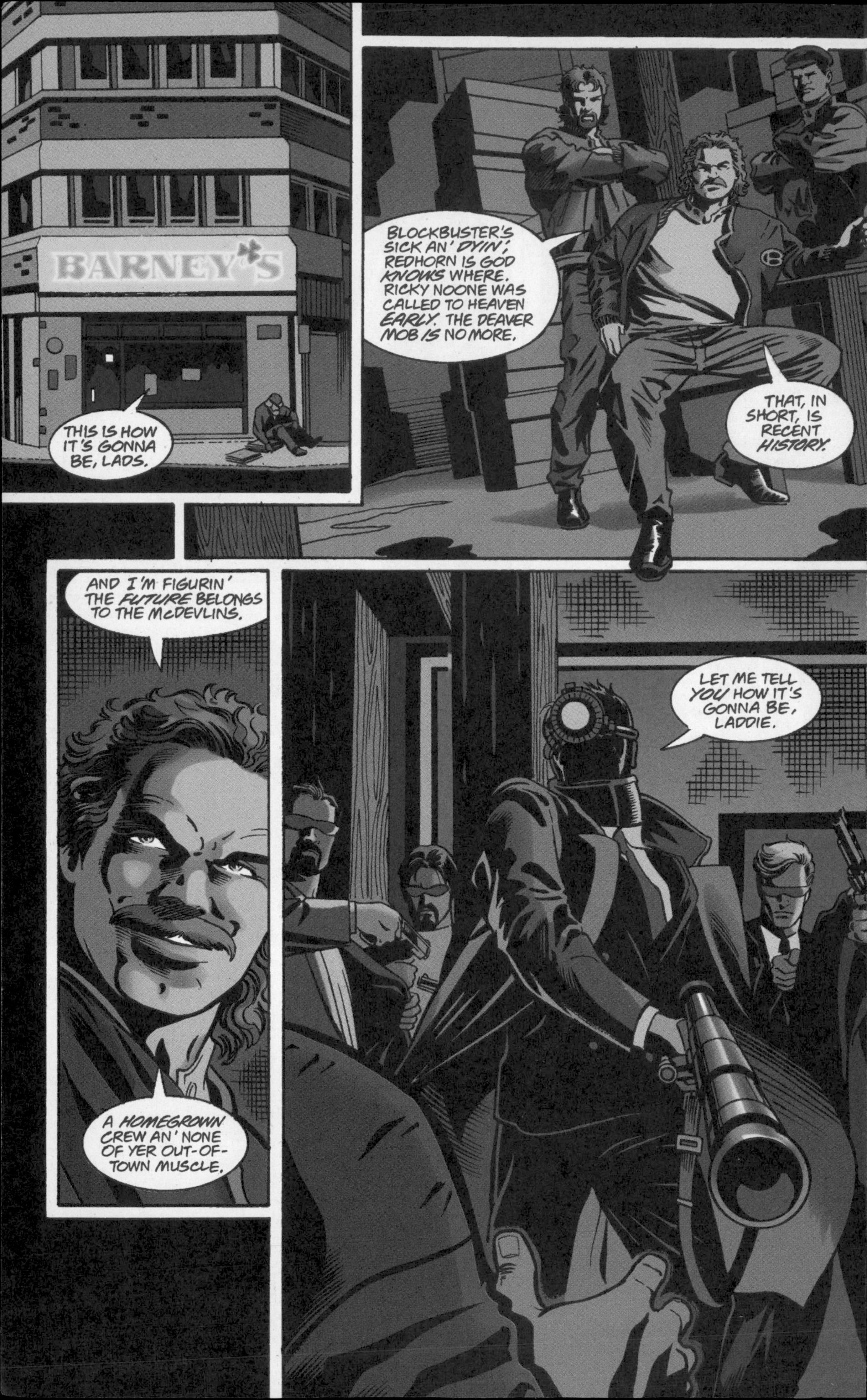
BARNEY'S
THIS IS HOW IT'S GONNA BE, LADS.
BLOCKBUSTER'S SICK AN' DYIN'; REDHORN IS GOD KNOWS WHERE. RICKY NOONE WAS CALLED TO HEAVEN EARLY. THE DEAVER MOB IS NO MORE.
THAT, IN SHORT, IS RECENT HISTORY.
AND I'M FIGURIN' THE FUTURE BELONGS TO THE McDEVLINS.
A HOMEGROWN CREW AN' NONE OF YER OUT-OF-TOWN MUSCLE.
LET ME TELL YOU HOW IT'S GONNA BE, LADDIE.

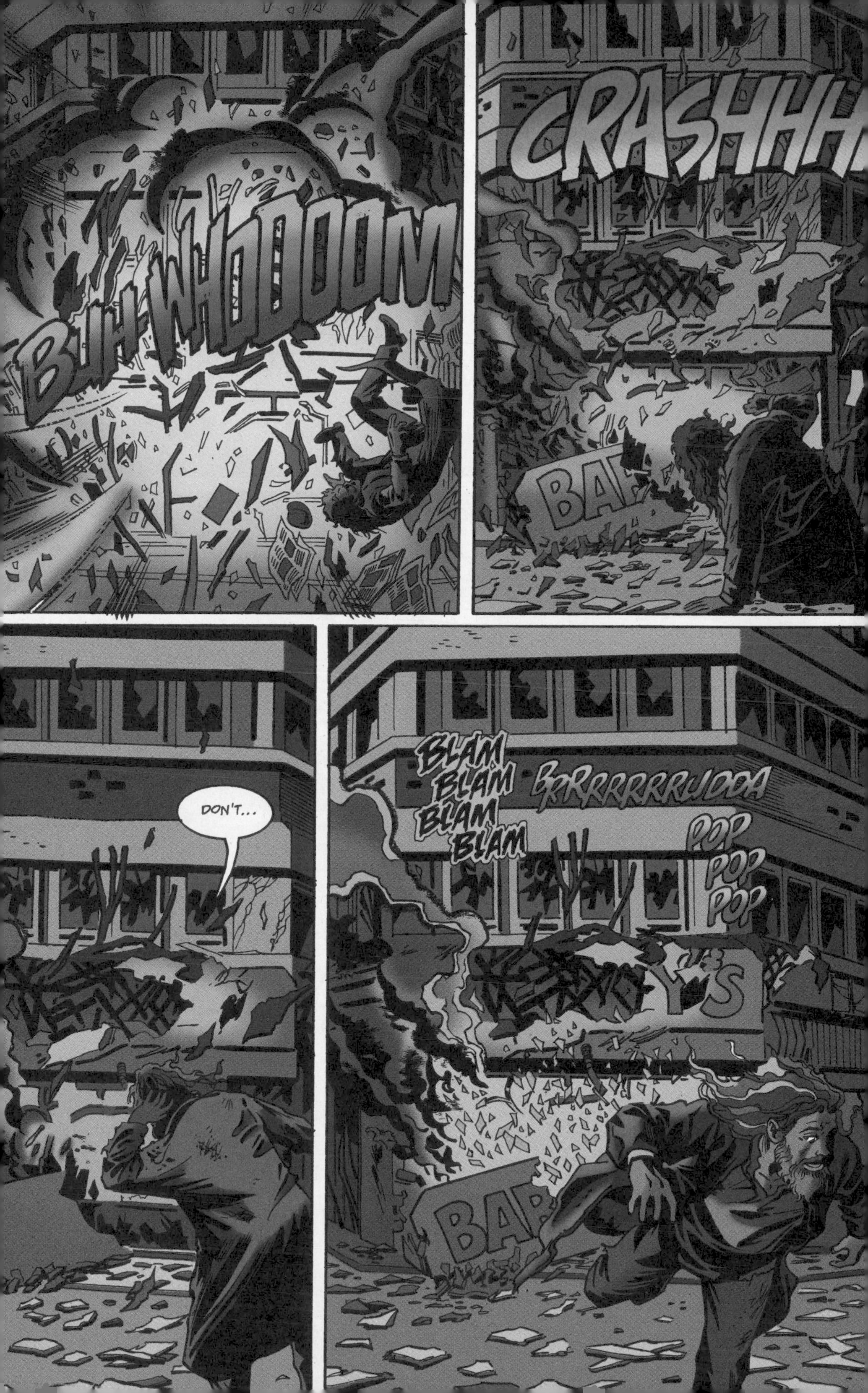
BUHWHOOOM
CRASHHH
BAR
DON'T...
BLAM
BLAM
BLAM
BLAM
BRRRRRRRRUDDA
POP
POP
POP
YS
BAR

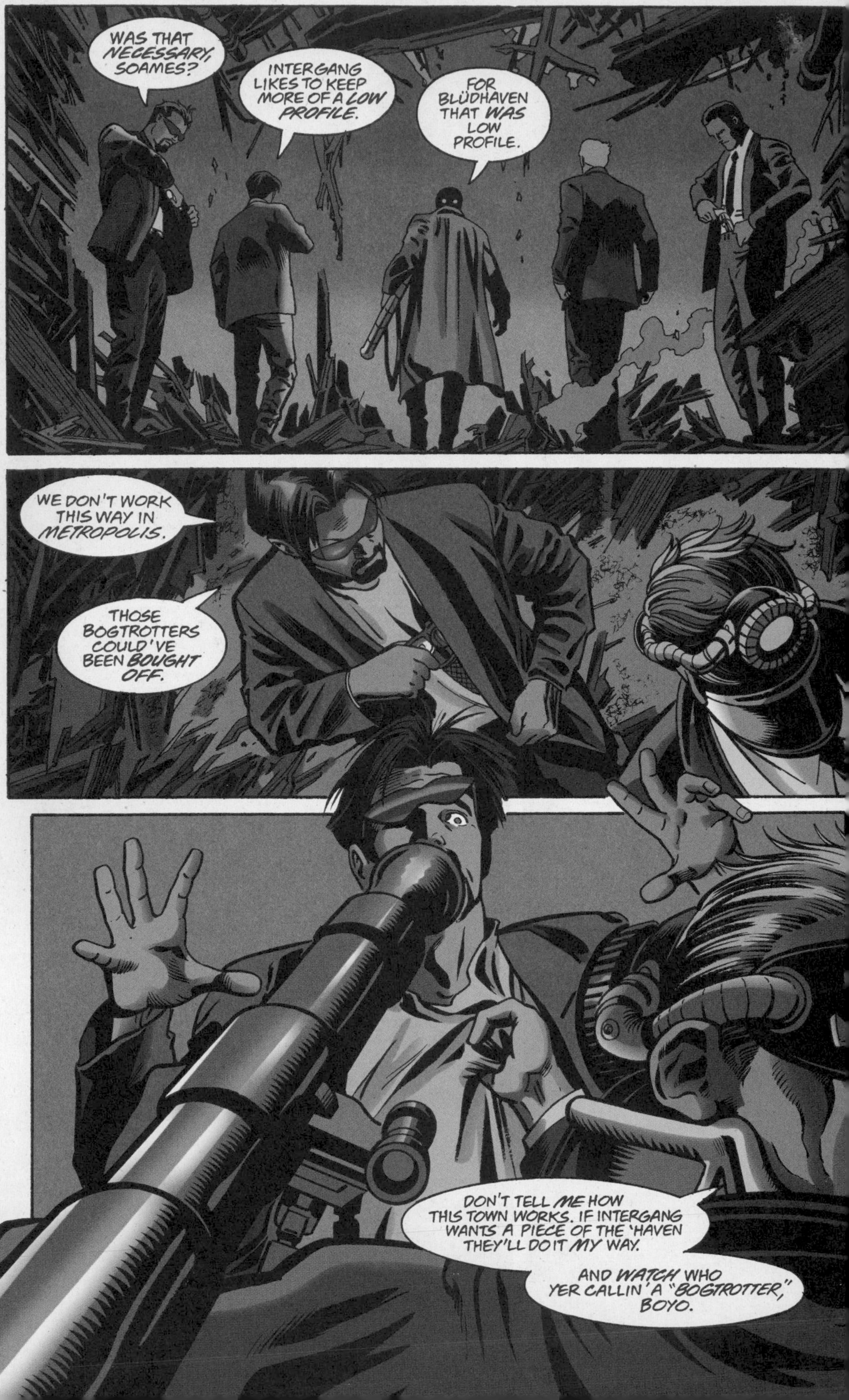
WAS THAT NECESSARY, SOAMES?
INTERGANG LIKES TO KEEP MORE OF A LOW PROFILE.
FOR BLÜDHAVEN THAT WAS LOW PROFILE.
WE DON'T WORK THIS WAY IN METROPOLIS.
THOSE BOGTROTTERS COULD'VE BEEN BOUGHT OFF.
DON'T TELL ME HOW THIS TOWN WORKS. IF INTERGANG WANTS A PIECE OF THE 'HAVEN THEY'LL DO IT MY WAY.
AND WATCH WHO YER CALLIN' A "BOGTROTTER," BOYO.

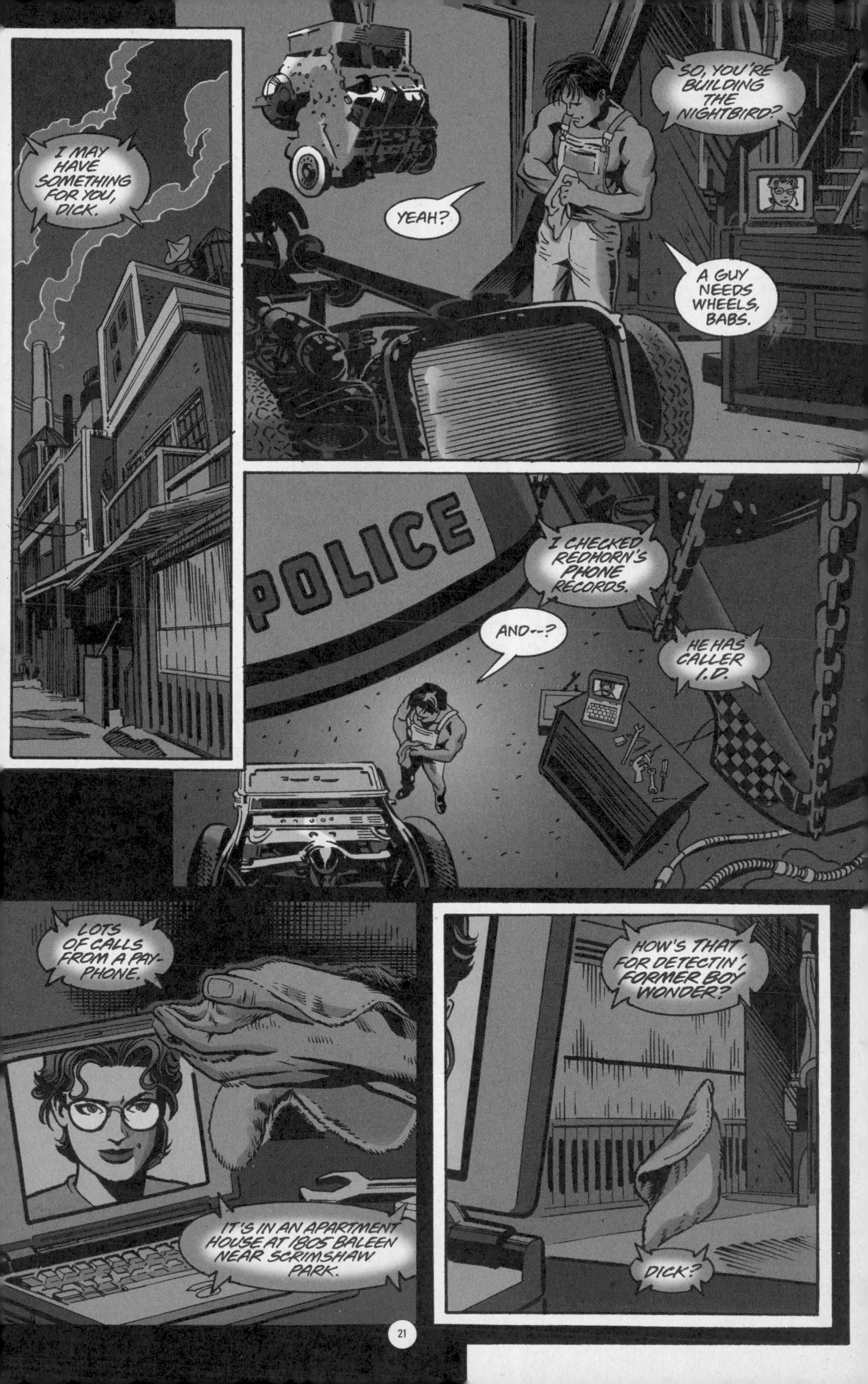
I MAY HAVE SOMETHING FOR YOU, DICK.
YEAH?
SO, YOU'RE BUILDING THE NIGHTBIRD?
A GUY NEEDS WHEELS, BABS.
POLICE
I CHECKED REDHORN'S PHONE RECORDS.
AND--?
HE HAS CALLER I.D.
LOTS OF CALLS FROM A PAY-PHONE.
IT'S IN AN APARTMENT HOUSE AT 1805 BALEEN NEAR SCRIMSHAW PARK.
HOW'S THAT FOR DETECTIN', FORMER BOY WONDER?
DICK?

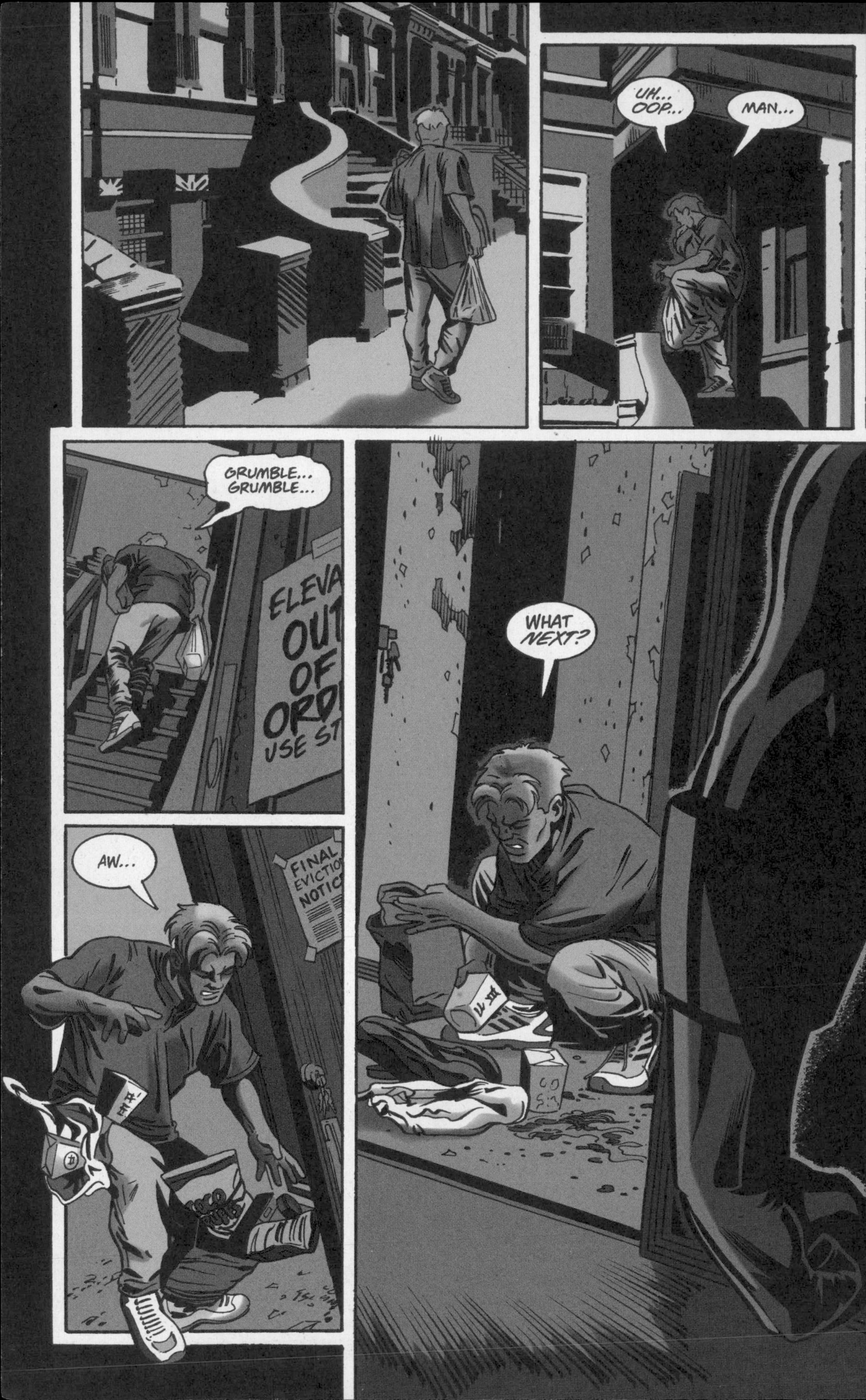
UH... OOP...
MAN...
GRUMBLE... GRUMBLE...
ELEVA
OUT OF ORD
USE ST
AW...
FINAL EVICTIO NOTIC
WHAT NEXT?

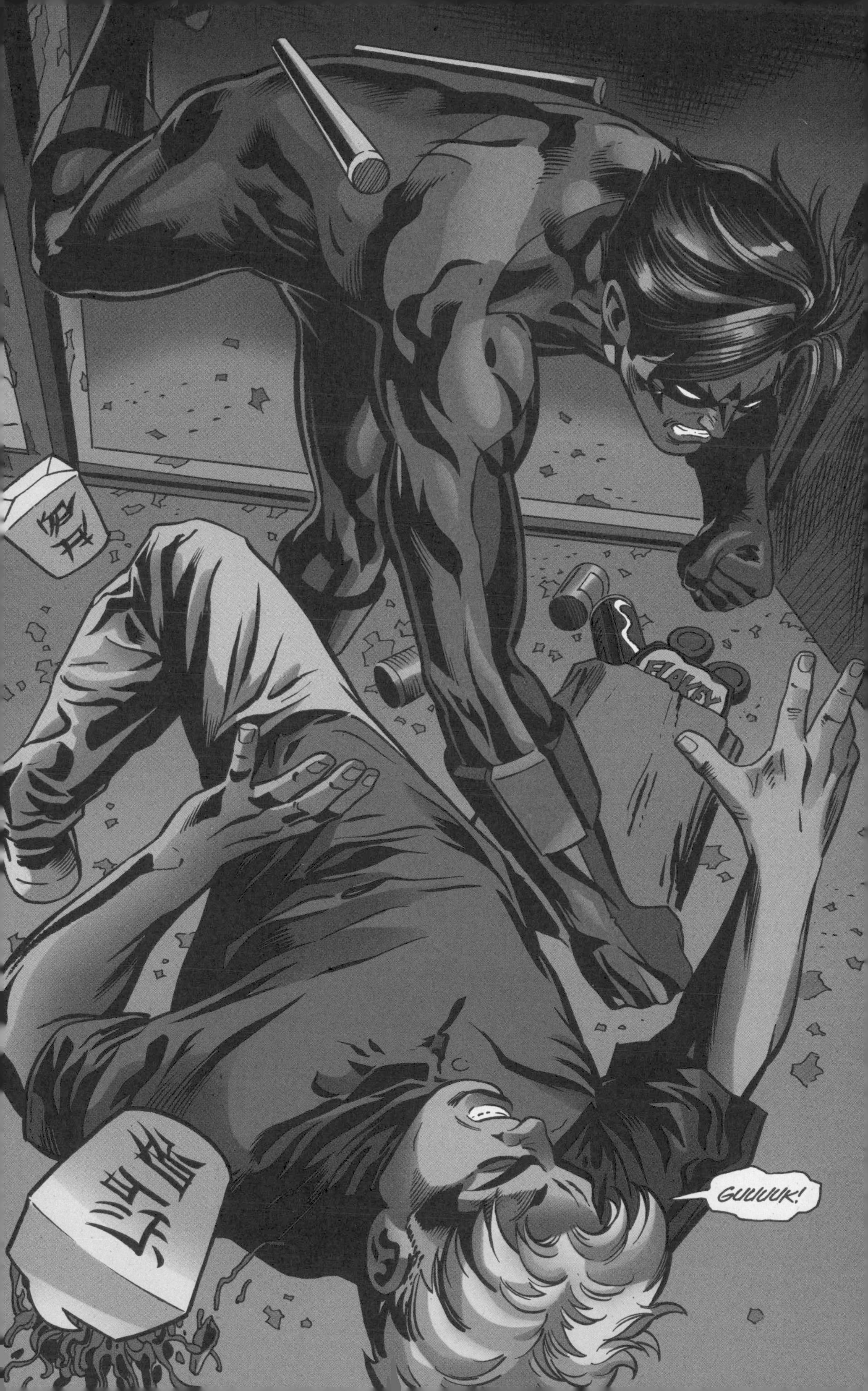
FLAKSY
GUUUUK!

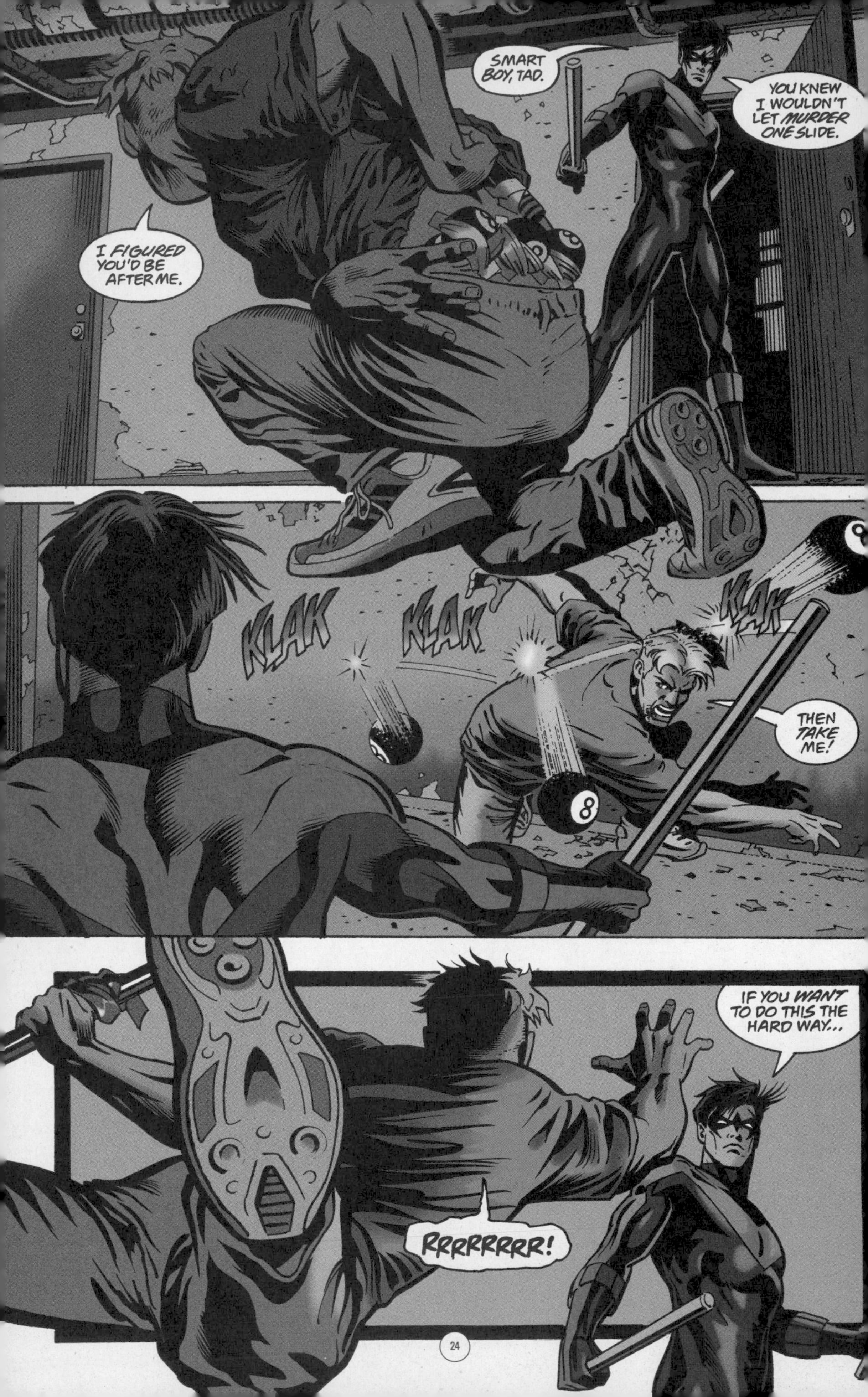
SMART BOY, TAD.
YOU KNEW I WOULDN'T LET MURDER ONE SLIDE.
I FIGURED YOU'D BE AFTER ME.
KLAK
KLAK
KLAK
THEN TAKE ME!
IF YOU WANT TO DO THIS THE HARD WAY...
RRRRRRRR!

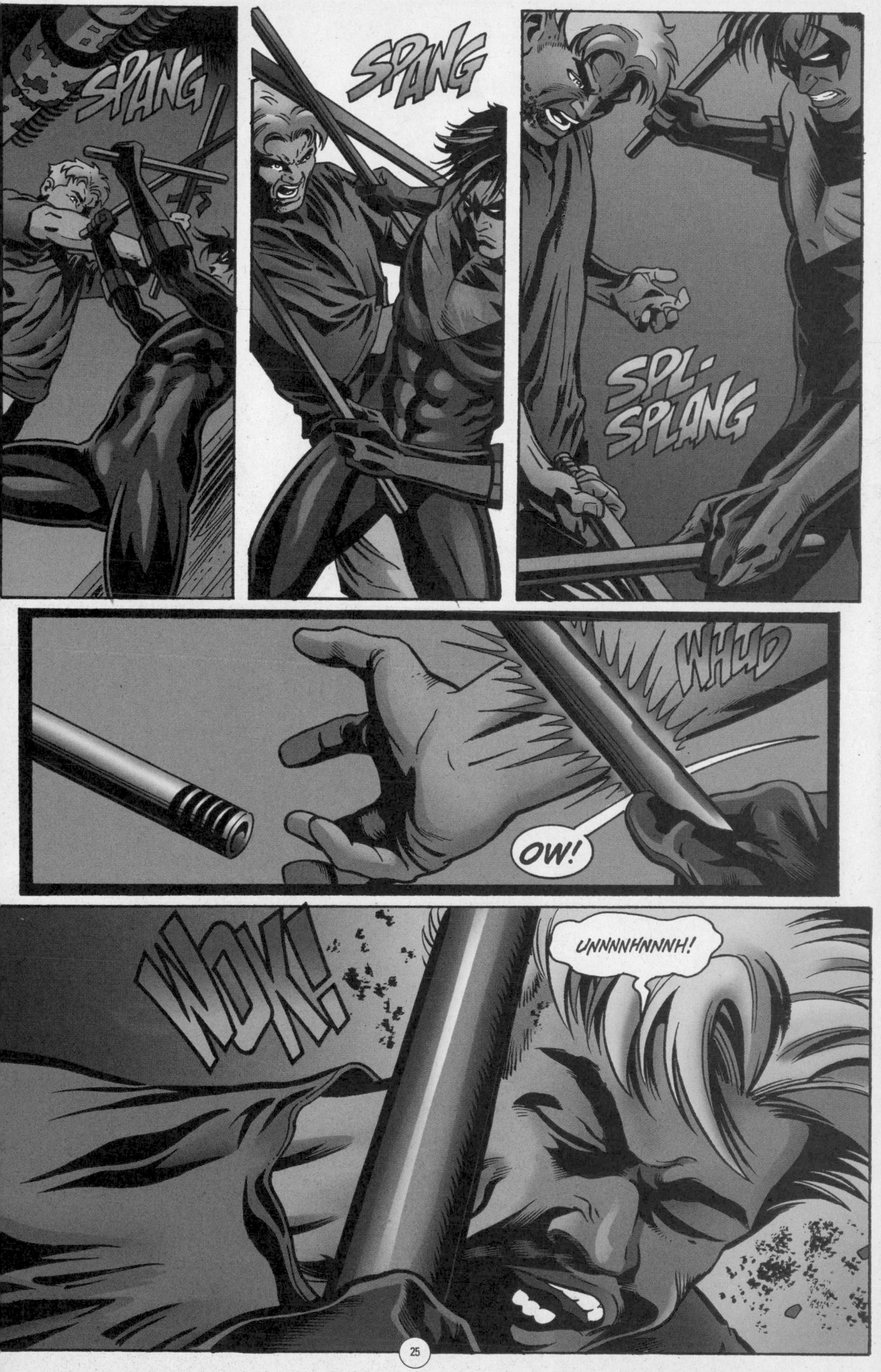
SPANG
SPANG
SPL-SPLANG
WHUD
OW!
WOK!
UNNNHNNNH!

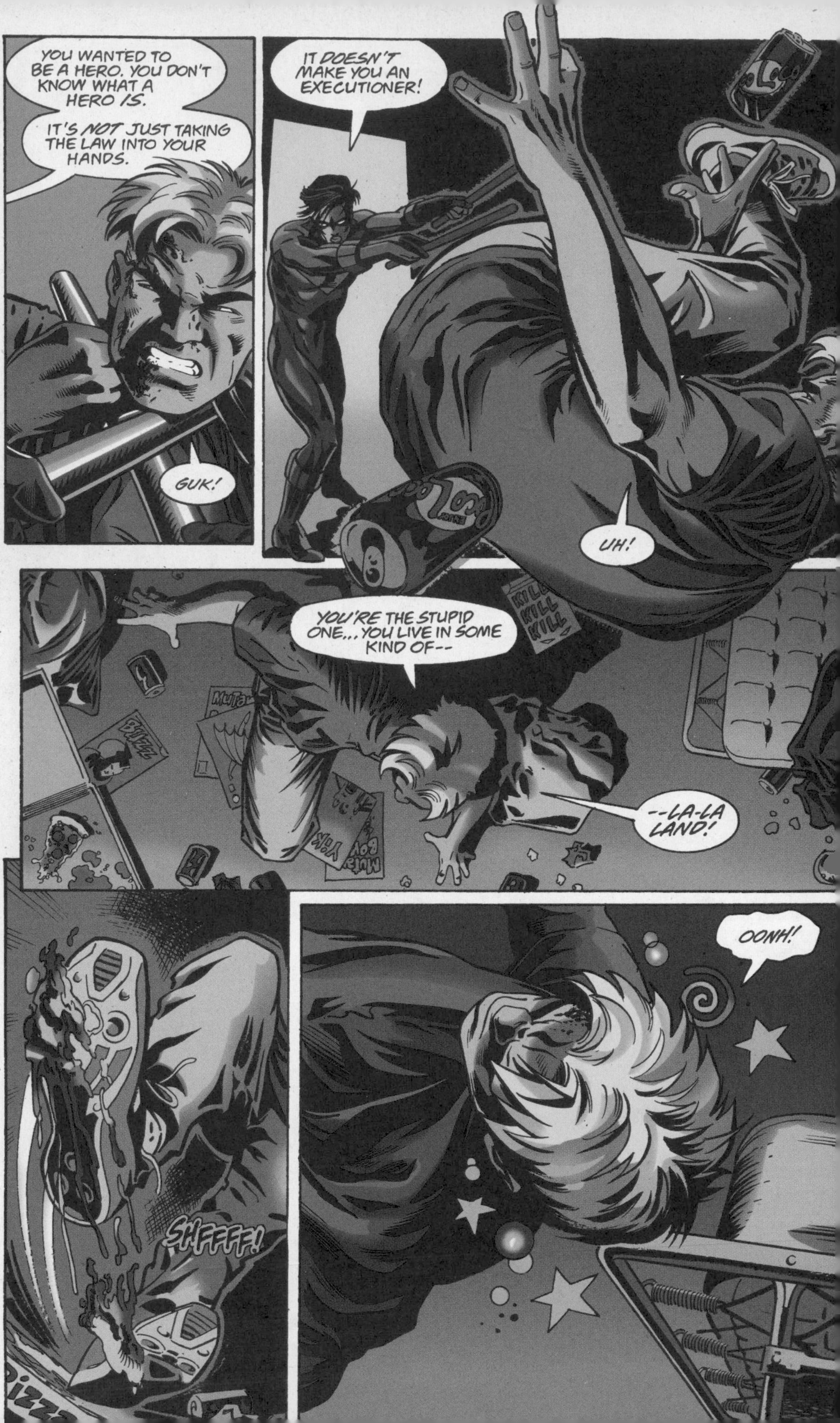
YOU WANTED TO BE A HERO. YOU DON'T KNOW WHAT A HERO IS.
IT'S NOT JUST TAKING THE LAW INTO YOUR HANDS.
GUK!
IT DOESN'T MAKE YOU AN EXECUTIONER!
UH!
KILL KILL KILL
YOU'RE THE STUPID ONE... YOU LIVE IN SOME KIND OF--
--LA-LA LAND!
OONH!
SHFFFF!

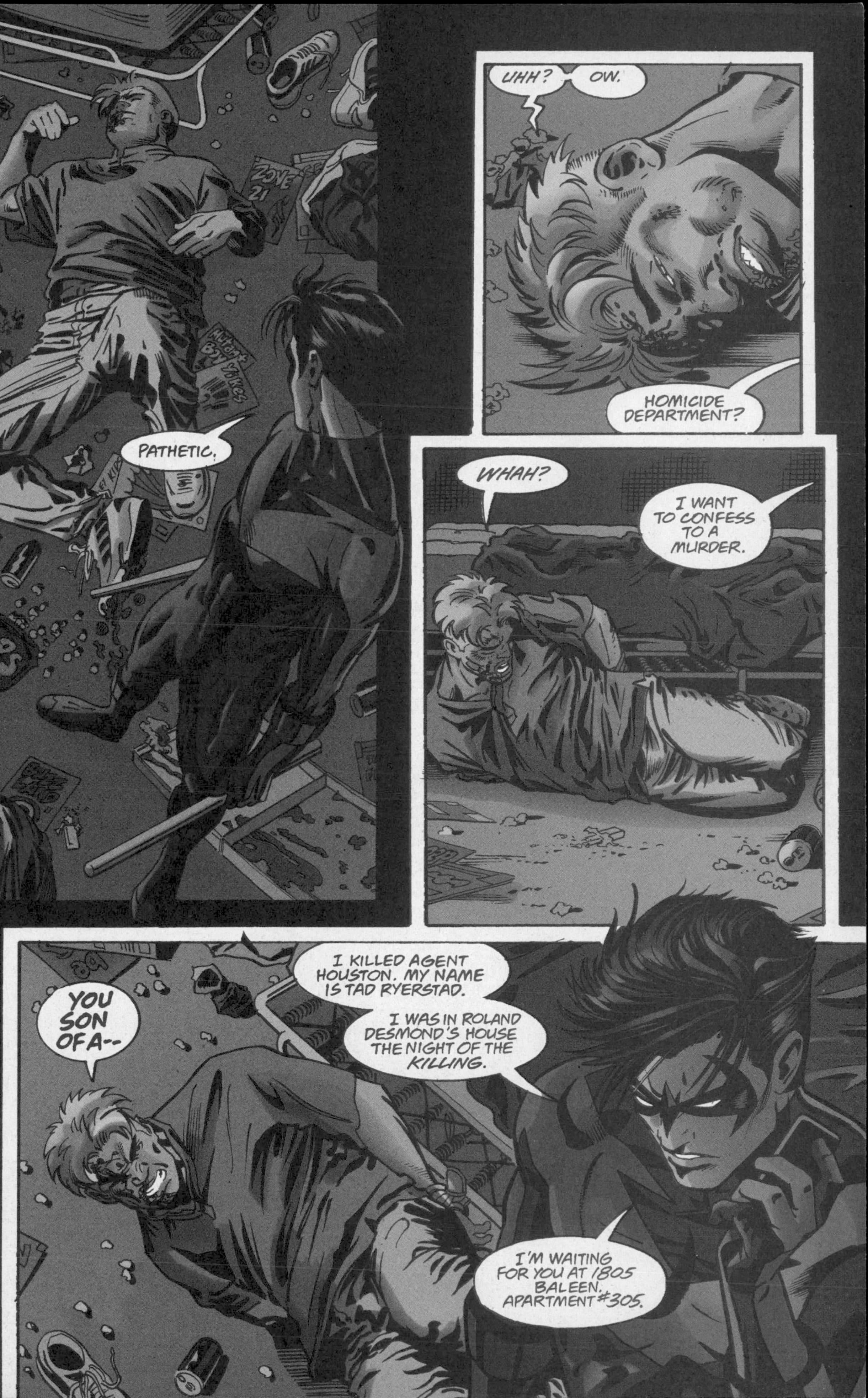

PATHETIC.
UHH?
OW.
HOMICIDE DEPARTMENT?
WHAH?
I WANT TO CONFESS TO A MURDER.
YOU SON OF A--
I KILLED AGENT HOUSTON. MY NAME IS TAD RYERSTAD.
I WAS IN ROLAND DESMOND'S HOUSE THE NIGHT OF THE *KILLING*.
I'M WAITING FOR YOU AT 1805 BALEEN. APARTMENT #305.

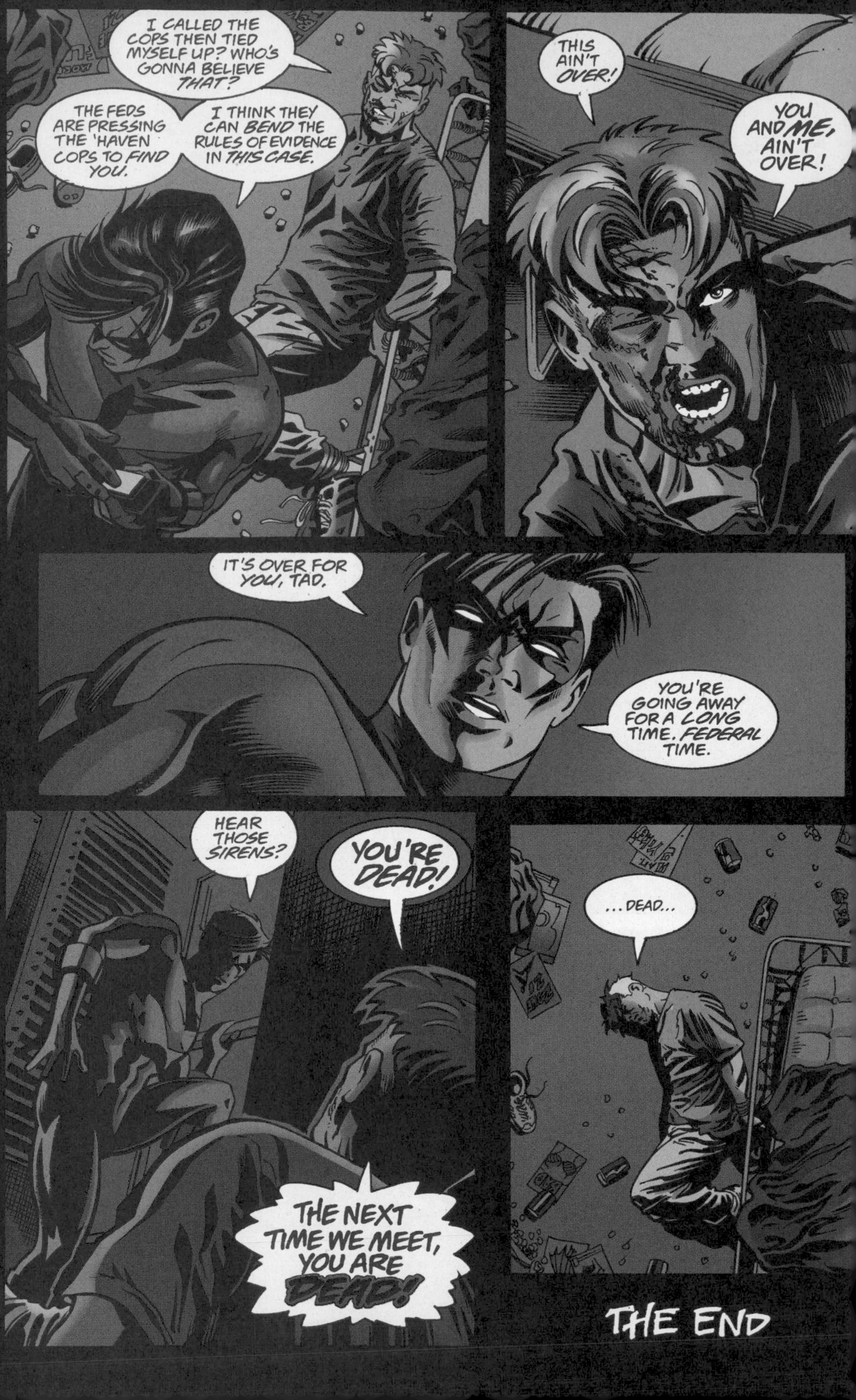
I CALLED THE COPS THEN TIED MYSELF UP? WHO'S GONNA BELIEVE *THAT*?
THE FEDS ARE PRESSING THE 'HAVEN COPS TO *FIND* YOU.
I THINK THEY CAN *BEND* THE RULES OF EVIDENCE IN *THIS CASE*.
THIS AIN'T *OVER*!
YOU AND *ME*, AIN'T OVER!
IT'S OVER FOR *YOU*, TAD.
YOU'RE GOING AWAY FOR A *LONG* TIME. *FEDERAL* TIME.
HEAR THOSE *SIRENS*?
YOU'RE DEAD!
THE NEXT TIME WE MEET, YOU ARE *DEAD*!
...DEAD...
THE END

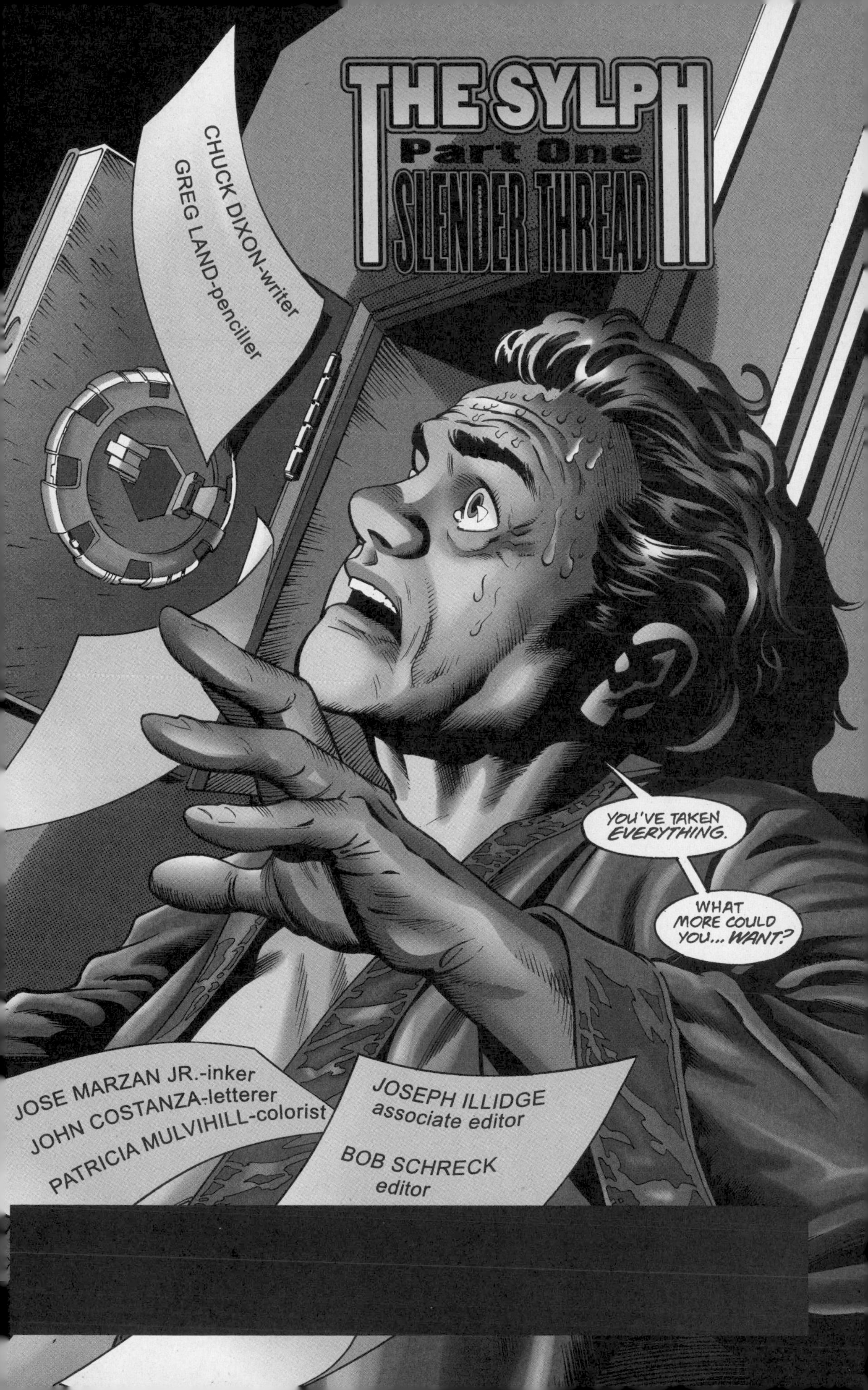

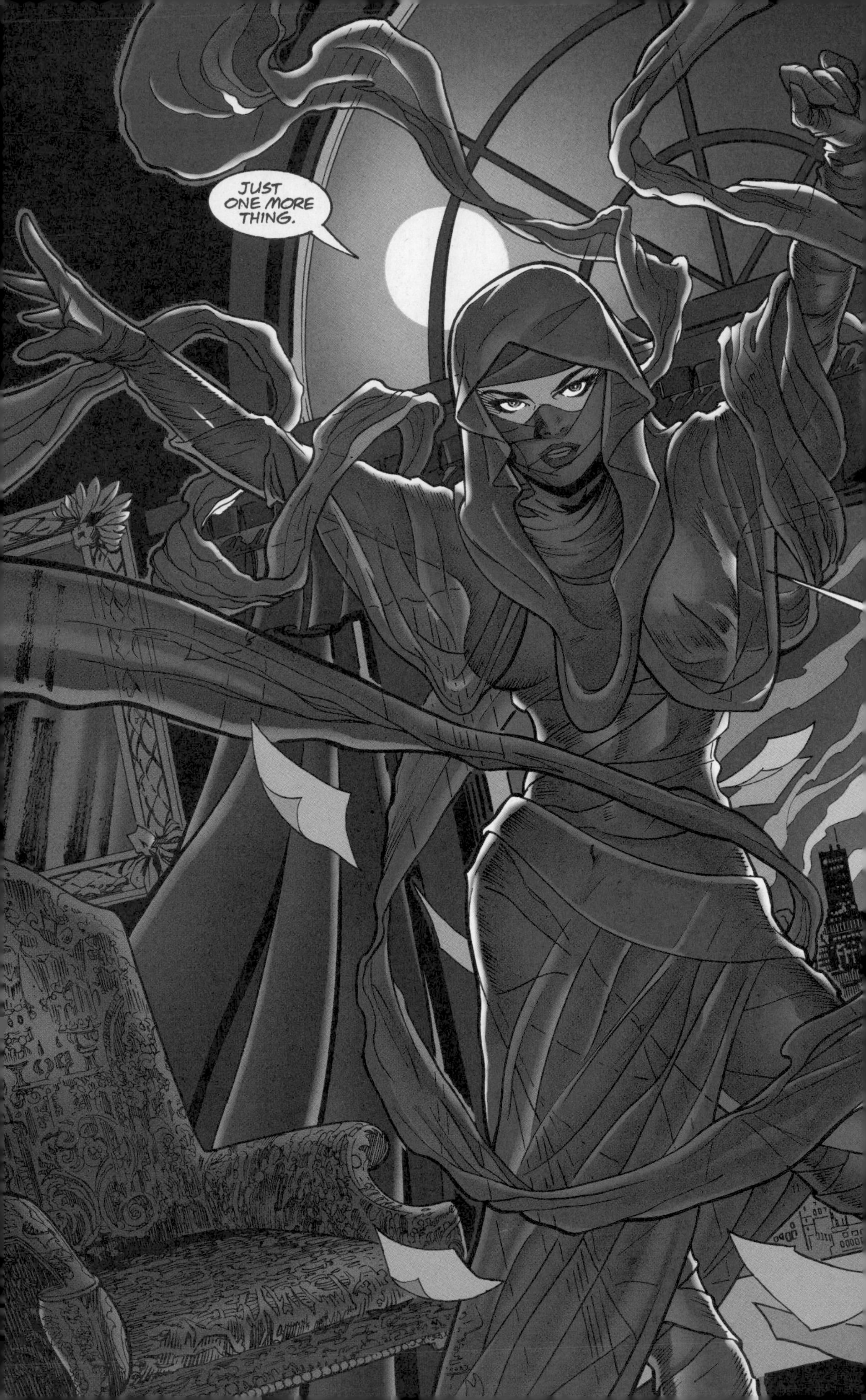
JUST ONE MORE THING.

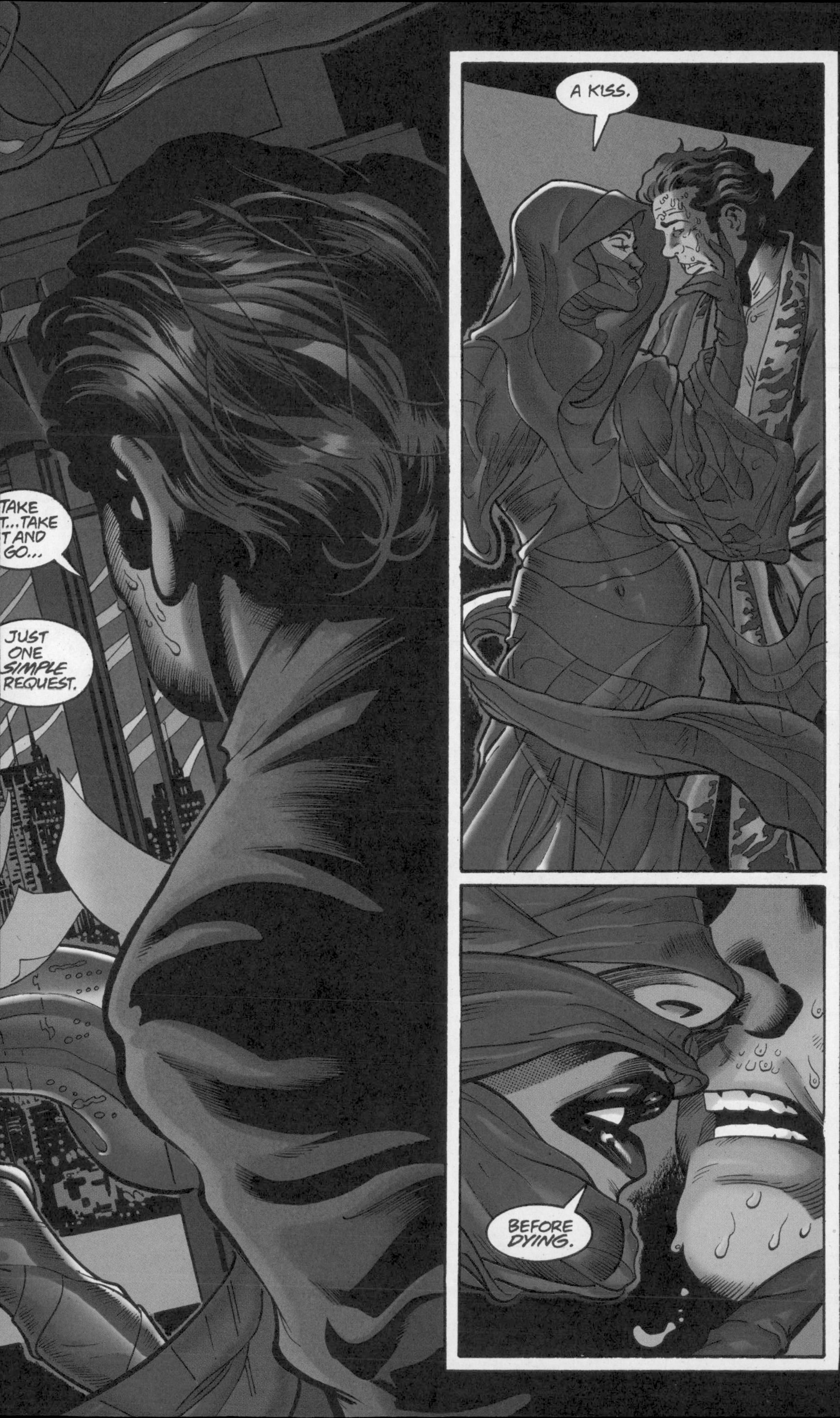
TAKE T...TAKE T AND GO...
JUST ONE *SIMPLE* REQUEST.
A KISS.
BEFORE *DYING*.

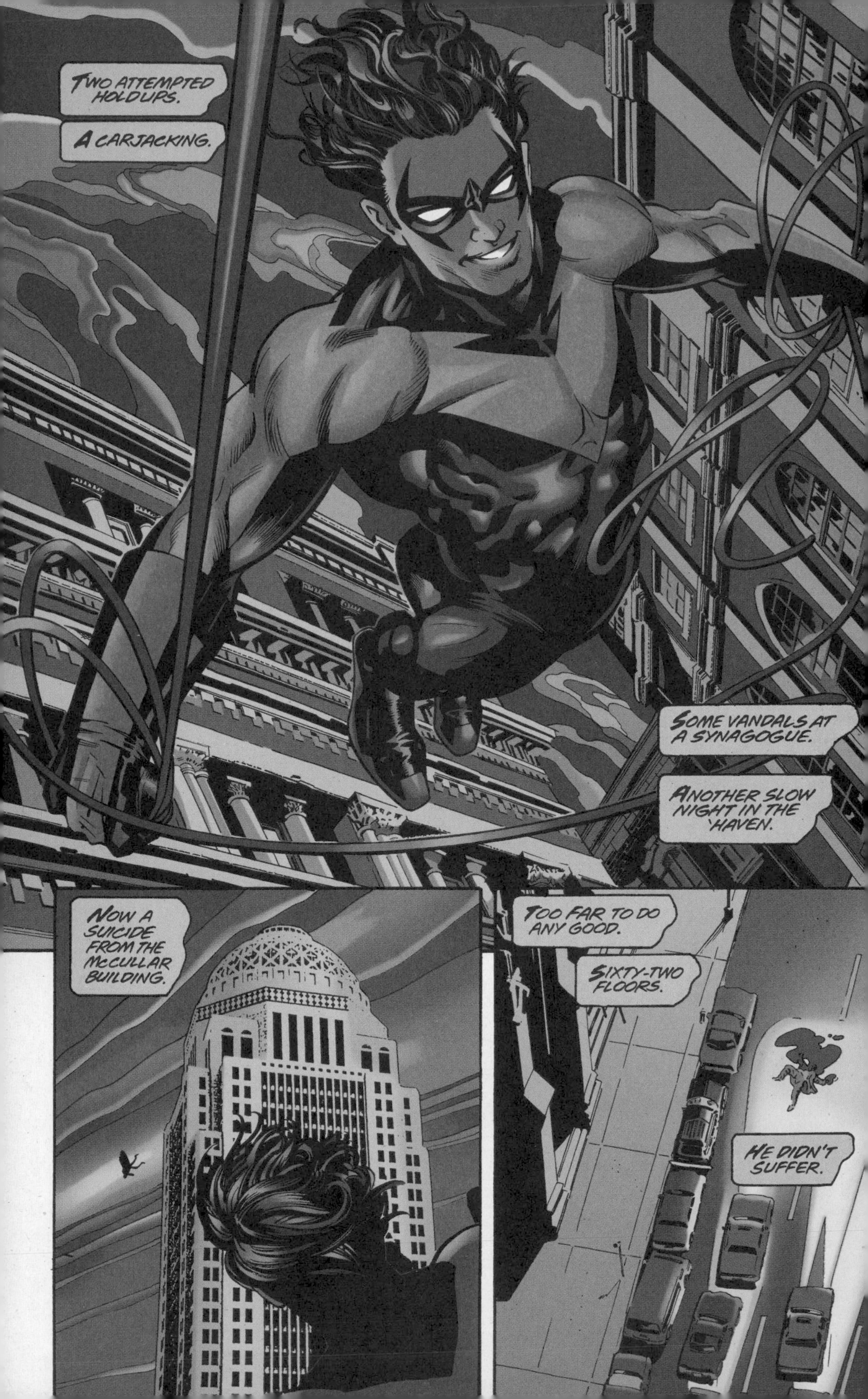
TWO ATTEMPTED HOLDUPS.
A CARJACKING.
SOME VANDALS AT A SYNAGOGUE.
ANOTHER SLOW NIGHT IN THE 'HAVEN.
NOW A SUICIDE FROM THE McCULLAR BUILDING.
TOO FAR TO DO ANY GOOD.
SIXTY-TWO FLOORS.
HE DIDN'T SUFFER.

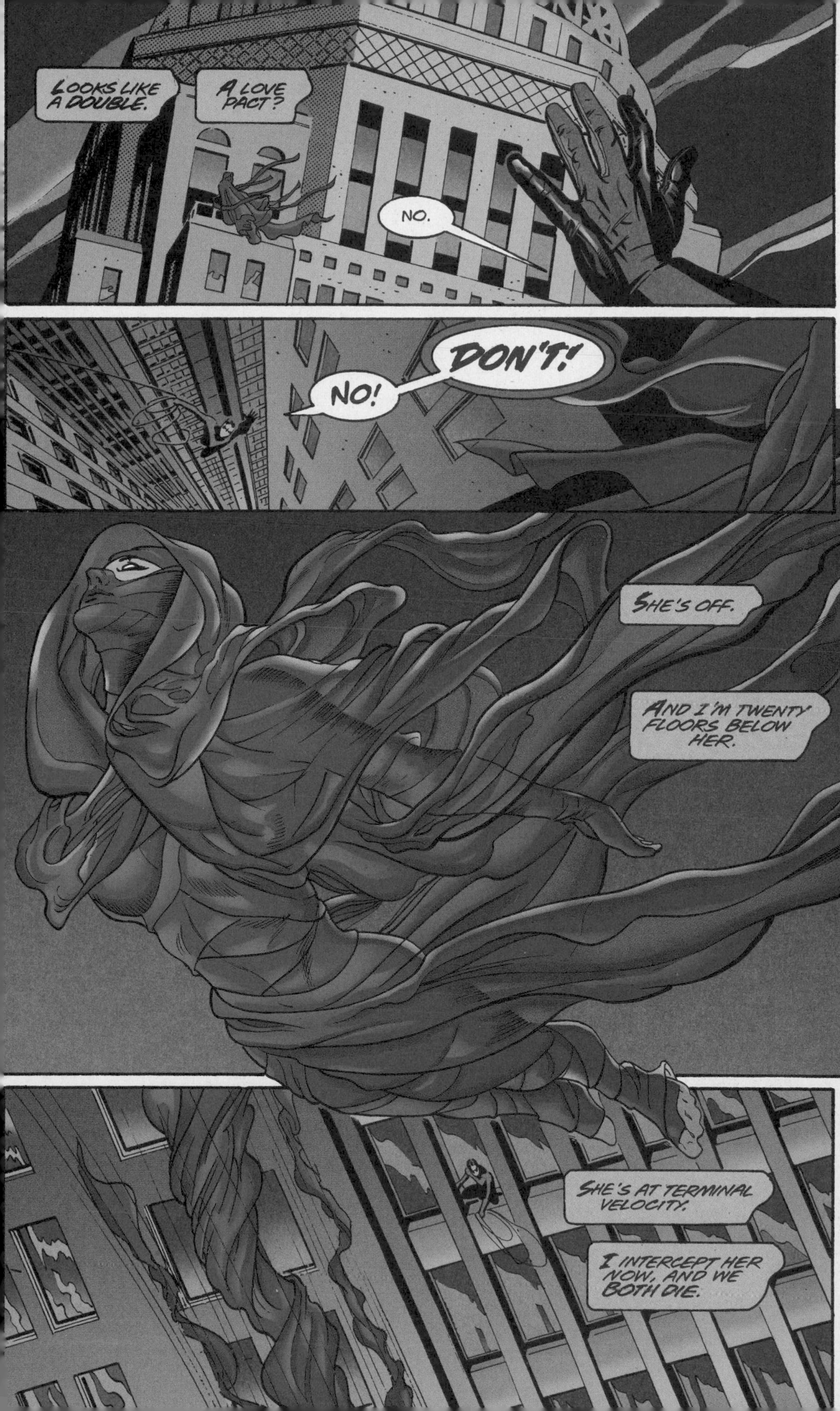
LOOKS LIKE A DOUBLE.
A LOVE PACT?
NO.
NO!
DON'T!
SHE'S OFF.
AND I'M TWENTY FLOORS BELOW HER.
SHE'S AT TERMINAL VELOCITY.
I INTERCEPT HER NOW, AND WE BOTH DIE.

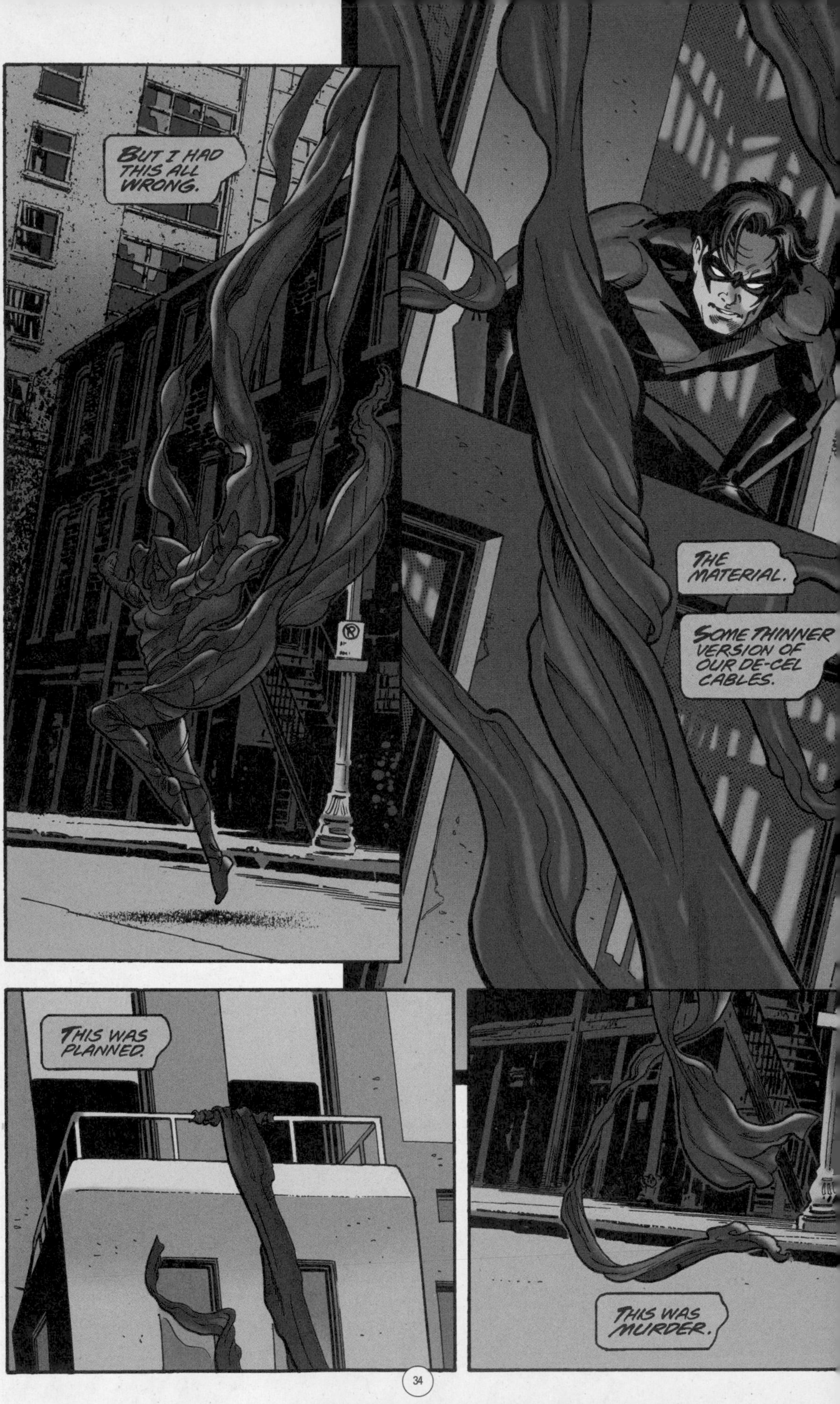
BUT I HAD THIS ALL WRONG.
THE MATERIAL.
SOME THINNER VERSION OF OUR DE-CEL CABLES.
THIS WAS PLANNED.
THIS WAS MURDER.

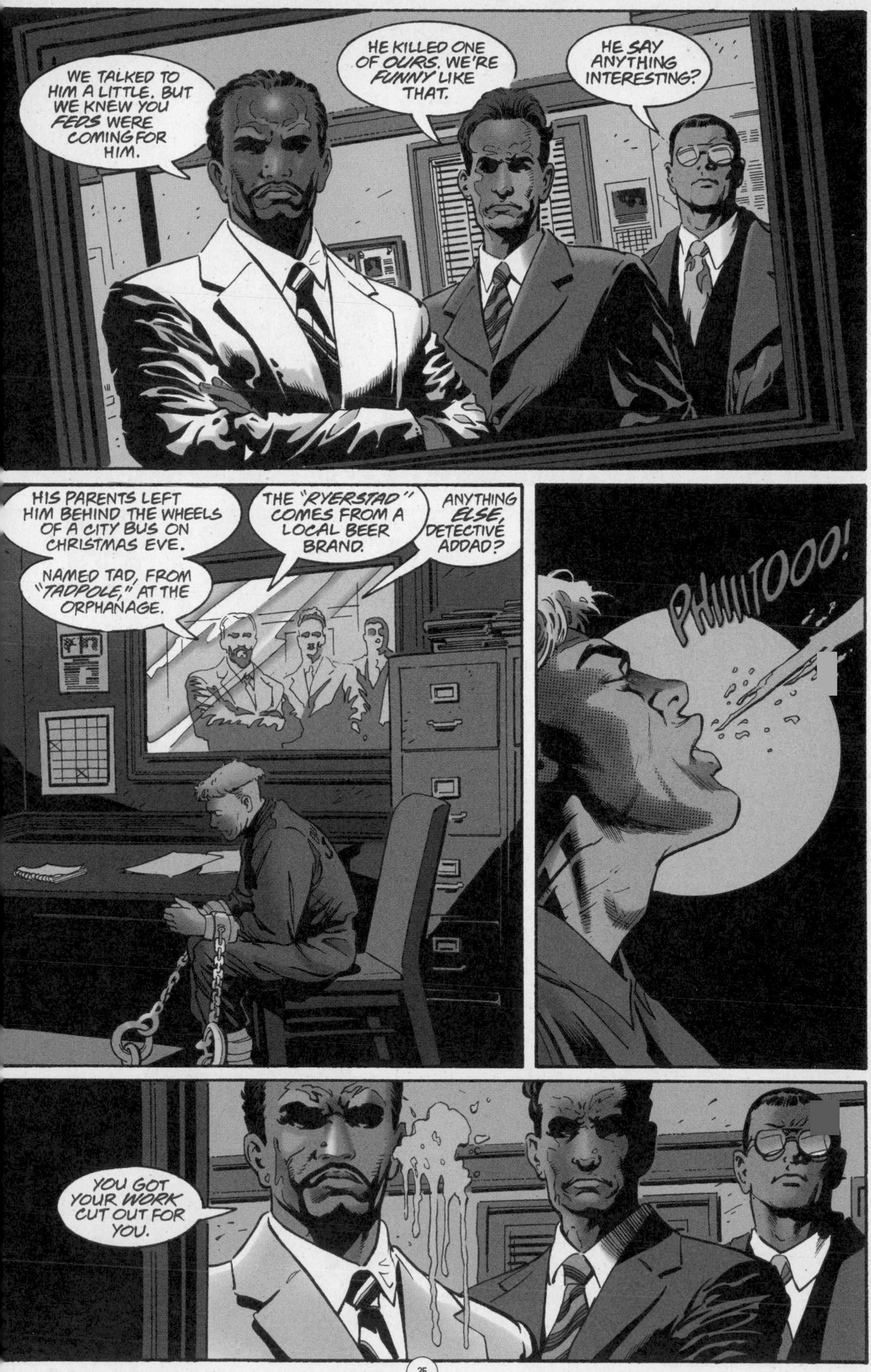
WE TALKED TO HIM A LITTLE. BUT WE KNEW YOU FEDS WERE COMING FOR HIM.
HE KILLED ONE OF OURS. WE'RE FUNNY LIKE THAT.
HE SAY ANYTHING INTERESTING?
HIS PARENTS LEFT HIM BEHIND THE WHEELS OF A CITY BUS ON CHRISTMAS EVE.
NAMED TAD, FROM "TADPOLE," AT THE ORPHANAGE.
THE "RYERSTAD" COMES FROM A LOCAL BEER BRAND.
ANYTHING ELSE, DETECTIVE ADDAD?
PHHHTOOO!
YOU GOT YOUR WORK CUT OUT FOR YOU.

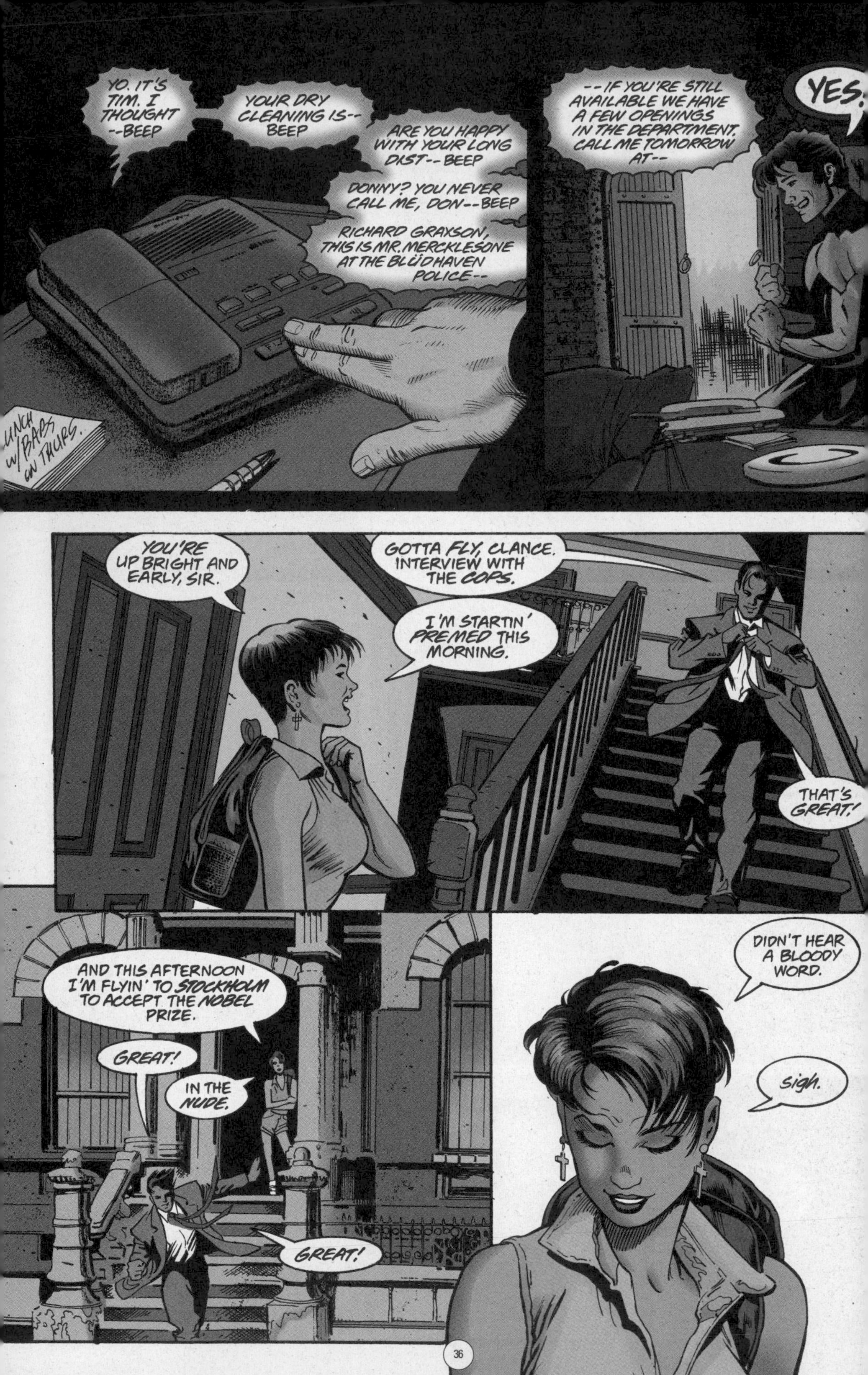
YO. IT'S TIM. I THOUGHT --BEEP
YOUR DRY CLEANING IS-- BEEP
ARE YOU HAPPY WITH YOUR LONG DIST-- BEEP
DONNY? YOU NEVER CALL ME, DON--BEEP
RICHARD GRAXSON, THIS IS MR. MERCKLESONE AT THE BLÜDHAVEN POLICE--
LUNCH W/BABS ON THURS
--IF YOU'RE STILL AVAILABLE WE HAVE A FEW OPENINGS IN THE DEPARTMENT. CALL ME TOMORROW AT--
YES!
YOU'RE UP BRIGHT AND EARLY, SIR.
GOTTA FLY, CLANCE. INTERVIEW WITH THE COPS.
I'M STARTIN' PREMED THIS MORNING.
THAT'S GREAT!
AND THIS AFTERNOON I'M FLYIN' TO STOCKHOLM TO ACCEPT THE NOBEL PRIZE.
GREAT!
IN THE NUDE.
GREAT!
DIDN'T HEAR A BLOODY WORD.
sigh.

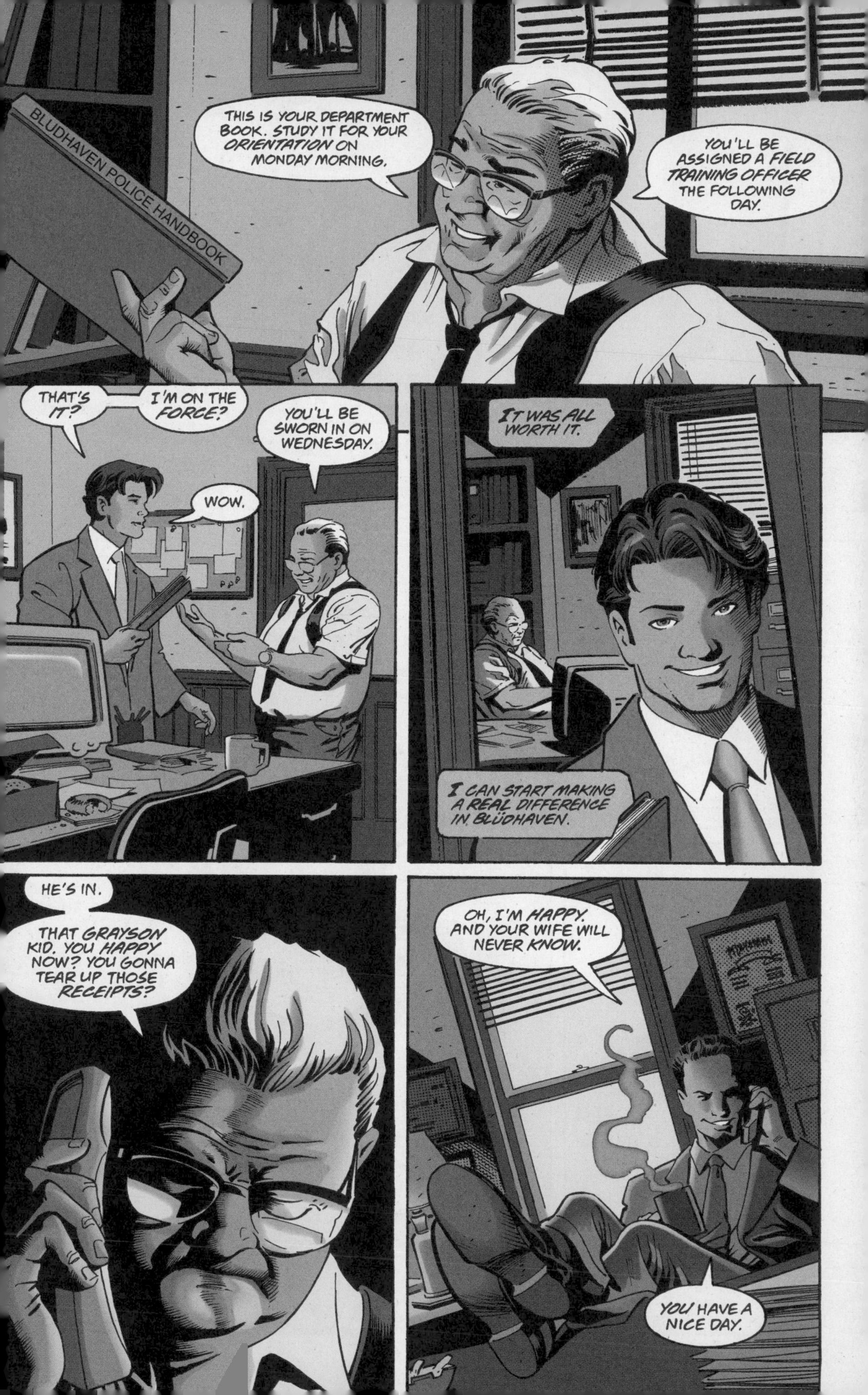

BLUDHAVEN POLICE HANDBOOK
THIS IS YOUR DEPARTMENT BOOK. STUDY IT FOR YOUR ORIENTATION ON MONDAY MORNING.
YOU'LL BE ASSIGNED A FIELD TRAINING OFFICER THE FOLLOWING DAY.
THAT'S IT?
I'M ON THE FORCE?
YOU'LL BE SWORN IN ON WEDNESDAY.
WOW.
IT WAS ALL WORTH IT.
I CAN START MAKING A REAL DIFFERENCE IN BLÜDHAVEN.
HE'S IN.
THAT GRAYSON KID. YOU HAPPY NOW? YOU GONNA TEAR UP THOSE RECEIPTS?
OH, I'M HAPPY. AND YOUR WIFE WILL NEVER KNOW.
YOU HAVE A NICE DAY.

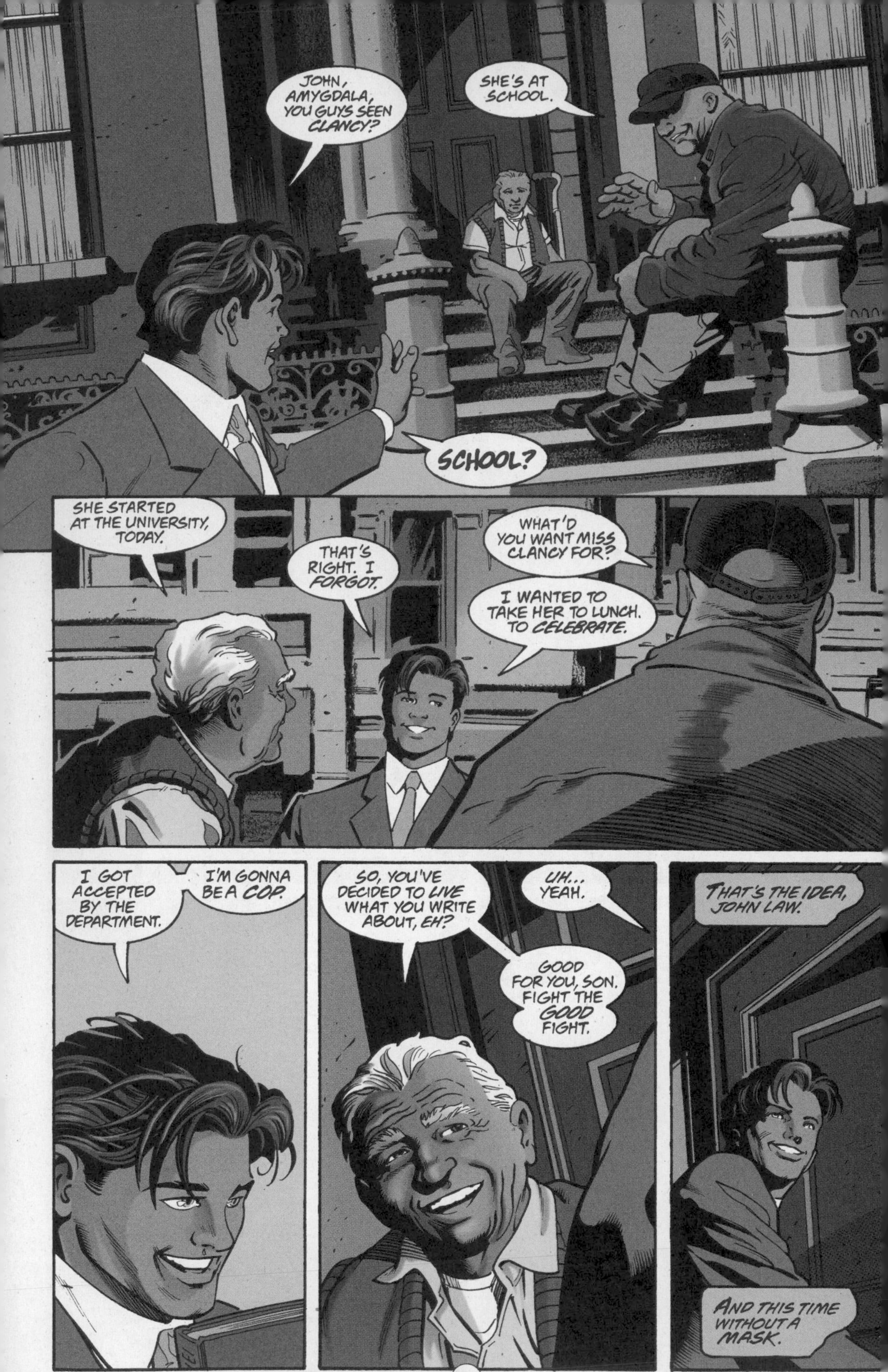
JOHN, AMYGDALA, YOU GUYS SEEN CLANCY?
SHE'S AT SCHOOL.
SCHOOL?
SHE STARTED AT THE UNIVERSITY, TODAY.
THAT'S RIGHT. I FORGOT.
WHAT'D YOU WANT MISS CLANCY FOR?
I WANTED TO TAKE HER TO LUNCH. TO CELEBRATE.
I GOT ACCEPTED BY THE DEPARTMENT.
I'M GONNA BE A COP.
SO, YOU'VE DECIDED TO LIVE WHAT YOU WRITE ABOUT, EH?
UH... YEAH.
GOOD FOR YOU, SON. FIGHT THE GOOD FIGHT.
THAT'S THE IDEA, JOHN LAW.
AND THIS TIME WITHOUT A MASK.

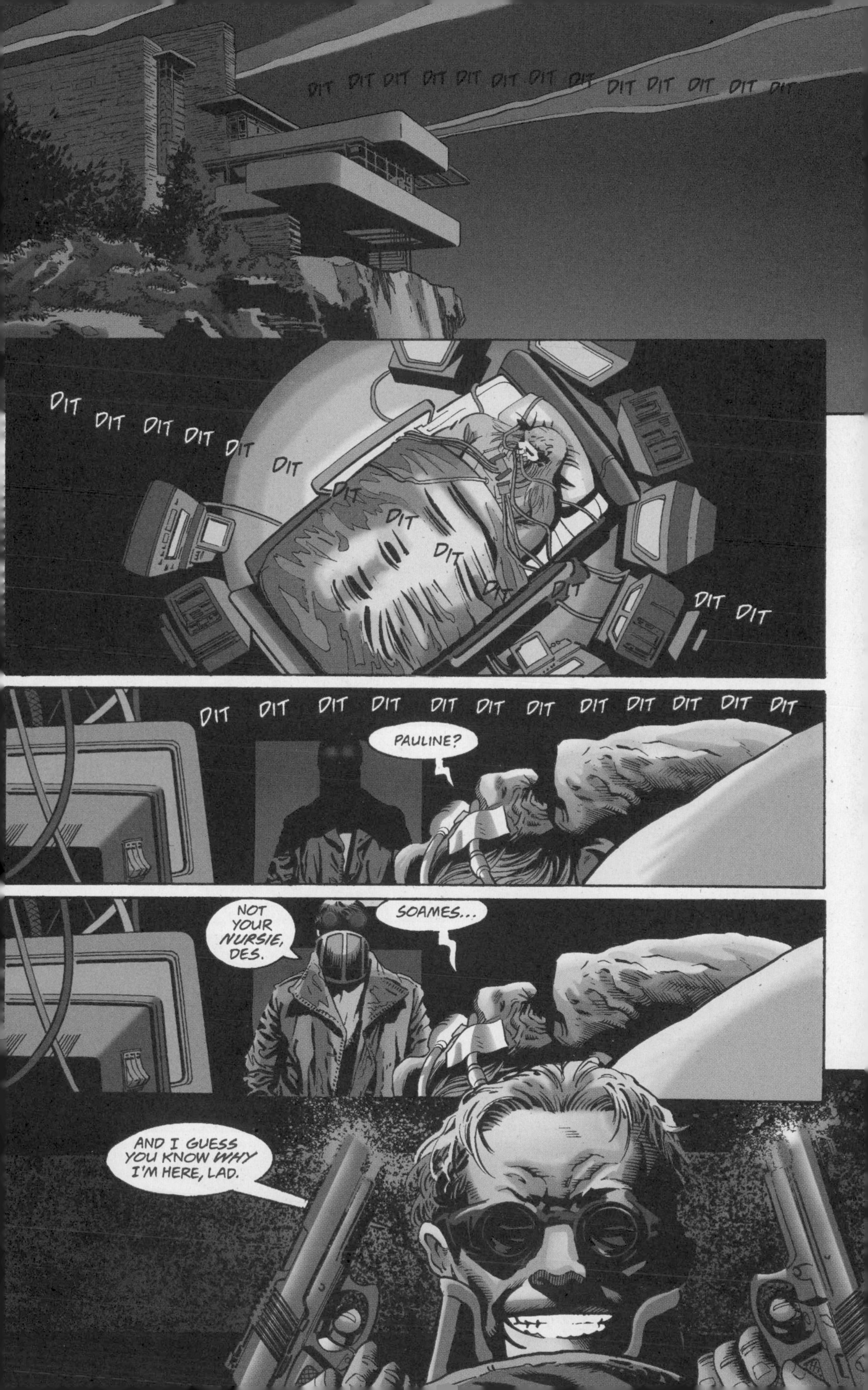
DIT DIT DIT DIT DIT DIT DIT DIT DIT DIT DIT DIT
DIT DIT DIT DIT DIT DIT DIT DIT DIT DIT DIT DIT
DIT DIT DIT DIT DIT DIT DIT DIT DIT DIT DIT DIT
PAULINE?
NOT YOUR NURSIE, DES.
SOAMES...
AND I GUESS YOU KNOW WHY I'M HERE, LAD.

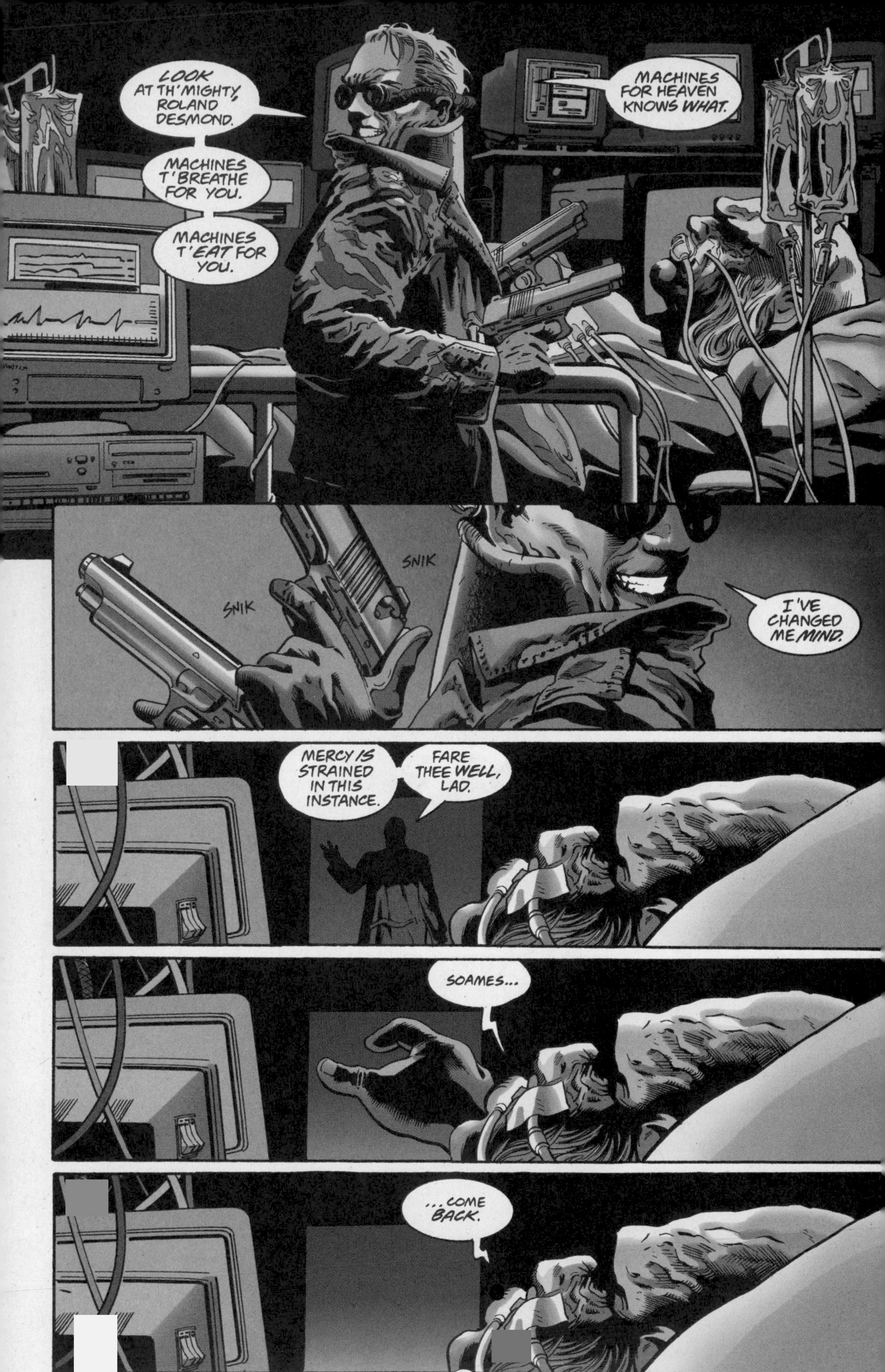
LOOK AT TH' MIGHTY, ROLAND DESMOND.
MACHINES T' BREATHE FOR YOU.
MACHINES T' EAT FOR YOU.
MACHINES FOR HEAVEN KNOWS WHAT.
SNIK
SNIK
I'VE CHANGED ME MIND.
MERCY IS STRAINED IN THIS INSTANCE.
FARE THEE WELL, LAD.
SOAMES...
...COME BACK.

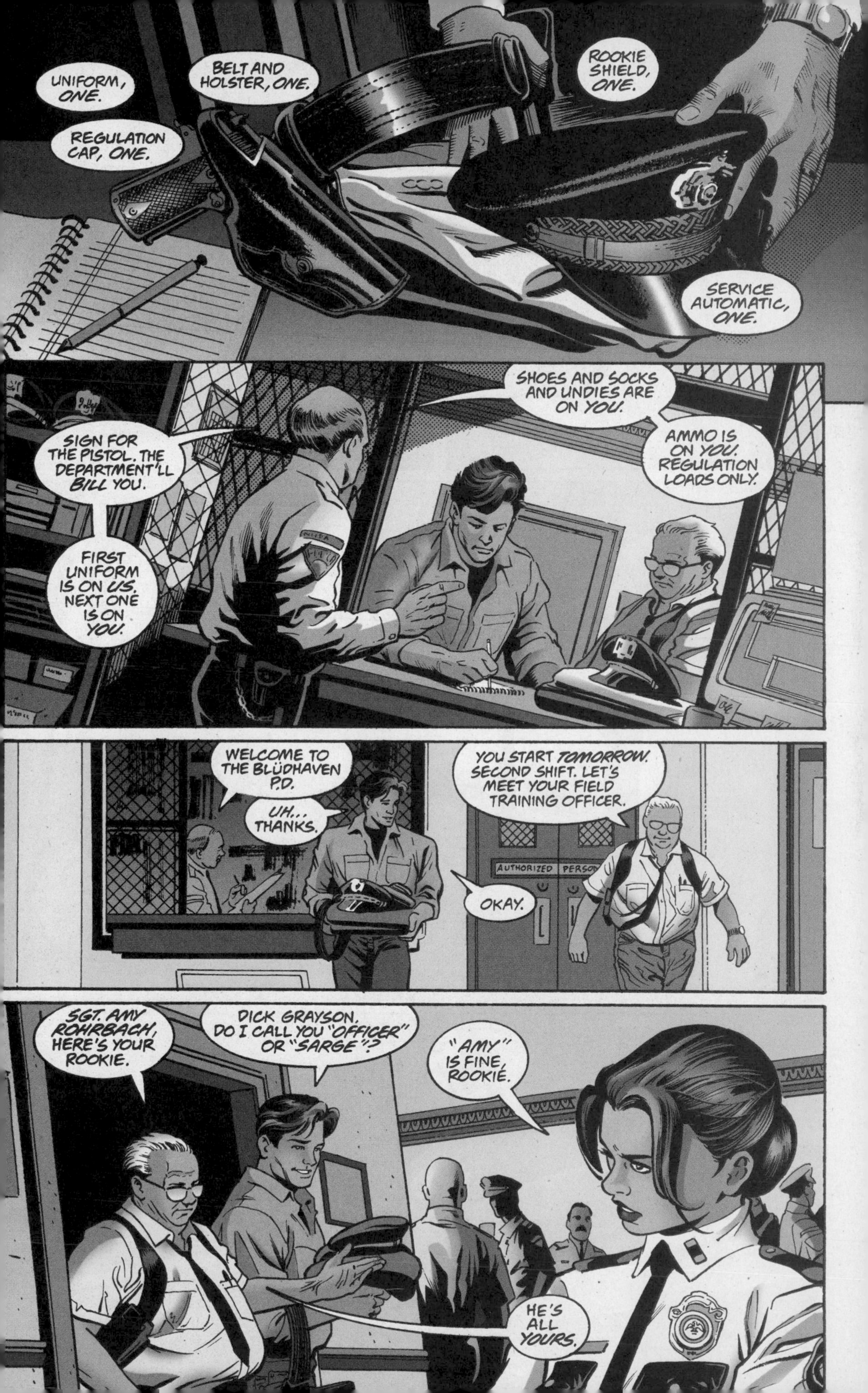
UNIFORM, ONE.
REGULATION CAP, ONE.
BELT AND HOLSTER, ONE.
ROOKIE SHIELD, ONE.
SERVICE AUTOMATIC, ONE.
SIGN FOR THE PISTOL. THE DEPARTMENT'LL BILL YOU.
FIRST UNIFORM IS ON US. NEXT ONE IS ON YOU.
SHOES AND SOCKS AND UNDIES ARE ON YOU.
AMMO IS ON YOU. REGULATION LOADS ONLY.
WELCOME TO THE BLÜDHAVEN P.D.
UH... THANKS.
YOU START TOMORROW. SECOND SHIFT. LET'S MEET YOUR FIELD TRAINING OFFICER.
OKAY.
AUTHORIZED PERSON
SGT. AMY ROHRBACH, HERE'S YOUR ROOKIE.
DICK GRAYSON. DO I CALL YOU "OFFICER" OR "SARGE"?
"AMY" IS FINE, ROOKIE.
HE'S ALL YOURS.

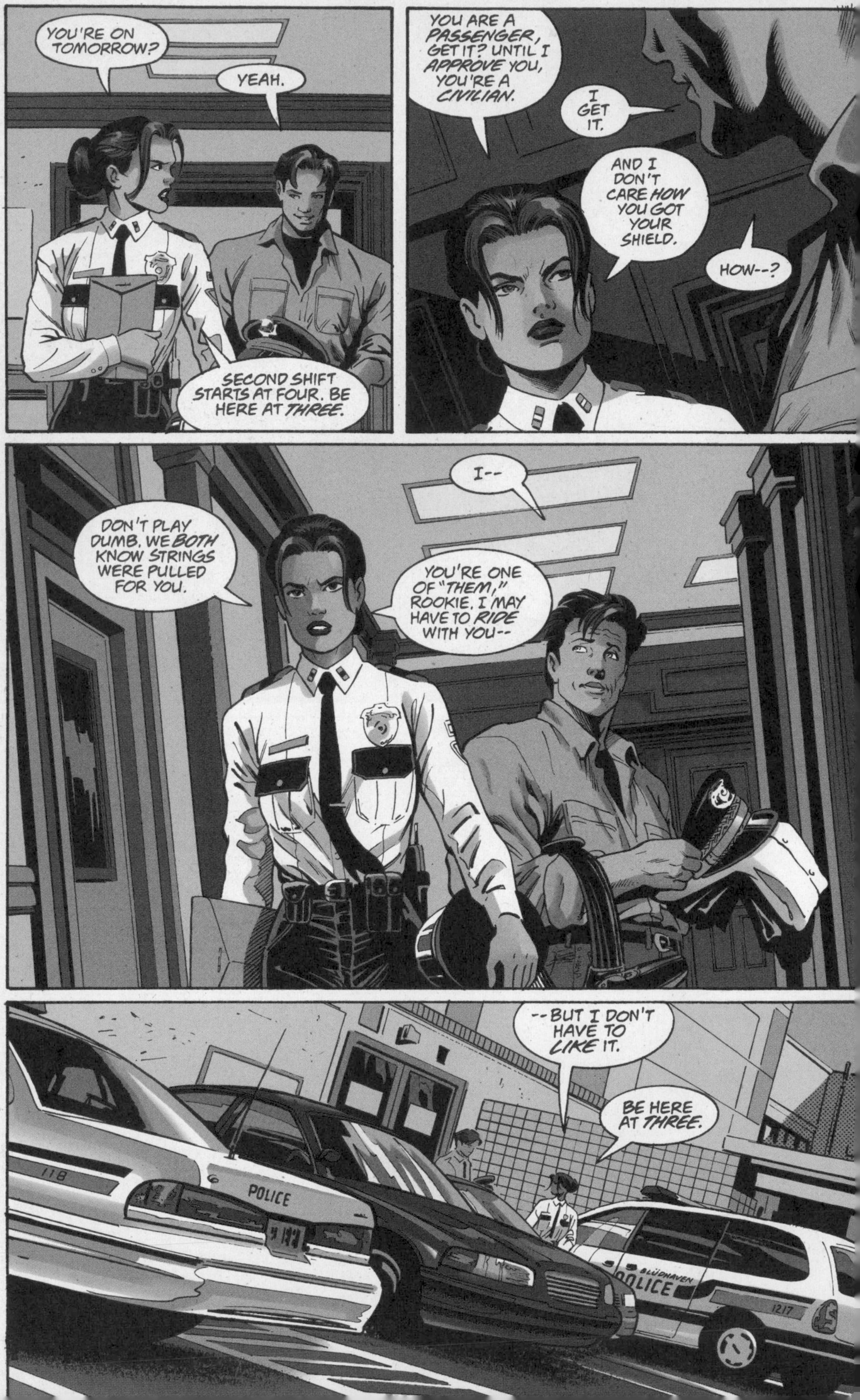
YOU'RE ON TOMORROW?
YEAH.
SECOND SHIFT STARTS AT FOUR. BE HERE AT THREE.
YOU ARE A PASSENGER, GET IT? UNTIL I APPROVE YOU, YOU'RE A CIVILIAN.
I GET IT.
AND I DON'T CARE HOW YOU GOT YOUR SHIELD.
HOW--?
I--
DON'T PLAY DUMB. WE BOTH KNOW STRINGS WERE PULLED FOR YOU.
YOU'RE ONE OF "THEM," ROOKIE. I MAY HAVE TO RIDE WITH YOU--
--BUT I DON'T HAVE TO LIKE IT.
BE HERE AT THREE.
118
POLICE
BLÜDHAVEN POLICE
1217

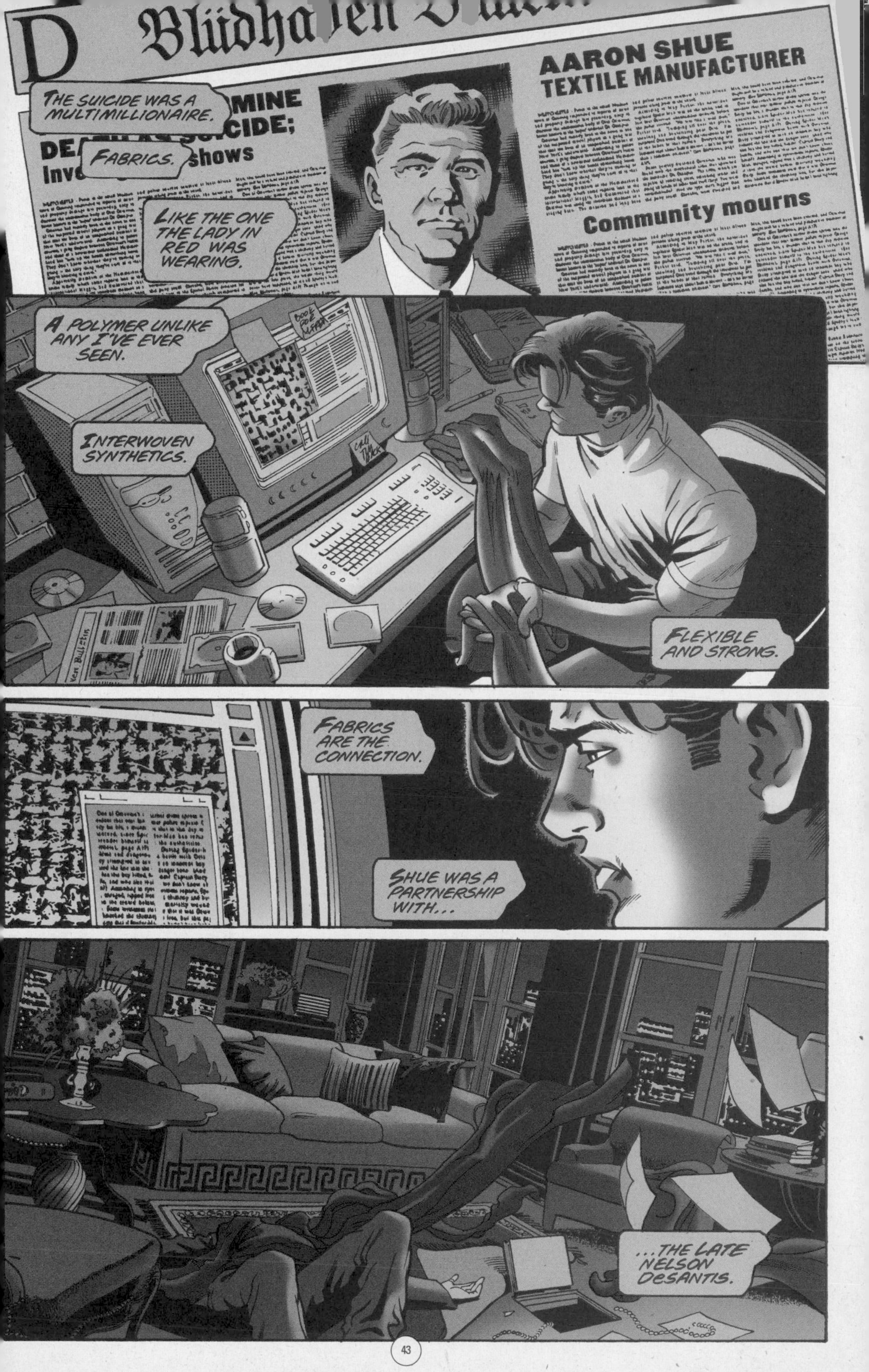

Blüdhaven
AARON SHUE
TEXTILE MANUFACTURER
THE SUICIDE WAS A MULTIMILLIONAIRE.
FABRICS.
LIKE THE ONE THE LADY IN RED WAS WEARING.
Community mourns
A POLYMER UNLIKE ANY I'VE EVER SEEN.
INTERWOVEN SYNTHETICS.
FLEXIBLE AND STRONG.
FABRICS ARE THE CONNECTION.
SHUE WAS A PARTNERSHIP WITH...
...THE LATE NELSON DeSANTIS.

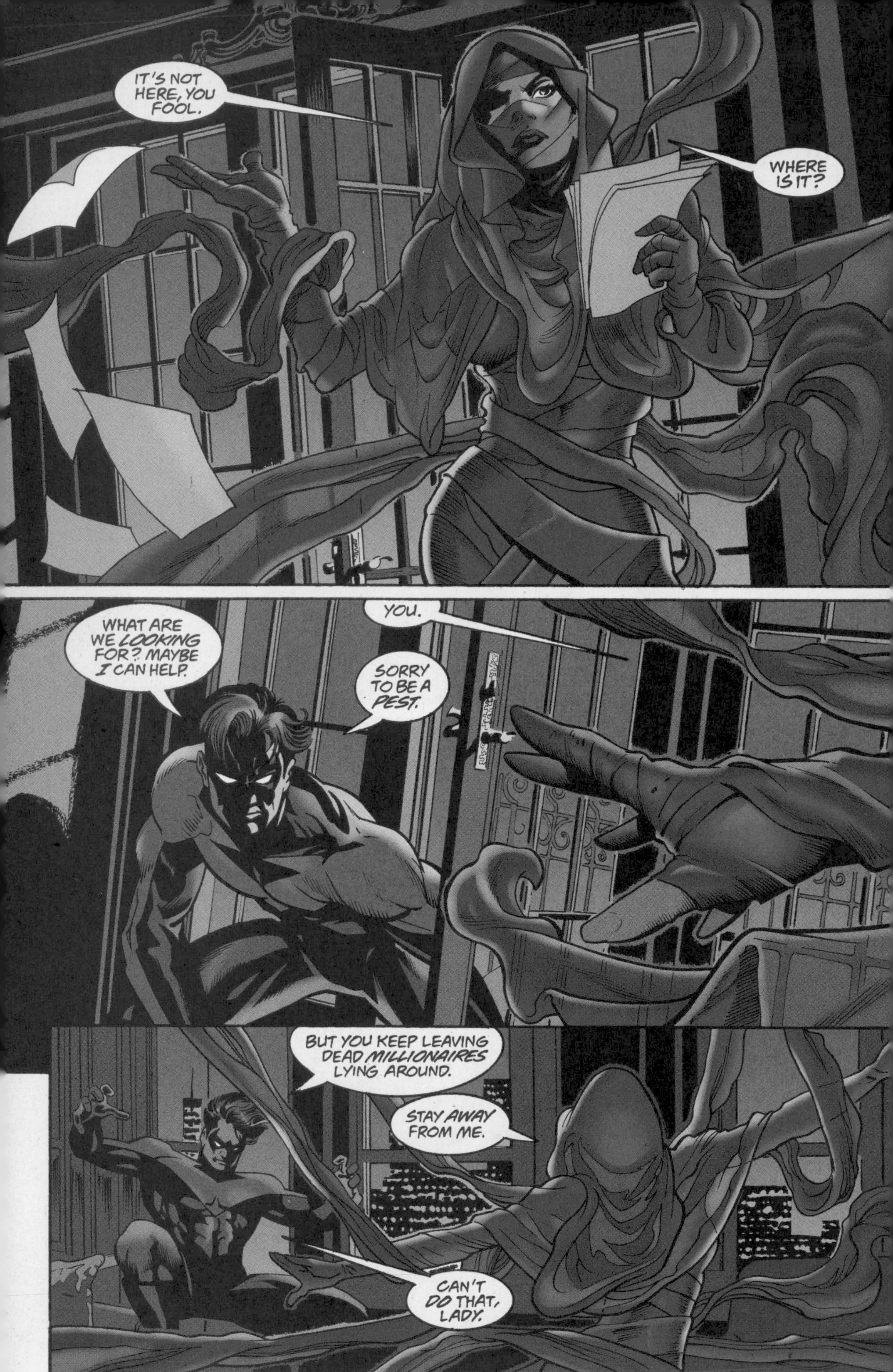
IT'S NOT HERE, YOU FOOL.
WHERE IS IT?
WHAT ARE WE LOOKING FOR? MAYBE I CAN HELP.
SORRY TO BE A PEST.
YOU.
BUT YOU KEEP LEAVING DEAD MILLIONAIRES LYING AROUND.
STAY AWAY FROM ME.
CAN'T DO THAT, LADY.

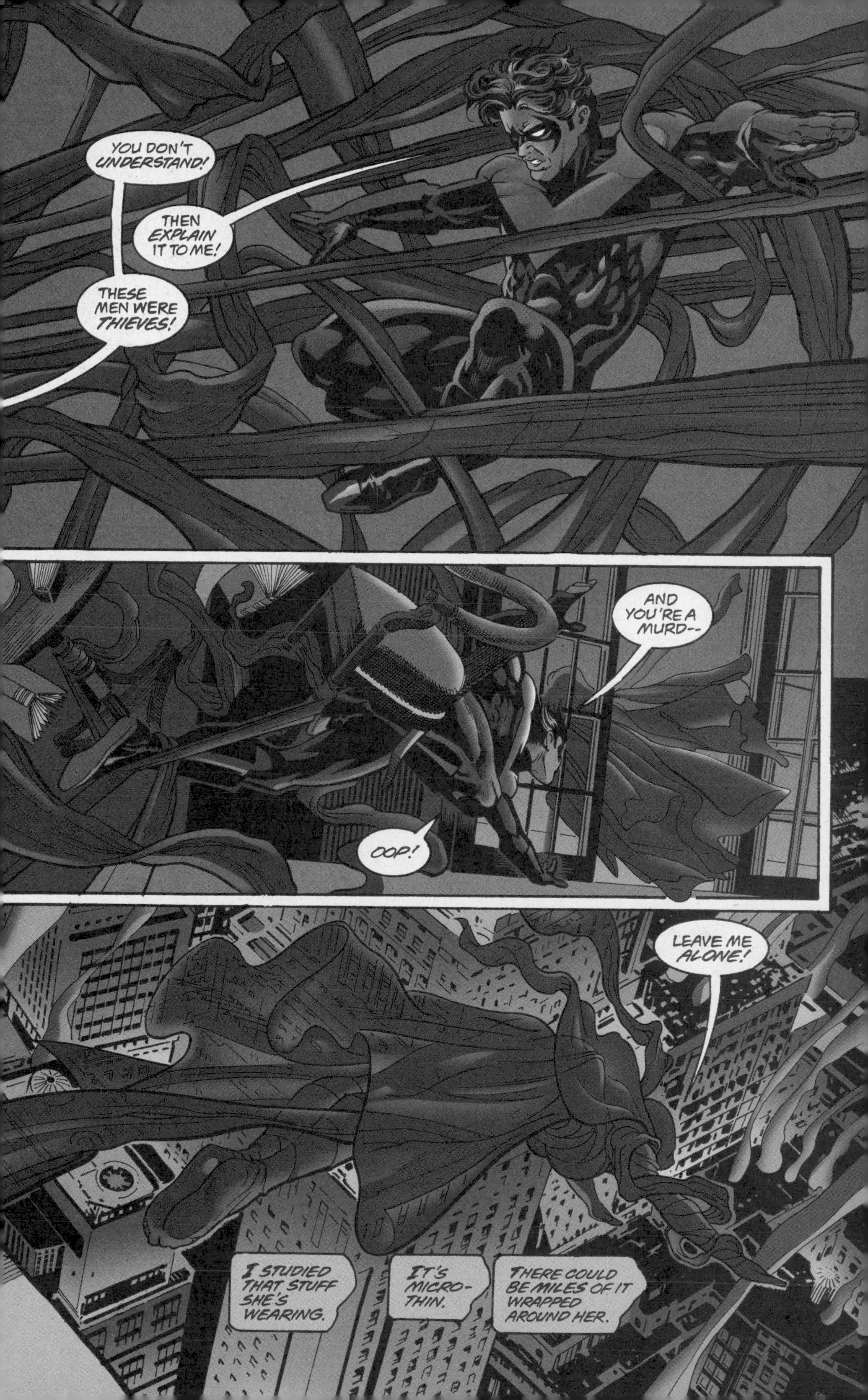
YOU DON'T UNDERSTAND!
THEN EXPLAIN IT TO ME!
THESE MEN WERE THIEVES!
AND YOU'RE A MURD--
OOP!
LEAVE ME ALONE!
I STUDIED THAT STUFF SHE'S WEARING.
IT'S MICRO-THIN.
THERE COULD BE MILES OF IT WRAPPED AROUND HER.

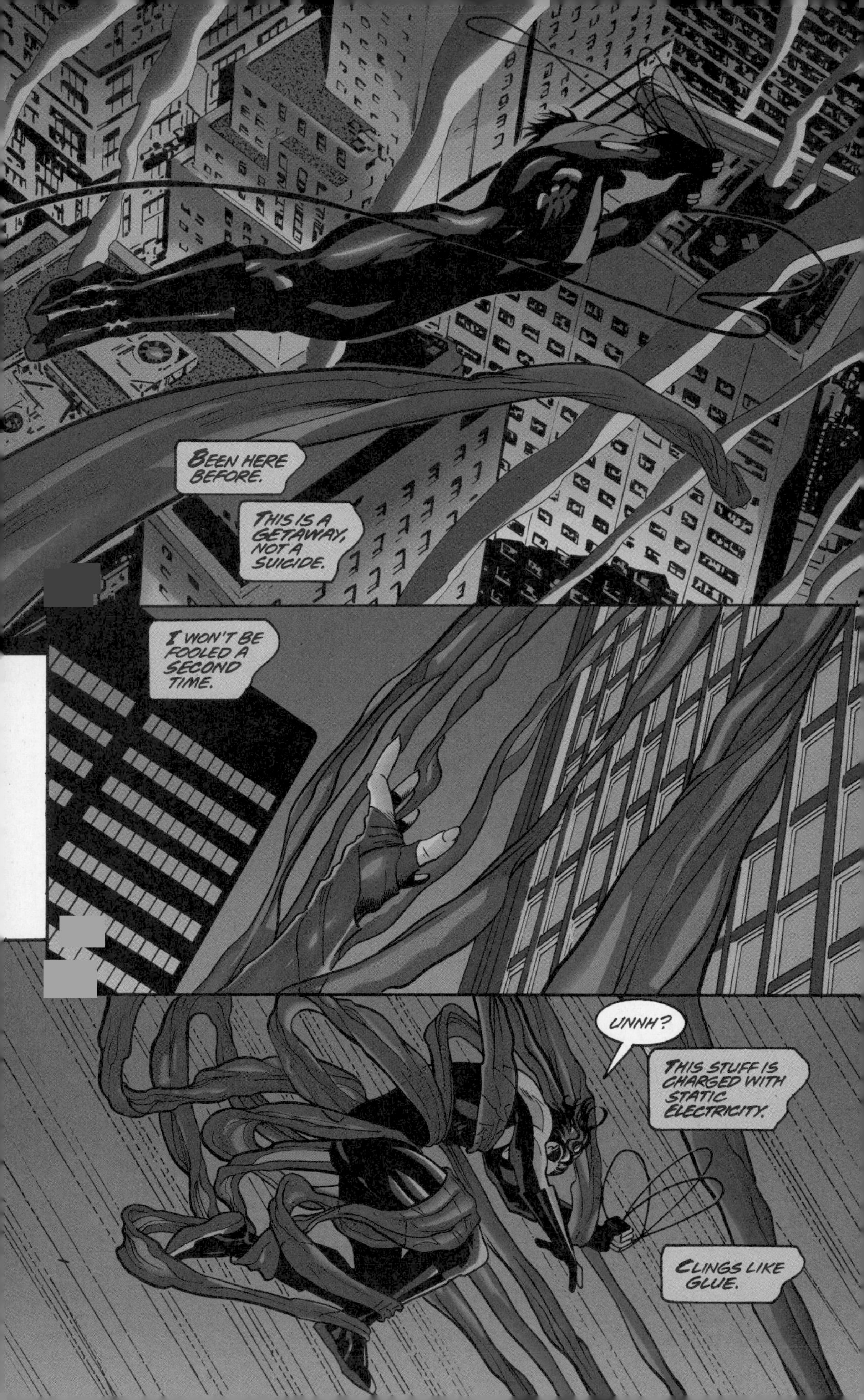
BEEN HERE BEFORE.
THIS IS A GETAWAY, NOT A SUICIDE.
I WON'T BE FOOLED A SECOND TIME.
UNNH?
THIS STUFF IS CHARGED WITH STATIC ELECTRICITY.
CLINGS LIKE GLUE.

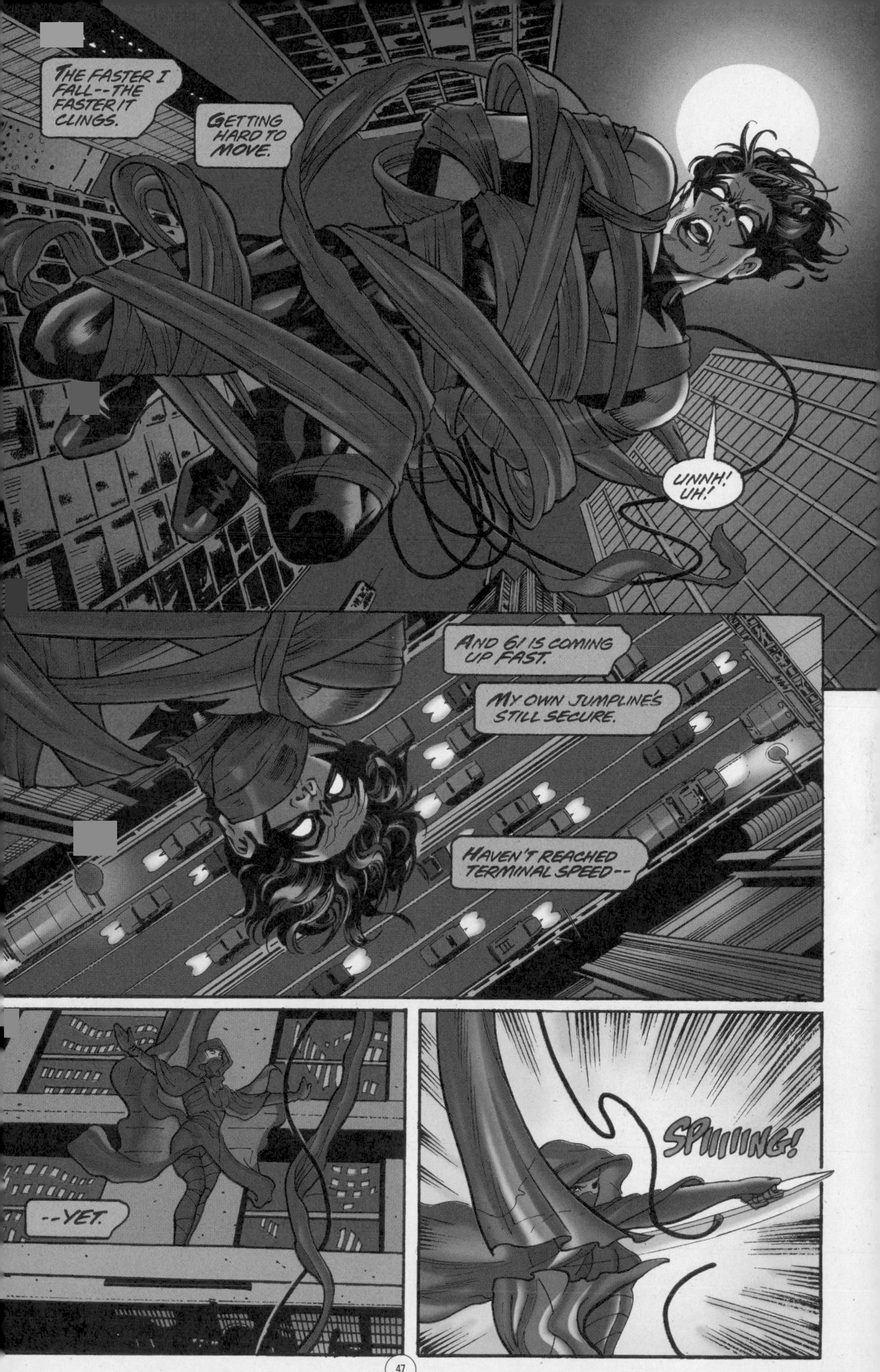
THE FASTER I FALL--THE FASTER IT CLINGS.
GETTING HARD TO MOVE.
UNNH! UH!
AND 61 IS COMING UP FAST.
MY OWN JUMPLINE'S STILL SECURE.
HAVEN'T REACHED TERMINAL SPEED--
--YET.
SPIIIIING!

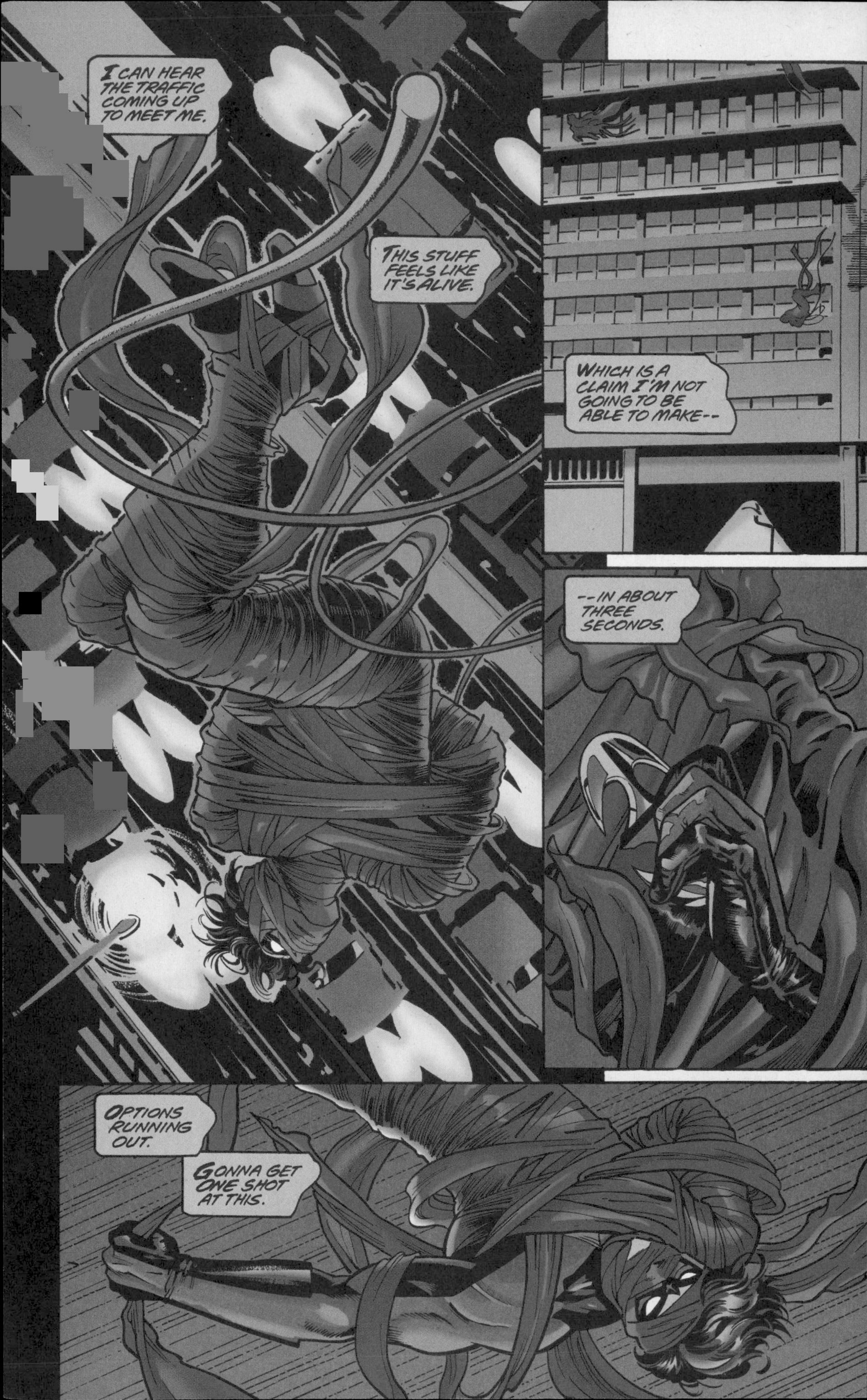
I CAN HEAR THE TRAFFIC COMING UP TO MEET ME.
THIS STUFF FEELS LIKE IT'S ALIVE.
WHICH IS A CLAIM I'M NOT GOING TO BE ABLE TO MAKE--
--IN ABOUT THREE SECONDS.
OPTIONS RUNNING OUT.
GONNA GET ONE SHOT AT THIS.

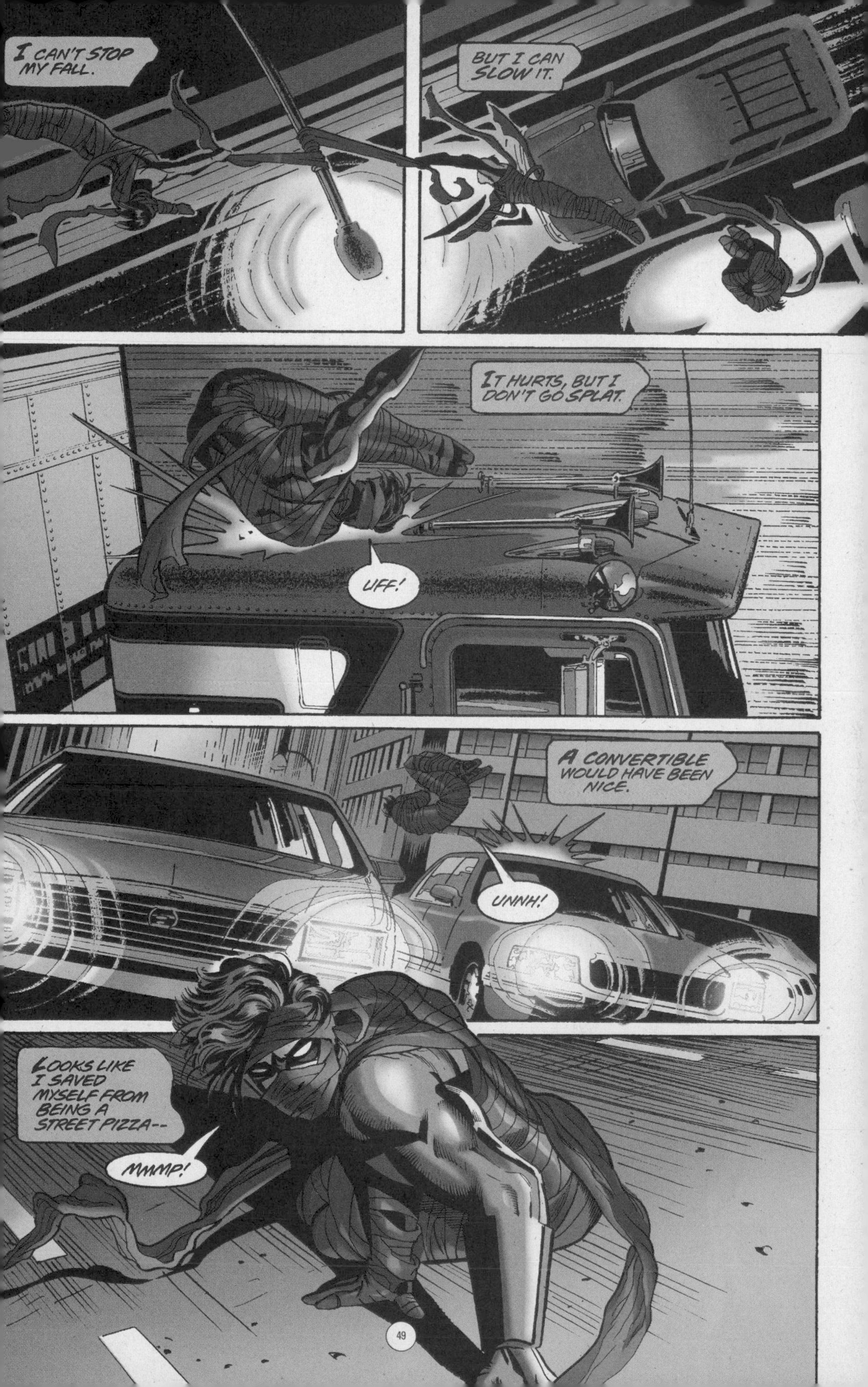
I CAN'T STOP MY FALL.
BUT I CAN SLOW IT.
IT HURTS, BUT I DON'T GO SPLAT.
UFF!
A CONVERTIBLE WOULD HAVE BEEN NICE.
UNNH!
LOOKS LIKE I SAVED MYSELF FROM BEING A STREET PIZZA--
MMMP!

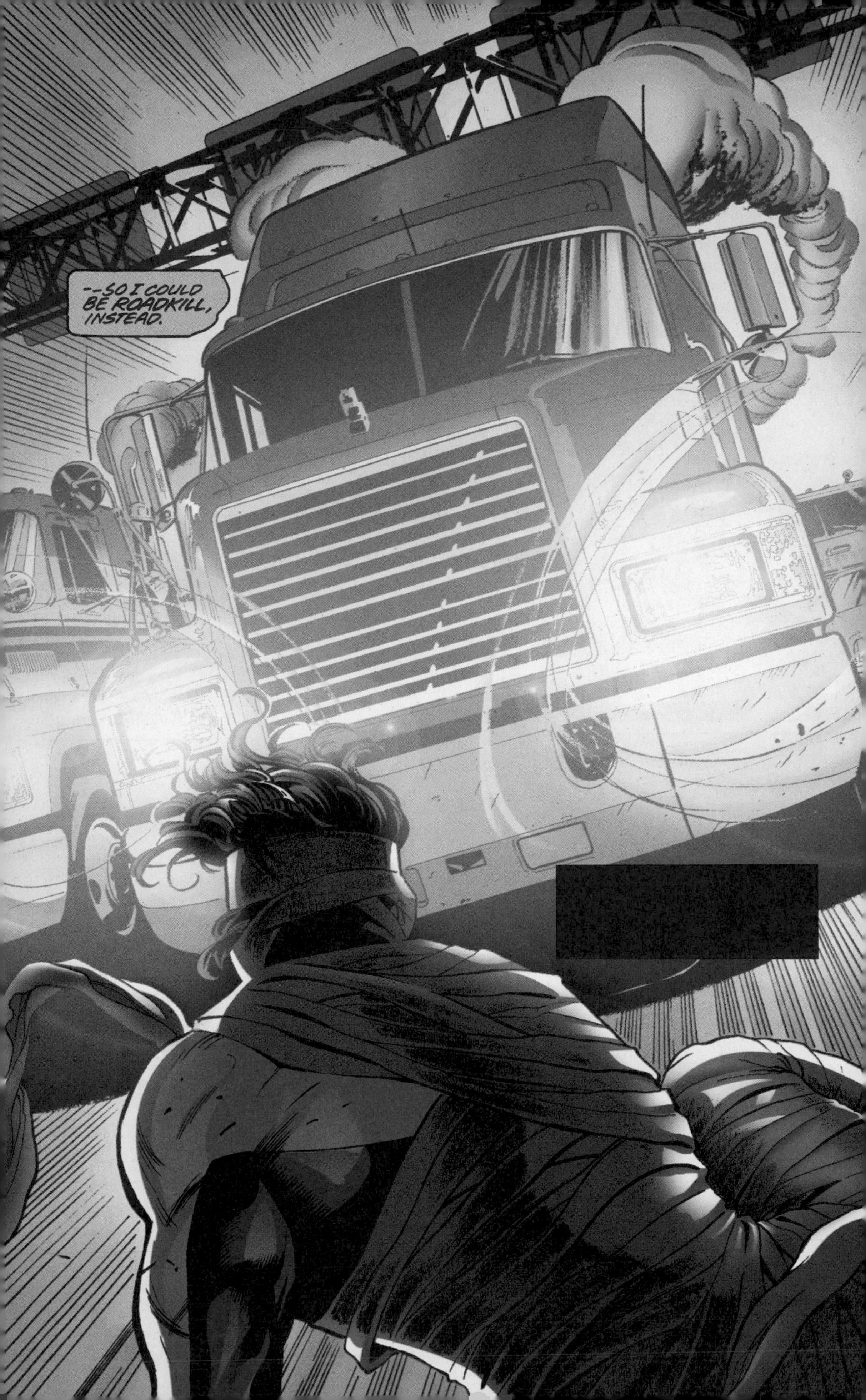
--SO I COULD BE ROADKILL, INSTEAD.
[redacted]

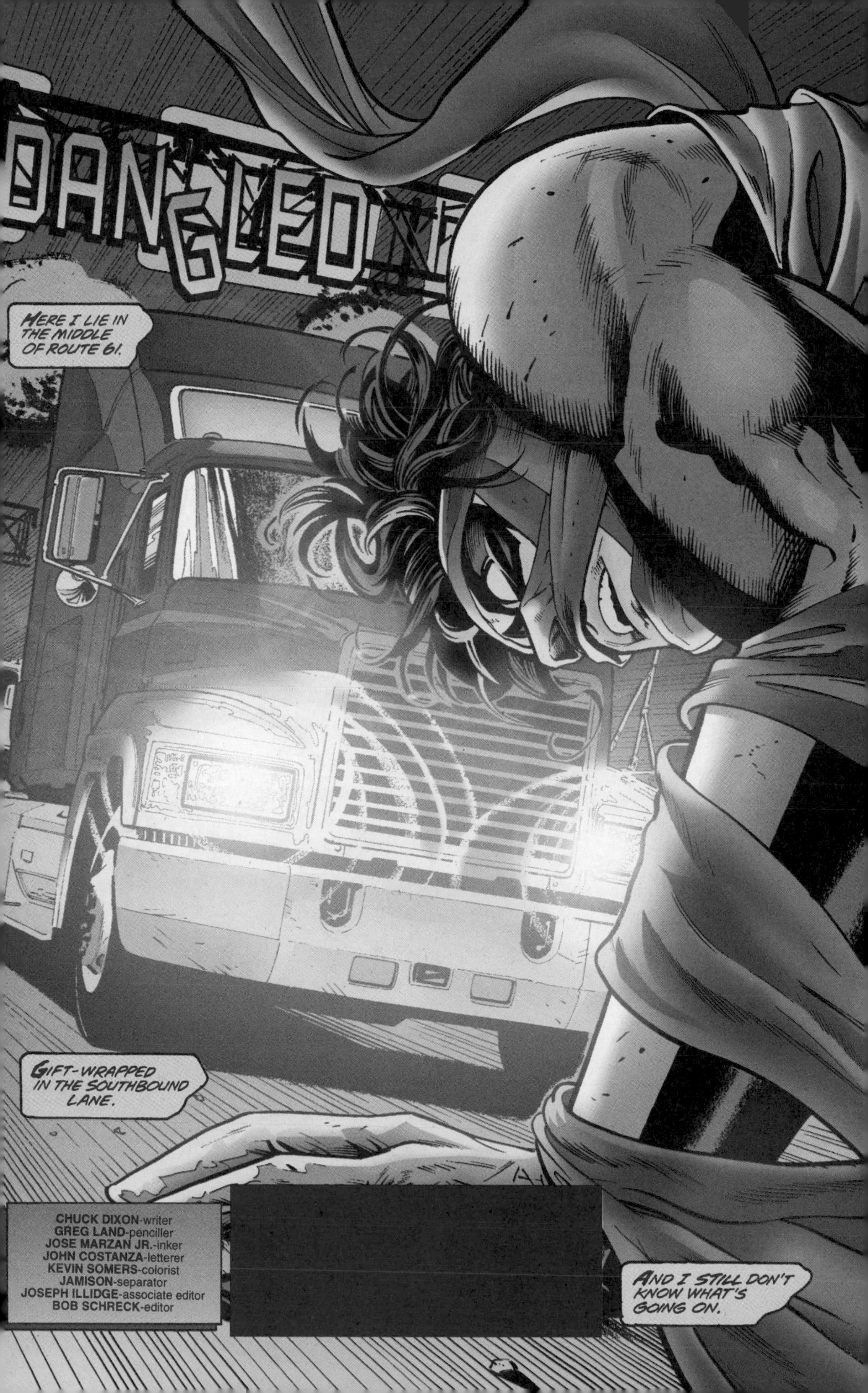
HERE I LIE IN THE MIDDLE OF ROUTE 61.
GIFT-WRAPPED IN THE SOUTHBOUND LANE.
CHUCK DIXON-writer
GREG LAND-penciller
JOSE MARZAN JR.-inker
JOHN COSTANZA-letterer
KEVIN SOMERS-colorist
JAMISON-separator
JOSEPH ILLIDGE-associate editor
BOB SCHRECK-editor
[redacted]
AND I STILL DON'T KNOW WHAT'S GOING ON.

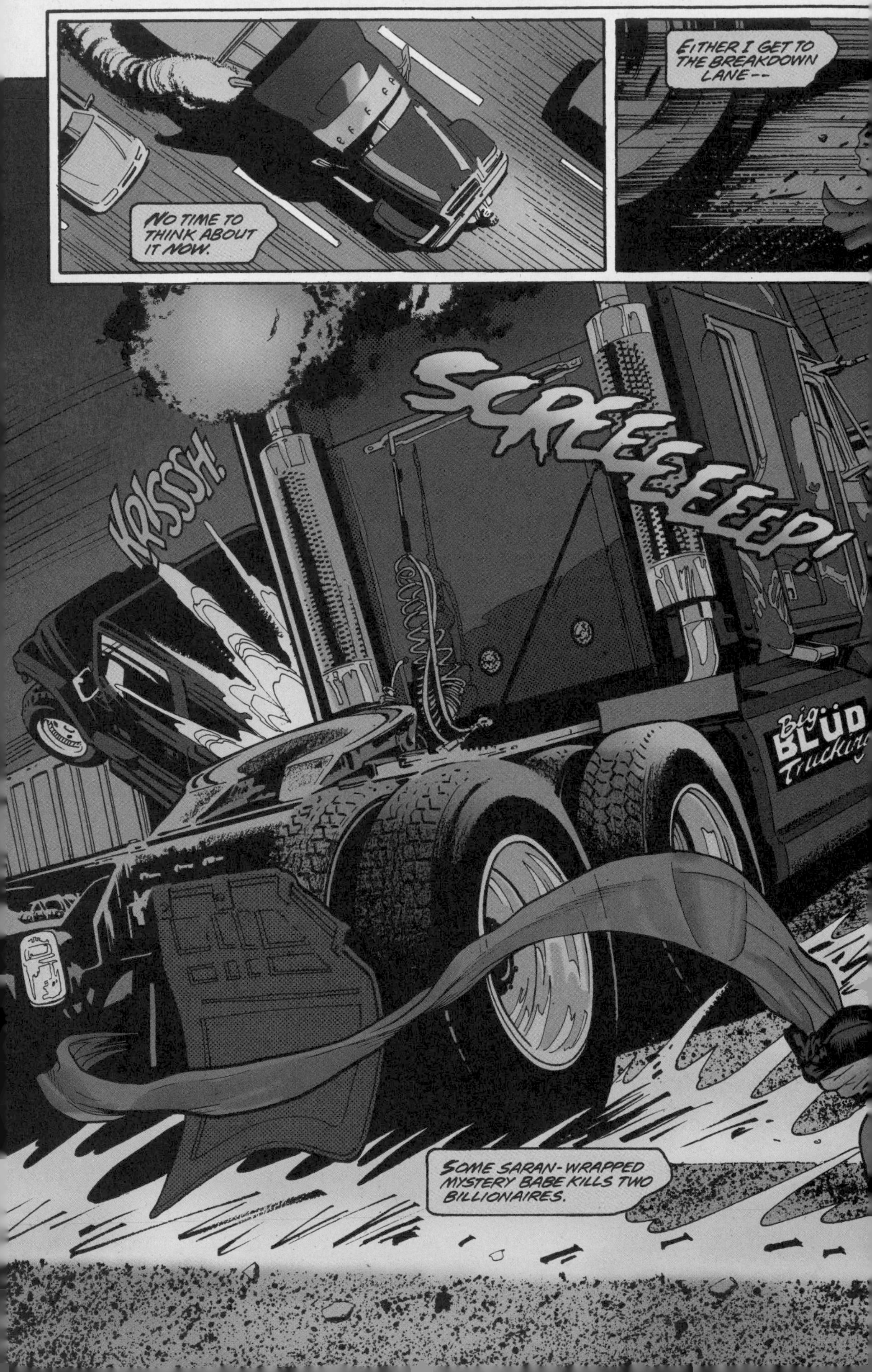
NO TIME TO THINK ABOUT IT NOW.
EITHER I GET TO THE BREAKDOWN LANE--
SCREEEEEEEP!
KRSSSH!
Big BLÜD Trucking
SOME SARAN-WRAPPED MYSTERY BABE KILLS TWO BILLIONAIRES.

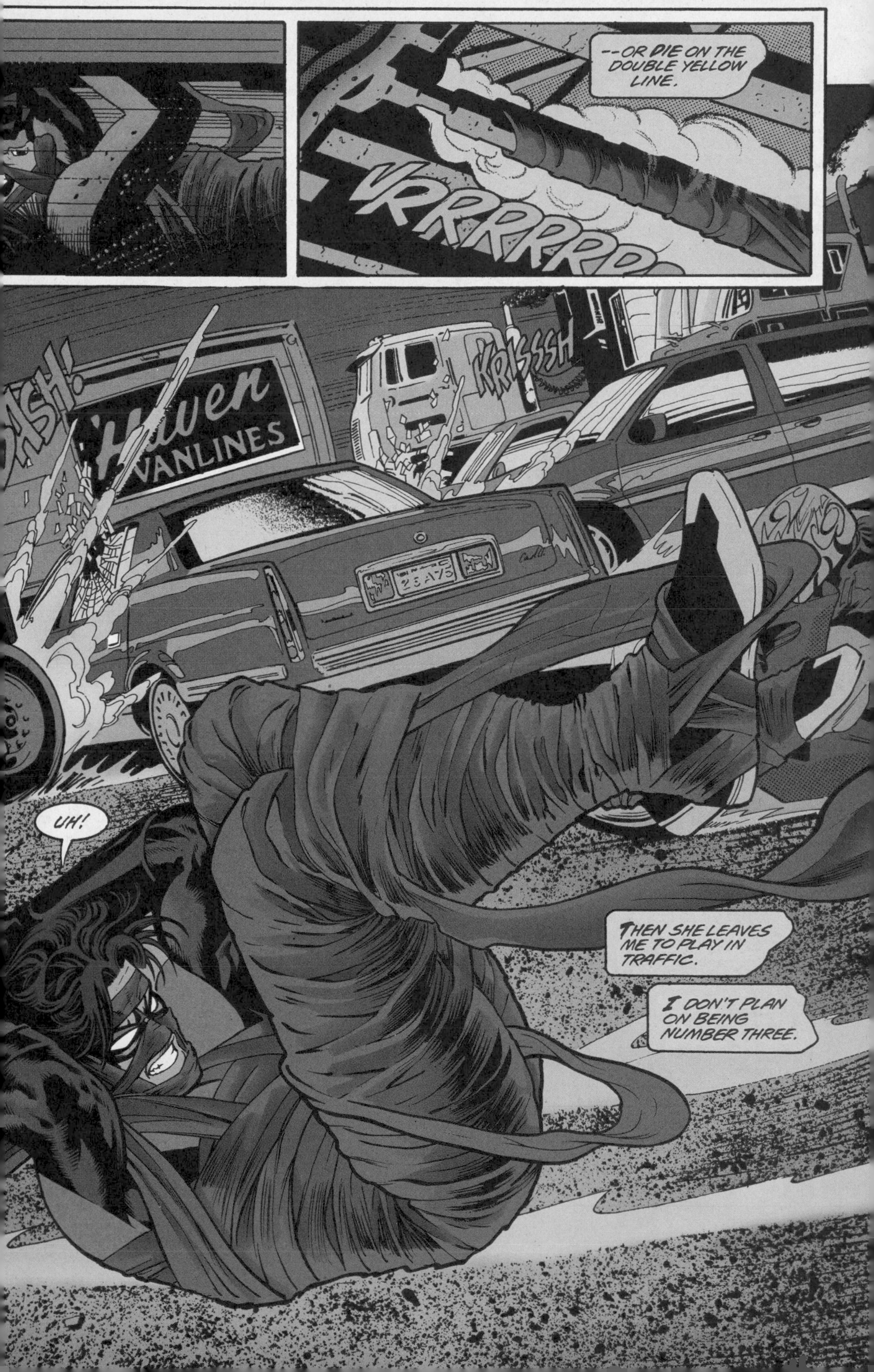
--OR DIE ON THE DOUBLE YELLOW LINE.
VRRRRRRD
ASH!
Haven VANLINES
KRISSSH
UH!
THEN SHE LEAVES ME TO PLAY IN TRAFFIC.
I DON'T PLAN ON BEING NUMBER THREE.

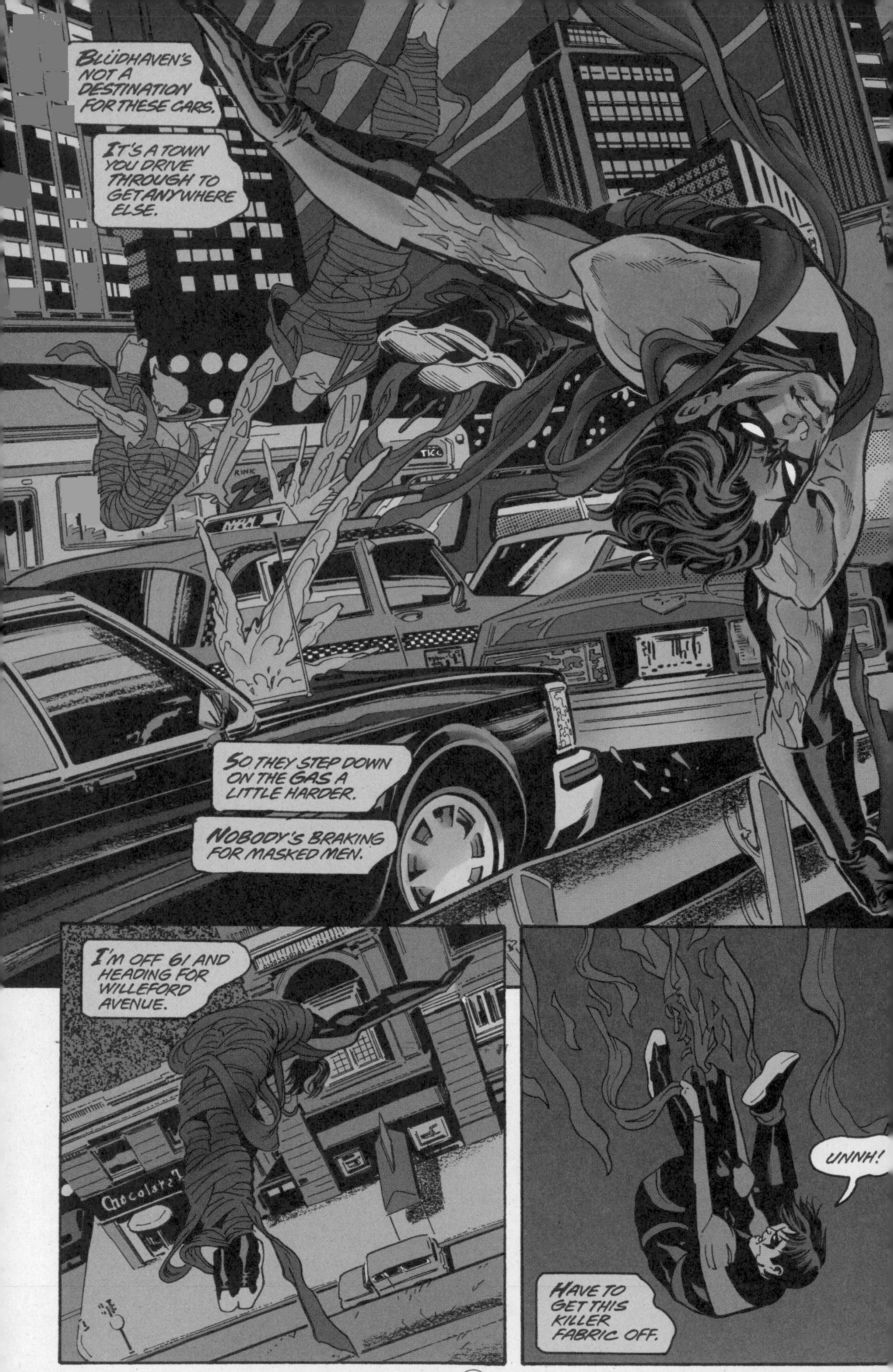
BLÜDHAVEN'S NOT A DESTINATION FOR THESE CARS.
IT'S A TOWN YOU DRIVE THROUGH TO GET ANYWHERE ELSE.
SO THEY STEP DOWN ON THE GAS A LITTLE HARDER.
NOBODY'S BRAKING FOR MASKED MEN.
I'M OFF 61 AND HEADING FOR WILLEFORD AVENUE.
Chocolate
UNNH!
HAVE TO GET THIS KILLER FABRIC OFF.

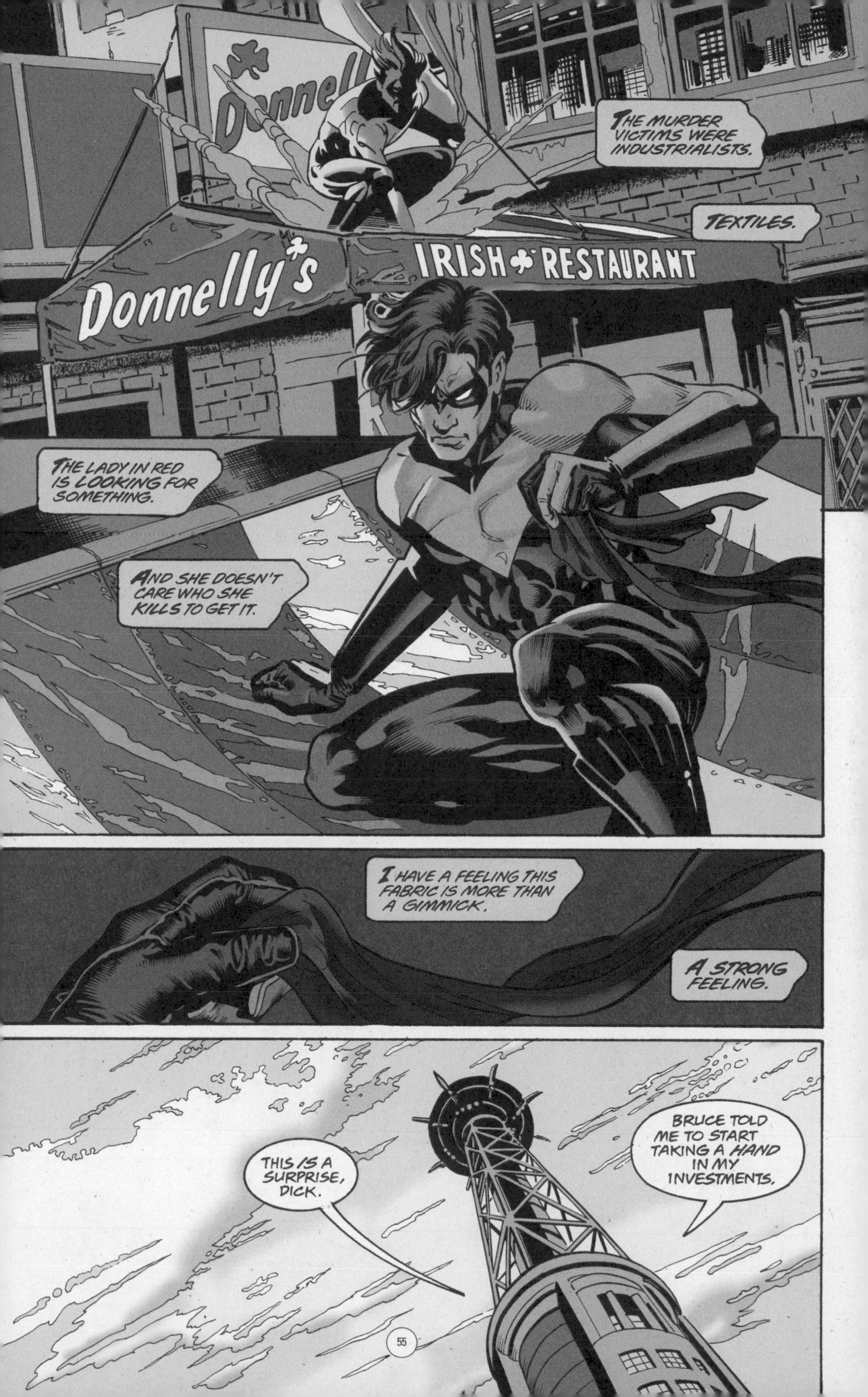
Donnelly's
THE MURDER VICTIMS WERE INDUSTRIALISTS.
TEXTILES.
Donnelly's IRISH RESTAURANT
THE LADY IN RED IS LOOKING FOR SOMETHING.
AND SHE DOESN'T CARE WHO SHE KILLS TO GET IT.
I HAVE A FEELING THIS FABRIC IS MORE THAN A GIMMICK.
A STRONG FEELING.
THIS IS A SURPRISE, DICK.
BRUCE TOLD ME TO START TAKING A HAND IN MY INVESTMENTS.

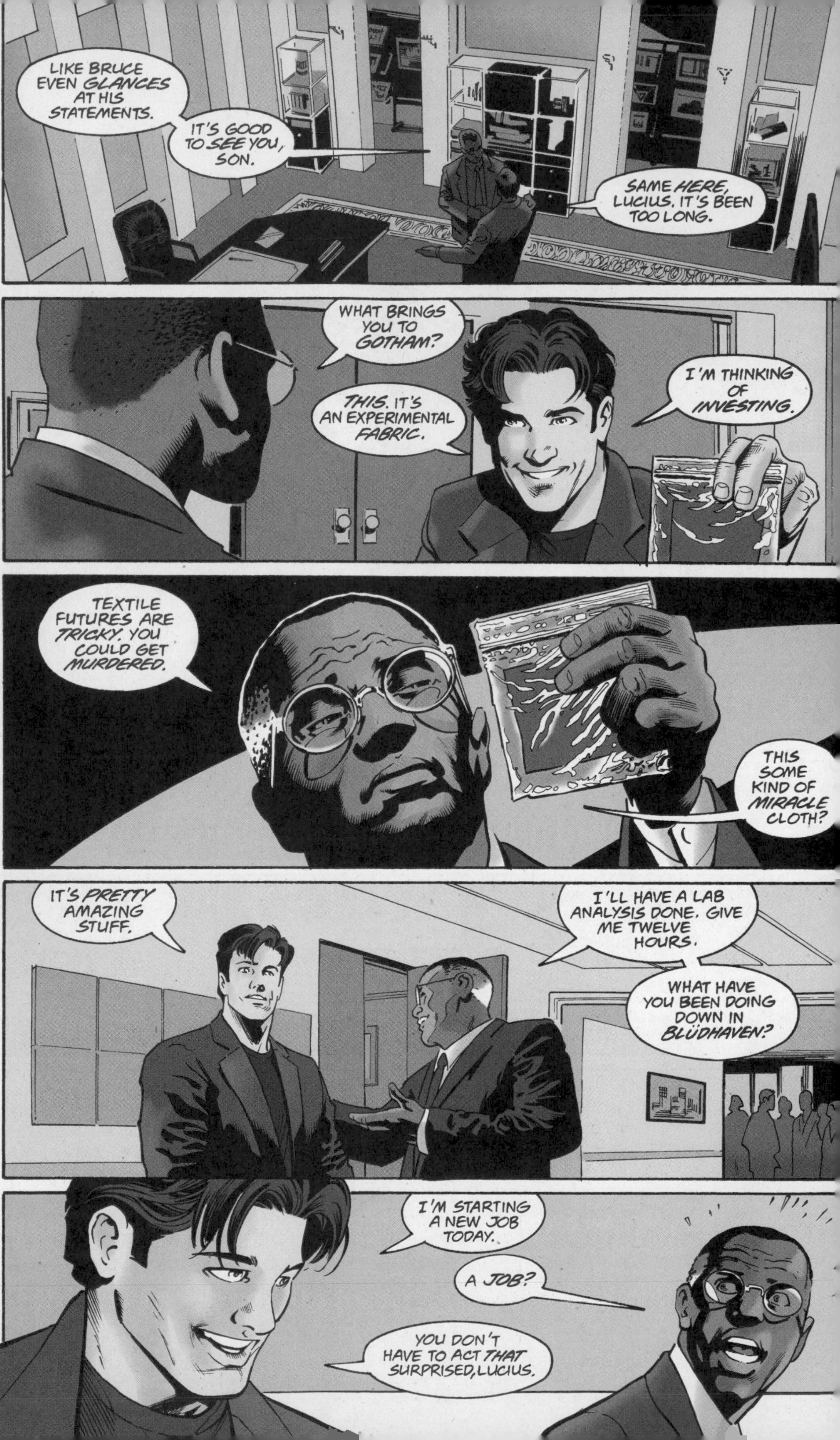
LIKE BRUCE EVEN GLANCES AT HIS STATEMENTS.
IT'S GOOD TO SEE YOU, SON.
SAME HERE, LUCIUS. IT'S BEEN TOO LONG.
WHAT BRINGS YOU TO GOTHAM?
THIS. IT'S AN EXPERIMENTAL FABRIC.
I'M THINKING OF INVESTING.
TEXTILE FUTURES ARE TRICKY. YOU COULD GET MURDERED.
THIS SOME KIND OF MIRACLE CLOTH?
IT'S PRETTY AMAZING STUFF.
I'LL HAVE A LAB ANALYSIS DONE. GIVE ME TWELVE HOURS.
WHAT HAVE YOU BEEN DOING DOWN IN BLÜDHAVEN?
I'M STARTING A NEW JOB TODAY.
A JOB?
YOU DON'T HAVE TO ACT THAT SURPRISED, LUCIUS.

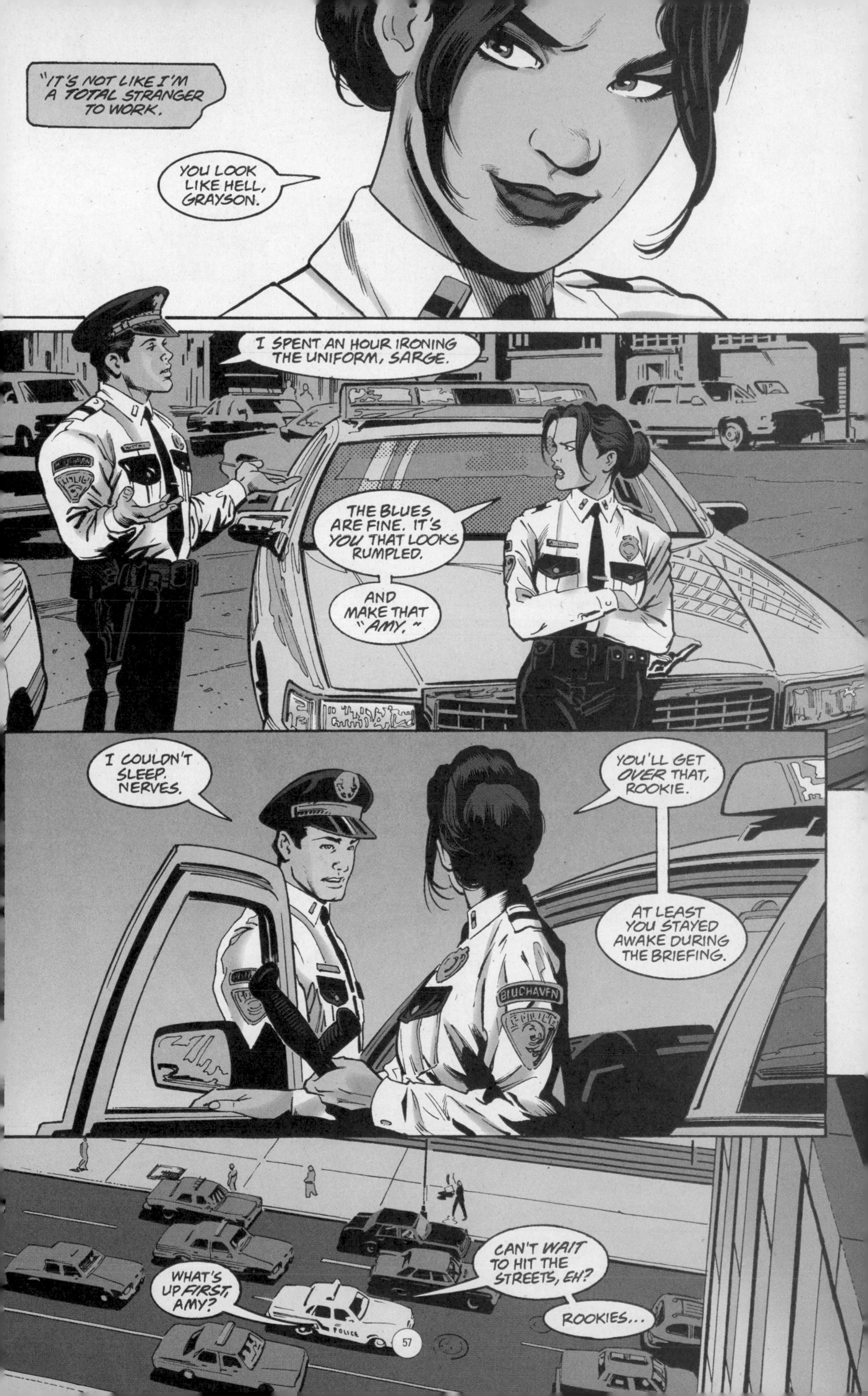
"IT'S NOT LIKE I'M A TOTAL STRANGER TO WORK.
YOU LOOK LIKE HELL, GRAYSON.
I SPENT AN HOUR IRONING THE UNIFORM, SARGE.
THE BLUES ARE FINE. IT'S YOU THAT LOOKS RUMPLED.
AND MAKE THAT "AMY."
I COULDN'T SLEEP. NERVES.
YOU'LL GET OVER THAT, ROOKIE.
AT LEAST YOU STAYED AWAKE DURING THE BRIEFING.
BLUDHAVEN
POLICE
CAN'T WAIT TO HIT THE STREETS, EH?
WHAT'S UP FIRST, AMY?
ROOKIES...
POLICE

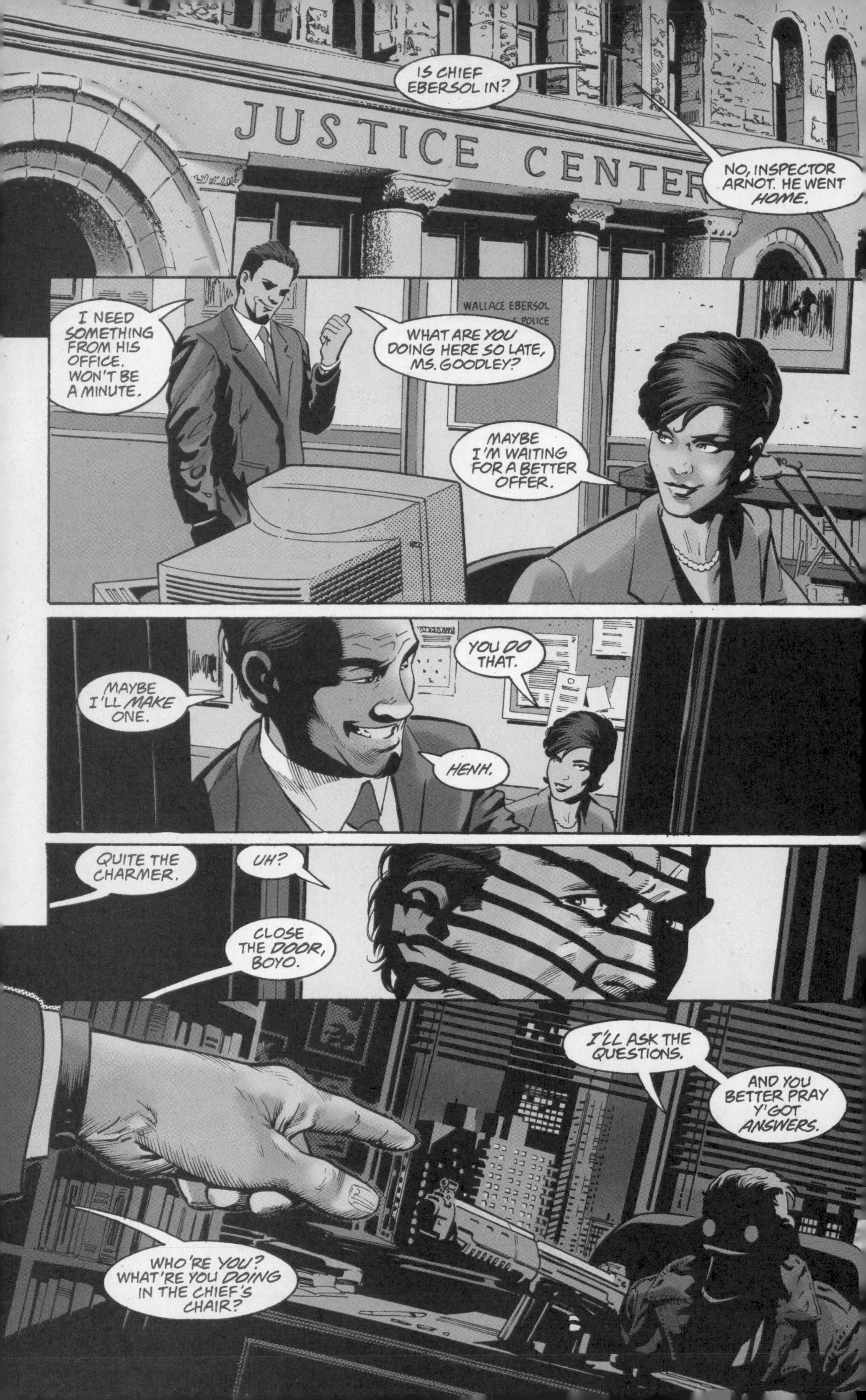
IS CHIEF EBERSOL IN?
JUSTICE CENTER
NO, INSPECTOR ARNOT. HE WENT HOME.
I NEED SOMETHING FROM HIS OFFICE. WON'T BE A MINUTE.
WHAT ARE YOU DOING HERE SO LATE, MS. GOODLEY?
WALLACE EBERSOL
MAYBE I'M WAITING FOR A BETTER OFFER.
MAYBE I'LL MAKE ONE.
YOU DO THAT.
HENH.
QUITE THE CHARMER.
UH?
CLOSE THE DOOR, BOYO.
I'LL ASK THE QUESTIONS.
AND YOU BETTER PRAY Y'GOT ANSWERS.
WHO'RE YOU? WHAT'RE YOU DOING IN THE CHIEF'S CHAIR?

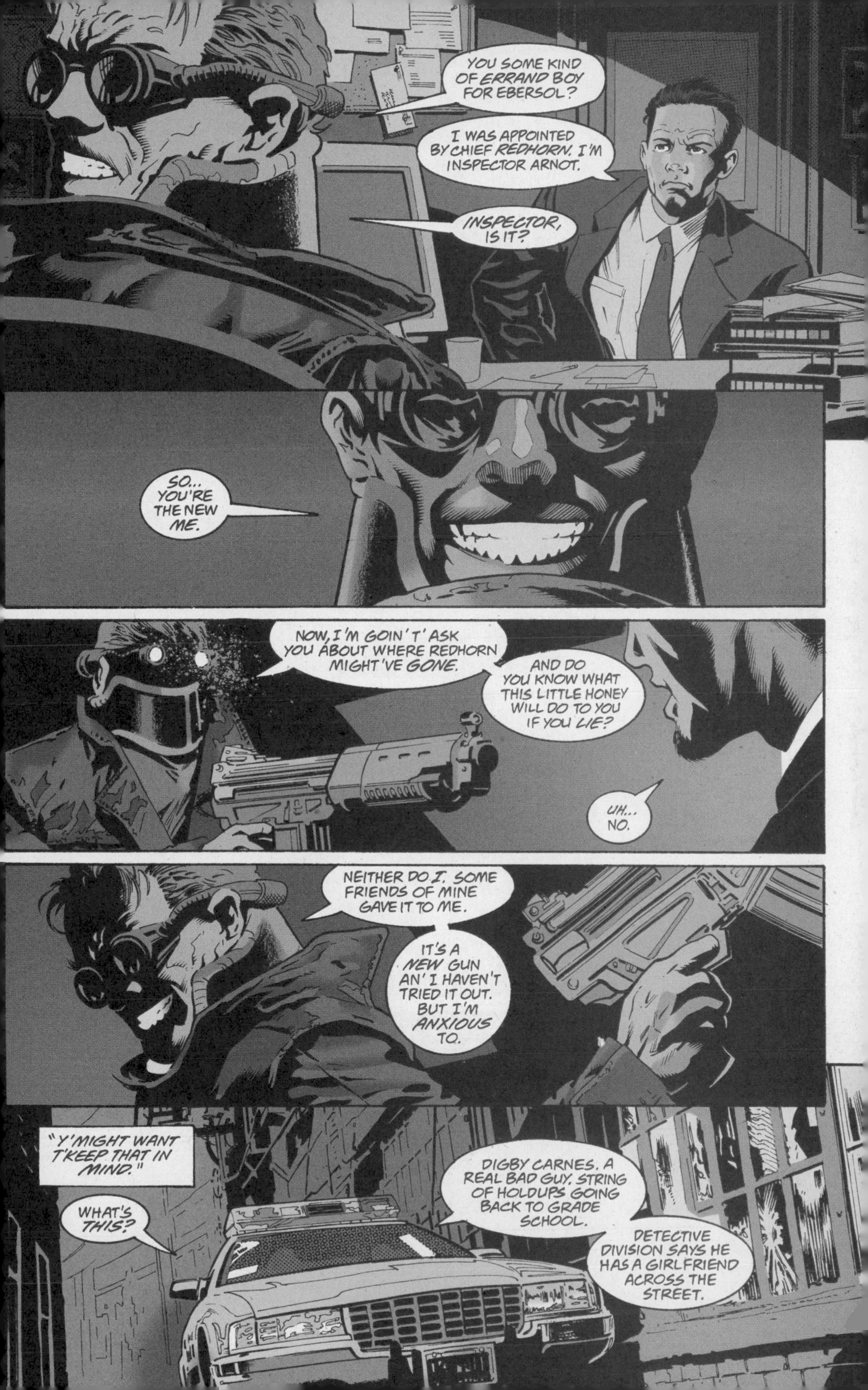
YOU SOME KIND OF ERRAND BOY FOR EBERSOL?
I WAS APPOINTED BY CHIEF REDHORN. I'M INSPECTOR ARNOT.
INSPECTOR, IS IT?
SO... YOU'RE THE NEW ME.
NOW, I'M GOIN' T' ASK YOU ABOUT WHERE REDHORN MIGHT'VE GONE.
AND DO YOU KNOW WHAT THIS LITTLE HONEY WILL DO TO YOU IF YOU LIE?
UH... NO.
NEITHER DO I. SOME FRIENDS OF MINE GAVE IT TO ME.
IT'S A NEW GUN AN' I HAVEN'T TRIED IT OUT. BUT I'M ANXIOUS TO.
"Y'MIGHT WANT T'KEEP THAT IN MIND."
WHAT'S THIS?
DIGBY CARNES. A REAL BAD GUY. STRING OF HOLDUPS GOING BACK TO GRADE SCHOOL.
DETECTIVE DIVISION SAYS HE HAS A GIRLFRIEND ACROSS THE STREET.

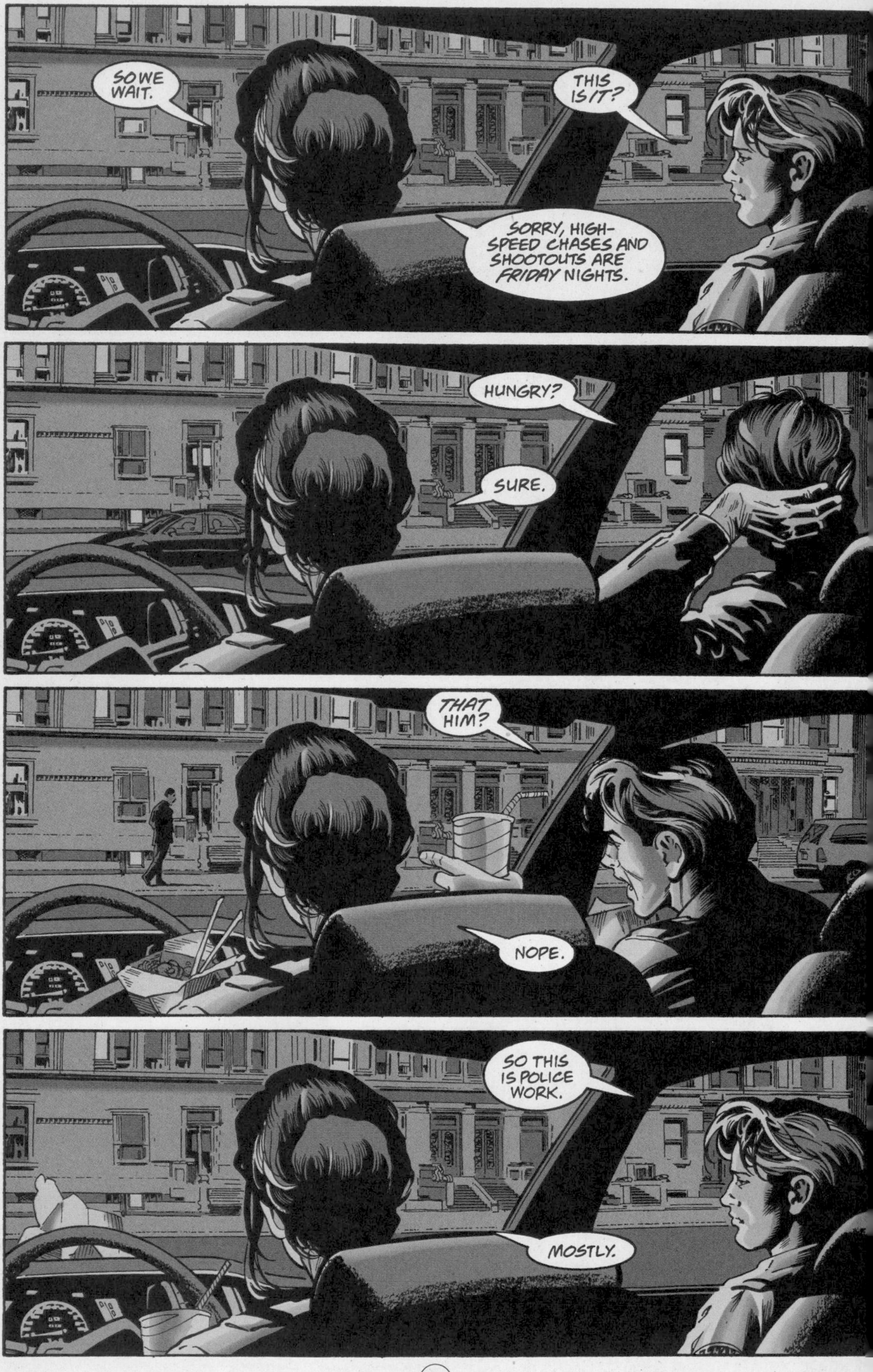
THIS IS IT?
SO WE WAIT.
SORRY, HIGH-SPEED CHASES AND SHOOTOUTS ARE FRIDAY NIGHTS.
HUNGRY?
SURE.
THAT HIM?
NOPE.
SO THIS IS POLICE WORK.
MOSTLY.

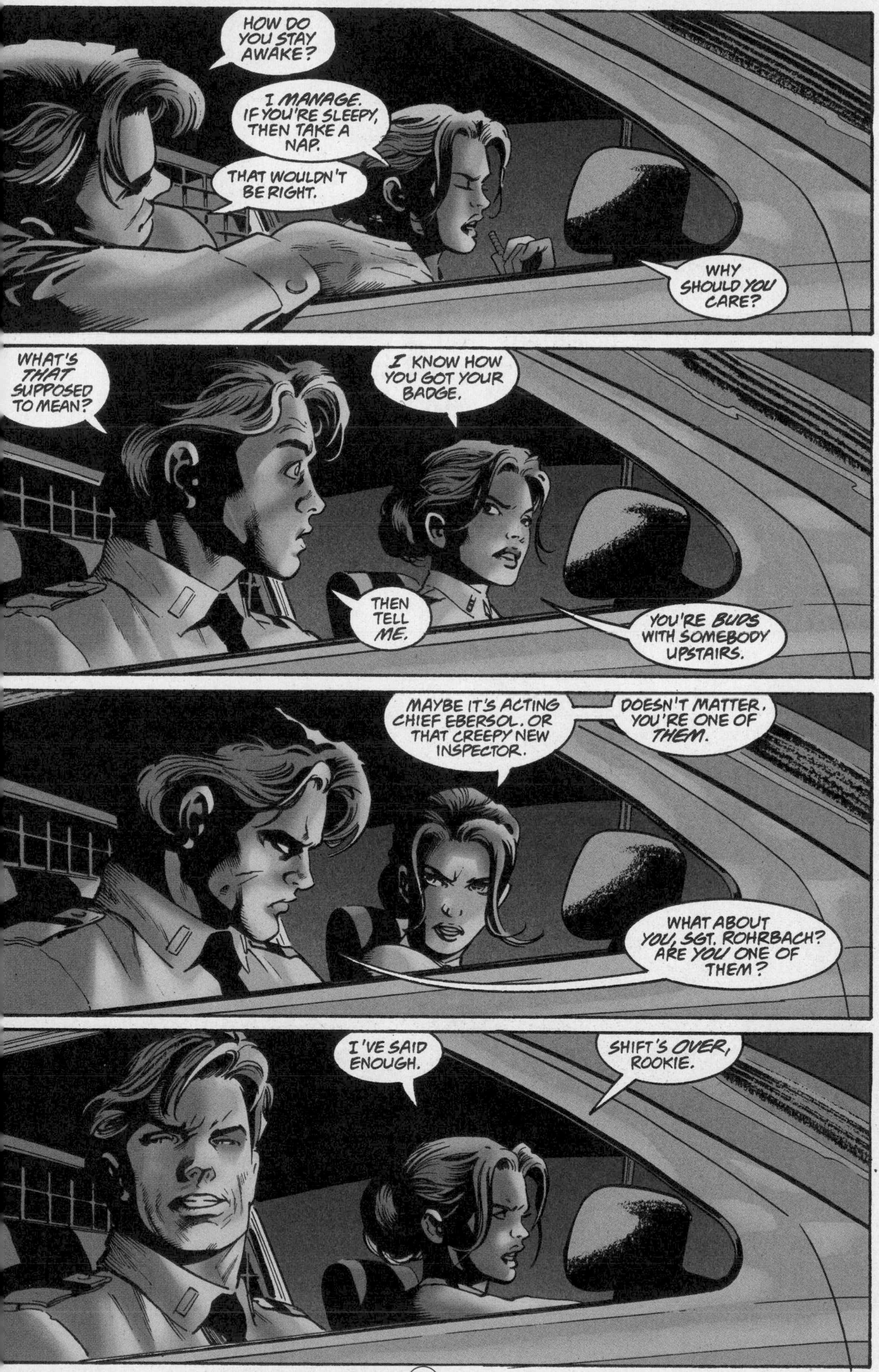
HOW DO YOU STAY AWAKE?
I MANAGE. IF YOU'RE SLEEPY, THEN TAKE A NAP.
THAT WOULDN'T BE RIGHT.
WHY SHOULD YOU CARE?
WHAT'S THAT SUPPOSED TO MEAN?
I KNOW HOW YOU GOT YOUR BADGE.
THEN TELL ME.
YOU'RE BUDS WITH SOMEBODY UPSTAIRS.
MAYBE IT'S ACTING CHIEF EBERSOL. OR THAT CREEPY NEW INSPECTOR.
DOESN'T MATTER. YOU'RE ONE OF THEM.
WHAT ABOUT YOU, SGT. ROHRBACH? ARE YOU ONE OF THEM?
I'VE SAID ENOUGH.
SHIFT'S OVER, ROOKIE.

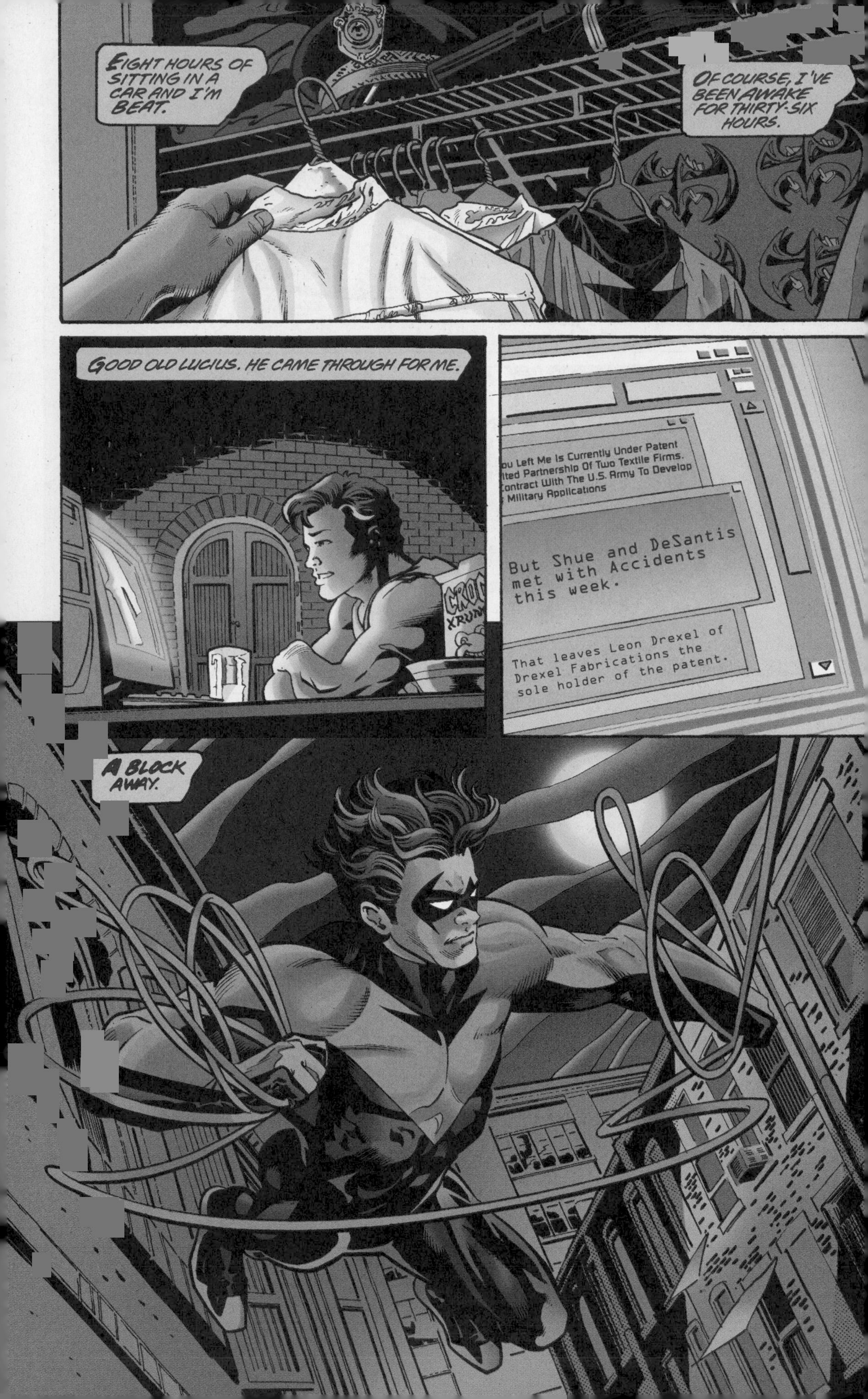
EIGHT HOURS OF SITTING IN A CAR AND I'M BEAT.
OF COURSE, I'VE BEEN AWAKE FOR THIRTY-SIX HOURS.
GOOD OLD LUCIUS. HE CAME THROUGH FOR ME.
CROC XRUN
ou Left Me Is Currently Under Patent
ited Partnership Of Two Textile Firms.
Contract With The U.S. Army To Develop
Military Applications
But Shue and DeSantis met with Accidents this week.
That leaves Leon Drexel of Drexel Fabrications the sole holder of the patent.
A BLOCK AWAY.

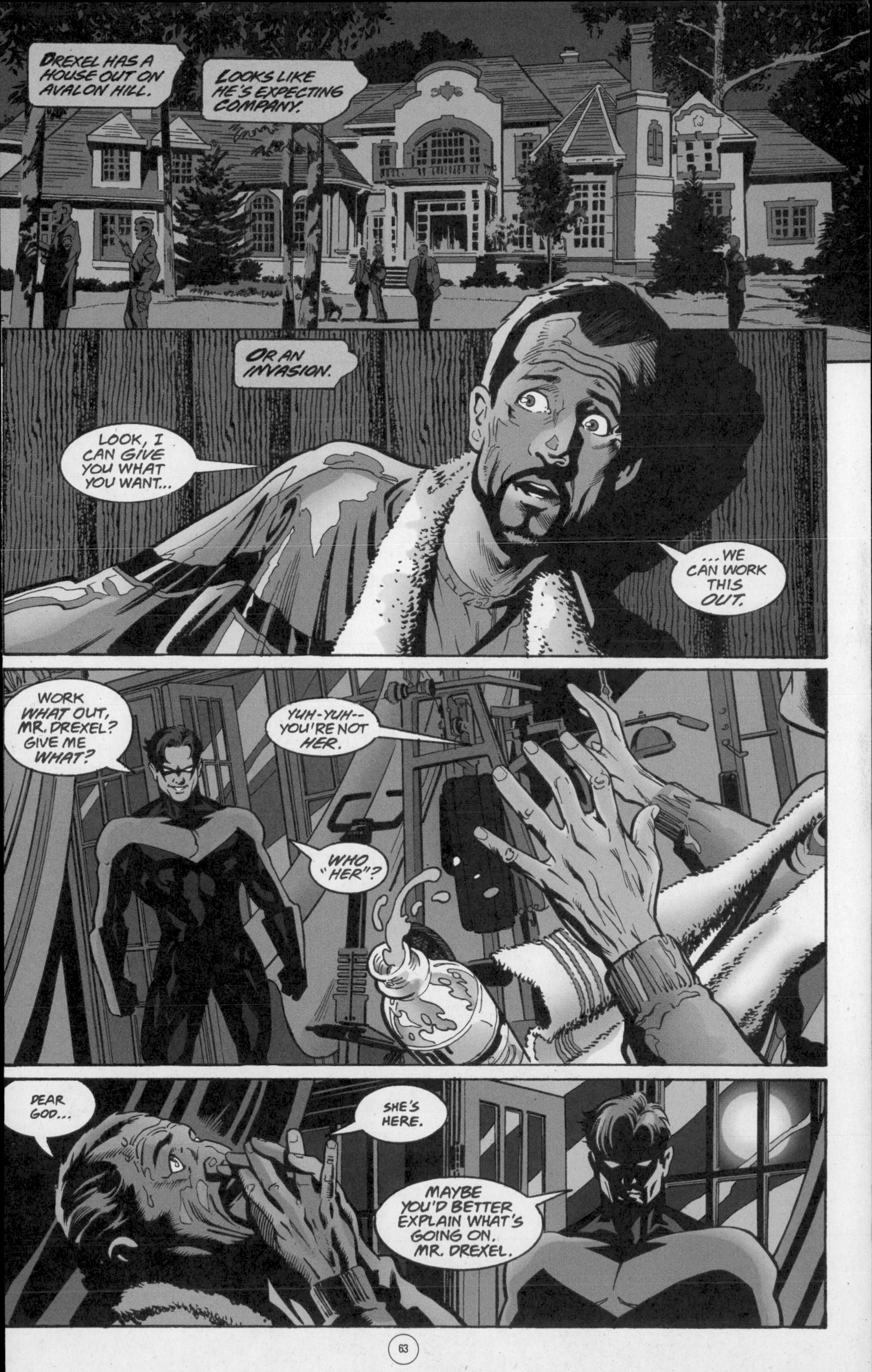
DREXEL HAS A HOUSE OUT ON AVALON HILL.
LOOKS LIKE HE'S EXPECTING COMPANY.
OR AN INVASION.
LOOK, I CAN GIVE YOU WHAT YOU WANT...
...WE CAN WORK THIS OUT.
WORK WHAT OUT, MR. DREXEL? GIVE ME WHAT?
YUH-YUH-- YOU'RE NOT HER.
WHO "HER"?
DEAR GOD...
SHE'S HERE.
MAYBE YOU'D BETTER EXPLAIN WHAT'S GOING ON, MR. DREXEL.

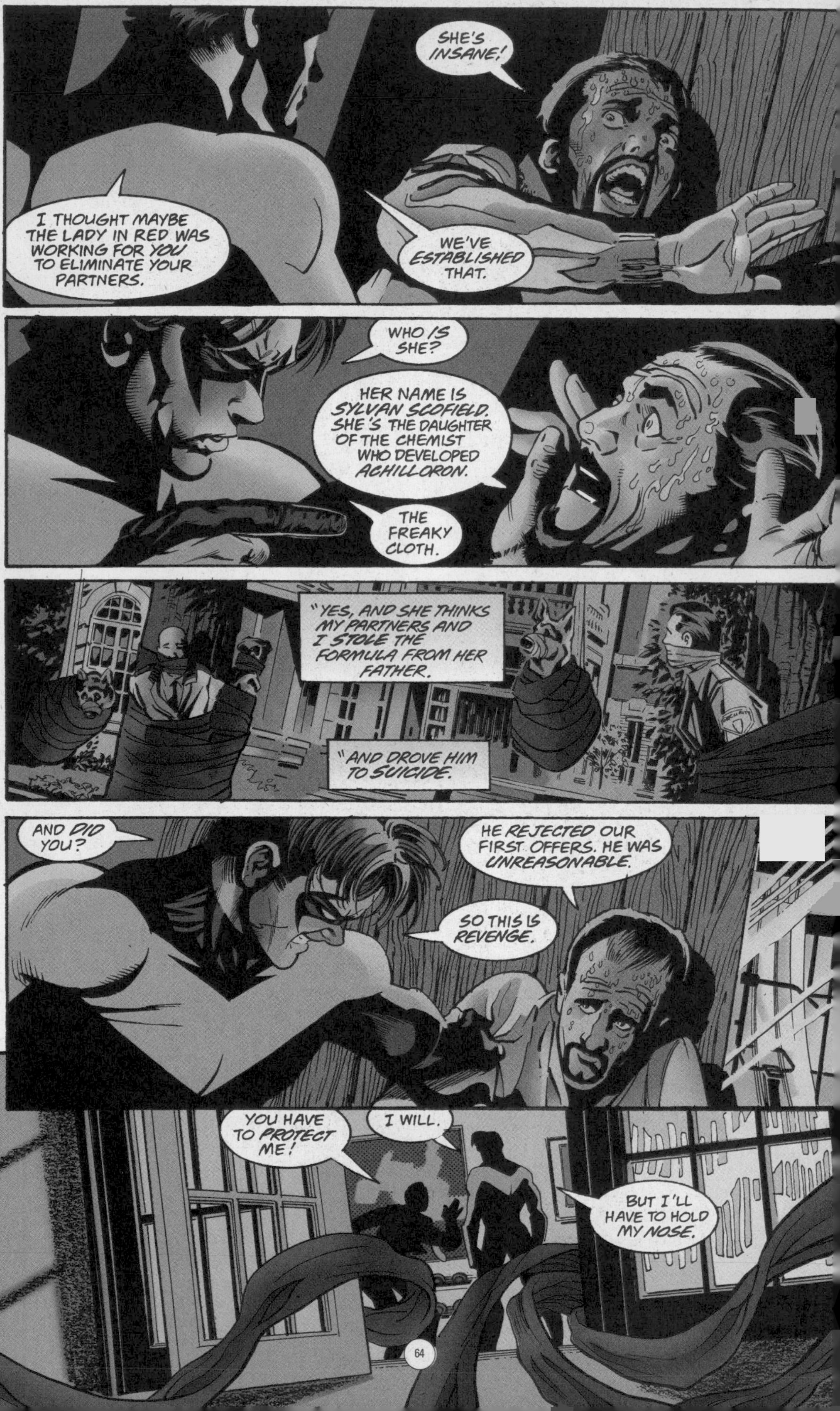
SHE'S INSANE!
I THOUGHT MAYBE THE LADY IN RED WAS WORKING FOR YOU TO ELIMINATE YOUR PARTNERS.
WE'VE ESTABLISHED THAT.
WHO IS SHE?
HER NAME IS SYLVAN SCOFIELD. SHE'S THE DAUGHTER OF THE CHEMIST WHO DEVELOPED ACHILLORON.
THE FREAKY CLOTH.
"YES, AND SHE THINKS MY PARTNERS AND I STOLE THE FORMULA FROM HER FATHER.
"AND DROVE HIM TO SUICIDE.
AND DID YOU?
HE REJECTED OUR FIRST OFFERS. HE WAS UNREASONABLE.
SO THIS IS REVENGE.
YOU HAVE TO PROTECT ME!
I WILL.
BUT I'LL HAVE TO HOLD MY NOSE.

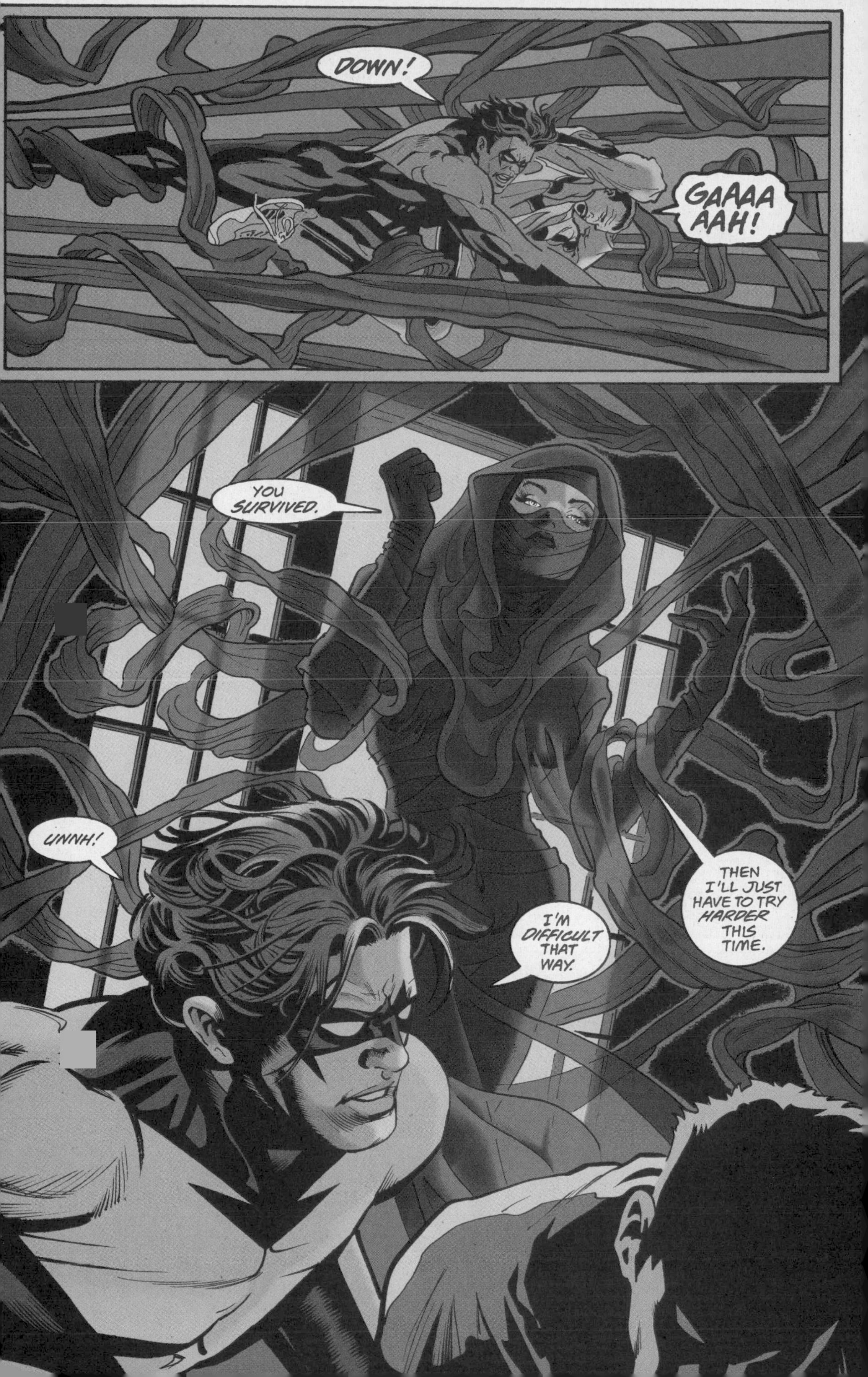
DOWN!
GAAAA AAH!
YOU SURVIVED.
UNNH!
I'M DIFFICULT THAT WAY.
THEN I'LL JUST HAVE TO TRY HARDER THIS TIME.

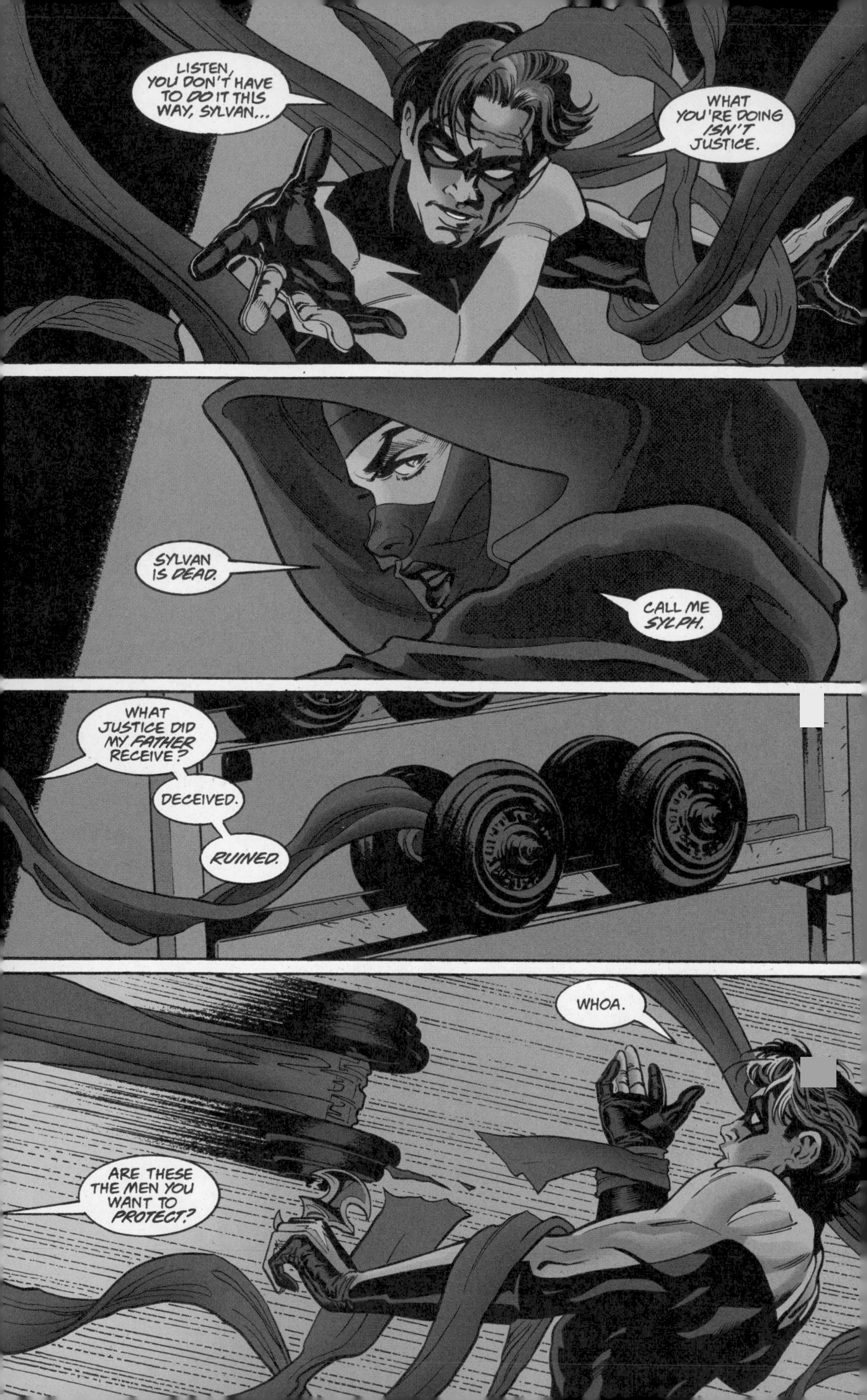
LISTEN, YOU DON'T HAVE TO DO IT THIS WAY, SYLVAN...
WHAT YOU'RE DOING ISN'T JUSTICE.
SYLVAN IS DEAD.
CALL ME SYLPH.
WHAT JUSTICE DID MY FATHER RECEIVE?
DECEIVED.
RUINED.
WHOA.
ARE THESE THE MEN YOU WANT TO PROTECT?

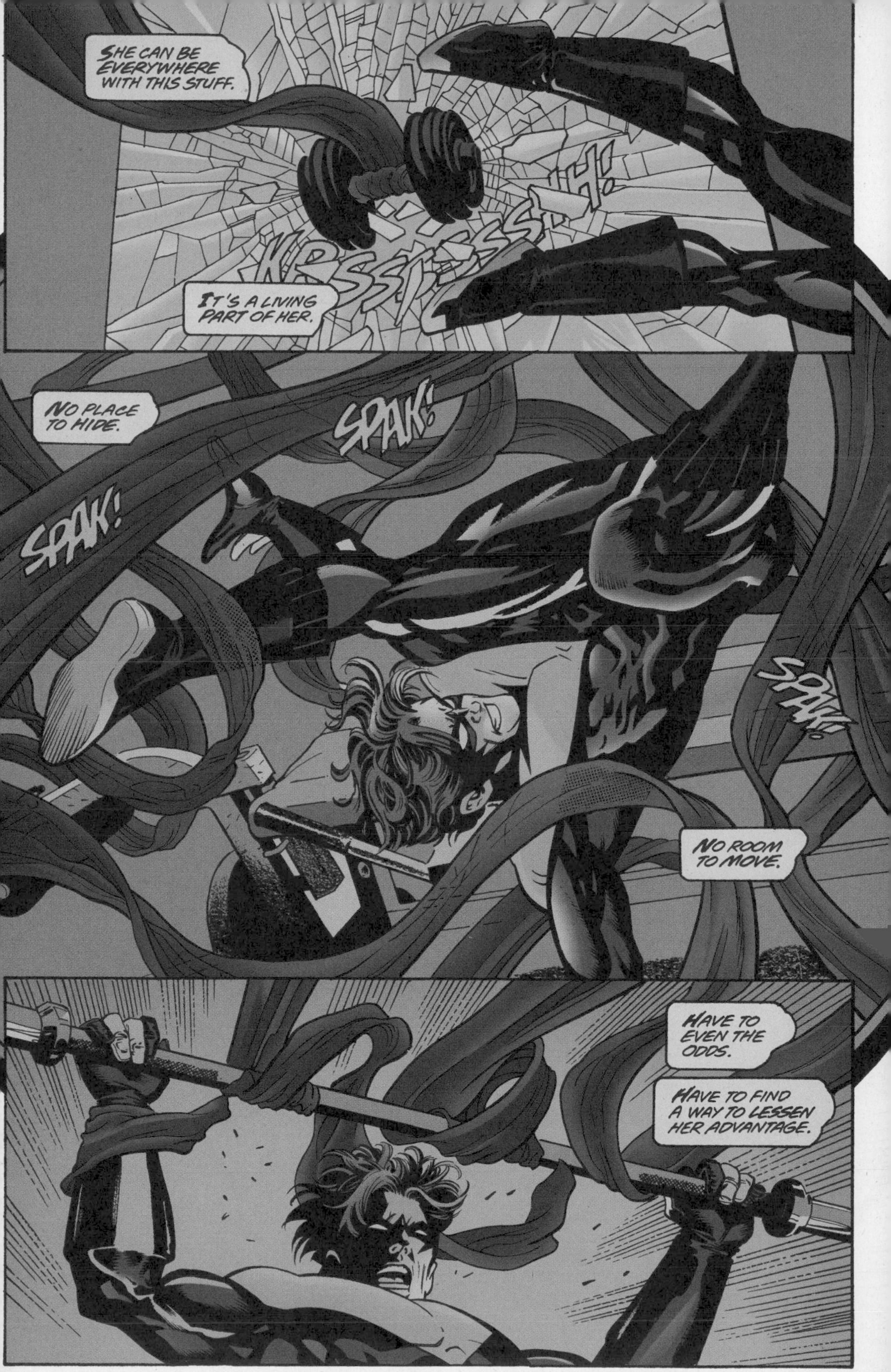
SHE CAN BE EVERYWHERE WITH THIS STUFF.
IT'S A LIVING PART OF HER.
NO PLACE TO HIDE.
SPAK!
SPAK!
SPAK!
NO ROOM TO MOVE.
HAVE TO EVEN THE ODDS.
HAVE TO FIND A WAY TO LESSEN HER ADVANTAGE.

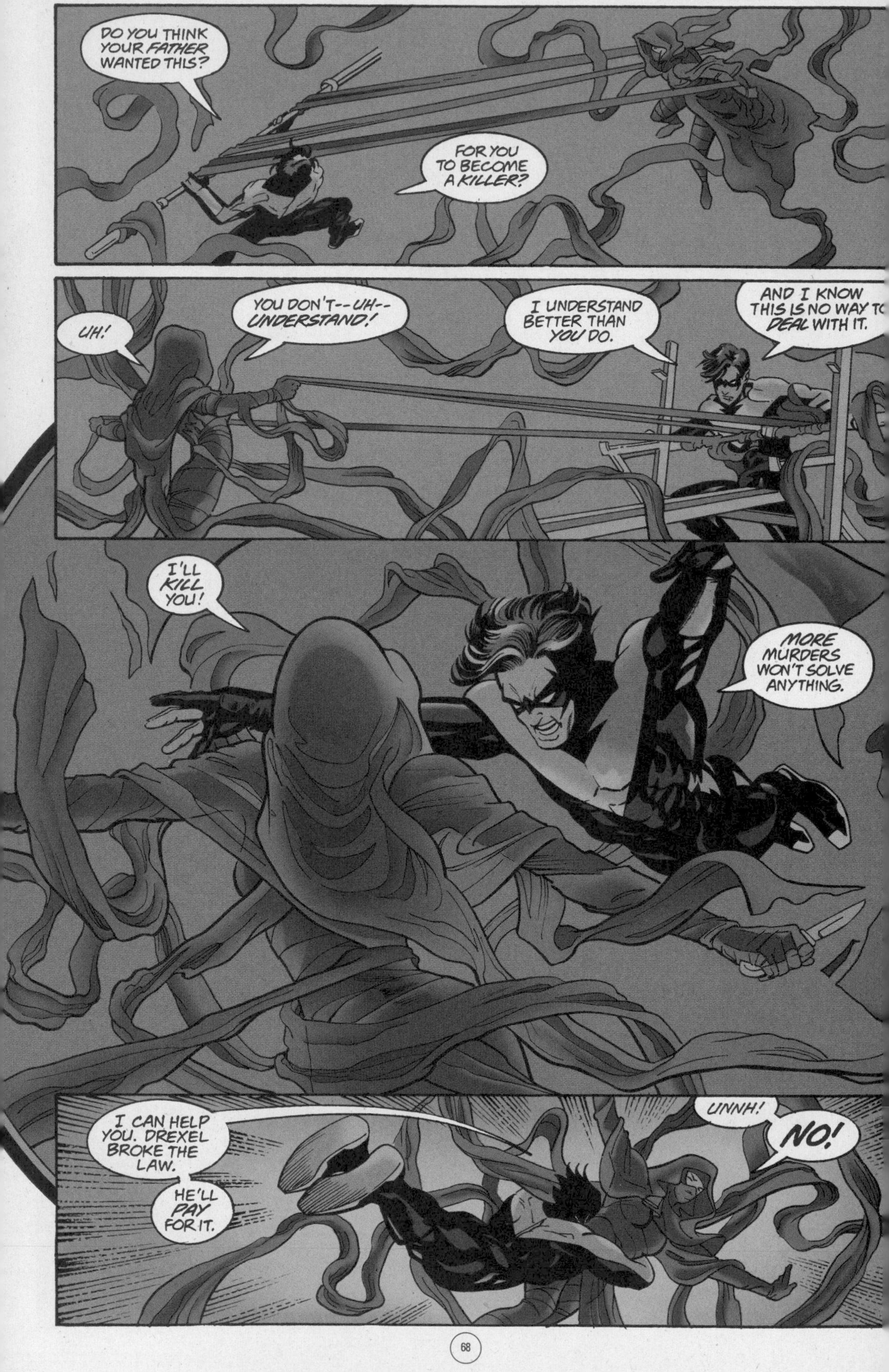
DO YOU THINK YOUR FATHER WANTED THIS?
FOR YOU TO BECOME A KILLER?
UH!
YOU DON'T--UH-- UNDERSTAND!
I UNDERSTAND BETTER THAN YOU DO.
AND I KNOW THIS IS NO WAY TO DEAL WITH IT.
I'LL KILL YOU!
MORE MURDERS WON'T SOLVE ANYTHING.
I CAN HELP YOU. DREXEL BROKE THE LAW.
HE'LL PAY FOR IT.
UNNH!
NO!

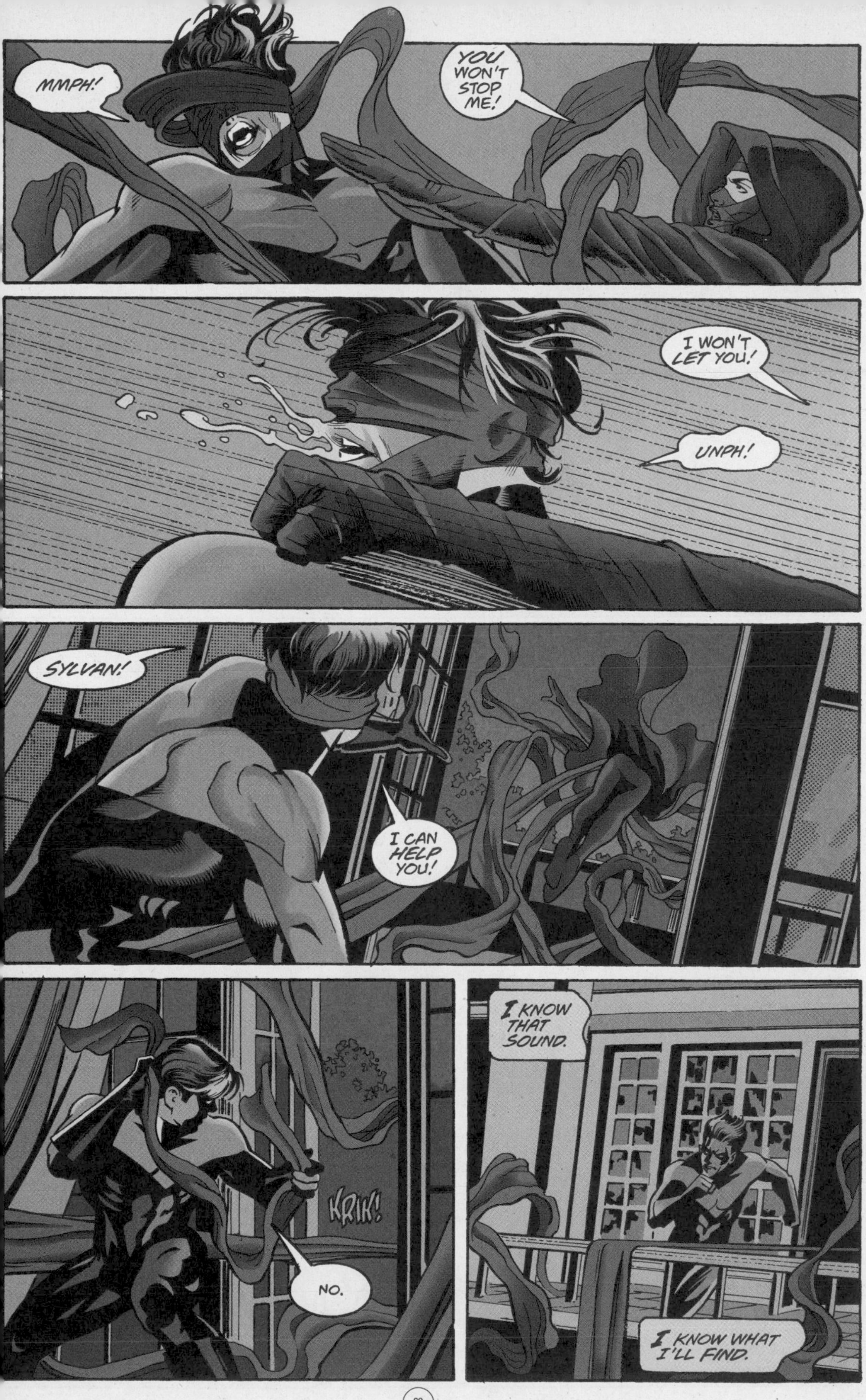
MMPH!
YOU WON'T STOP ME!
I WON'T LET YOU!
UNPH!
SYLVAN!
I CAN HELP YOU!
KRIK!
NO.
I KNOW THAT SOUND.
I KNOW WHAT I'LL FIND.

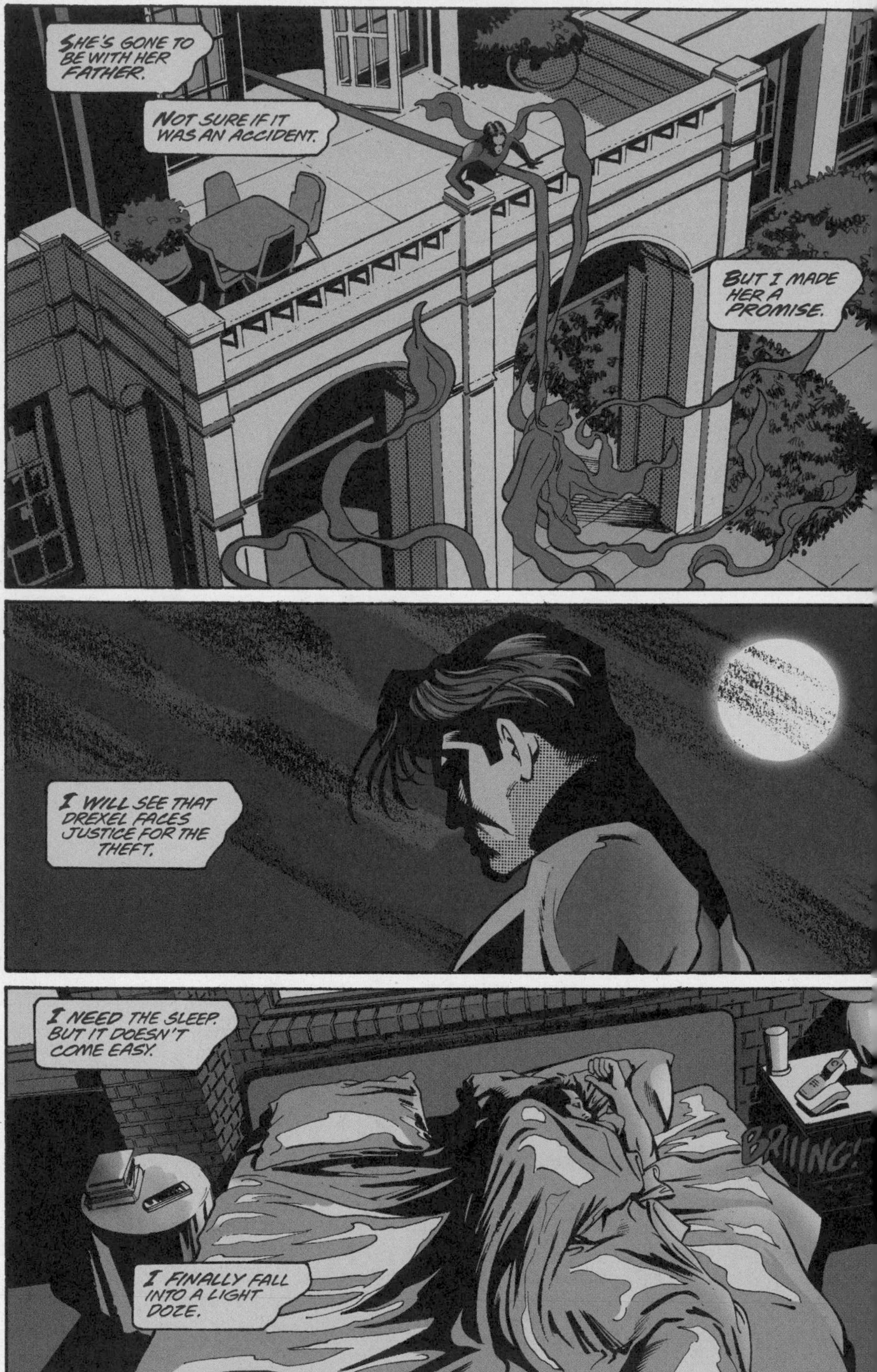
SHE'S GONE TO BE WITH HER FATHER.
NOT SURE IF IT WAS AN ACCIDENT.
BUT I MADE HER A PROMISE.
I WILL SEE THAT DREXEL FACES JUSTICE FOR THE THEFT.
I NEED THE SLEEP. BUT IT DOESN'T COME EASY.
BRIIING!
I FINALLY FALL INTO A LIGHT DOZE.

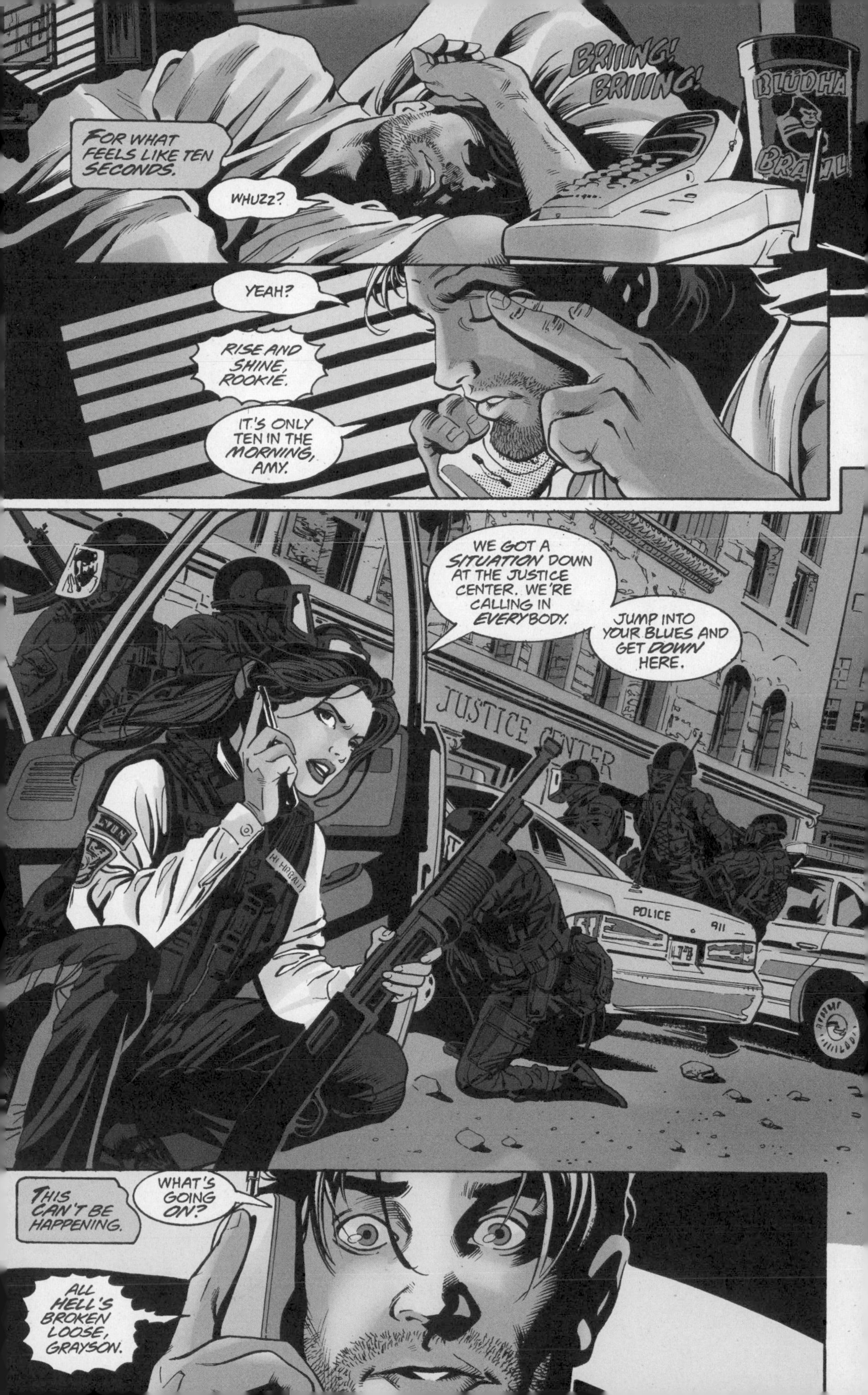
BRIIING! BRIIING!
BLÜDHA
BRAWL
FOR WHAT FEELS LIKE TEN SECONDS.
WHUZZ?
YEAH?
RISE AND SHINE, ROOKIE.
IT'S ONLY TEN IN THE MORNING, AMY.
WE GOT A SITUATION DOWN AT THE JUSTICE CENTER. WE'RE CALLING IN EVERYBODY.
JUMP INTO YOUR BLUES AND GET DOWN HERE.
JUSTICE CENTER
POLICE 911
THIS CAN'T BE HAPPENING.
WHAT'S GOING ON?
ALL HELL'S BROKEN LOOSE, GRAYSON.

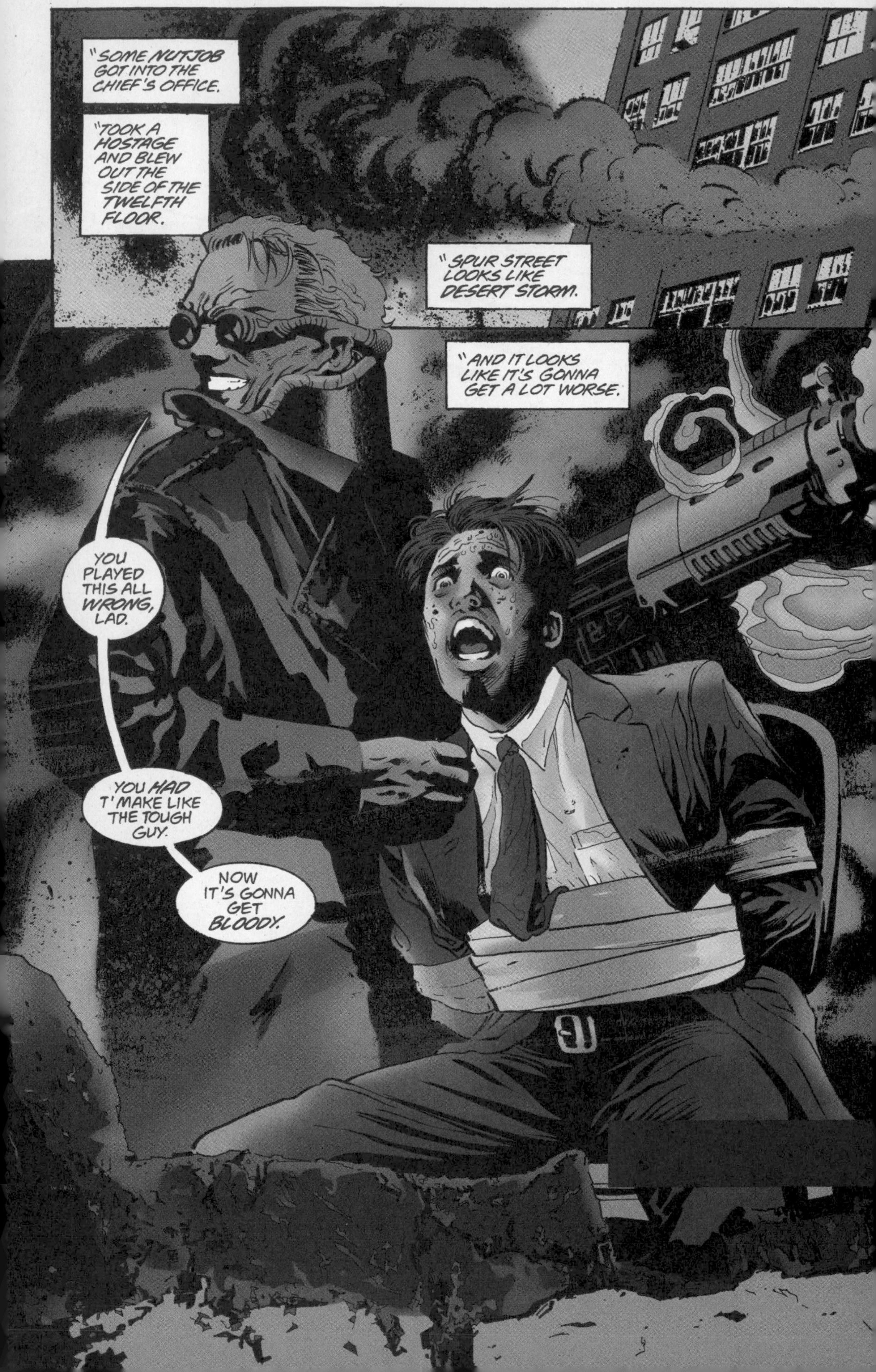
"SOME NUTJOB GOT INTO THE CHIEF'S OFFICE.
"TOOK A HOSTAGE AND BLEW OUT THE SIDE OF THE TWELFTH FLOOR.
"SPUR STREET LOOKS LIKE DESERT STORM.
"AND IT LOOKS LIKE IT'S GONNA GET A LOT WORSE.
YOU PLAYED THIS ALL WRONG, LAD.
YOU HAD T' MAKE LIKE THE TOUGH GUY.
NOW IT'S GONNA GET BLOODY.

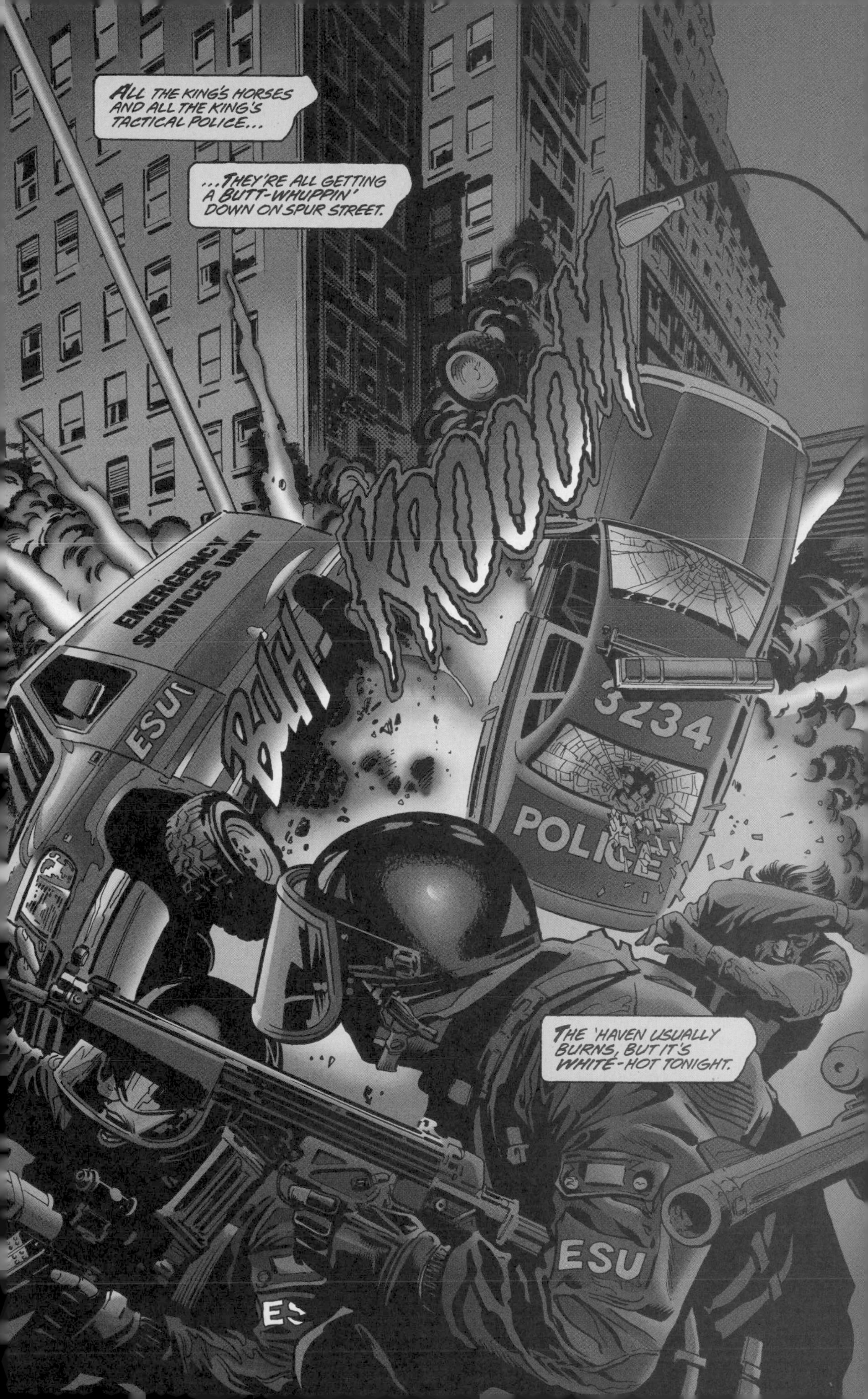
ALL THE KING'S HORSES AND ALL THE KING'S TACTICAL POLICE...
...THEY'RE ALL GETTING A BUTT-WHUPPIN' DOWN ON SPUR STREET.
BUH-KROOOOOM
EMERGENCY SERVICES UNIT
ESU
3234
POLICE
THE 'HAVEN USUALLY BURNS, BUT IT'S WHITE-HOT TONIGHT.
ESU
ES

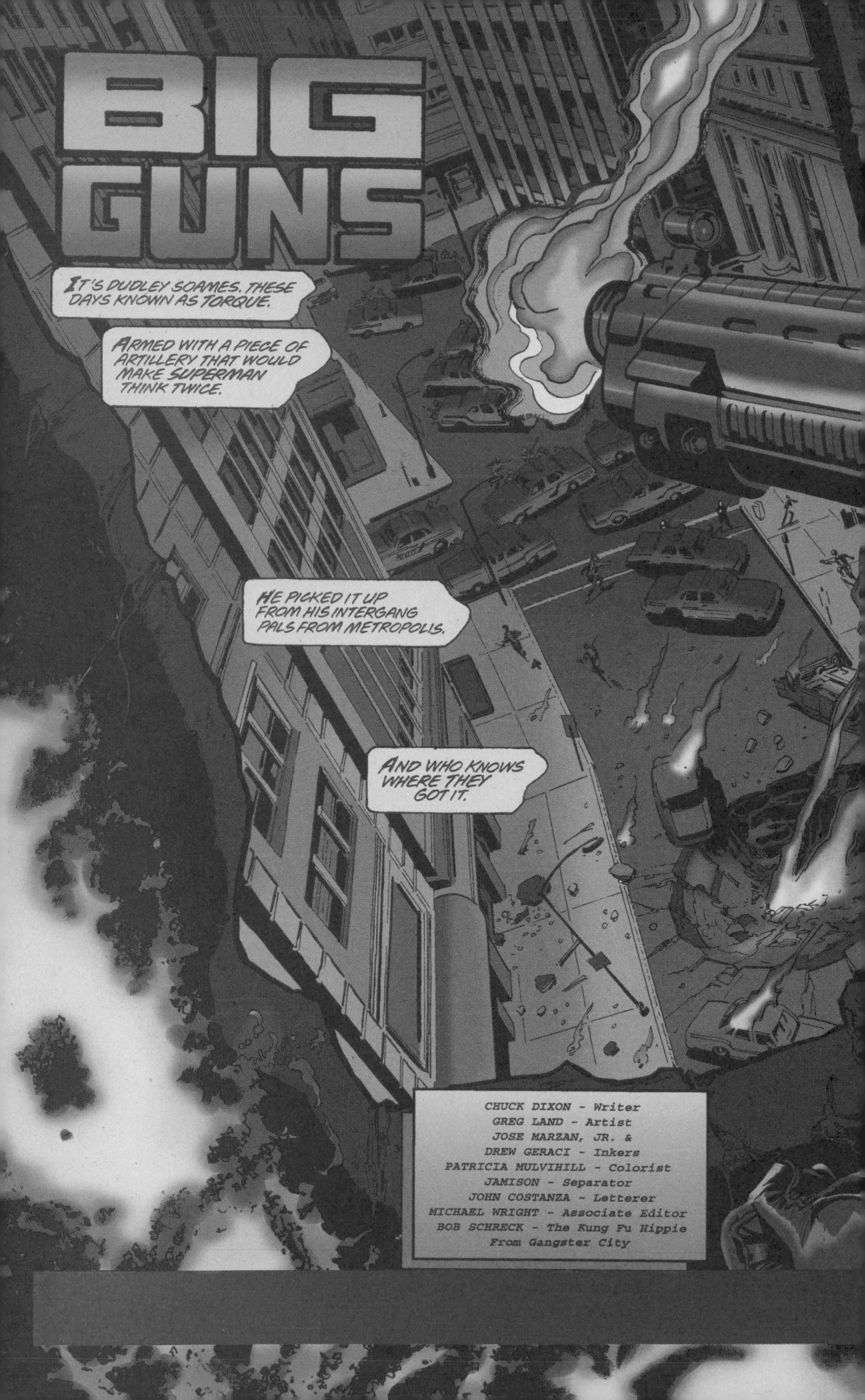
BIG GUNS
IT'S DUDLEY SOAMES. THESE DAYS KNOWN AS TORQUE.
ARMED WITH A PIECE OF ARTILLERY THAT WOULD MAKE SUPERMAN THINK TWICE.
HE PICKED IT UP FROM HIS INTERGANG PALS FROM METROPOLIS.
AND WHO KNOWS WHERE THEY GOT IT.
CHUCK DIXON - Writer
GREG LAND - Artist
JOSE MARZAN, JR. &
DREW GERACI - Inkers
PATRICIA MULVIHILL - Colorist
JAMISON - Separator
JOHN COSTANZA - Letterer
MICHAEL WRIGHT - Associate Editor
BOB SCHRECK - The Kung Fu Hippie
From Gangster City

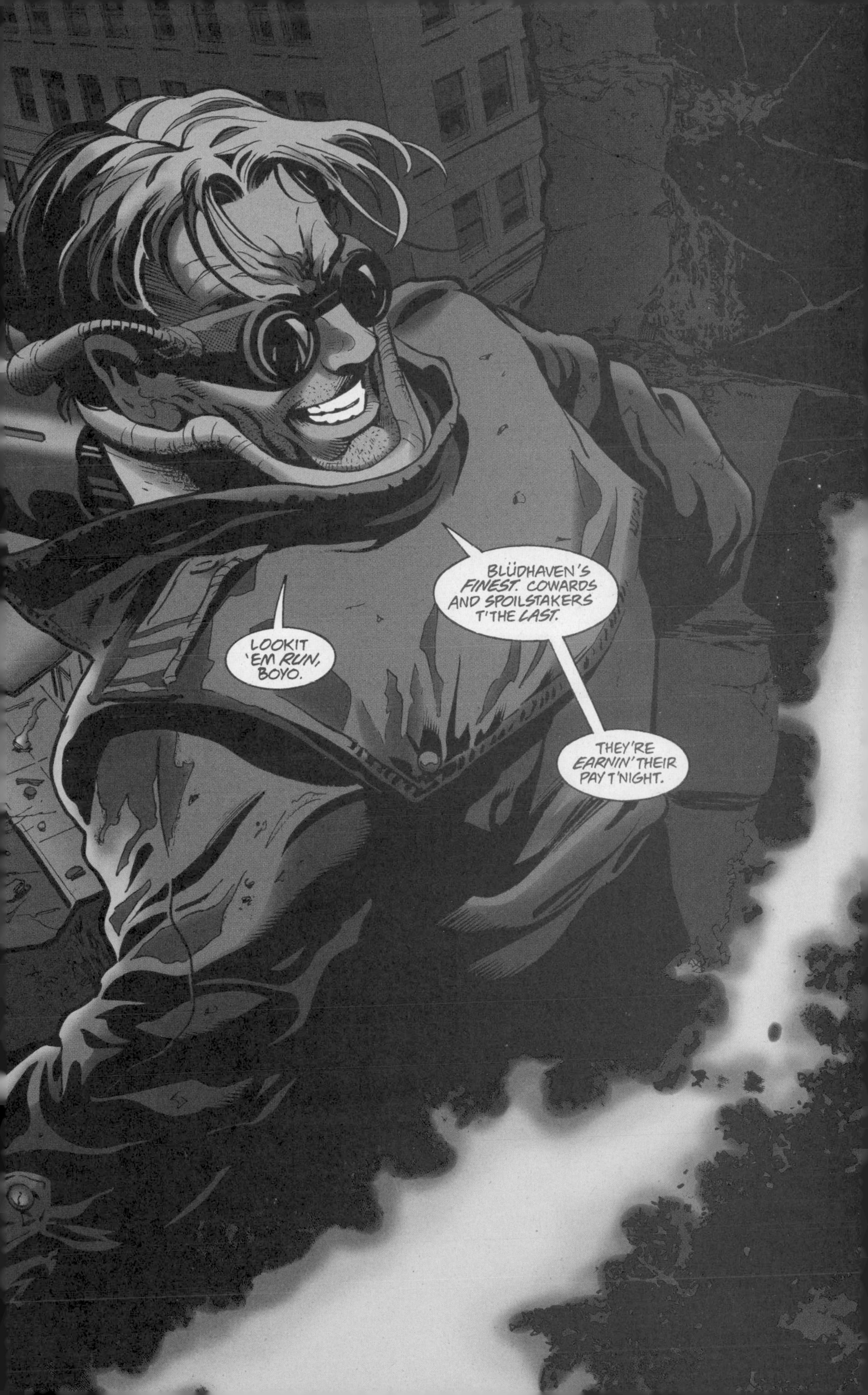
LOOKIT 'EM *RUN*, BOYO.
BLÜDHAVEN'S *FINEST.* COWARDS AND SPOILSTAKERS T'THE *LAST.*
THEY'RE *EARNIN'* THEIR PAY T'NIGHT.

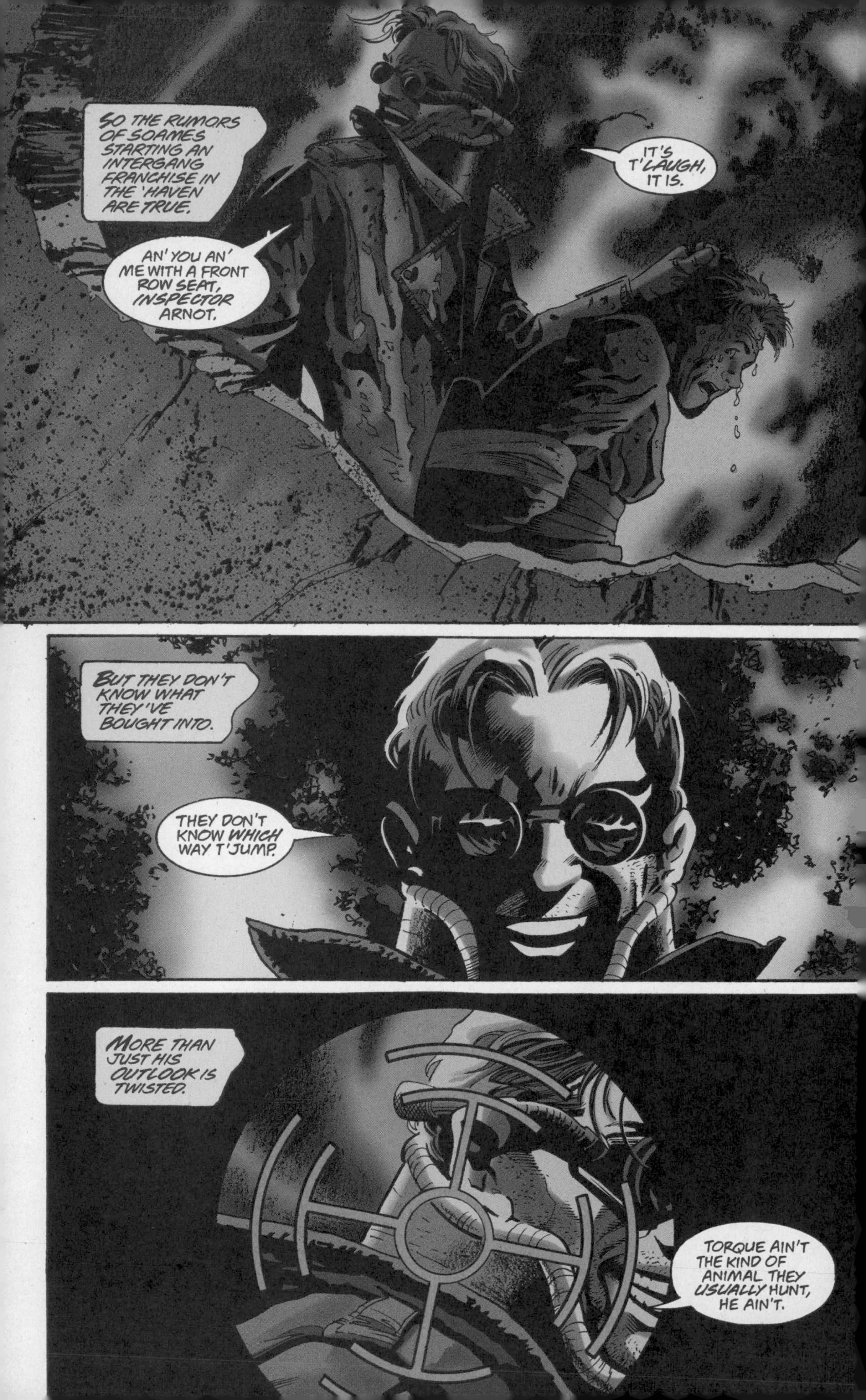
SO THE RUMORS OF SOAMES STARTING AN INTERGANG FRANCHISE IN THE 'HAVEN ARE TRUE.
IT'S T'LAUGH, IT IS.
AN' YOU AN' ME WITH A FRONT ROW SEAT, INSPECTOR ARNOT.
BUT THEY DON'T KNOW WHAT THEY'VE BOUGHT INTO.
THEY DON'T KNOW WHICH WAY T'JUMP.
MORE THAN JUST HIS OUTLOOK IS TWISTED.
TORQUE AIN'T THE KIND OF ANIMAL THEY USUALLY HUNT, HE AIN'T.

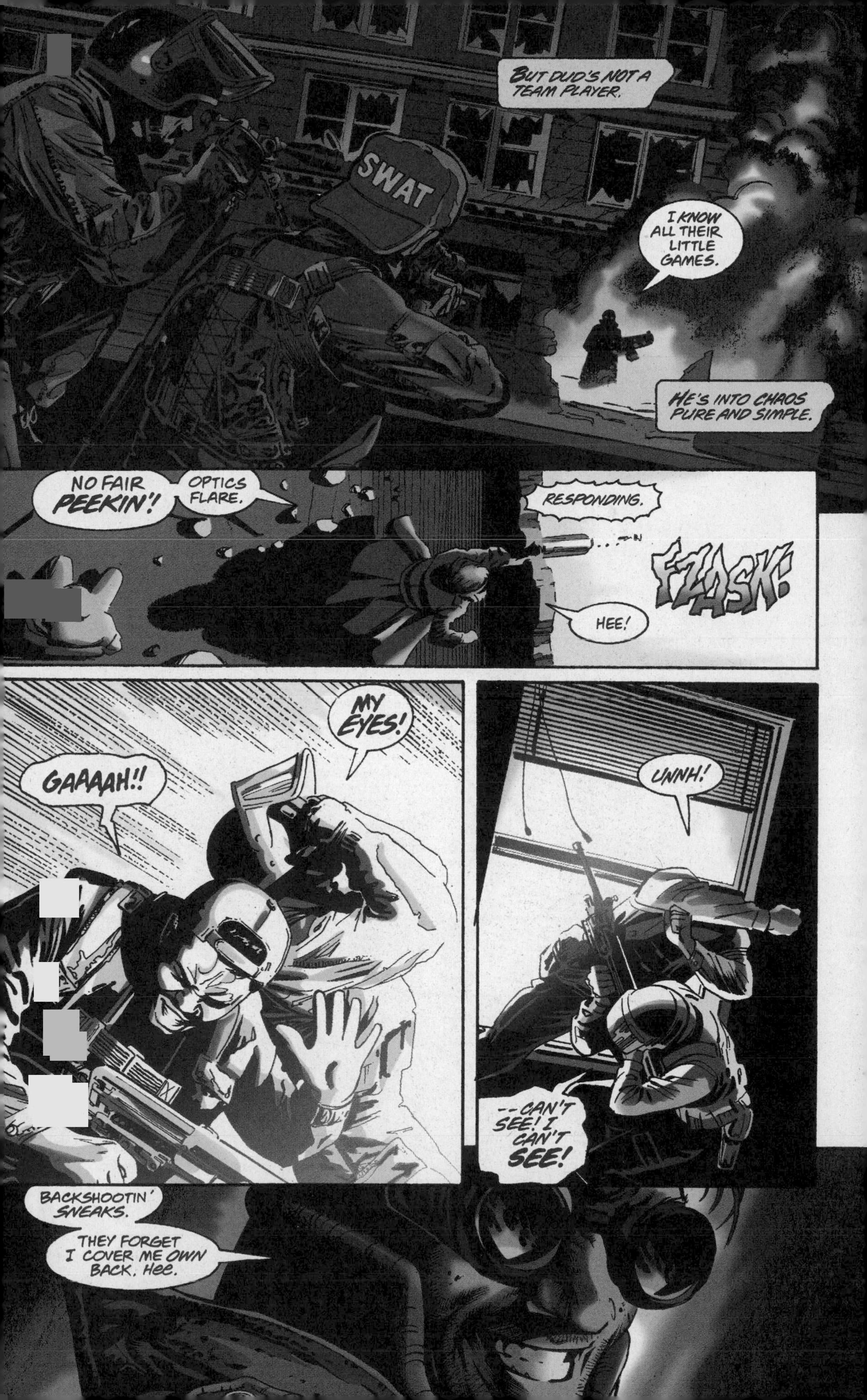
BUT DUD'S NOT A TEAM PLAYER.
SWAT
I KNOW ALL THEIR LITTLE GAMES.
HE'S INTO CHAOS PURE AND SIMPLE.
NO FAIR PEEKIN'!
OPTICS FLARE.
RESPONDING.
FZASK!
HEE!
GAAAAH!!
MY EYES!
UNNH!
--CAN'T SEE! I CAN'T SEE!
BACKSHOOTIN' SNEAKS.
THEY FORGET I COVER ME OWN BACK. Hee.

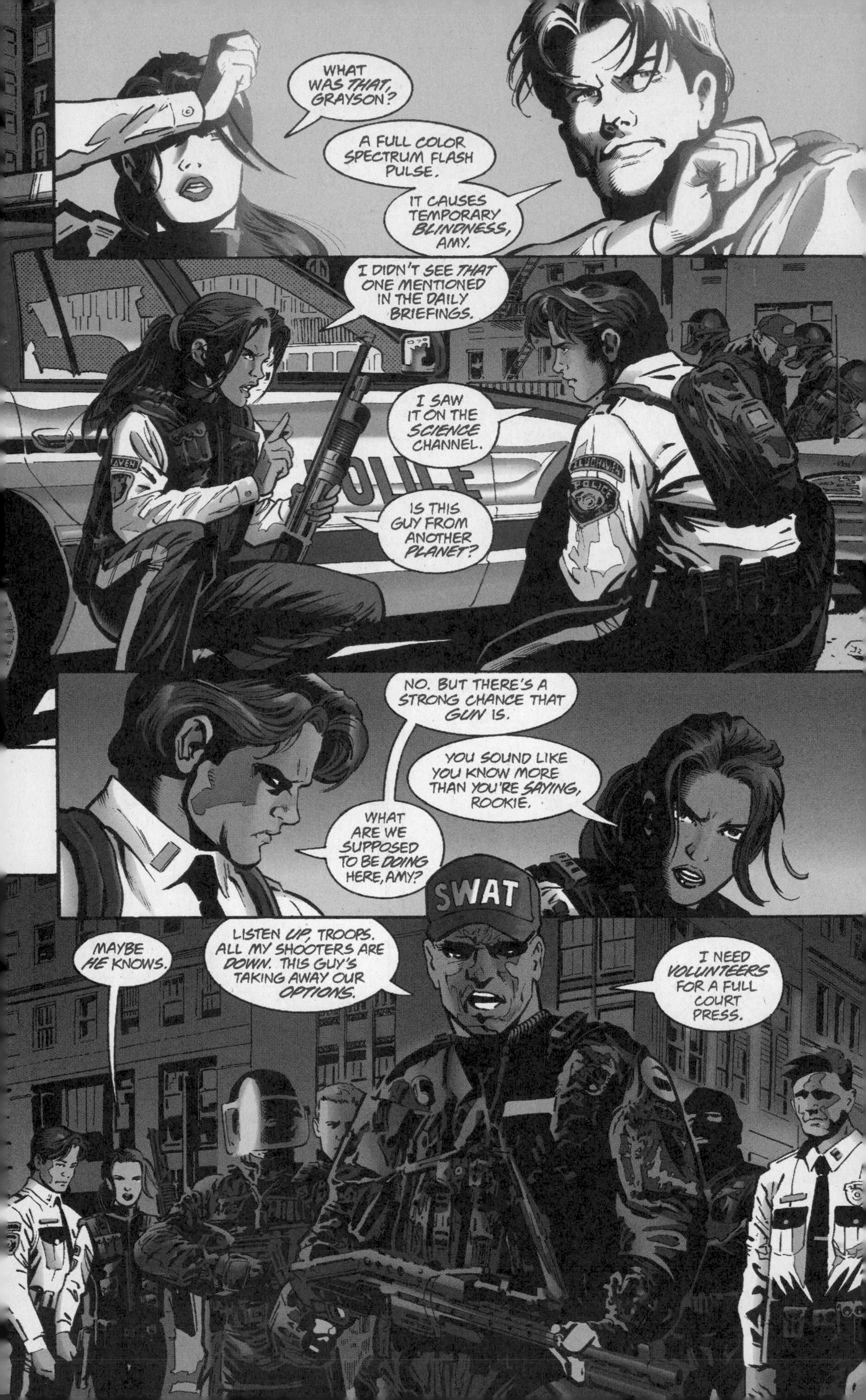
WHAT WAS THAT, GRAYSON?
A FULL COLOR SPECTRUM FLASH PULSE.
IT CAUSES TEMPORARY BLINDNESS, AMY.
I DIDN'T SEE THAT ONE MENTIONED IN THE DAILY BRIEFINGS.
I SAW IT ON THE SCIENCE CHANNEL.
IS THIS GUY FROM ANOTHER PLANET?
POLICE
NO. BUT THERE'S A STRONG CHANCE THAT GUN IS.
YOU SOUND LIKE YOU KNOW MORE THAN YOU'RE SAYING, ROOKIE.
WHAT ARE WE SUPPOSED TO BE DOING HERE, AMY?
SWAT
MAYBE HE KNOWS.
LISTEN UP, TROOPS. ALL MY SHOOTERS ARE DOWN. THIS GUY'S TAKING AWAY OUR OPTIONS.
I NEED VOLUNTEERS FOR A FULL COURT PRESS.

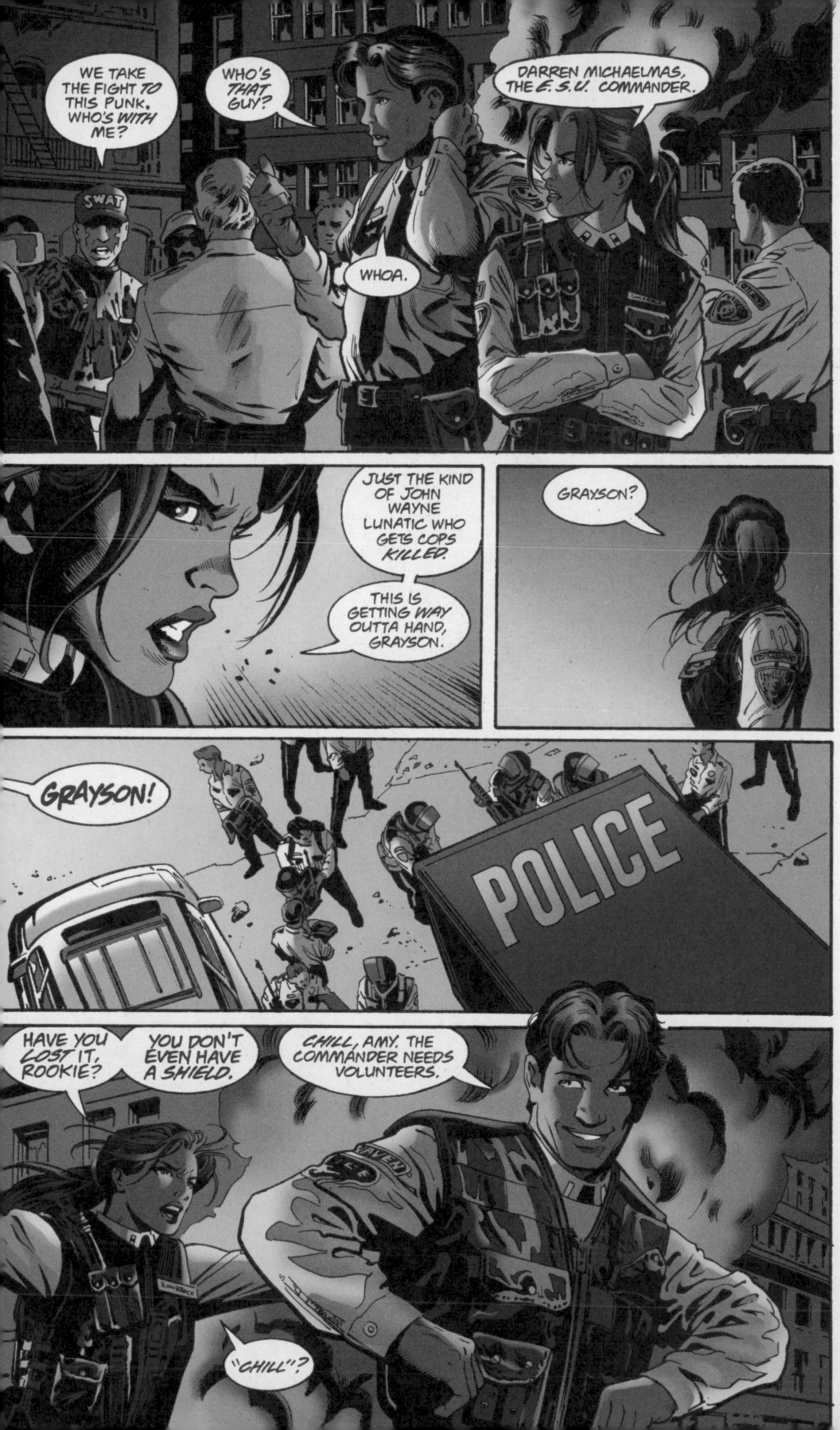
WE TAKE THE FIGHT TO THIS PUNK. WHO'S WITH ME?
WHO'S THAT GUY?
DARREN MICHAELMAS, THE E.S.U. COMMANDER.
WHOA.
SWAT
JUST THE KIND OF JOHN WAYNE LUNATIC WHO GETS COPS KILLED.
THIS IS GETTING WAY OUTTA HAND, GRAYSON.
GRAYSON?
GRAYSON!
POLICE
HAVE YOU LOST IT, ROOKIE?
YOU DON'T EVEN HAVE A SHIELD.
CHILL, AMY. THE COMMANDER NEEDS VOLUNTEERS.
"CHILL"?

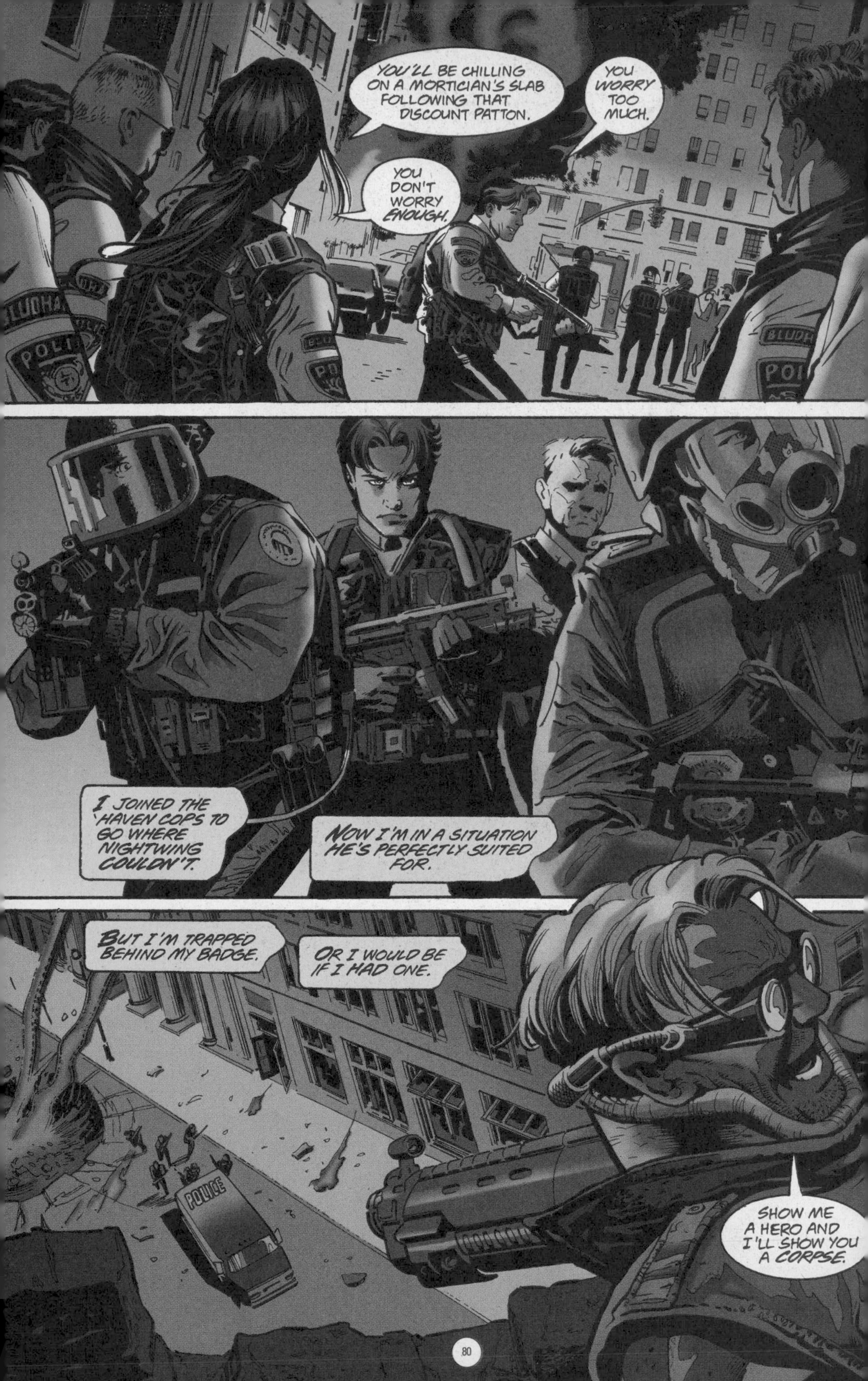
YOU'LL BE CHILLING ON A MORTICIAN'S SLAB FOLLOWING THAT DISCOUNT PATTON.
YOU WORRY TOO MUCH.
YOU DON'T WORRY ENOUGH.
BLUDHA
POLI
POLI
BLUDH
POLI
I JOINED THE HAVEN COPS TO GO WHERE NIGHTWING COULDN'T.
NOW I'M IN A SITUATION HE'S PERFECTLY SUITED FOR.
BUT I'M TRAPPED BEHIND MY BADGE.
OR I WOULD BE IF I HAD ONE.
POLICE
SHOW ME A HERO AND I'LL SHOW YOU A CORPSE.

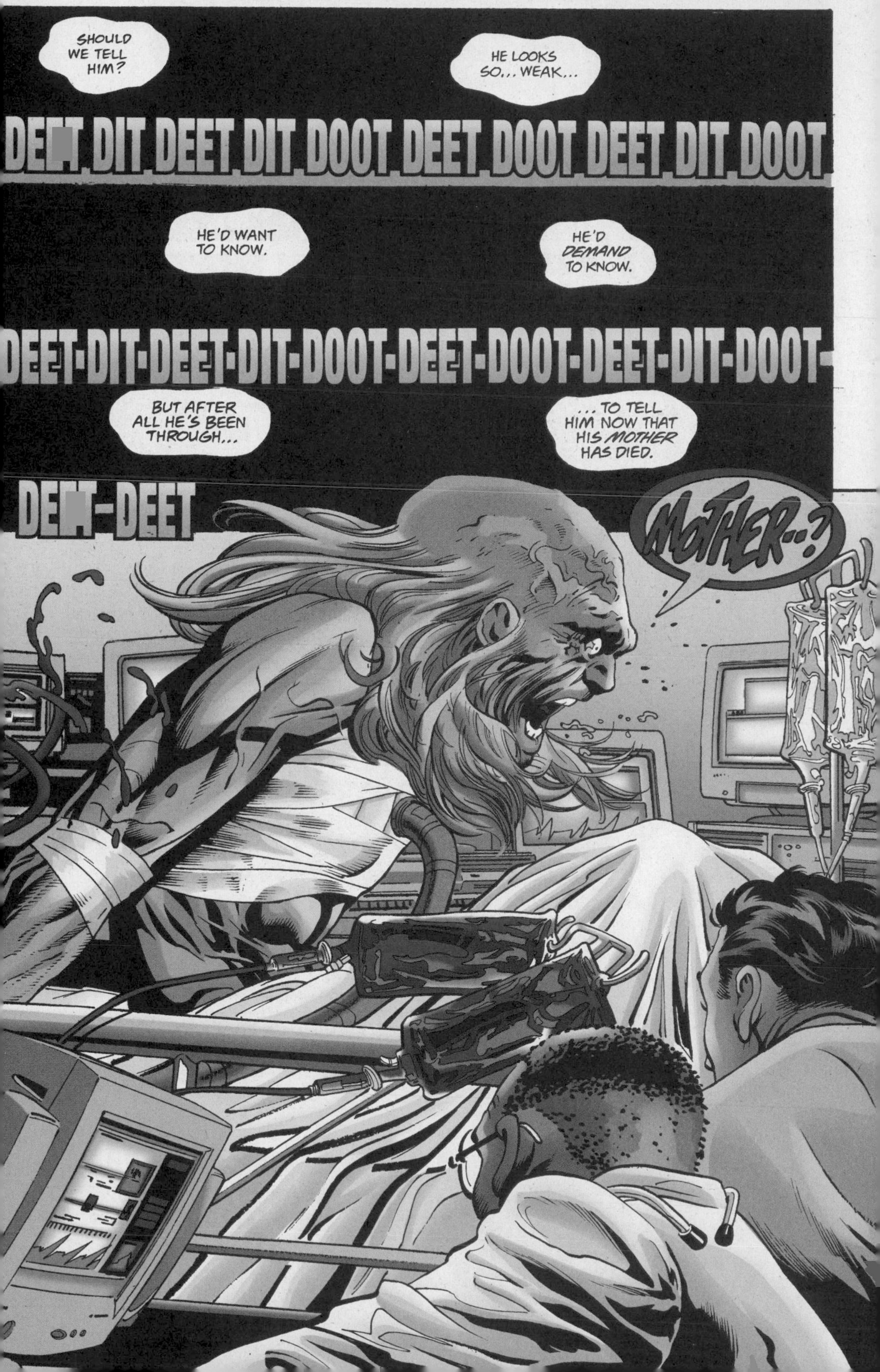

SHOULD WE TELL HIM?
HE LOOKS SO... WEAK...
DEET DIT DEET DIT DOOT DEET DOOT DEET DIT DOOT
HE'D WANT TO KNOW.
HE'D DEMAND TO KNOW.
DEET-DIT-DEET-DIT-DOOT-DEET-DOOT-DEET-DIT-DOOT-
BUT AFTER ALL HE'S BEEN THROUGH...
...TO TELL HIM NOW THAT HIS MOTHER HAS DIED.
DEET-DEET
MOTHER--?

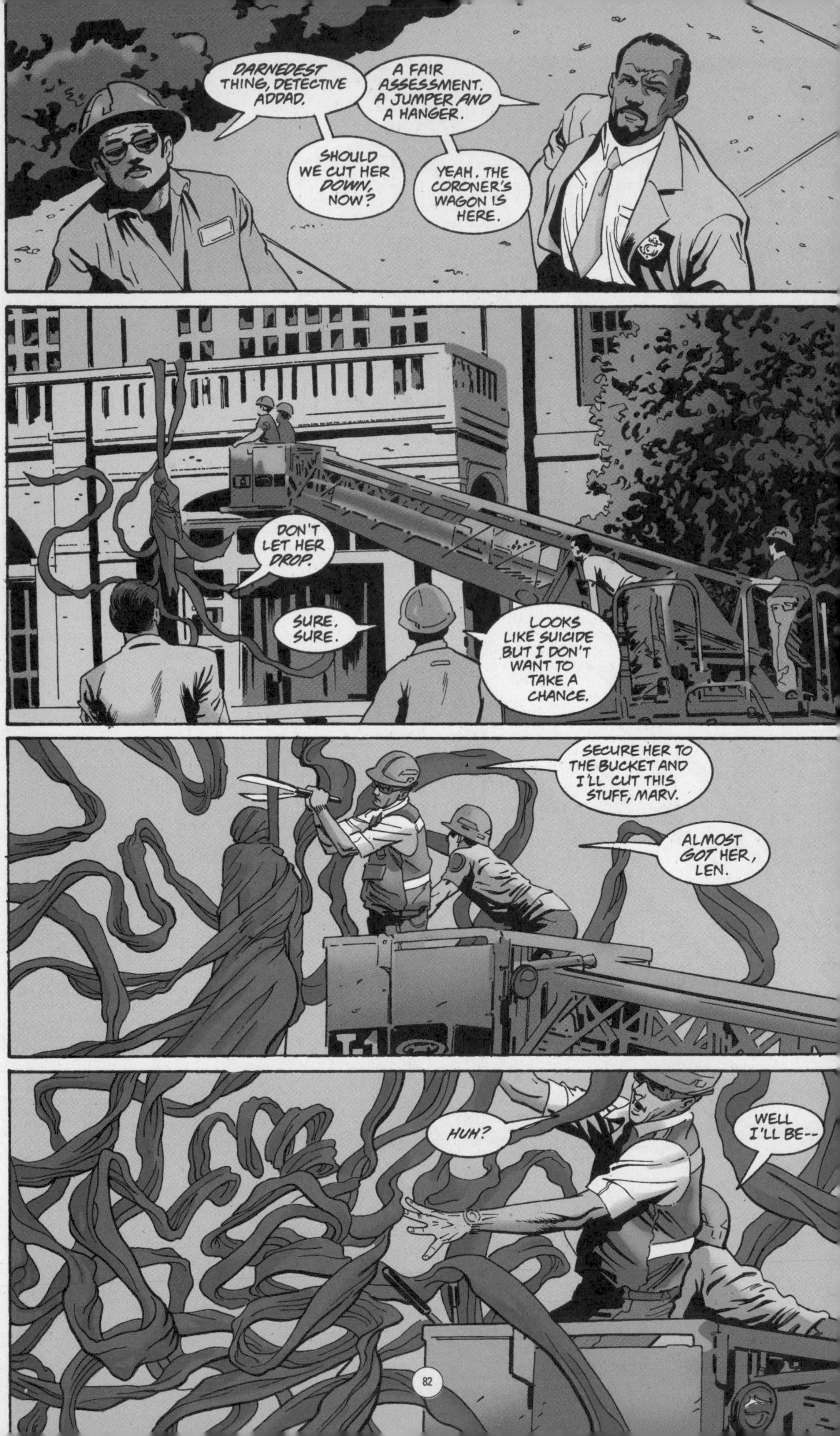
DARNEDEST THING, DETECTIVE ADDAD.
A FAIR ASSESSMENT. A JUMPER AND A HANGER.
SHOULD WE CUT HER DOWN, NOW?
YEAH. THE CORONER'S WAGON IS HERE.
DON'T LET HER DROP.
SURE, SURE.
LOOKS LIKE SUICIDE BUT I DON'T WANT TO TAKE A CHANCE.
SECURE HER TO THE BUCKET AND I'LL CUT THIS STUFF, MARV.
ALMOST GOT HER, LEN.
T-1
HUH?
WELL I'LL BE--

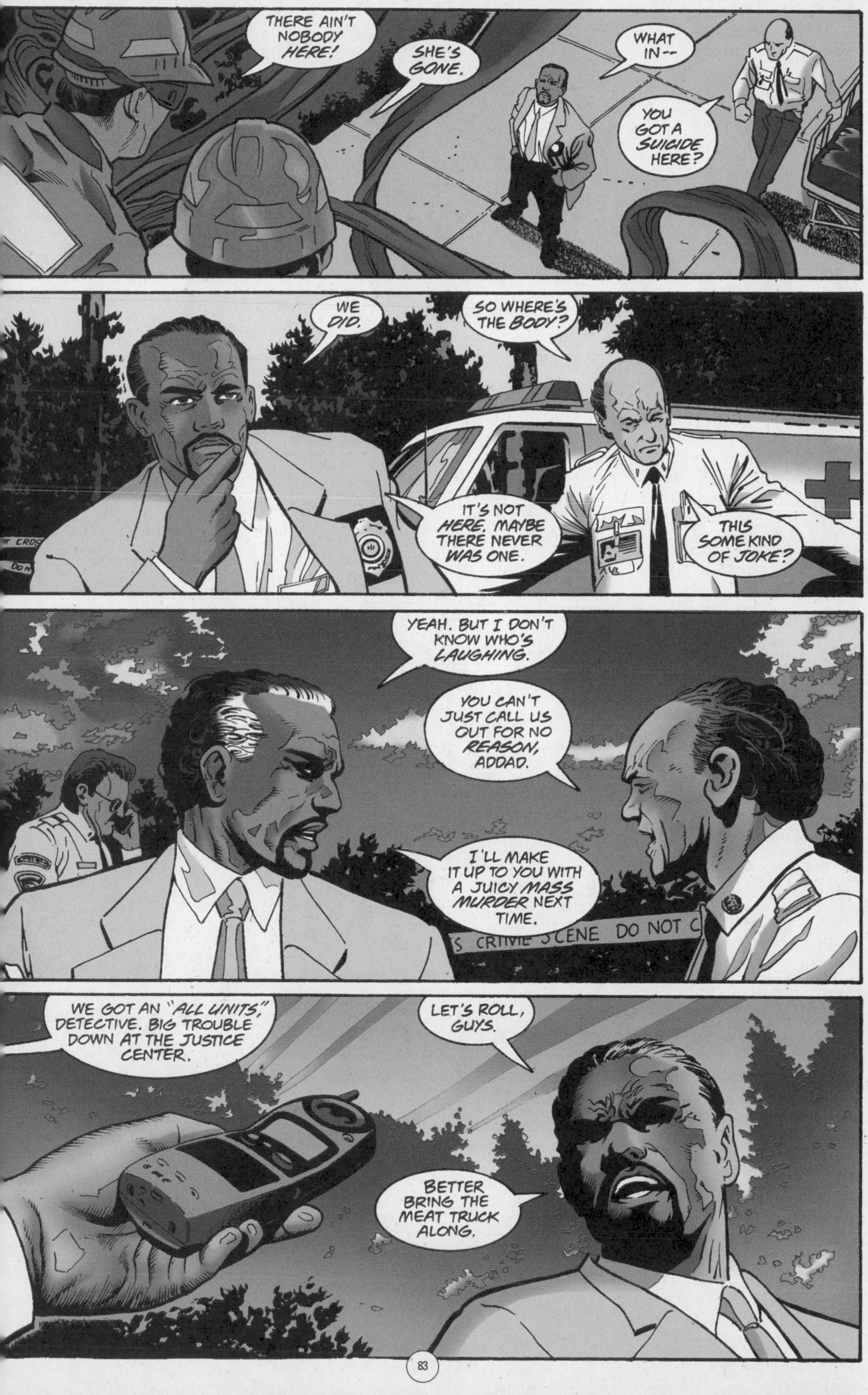
THERE AIN'T NOBODY HERE!
SHE'S GONE.
WHAT IN--
YOU GOT A SUICIDE HERE?
WE DID.
SO WHERE'S THE BODY?
IT'S NOT HERE. MAYBE THERE NEVER WAS ONE.
THIS SOME KIND OF JOKE?
YEAH. BUT I DON'T KNOW WHO'S LAUGHING.
YOU CAN'T JUST CALL US OUT FOR NO REASON, ADDAD.
I'LL MAKE IT UP TO YOU WITH A JUICY MASS MURDER NEXT TIME.
CRIME SCENE DO NOT C
WE GOT AN "ALL UNITS," DETECTIVE. BIG TROUBLE DOWN AT THE JUSTICE CENTER.
LET'S ROLL, GUYS.
BETTER BRING THE MEAT TRUCK ALONG.

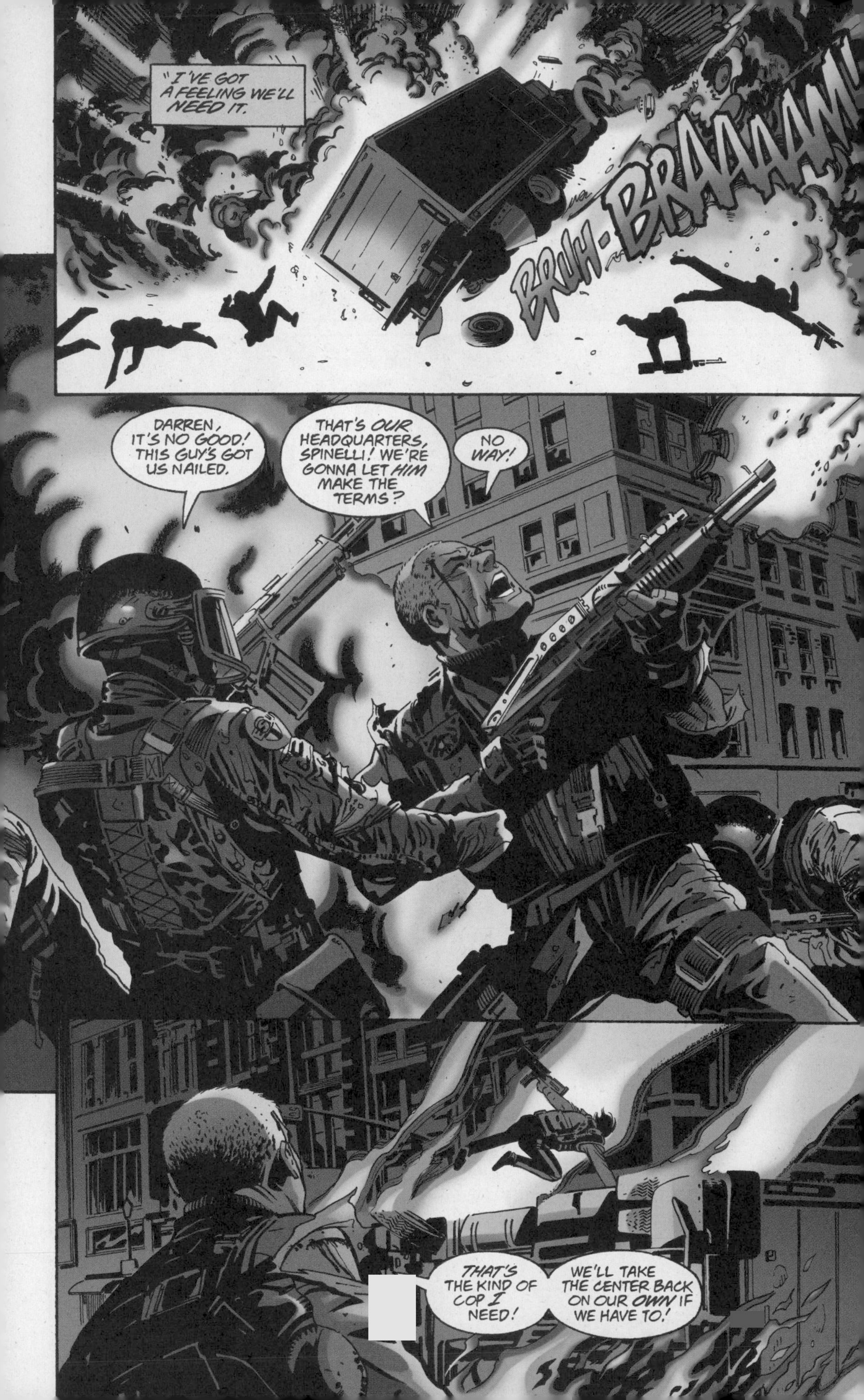
"I'VE GOT A FEELING WE'LL NEED IT.
BRUH-BRAAAAM!
DARREN, IT'S NO GOOD! THIS GUY'S GOT US NAILED.
THAT'S OUR HEADQUARTERS, SPINELLI! WE'RE GONNA LET HIM MAKE THE TERMS?
NO WAY!
THAT'S THE KIND OF COP I NEED!
WE'LL TAKE THE CENTER BACK ON OUR OWN IF WE HAVE TO!

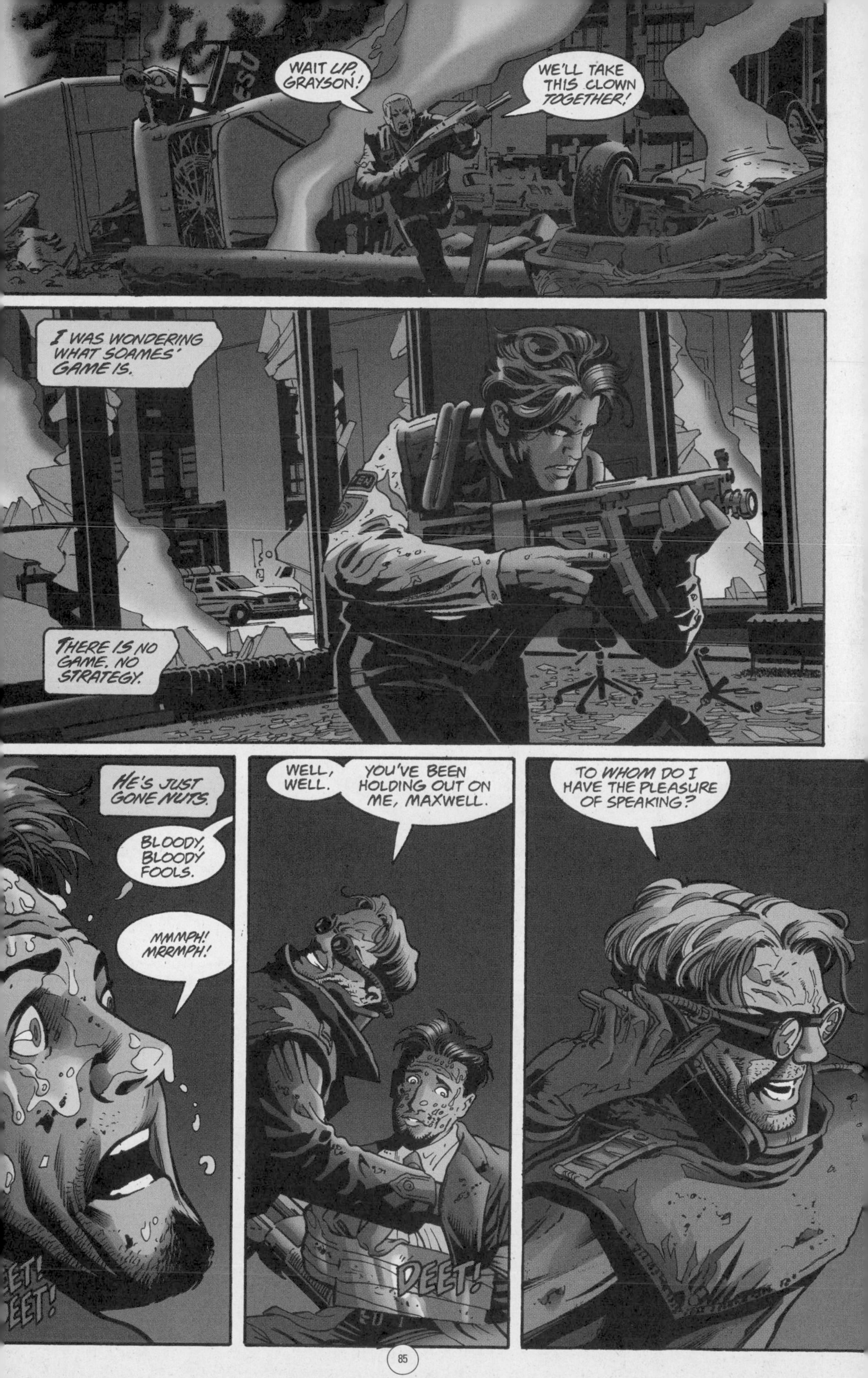
WAIT UP, GRAYSON!
WE'LL TAKE THIS CLOWN TOGETHER!
I WAS WONDERING WHAT SOAMES' GAME IS.
THERE IS NO GAME. NO STRATEGY.
HE'S JUST GONE NUTS.
BLOODY, BLOODY FOOLS.
MMMPH! MRRMPH!
EET! EET!
WELL, WELL.
YOU'VE BEEN HOLDING OUT ON ME, MAXWELL.
DEET!
TO WHOM DO I HAVE THE PLEASURE OF SPEAKING?

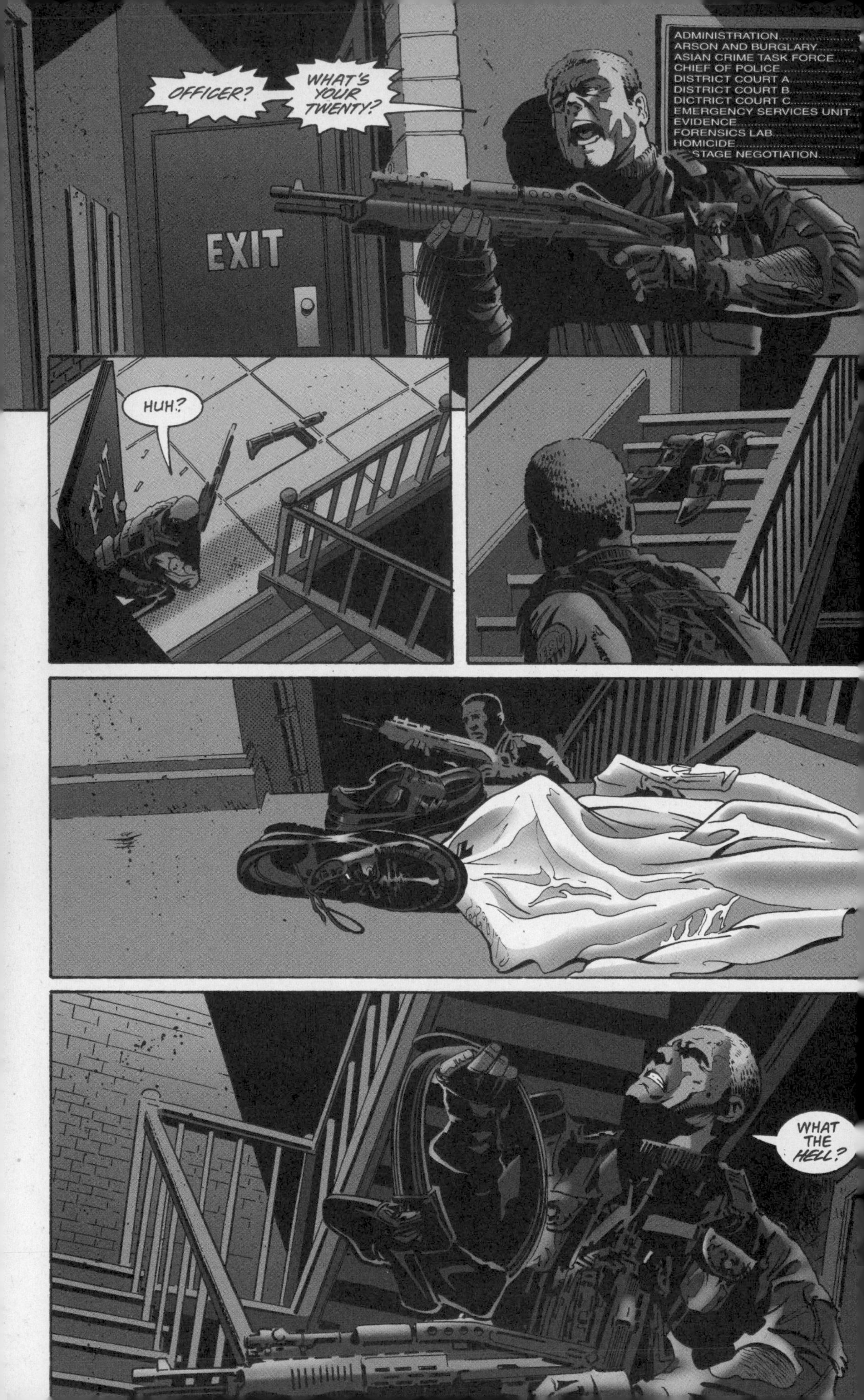
ADMINISTRATION
ARSON AND BURGLARY
ASIAN CRIME TASK FORCE
CHIEF OF POLICE
DISTRICT COURT A
DISTRICT COURT B
DICTRICT COURT C
EMERGENCY SERVICES UNIT
EVIDENCE
FORENSICS LAB
HOMICIDE
STAGE NEGOTIATION
OFFICER?
WHAT'S YOUR TWENTY?
EXIT
HUH?
WHAT THE HELL?

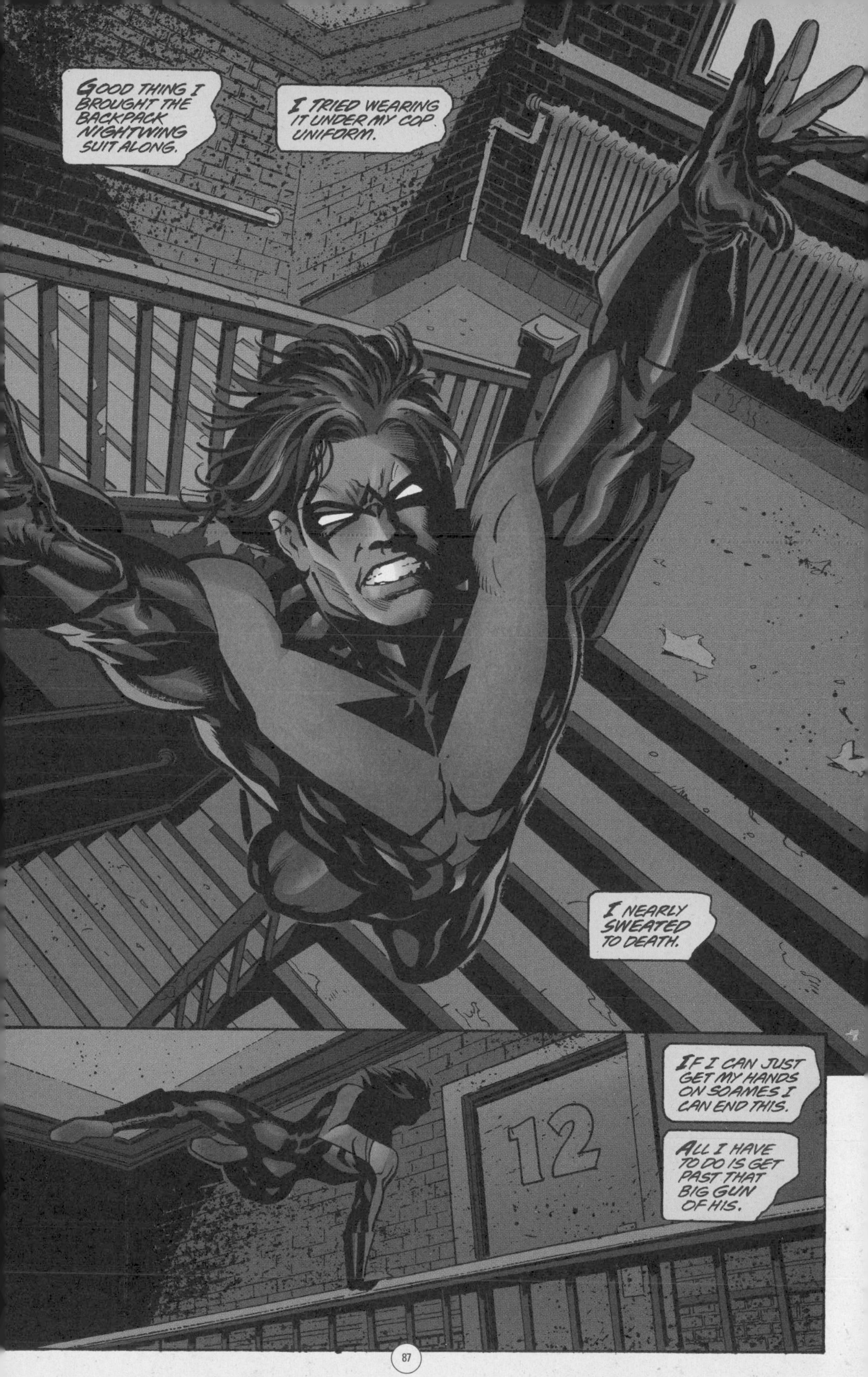
GOOD THING I BROUGHT THE BACKPACK NIGHTWING SUIT ALONG.
I TRIED WEARING IT UNDER MY COP UNIFORM.
I NEARLY SWEATED TO DEATH.
IF I CAN JUST GET MY HANDS ON SOAMES I CAN END THIS.
ALL I HAVE TO DO IS GET PAST THAT BIG GUN OF HIS.
12

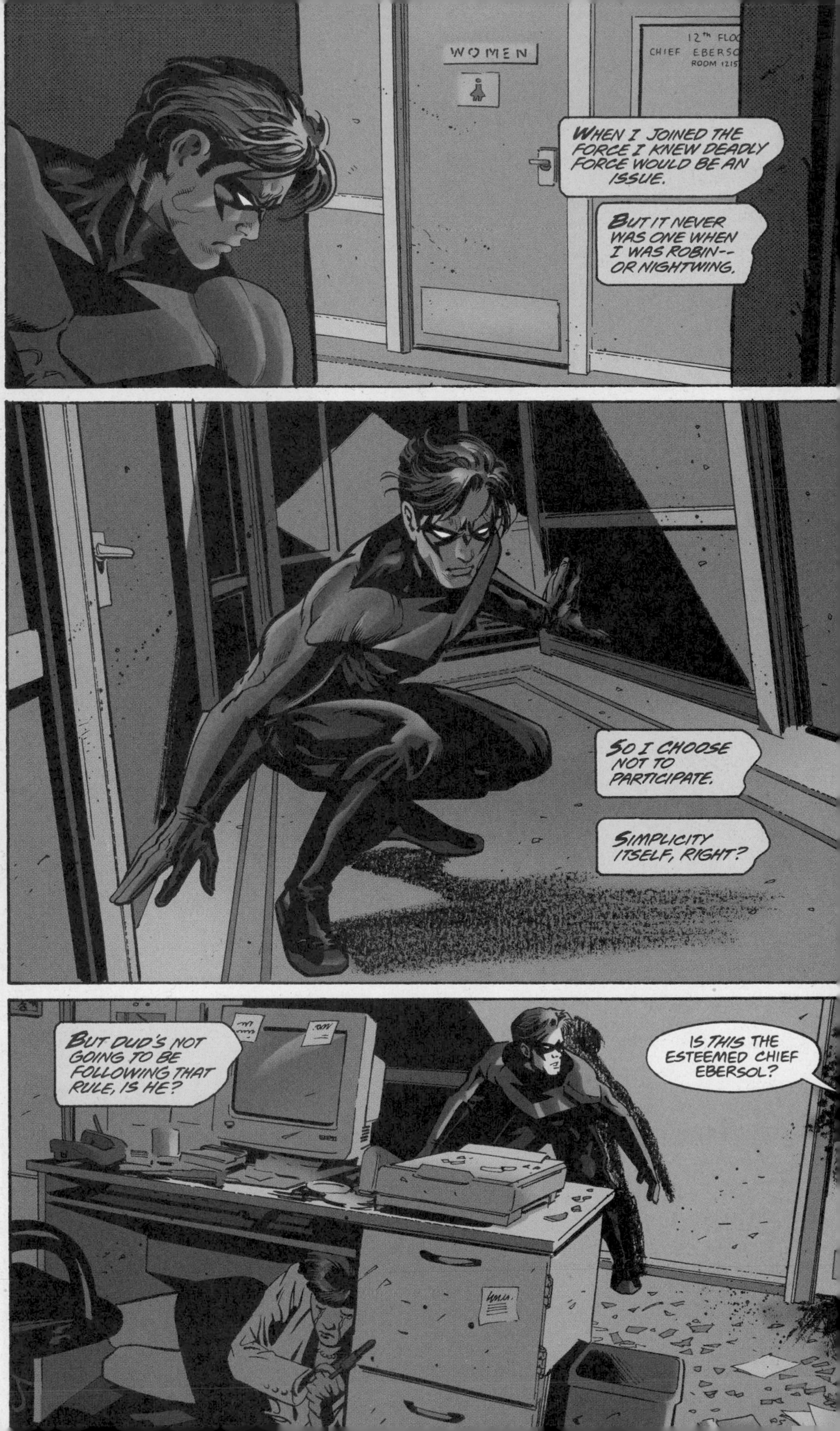
WOMEN
12th FLO
CHIEF EBERSO
ROOM 1215
WHEN I JOINED THE FORCE I KNEW DEADLY FORCE WOULD BE AN ISSUE.
BUT IT NEVER WAS ONE WHEN I WAS ROBIN-- OR NIGHTWING.
SO I CHOOSE NOT TO PARTICIPATE.
SIMPLICITY ITSELF, RIGHT?
BUT DUD'S NOT GOING TO BE FOLLOWING THAT RULE, IS HE?
IS THIS THE ESTEEMED CHIEF EBERSOL?

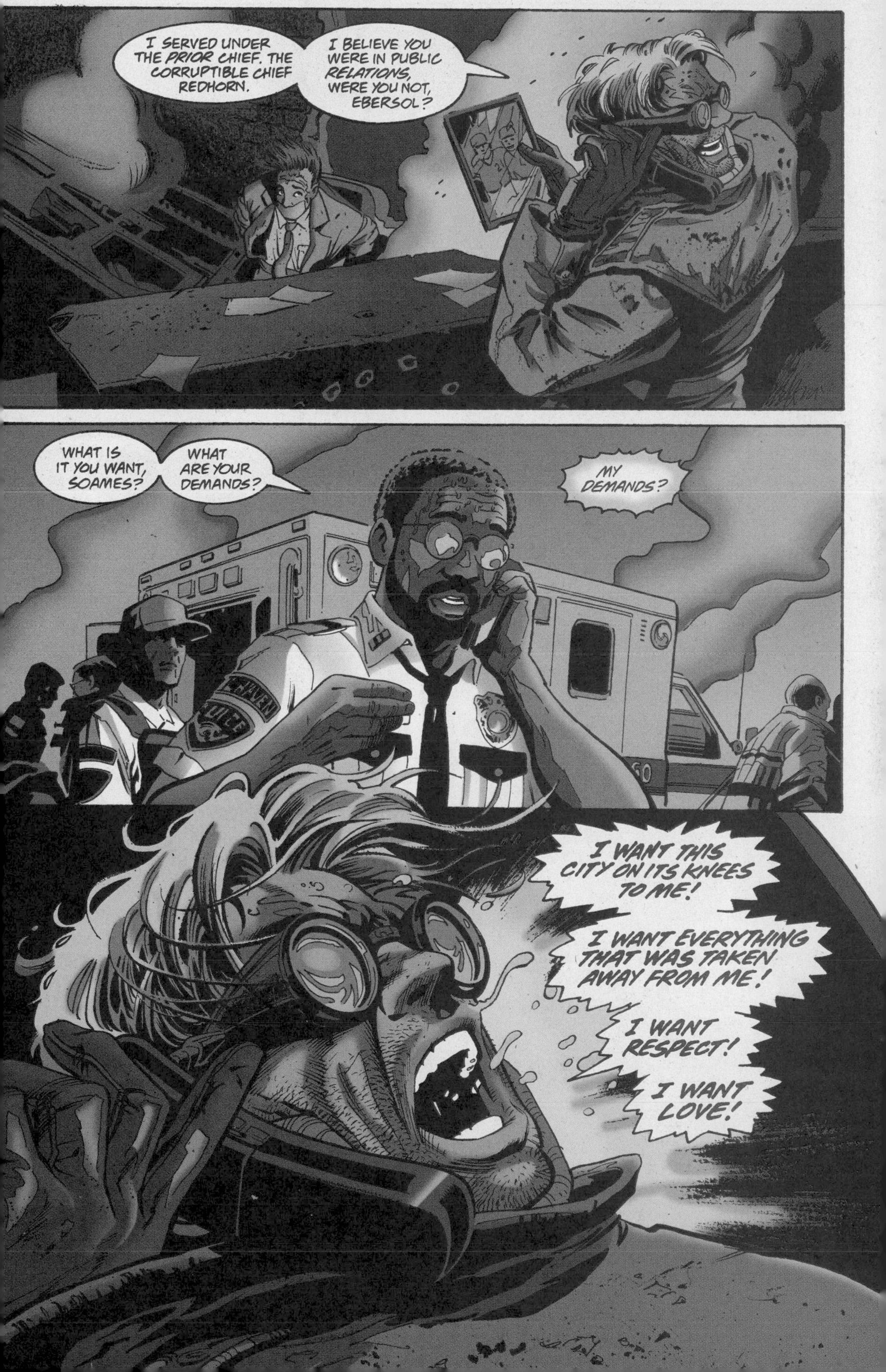
I SERVED UNDER THE PRIOR CHIEF. THE CORRUPTIBLE CHIEF REDHORN.
I BELIEVE YOU WERE IN PUBLIC RELATIONS, WERE YOU NOT, EBERSOL?
WHAT IS IT YOU WANT, SOAMES?
WHAT ARE YOUR DEMANDS?
MY DEMANDS?
I WANT THIS CITY ON ITS KNEES TO ME!
I WANT EVERYTHING THAT WAS TAKEN AWAY FROM ME!
I WANT RESPECT!
I WANT LOVE!

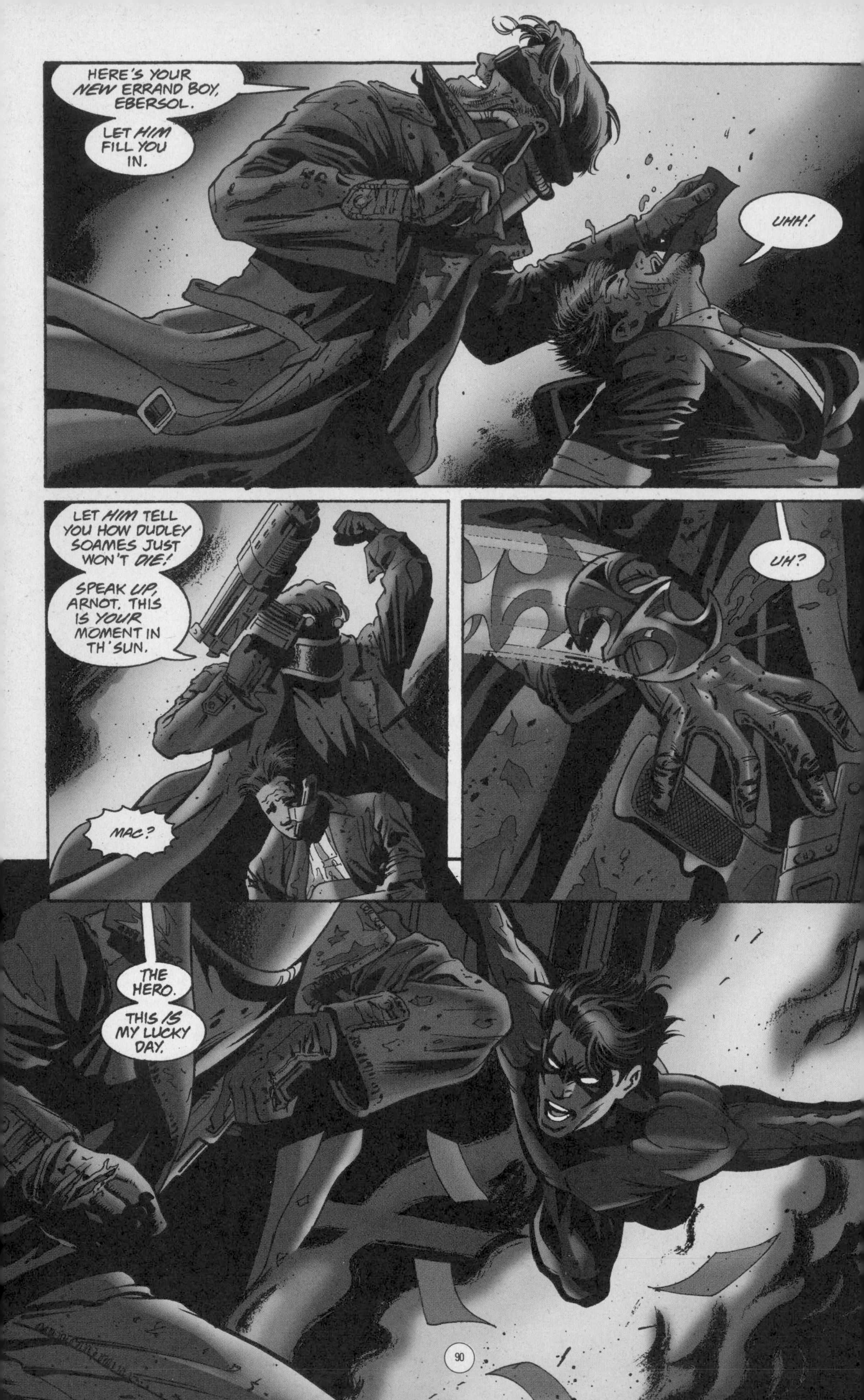
HERE'S YOUR NEW ERRAND BOY, EBERSOL.
LET HIM FILL YOU IN.
UHH!
LET HIM TELL YOU HOW DUDLEY SOAMES JUST WON'T DIE!
SPEAK UP, ARNOT. THIS IS YOUR MOMENT IN TH' SUN.
MAC?
UH?
THE HERO.
THIS IS MY LUCKY DAY.

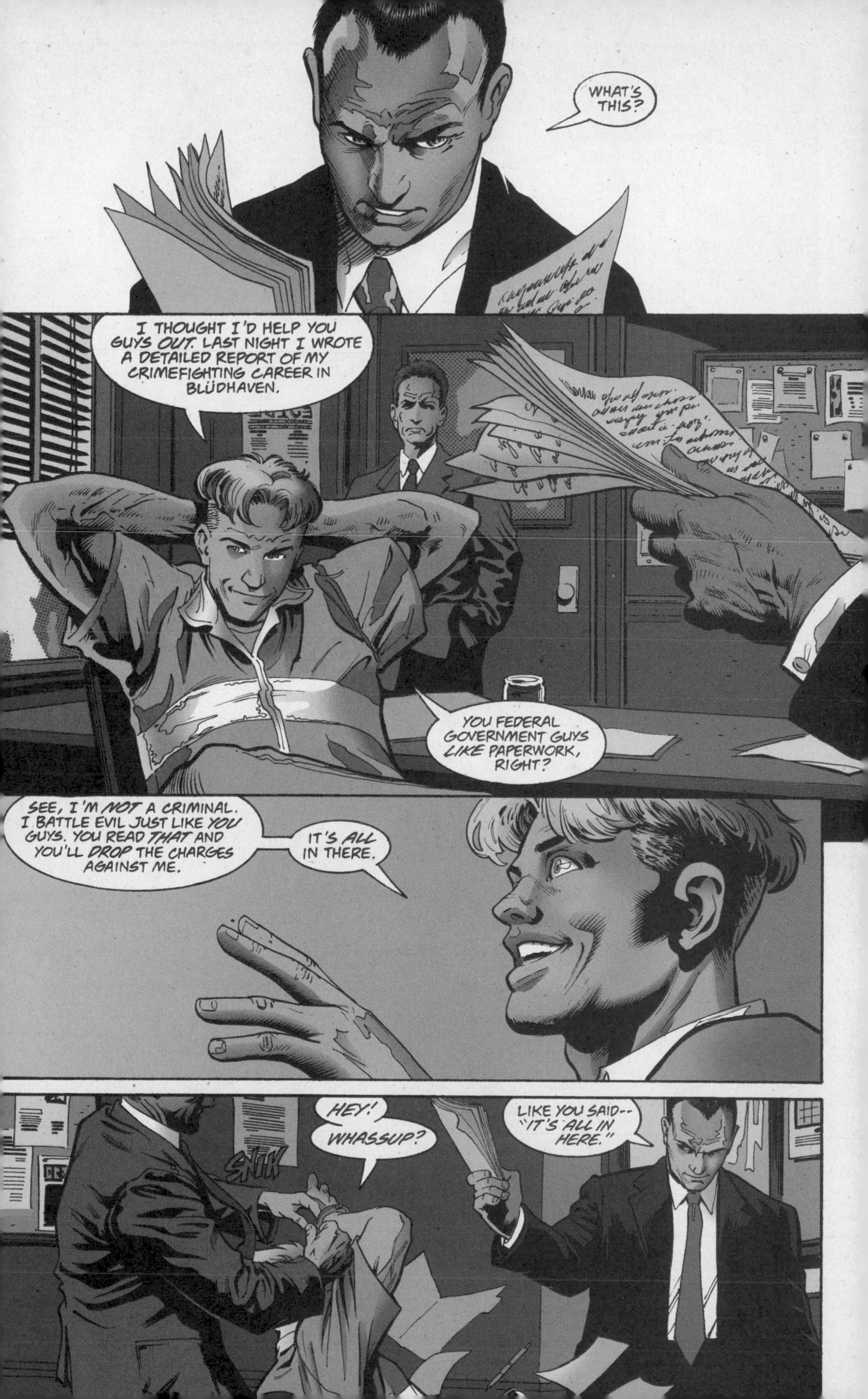
WHAT'S THIS?
I THOUGHT I'D HELP YOU GUYS OUT. LAST NIGHT I WROTE A DETAILED REPORT OF MY CRIMEFIGHTING CAREER IN BLÜDHAVEN.
YOU FEDERAL GOVERNMENT GUYS LIKE PAPERWORK, RIGHT?
SEE, I'M NOT A CRIMINAL. I BATTLE EVIL JUST LIKE YOU GUYS. YOU READ THAT AND YOU'LL DROP THE CHARGES AGAINST ME.
IT'S ALL IN THERE.
HEY! WHASSUP?
LIKE YOU SAID-- "IT'S ALL IN HERE."

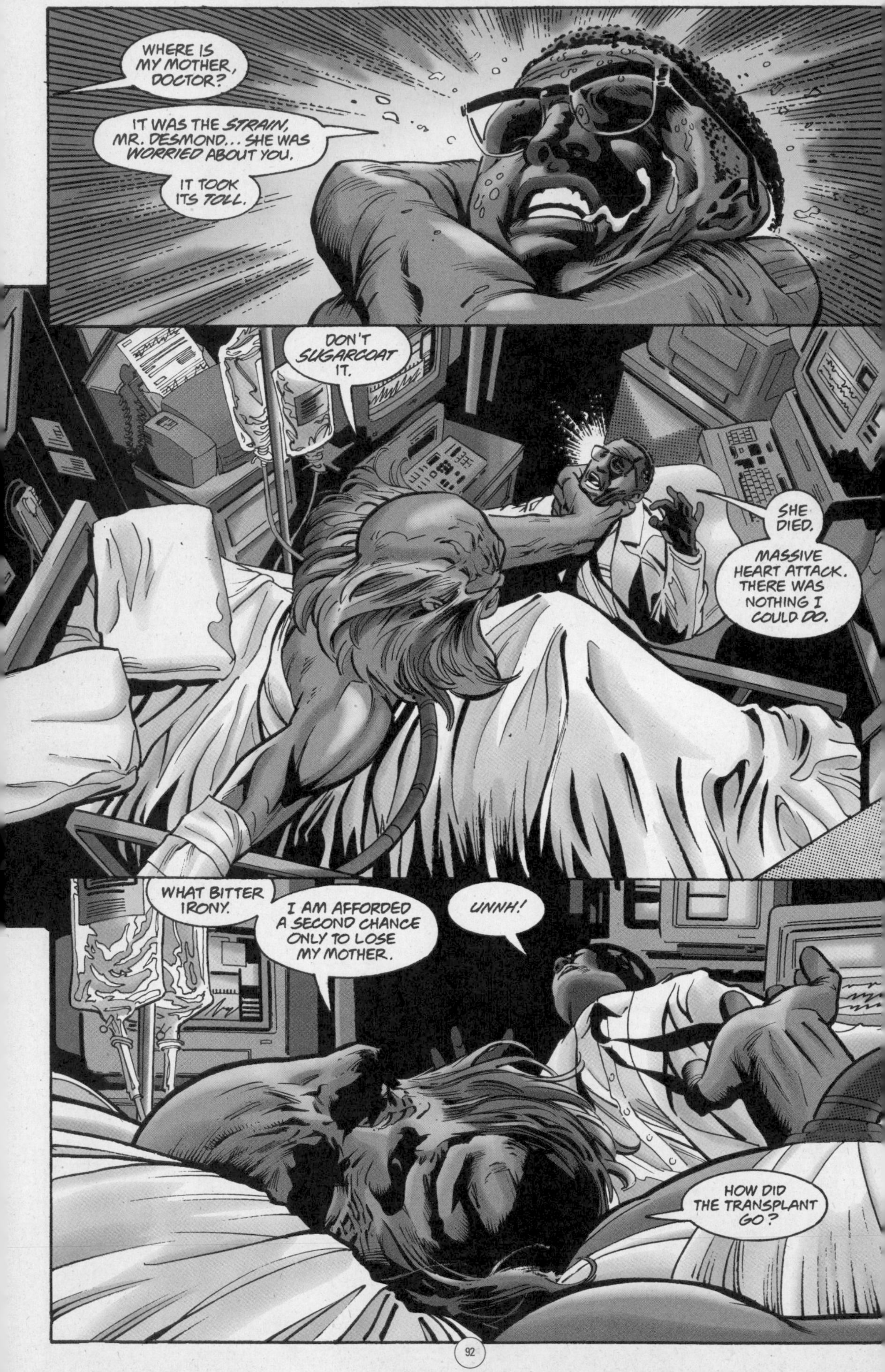
WHERE IS MY MOTHER, DOCTOR?
IT WAS THE STRAIN, MR. DESMOND... SHE WAS WORRIED ABOUT YOU.
IT TOOK ITS TOLL.
DON'T SUGARCOAT IT.
SHE DIED.
MASSIVE HEART ATTACK. THERE WAS NOTHING I COULD DO.
WHAT BITTER IRONY.
I AM AFFORDED A SECOND CHANCE ONLY TO LOSE MY MOTHER.
UNNH!
HOW DID THE TRANSPLANT GO?

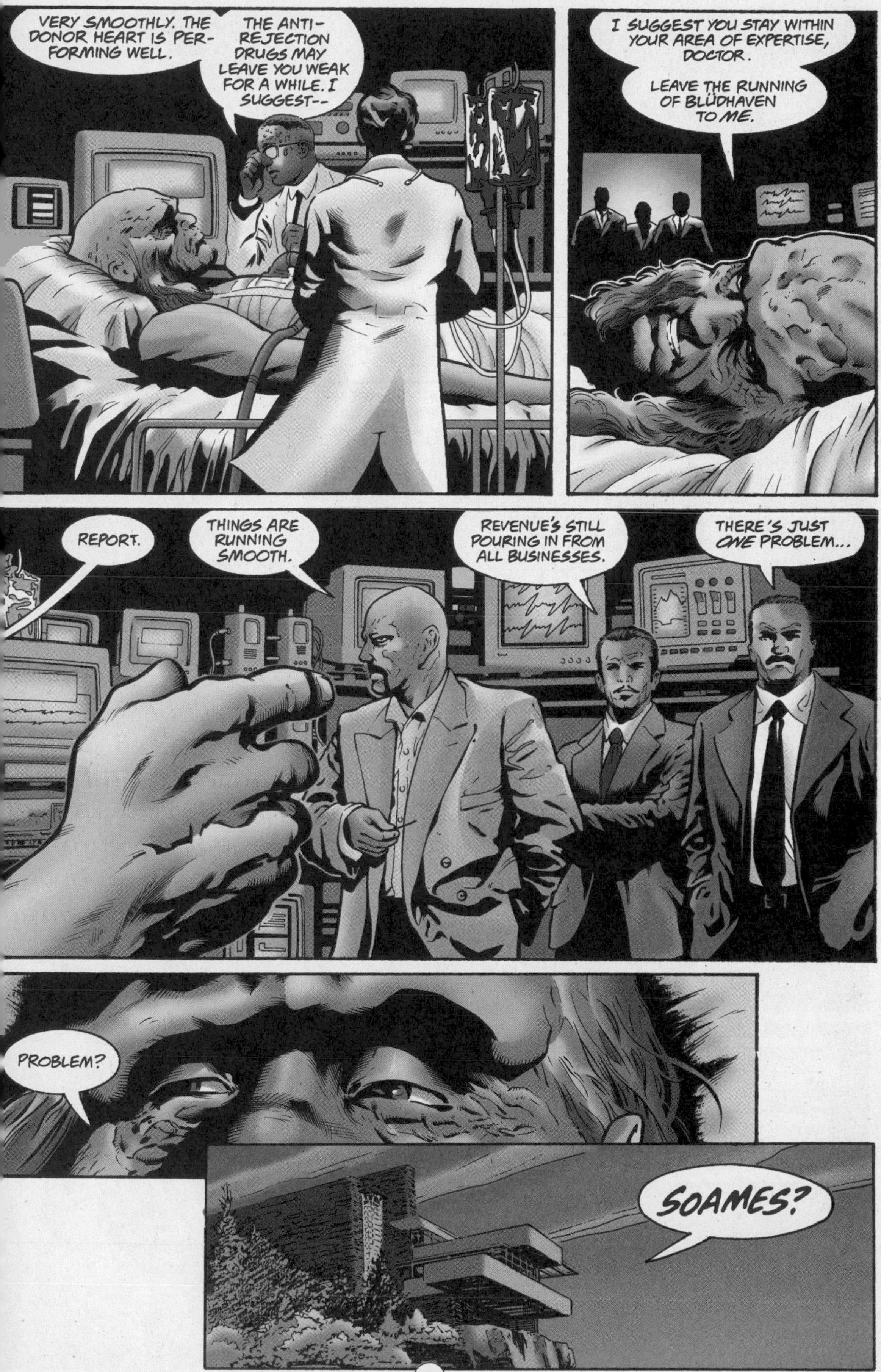
VERY SMOOTHLY. THE DONOR HEART IS PERFORMING WELL.
THE ANTI-REJECTION DRUGS MAY LEAVE YOU WEAK FOR A WHILE. I SUGGEST--
I SUGGEST YOU STAY WITHIN YOUR AREA OF EXPERTISE, DOCTOR.
LEAVE THE RUNNING OF BLÜDHAVEN TO *ME*.
REPORT.
THINGS ARE RUNNING SMOOTH.
REVENUE'S STILL POURING IN FROM ALL BUSINESSES.
THERE'S JUST *ONE* PROBLEM...
PROBLEM?
SOAMES?

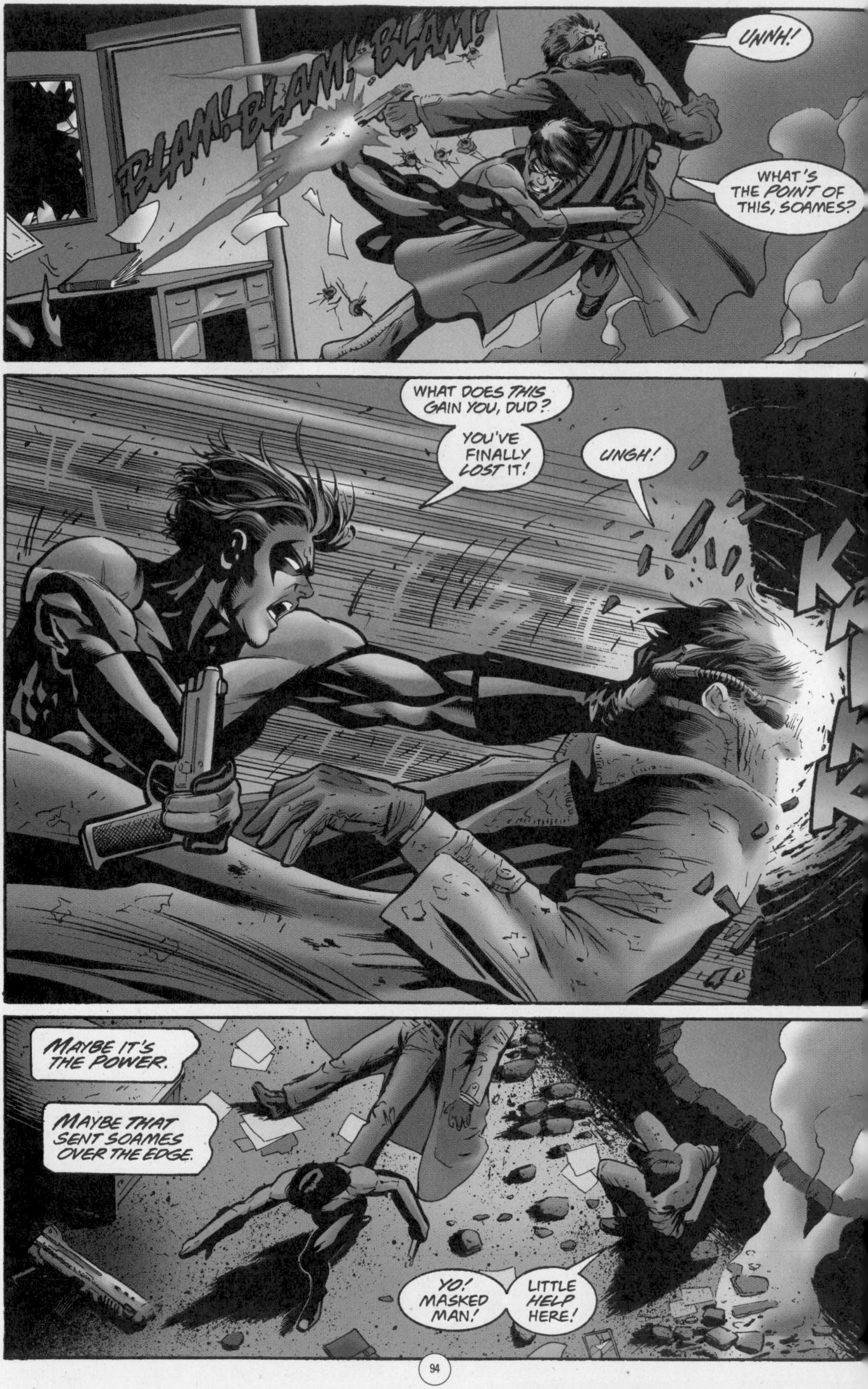
BLAM! BLAM! BLAM! BLAM!
UNNH!
WHAT'S THE POINT OF THIS, SOAMES?
WHAT DOES THIS GAIN YOU, DUD?
YOU'VE FINALLY LOST IT!
UNGH!
MAYBE IT'S THE POWER.
MAYBE THAT SENT SOAMES OVER THE EDGE.
YO! MASKED MAN!
LITTLE HELP HERE!

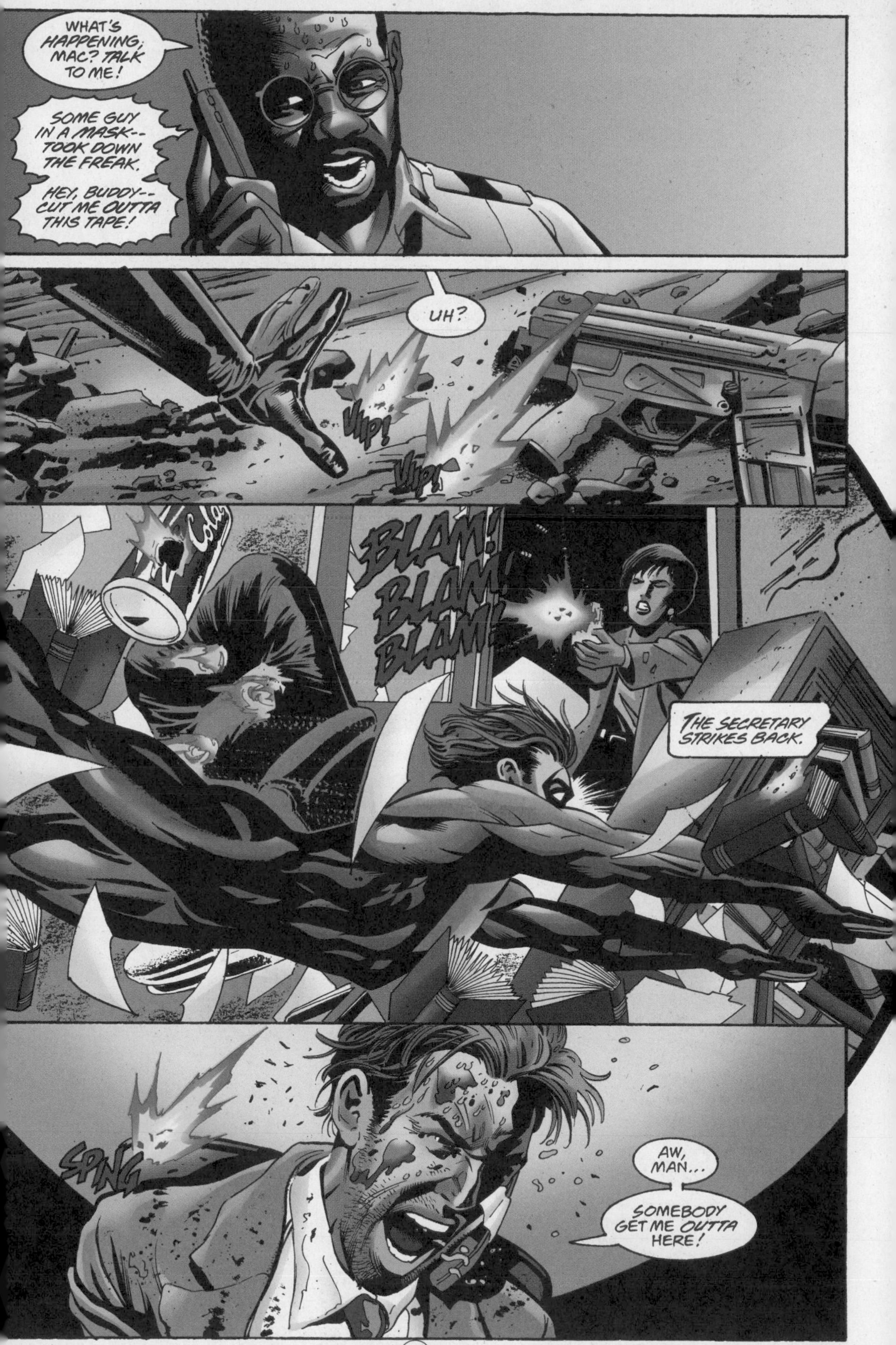
WHAT'S HAPPENING, MAC? TALK TO ME!
SOME GUY IN A MASK-- TOOK DOWN THE FREAK.
HEY, BUDDY-- CUT ME OUTTA THIS TAPE!
UH?
VIIP!
VIIP!
BLAM! BLAM! BLAM!
THE SECRETARY STRIKES BACK.
SPING
AW, MAN...
SOMEBODY GET ME OUTTA HERE!

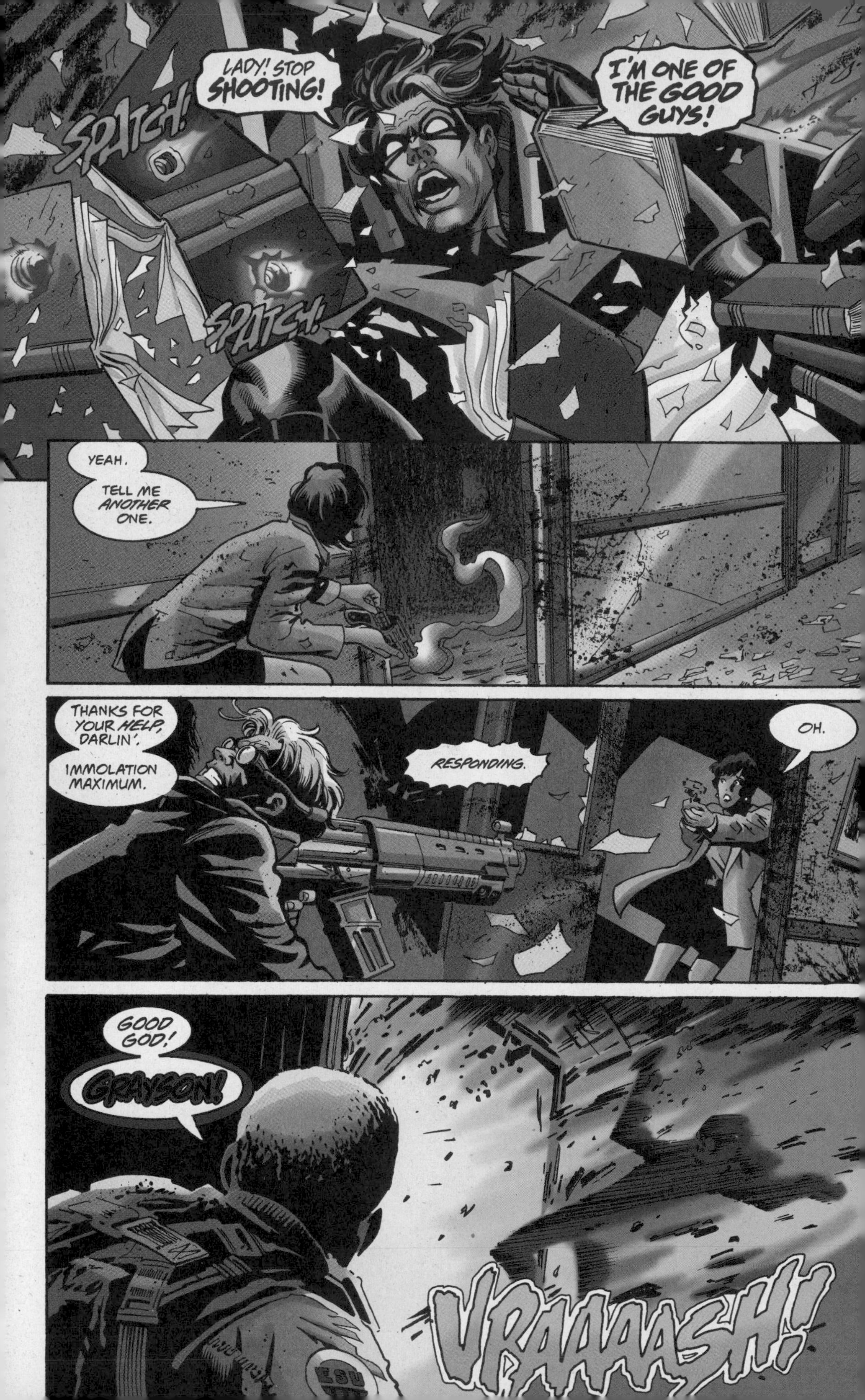
LADY! STOP SHOOTING!
SPATCH!
I'M ONE OF THE GOOD GUYS!
SPATCH!
YEAH.
TELL ME ANOTHER ONE.
THANKS FOR YOUR HELP, DARLIN'.
IMMOLATION MAXIMUM.
RESPONDING.
OH.
GOOD GOD!
GRAYSON!
VRAAAASH!

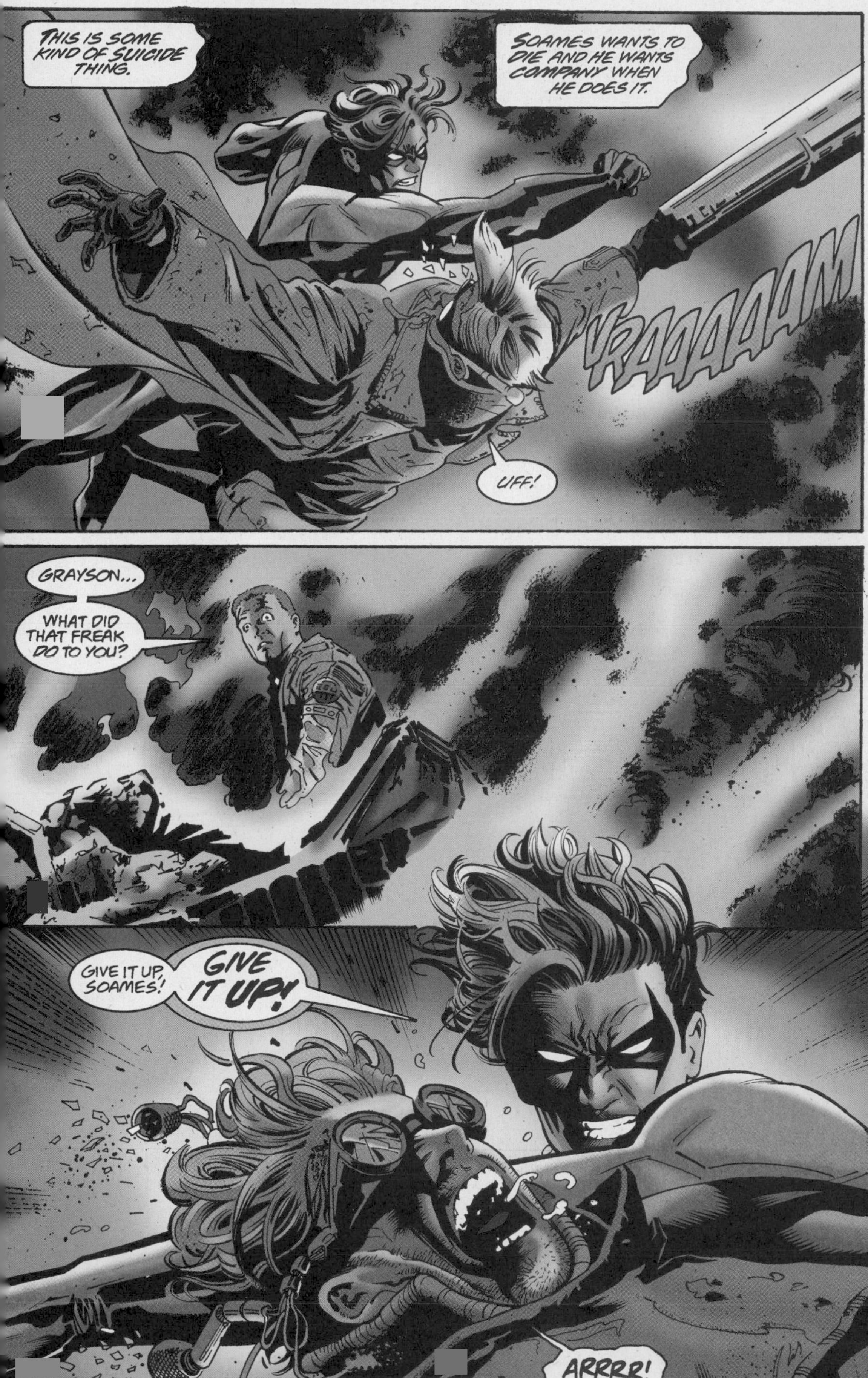
THIS IS SOME KIND OF SUICIDE THING.
SOAMES WANTS TO DIE AND HE WANTS COMPANY WHEN HE DOES IT.
VRAAAAAAM
UFF!
GRAYSON...
WHAT DID THAT FREAK DO TO YOU?
GIVE IT UP, SOAMES!
GIVE IT UP!
ARRRR!

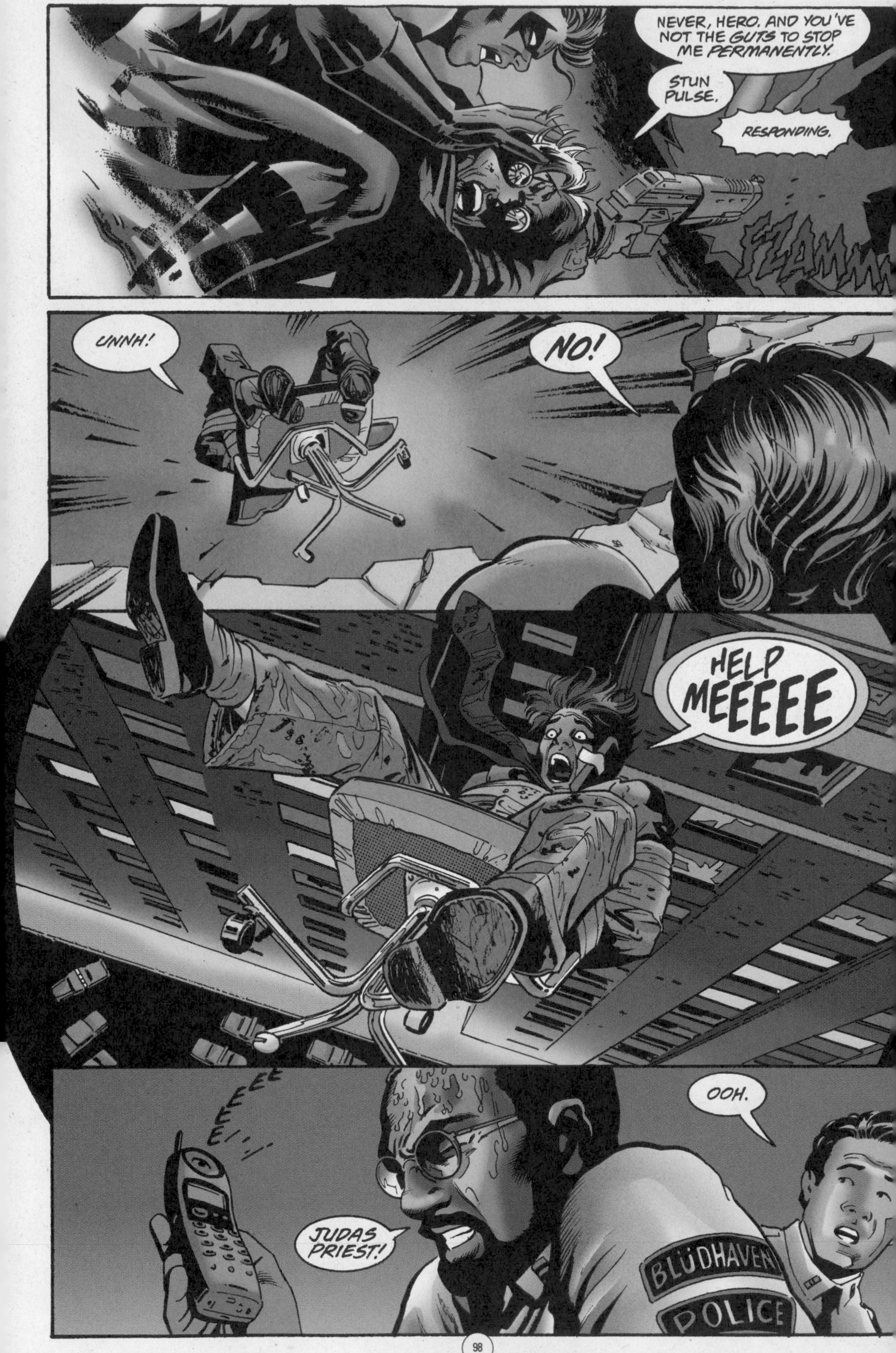
NEVER, HERO. AND YOU'VE NOT THE GUTS TO STOP ME PERMANENTLY.
STUN PULSE.
RESPONDING.
FZAMM
UNNH!
NO!
HELP MEEEEE
EEEEE
OOH.
JUDAS PRIEST!
BLÜDHAVEN
POLICE

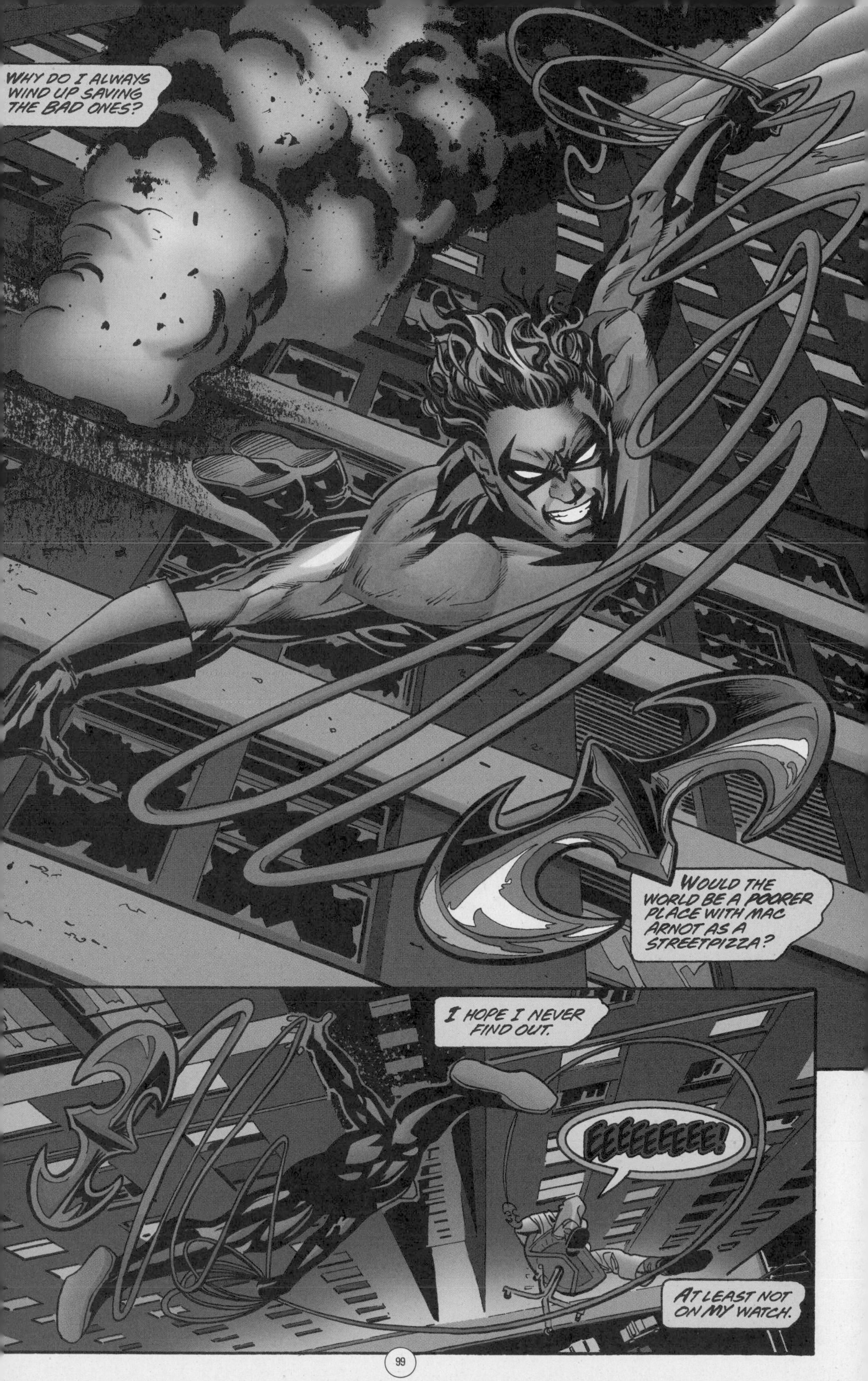

WHY DO I ALWAYS WIND UP SAVING THE BAD ONES?
WOULD THE WORLD BE A POORER PLACE WITH MAC ARNOT AS A STREETPIZZA?
I HOPE I NEVER FIND OUT.
EEEEEEEEE!
AT LEAST NOT ON MY WATCH.

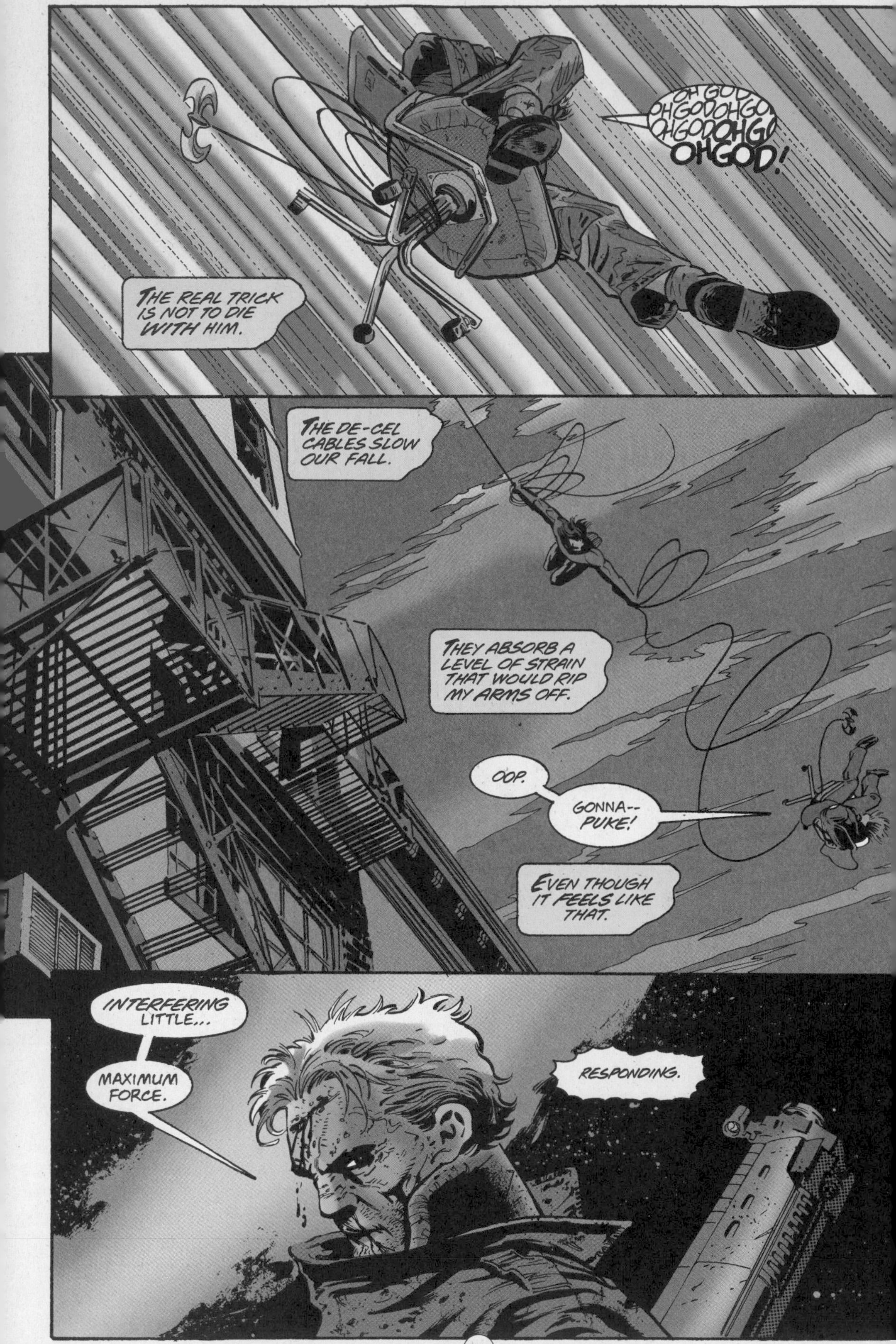
OHGODOHGODOHGO
OHGODOHGODOHG
OHGOD!
THE REAL TRICK IS NOT TO DIE WITH HIM.
THE DE-CEL CABLES SLOW OUR FALL.
THEY ABSORB A LEVEL OF STRAIN THAT WOULD RIP MY ARMS OFF.
OOP.
GONNA-- PUKE!
EVEN THOUGH IT FEELS LIKE THAT.
INTERFERING LITTLE...
MAXIMUM FORCE.
RESPONDING.

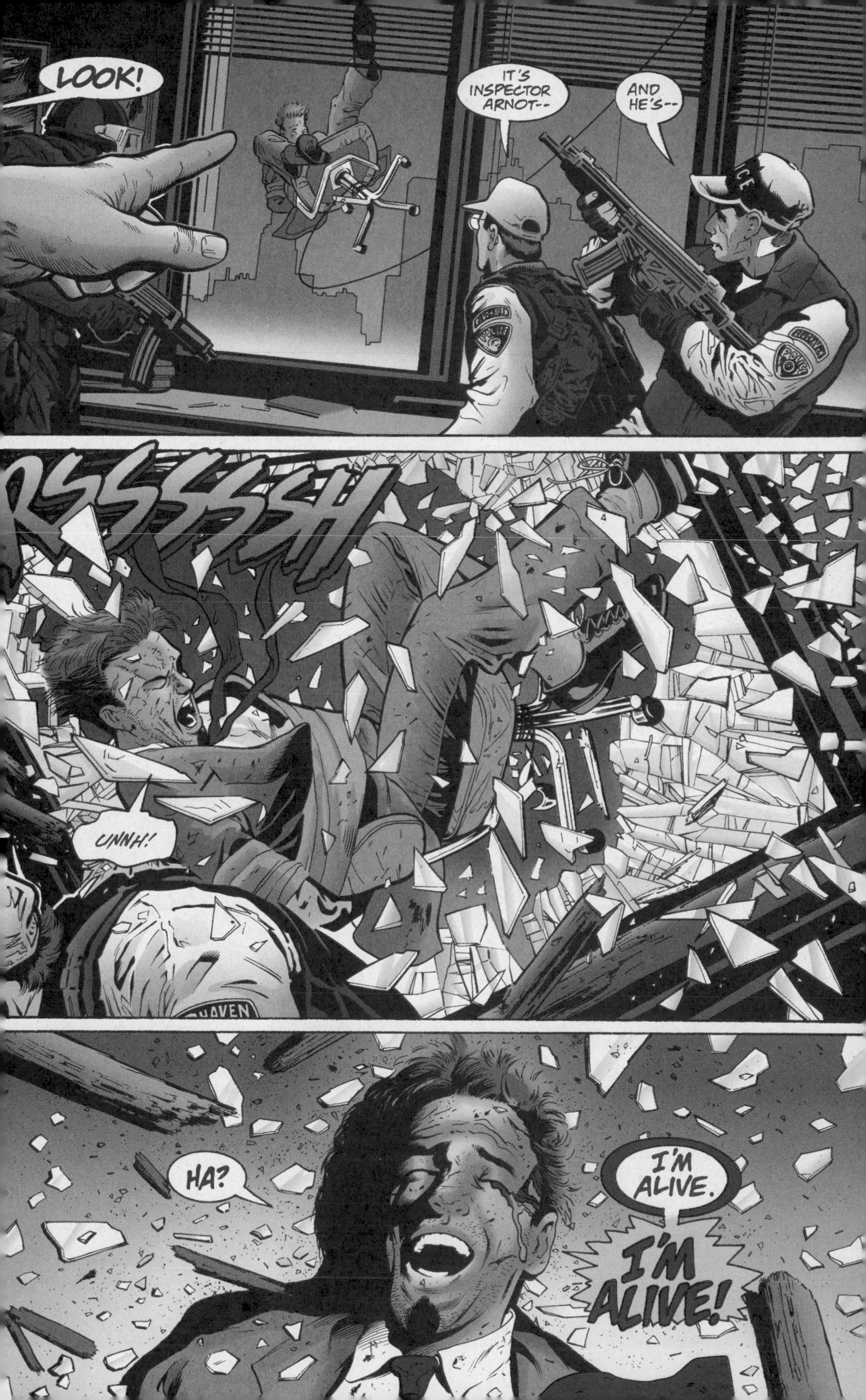
LOOK!
IT'S INSPECTOR ARNOT--
AND HE'S--
RSSSSSH
UNNH!
HA?
I'M ALIVE.
I'M ALIVE!

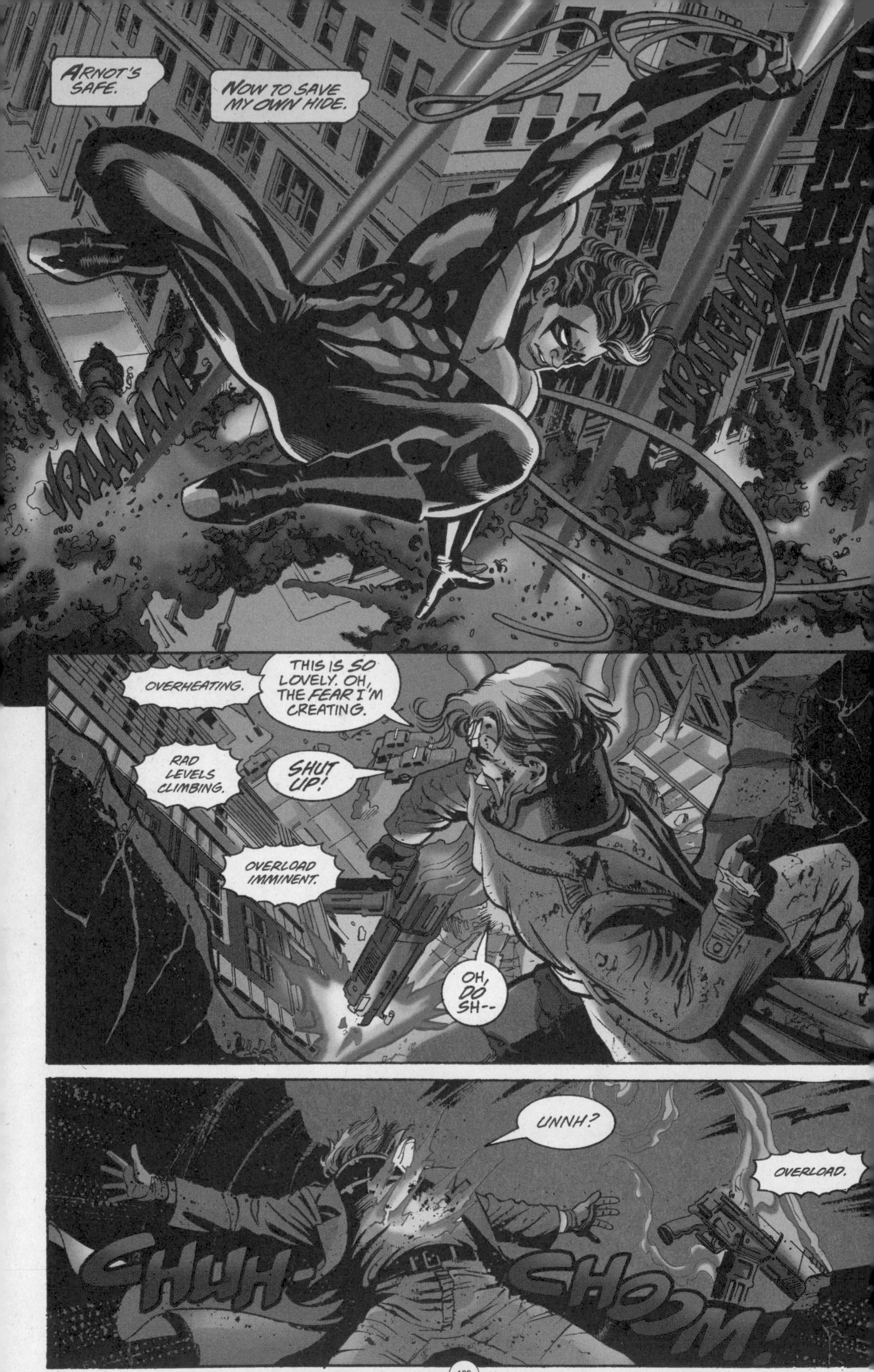
ARNOT'S SAFE.
NOW TO SAVE MY OWN HIDE.
VRAAAAM
VRAAAAM
OVERHEATING.
THIS IS SO LOVELY. OH, THE FEAR I'M CREATING.
RAD LEVELS CLIMBING.
SHUT UP!
OVERLOAD IMMINENT.
OH, DO SH--
UNNH?
OVERLOAD.
CHUH-
CHOOM!

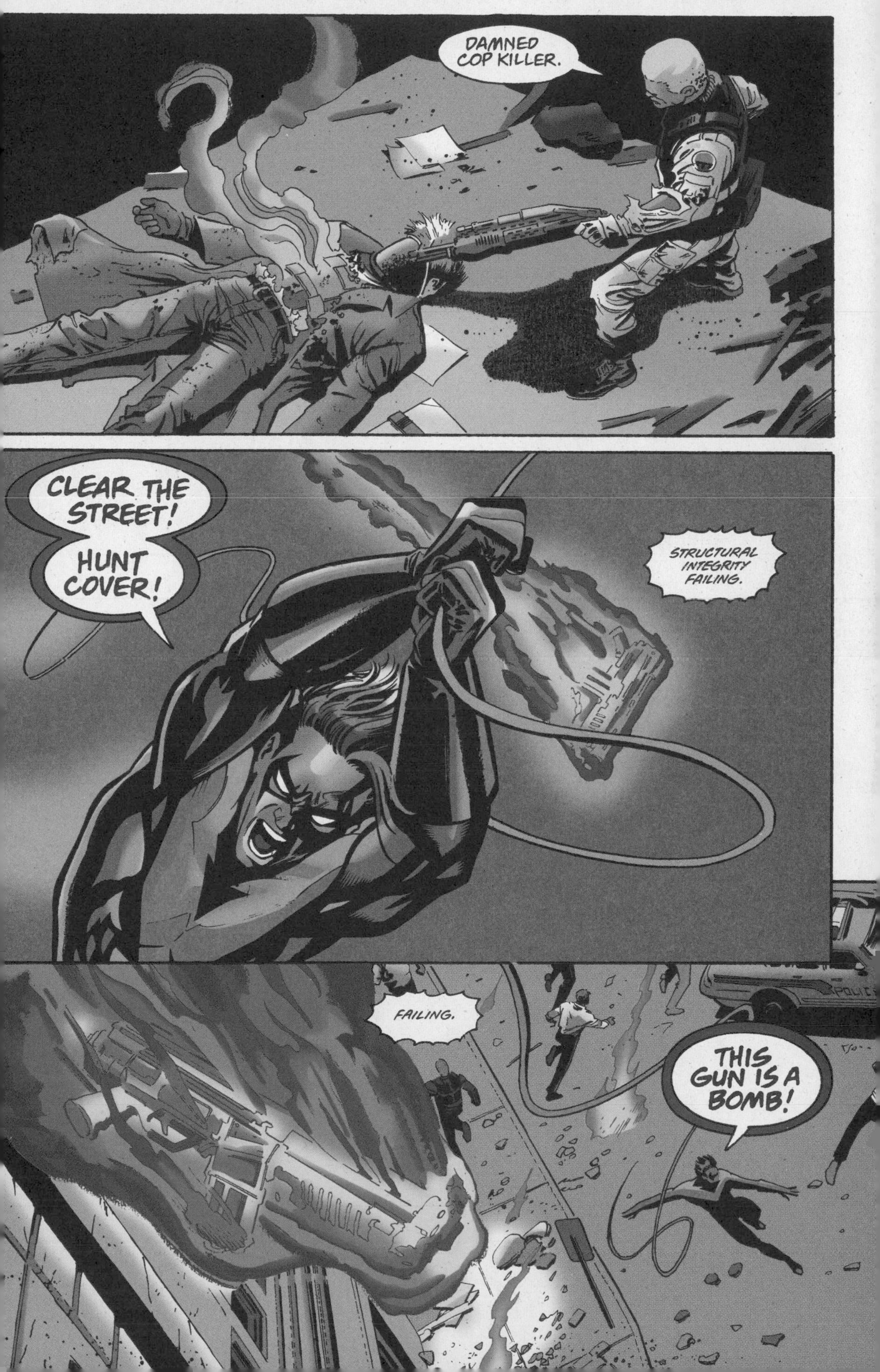
DAMNED COP KILLER.
CLEAR THE STREET!
HUNT COVER!
STRUCTURAL INTEGRITY FAILING.
FAILING.
THIS GUN IS A BOMB!

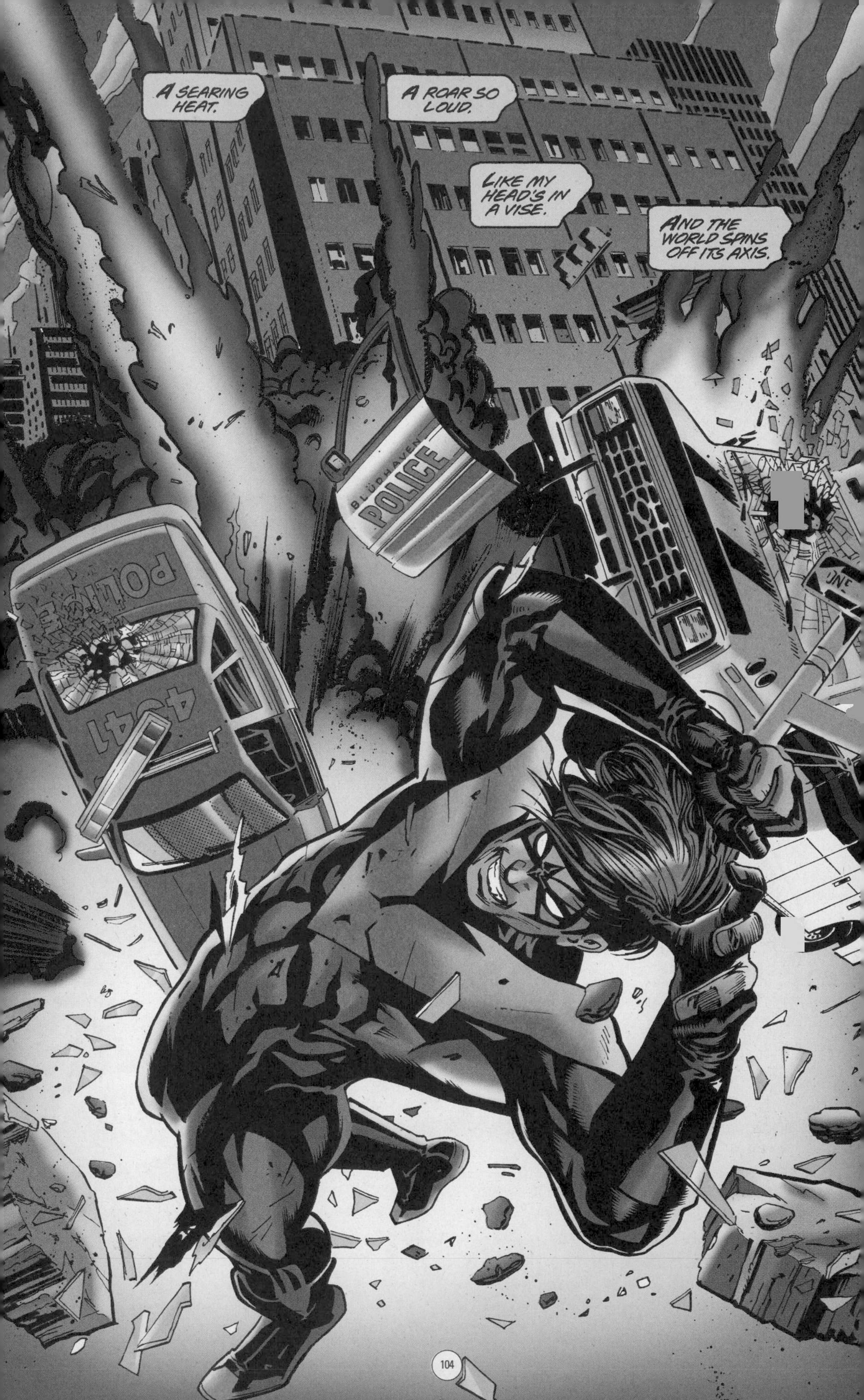
A SEARING HEAT.
A ROAR SO LOUD.
LIKE MY HEAD'S IN A VISE.
AND THE WORLD SPINS OFF ITS AXIS.
BLÜDHAVEN POLICE
POLI
4041

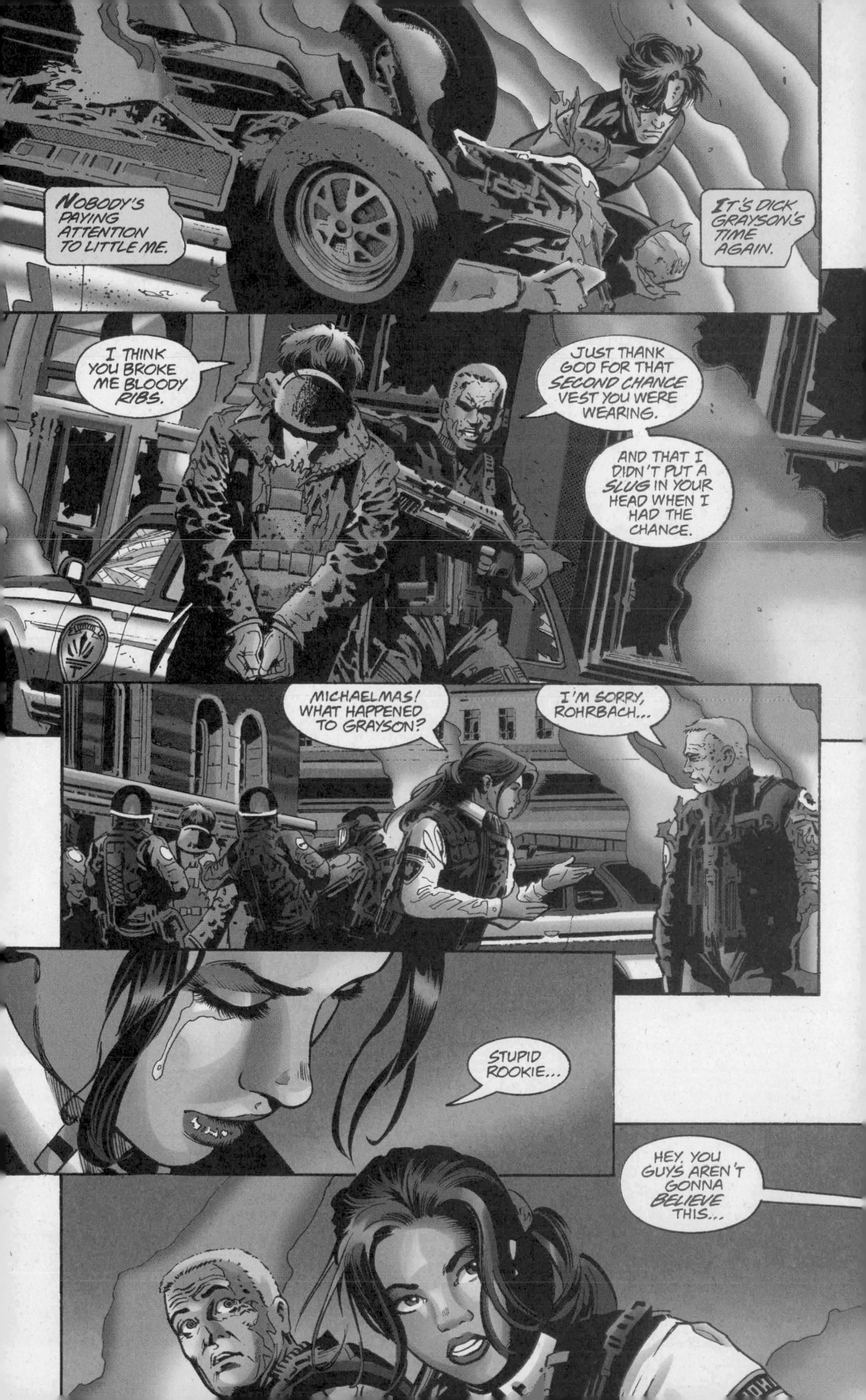
NOBODY'S PAYING ATTENTION TO LITTLE ME.
IT'S DICK GRAYSON'S TIME AGAIN.
I THINK YOU BROKE ME BLOODY RIBS.
JUST THANK GOD FOR THAT SECOND CHANCE VEST YOU WERE WEARING.
AND THAT I DIDN'T PUT A SLUG IN YOUR HEAD WHEN I HAD THE CHANCE.
MICHAELMAS! WHAT HAPPENED TO GRAYSON?
I'M SORRY, ROHRBACH...
STUPID ROOKIE...
HEY. YOU GUYS AREN'T GONNA BELIEVE THIS...

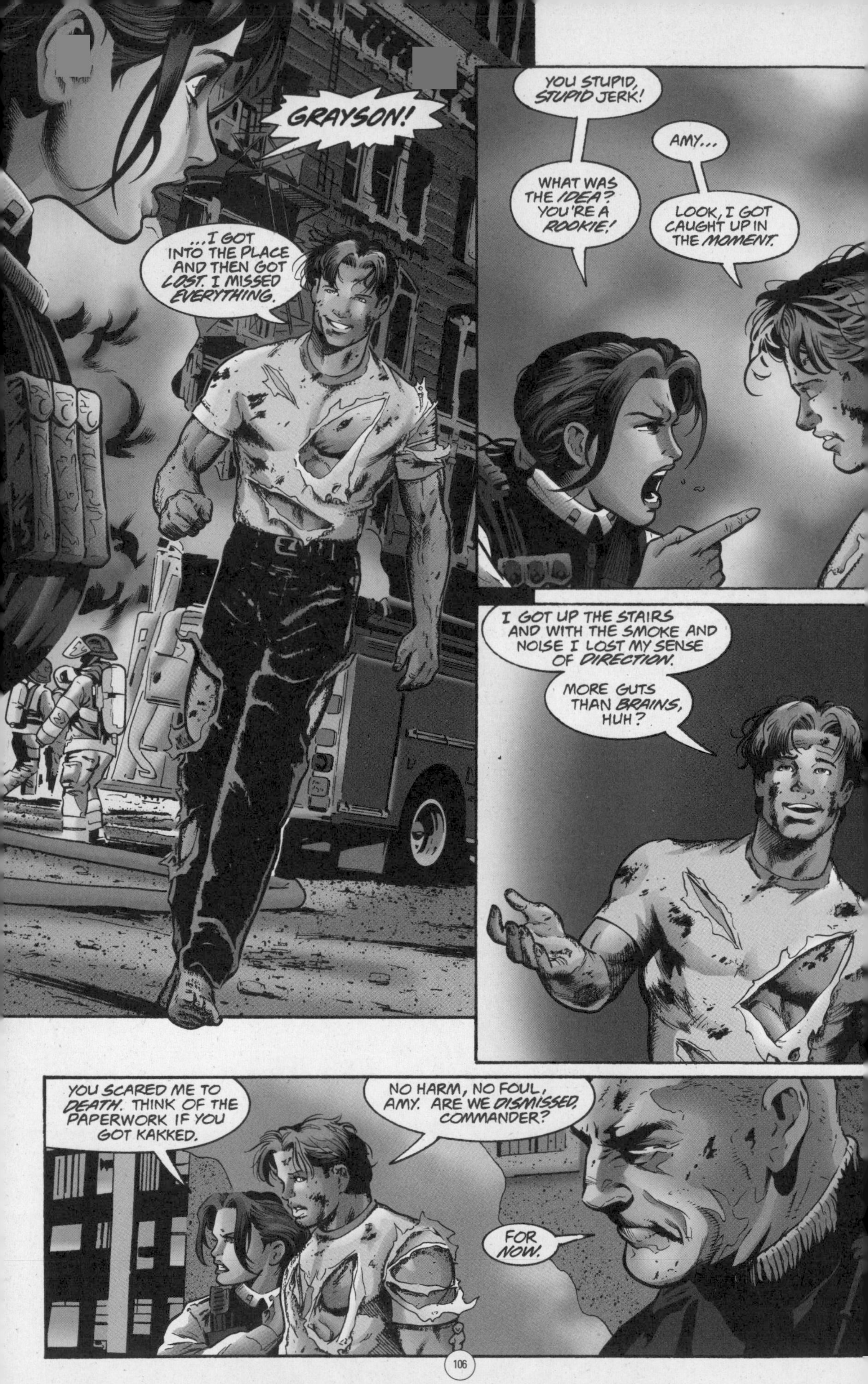
GRAYSON!
...I GOT INTO THE PLACE AND THEN GOT LOST. I MISSED EVERYTHING.
YOU STUPID, STUPID JERK!
WHAT WAS THE IDEA? YOU'RE A ROOKIE!
AMY...
LOOK, I GOT CAUGHT UP IN THE MOMENT.
I GOT UP THE STAIRS AND WITH THE SMOKE AND NOISE I LOST MY SENSE OF DIRECTION.
MORE GUTS THAN BRAINS, HUH?
YOU SCARED ME TO DEATH. THINK OF THE PAPERWORK IF YOU GOT KAKKED.
NO HARM, NO FOUL, AMY. ARE WE DISMISSED, COMMANDER?
FOR NOW.

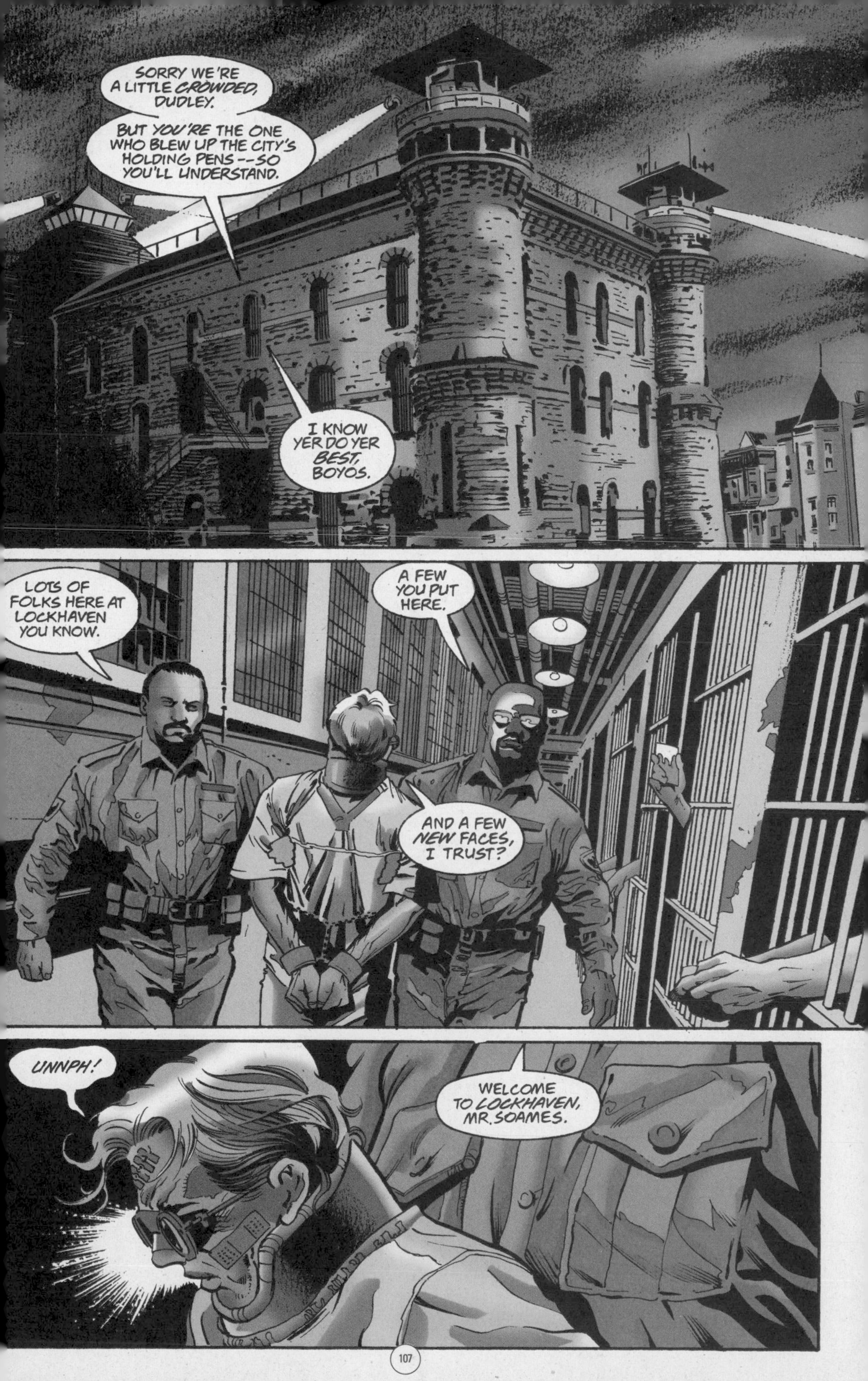
SORRY WE'RE A LITTLE CROWDED, DUDLEY.
BUT YOU'RE THE ONE WHO BLEW UP THE CITY'S HOLDING PENS--SO YOU'LL UNDERSTAND.
I KNOW YER DO YER BEST, BOYOS.
LOTS OF FOLKS HERE AT LOCKHAVEN YOU KNOW.
A FEW YOU PUT HERE.
AND A FEW NEW FACES, I TRUST?
UNNPH!
WELCOME TO LOCKHAVEN, MR. SOAMES.

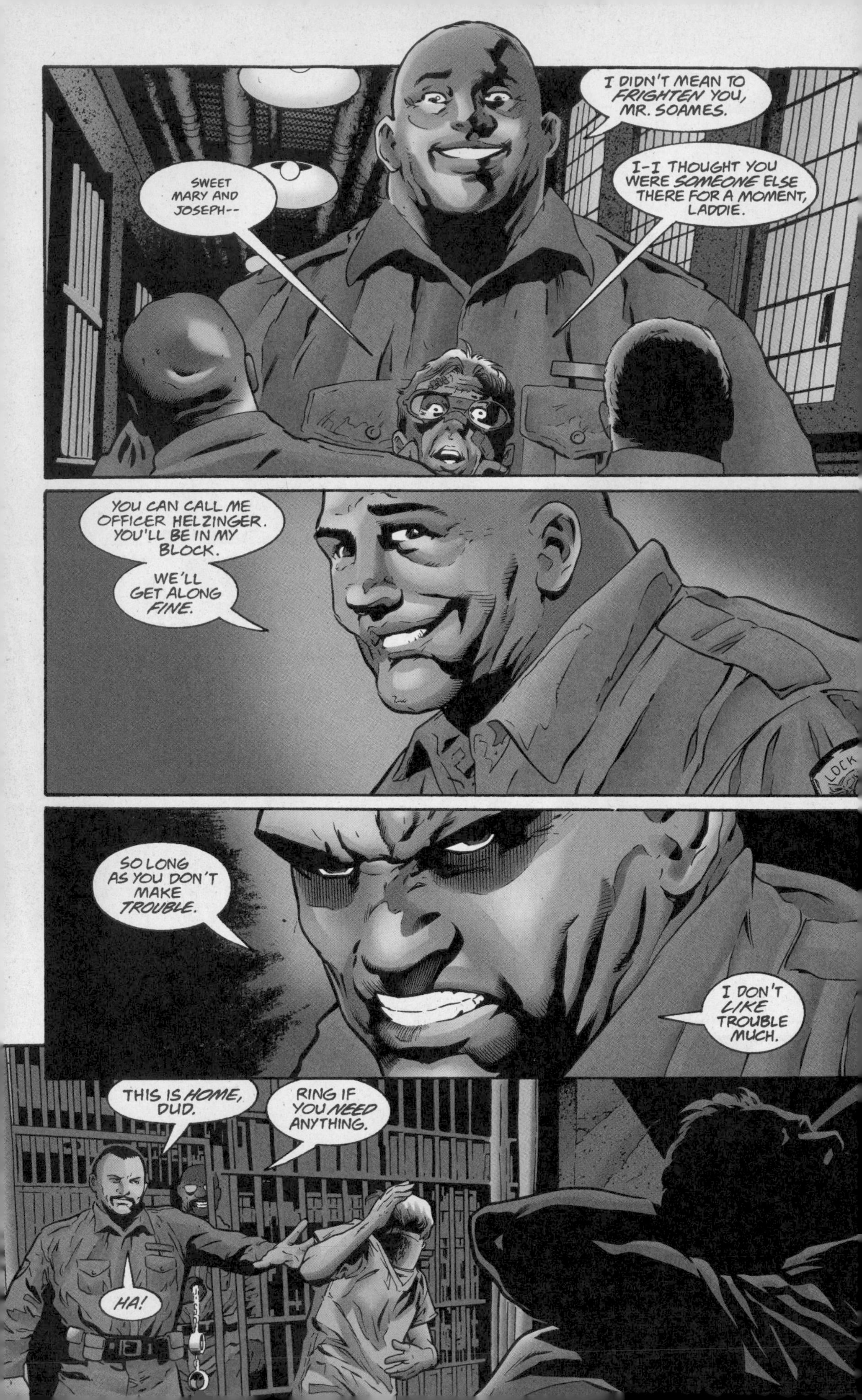
SWEET MARY AND JOSEPH--
I DIDN'T MEAN TO FRIGHTEN YOU, MR. SOAMES.
I-I THOUGHT YOU WERE SOMEONE ELSE THERE FOR A MOMENT, LADDIE.
YOU CAN CALL ME OFFICER HELZINGER. YOU'LL BE IN MY BLOCK.
WE'LL GET ALONG FINE.
LOCK
SO LONG AS YOU DON'T MAKE TROUBLE.
I DON'T LIKE TROUBLE MUCH.
THIS IS HOME, DUD.
RING IF YOU NEED ANYTHING.
HA!

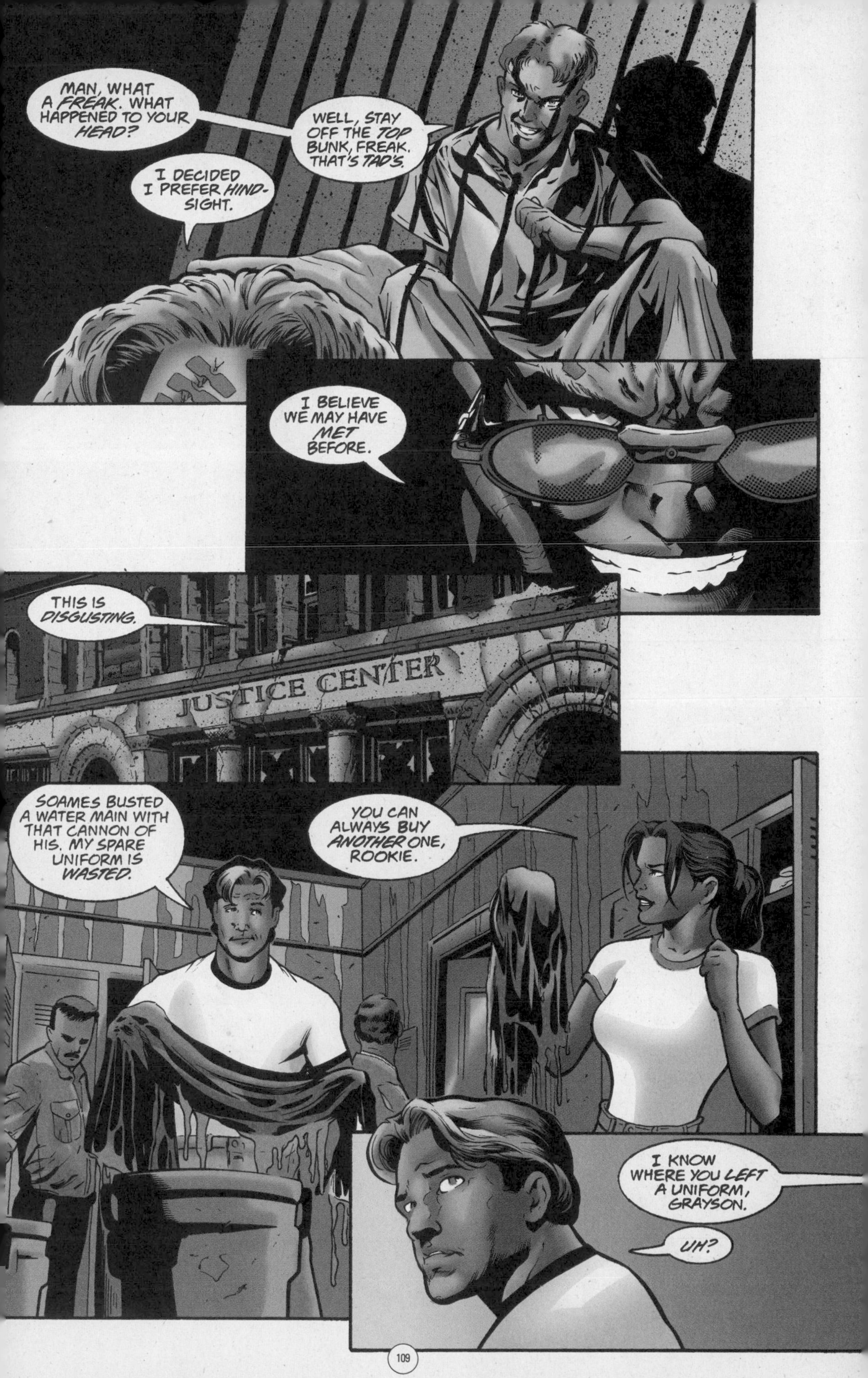

MAN, WHAT A FREAK. WHAT HAPPENED TO YOUR HEAD?
I DECIDED I PREFER HIND-SIGHT.
WELL, STAY OFF THE TOP BUNK, FREAK. THAT'S TAD'S.
I BELIEVE WE MAY HAVE MET BEFORE.
THIS IS DISGUSTING.
JUSTICE CENTER
SOAMES BUSTED A WATER MAIN WITH THAT CANNON OF HIS. MY SPARE UNIFORM IS WASTED.
YOU CAN ALWAYS BUY ANOTHER ONE, ROOKIE.
I KNOW WHERE YOU LEFT A UNIFORM, GRAYSON.
UH?

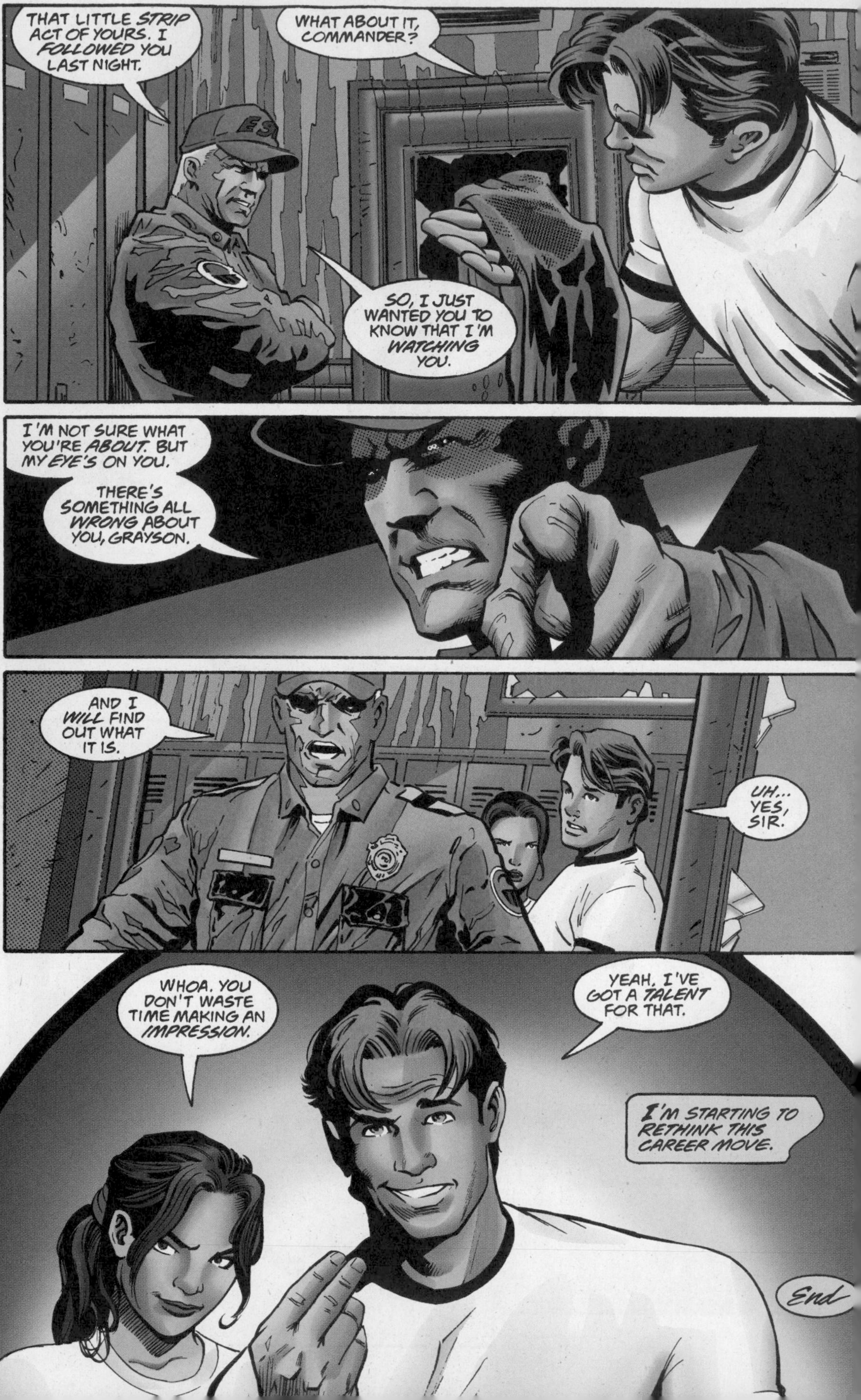
THAT LITTLE STRIP ACT OF YOURS. I FOLLOWED YOU LAST NIGHT.
WHAT ABOUT IT, COMMANDER?
SO, I JUST WANTED YOU TO KNOW THAT I'M WATCHING YOU.
I'M NOT SURE WHAT YOU'RE ABOUT. BUT MY EYE'S ON YOU.
THERE'S SOMETHING ALL WRONG ABOUT YOU, GRAYSON.
AND I WILL FIND OUT WHAT IT IS.
UH... YES, SIR.
WHOA. YOU DON'T WASTE TIME MAKING AN IMPRESSION.
YEAH, I'VE GOT A TALENT FOR THAT.
I'M STARTING TO RETHINK THIS CAREER MOVE.
End

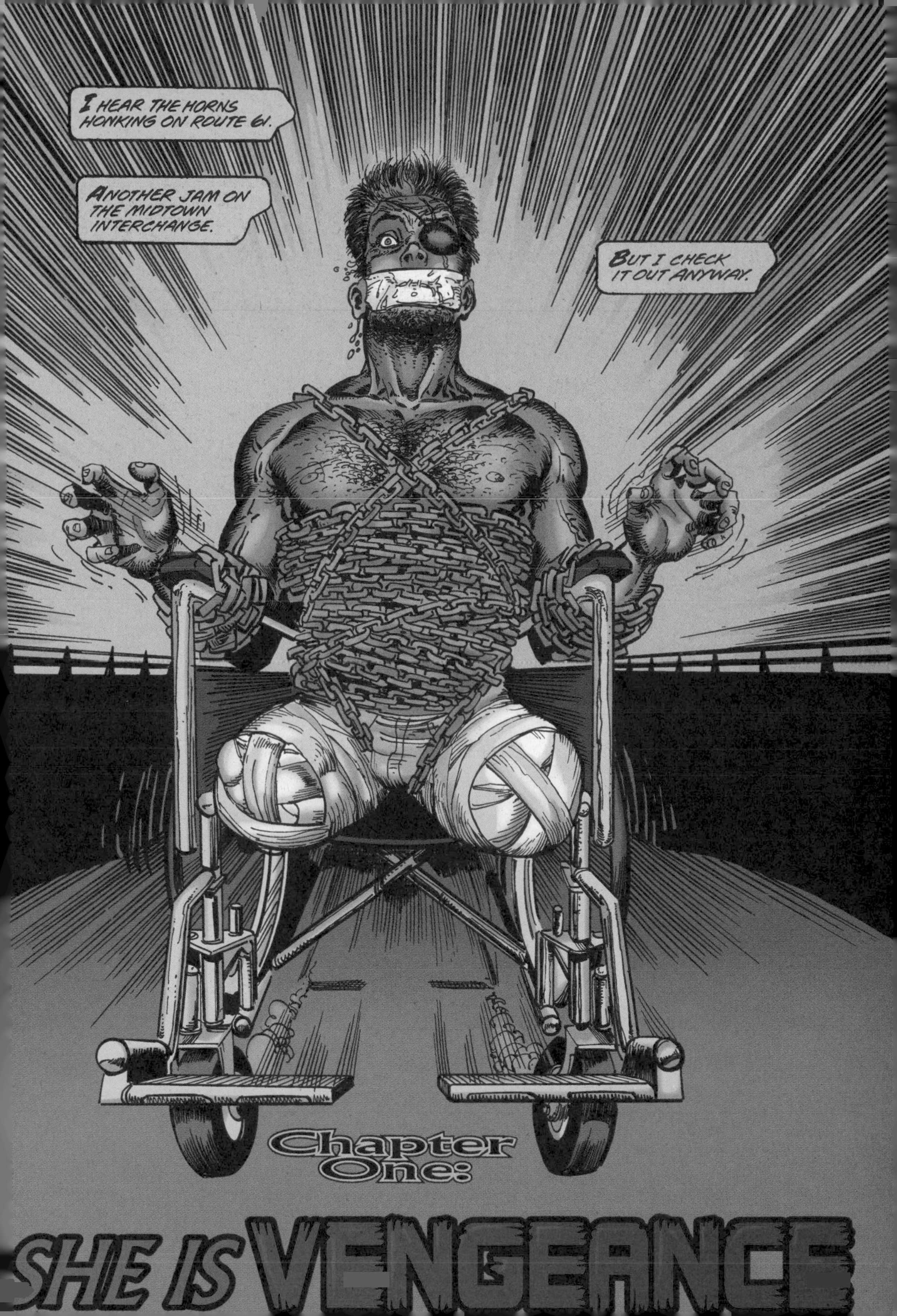
I HEAR THE HORNS HONKING ON ROUTE 61.
ANOTHER JAM ON THE MIDTOWN INTERCHANGE.
BUT I CHECK IT OUT ANYWAY.
Chapter One:
SHE IS VENGEANCE

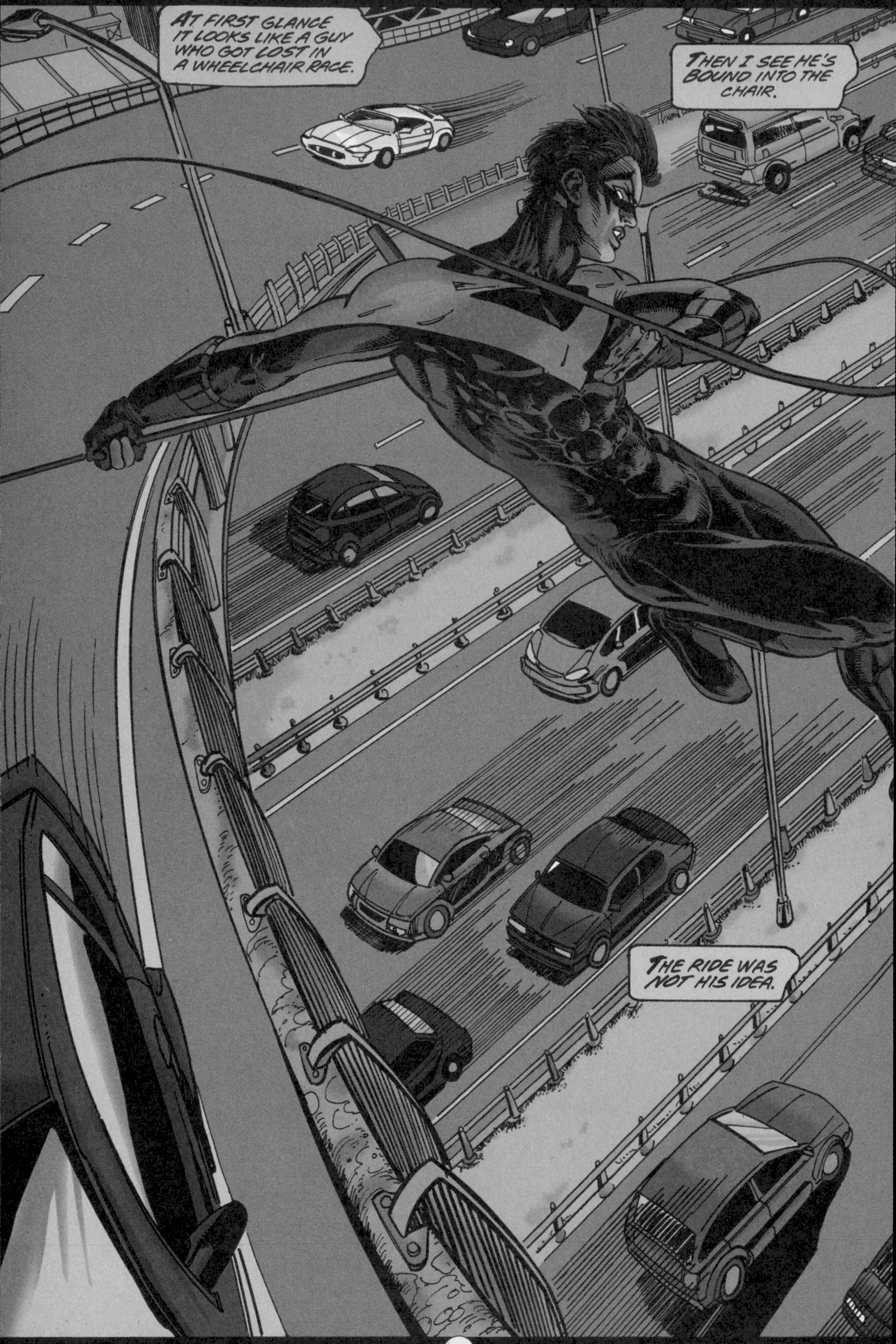
AT FIRST GLANCE IT LOOKS LIKE A GUY WHO GOT LOST IN A WHEELCHAIR RACE.
THEN I SEE HE'S BOUND INTO THE CHAIR.
THE RIDE WAS NOT HIS IDEA.

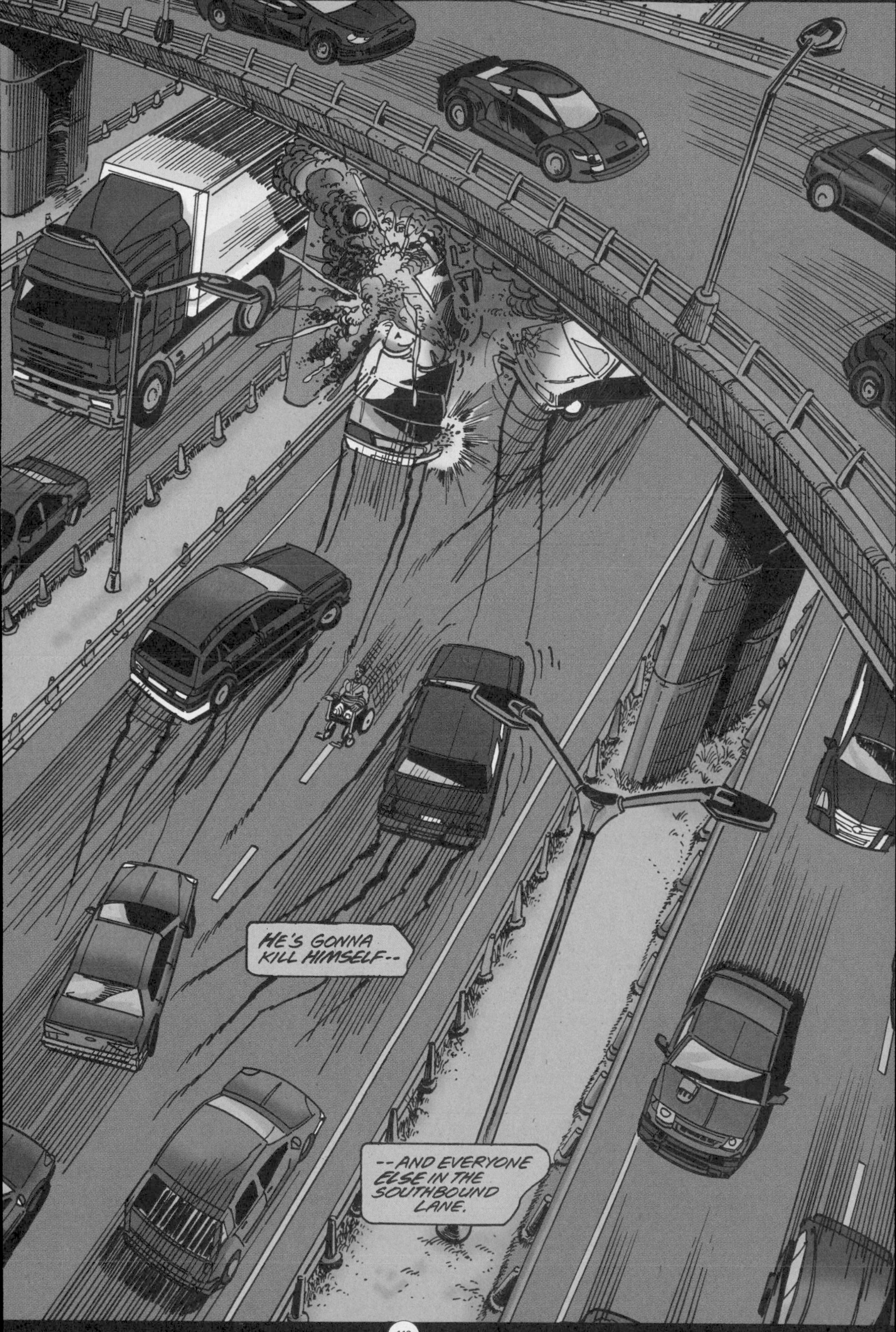
HE'S GONNA KILL HIMSELF--
--AND EVERYONE ELSE IN THE SOUTHBOUND LANE.

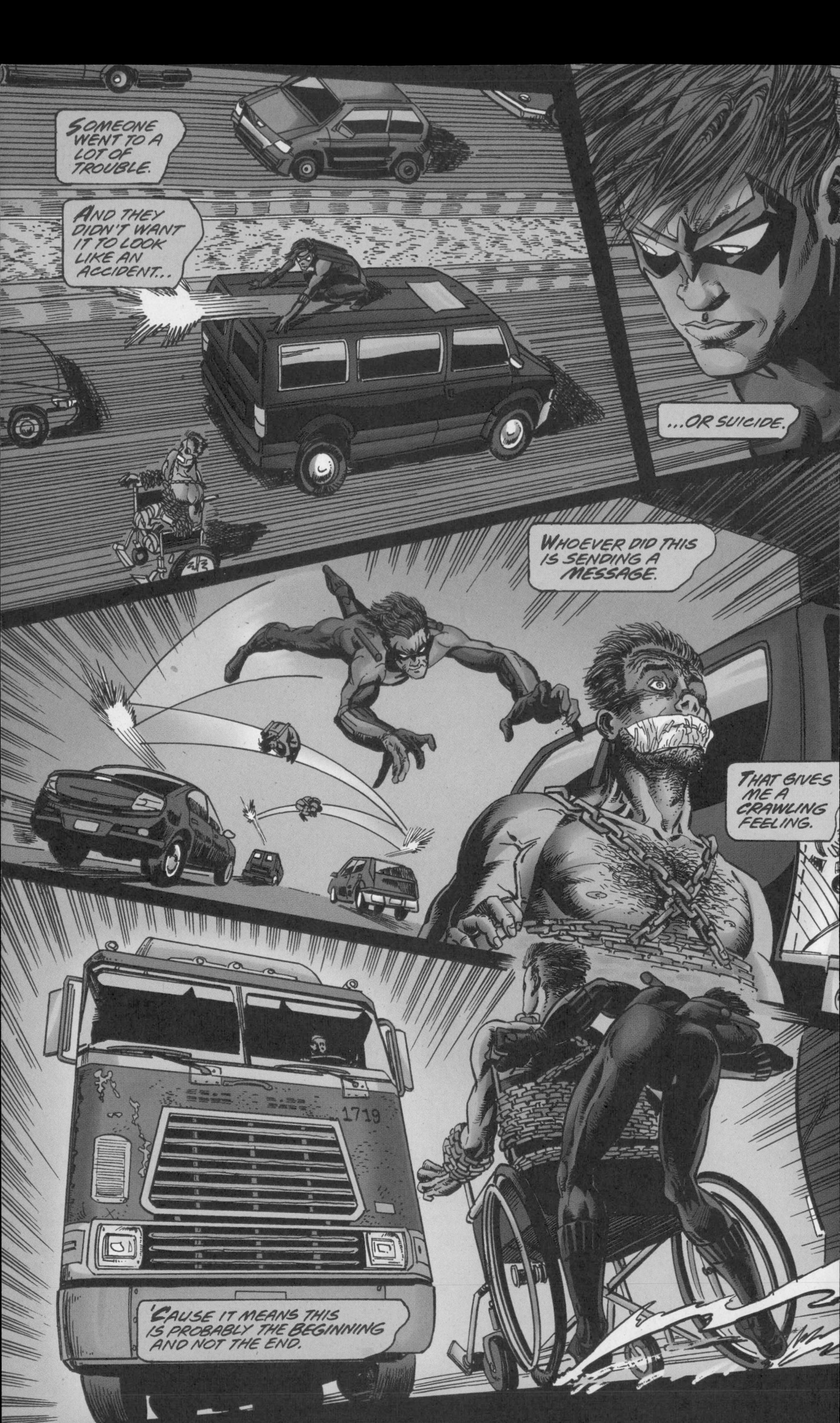
SOMEONE WENT TO A LOT OF TROUBLE.
AND THEY DIDN'T WANT IT TO LOOK LIKE AN ACCIDENT...
...OR SUICIDE.
WHOEVER DID THIS IS SENDING A MESSAGE.
THAT GIVES ME A CRAWLING FEELING.
1719
'CAUSE IT MEANS THIS IS PROBABLY THE BEGINNING AND NOT THE END.

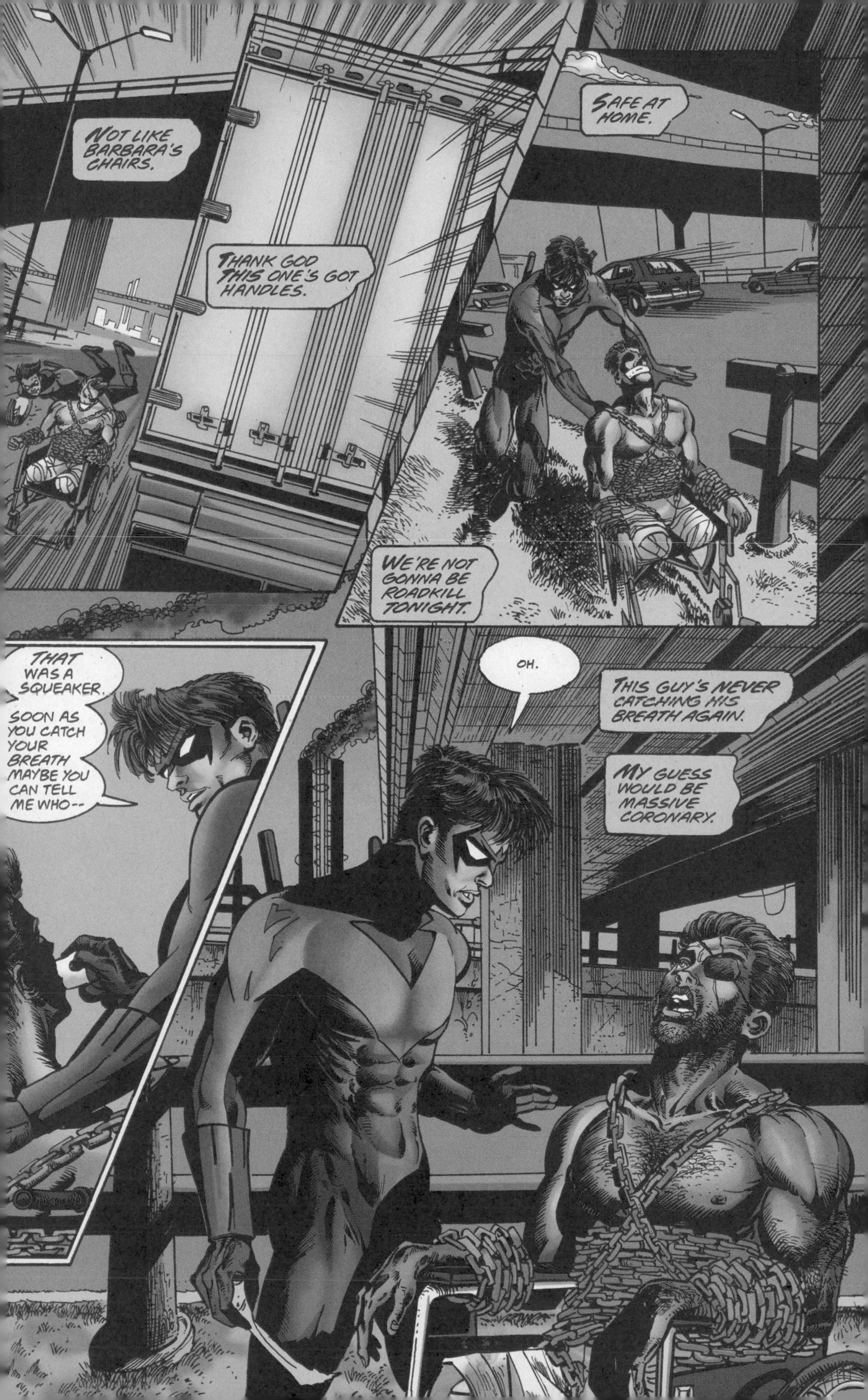
NOT LIKE BARBARA'S CHAIRS.
THANK GOD THIS ONE'S GOT HANDLES.
SAFE AT HOME.
WE'RE NOT GONNA BE ROADKILL TONIGHT.
THAT WAS A SQUEAKER.
SOON AS YOU CATCH YOUR BREATH MAYBE YOU CAN TELL ME WHO--
OH.
THIS GUY'S NEVER CATCHING HIS BREATH AGAIN.
MY GUESS WOULD BE MASSIVE CORONARY.

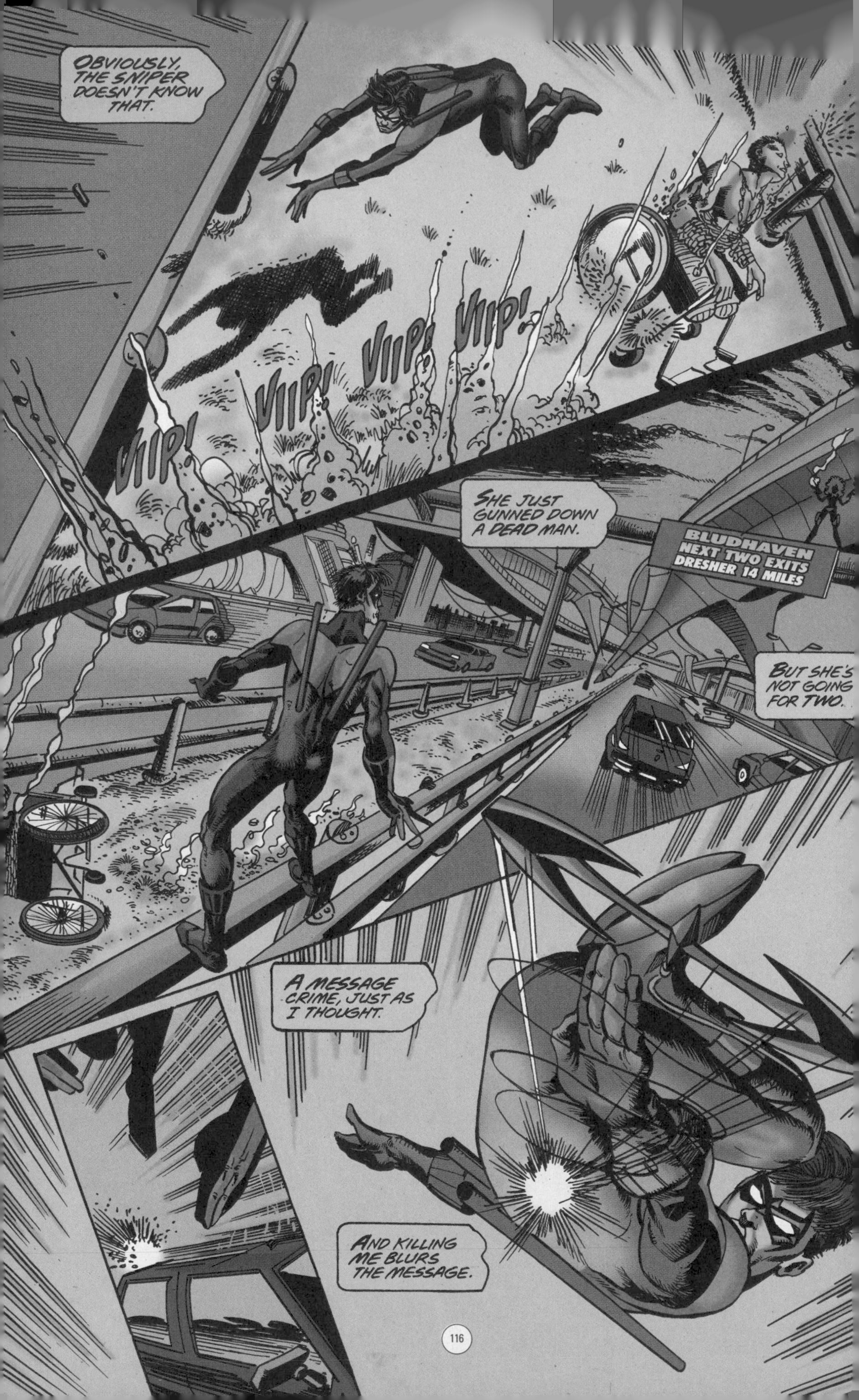

OBVIOUSLY, THE SNIPER DOESN'T KNOW THAT.
VIIP! VIIP! VIIP! VIIP! VIIP!
SHE JUST GUNNED DOWN A DEAD MAN.
BLUDHAVEN NEXT TWO EXITS DRESHER 14 MILES
BUT SHE'S NOT GOING FOR TWO.
A MESSAGE CRIME, JUST AS I THOUGHT.
AND KILLING ME BLURS THE MESSAGE.

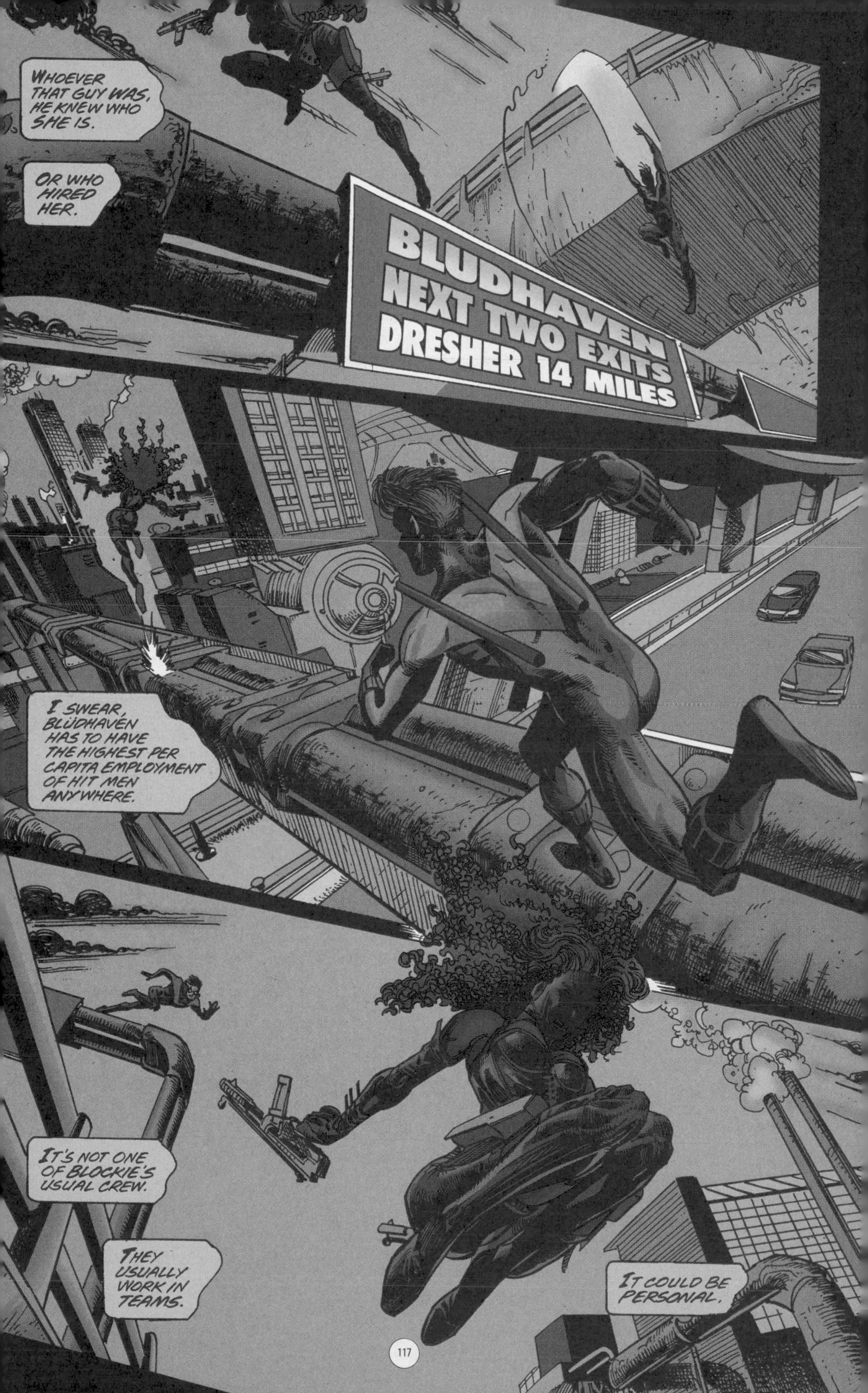
WHOEVER THAT GUY WAS, HE KNEW WHO SHE IS.
OR WHO HIRED HER.
BLUDHAVEN NEXT TWO EXITS DRESHER 14 MILES
I SWEAR, BLÜDHAVEN HAS TO HAVE THE HIGHEST PER CAPITA EMPLOYMENT OF HIT MEN ANYWHERE.
IT'S NOT ONE OF BLOCKIE'S USUAL CREW.
THEY USUALLY WORK IN TEAMS.
IT COULD BE PERSONAL.

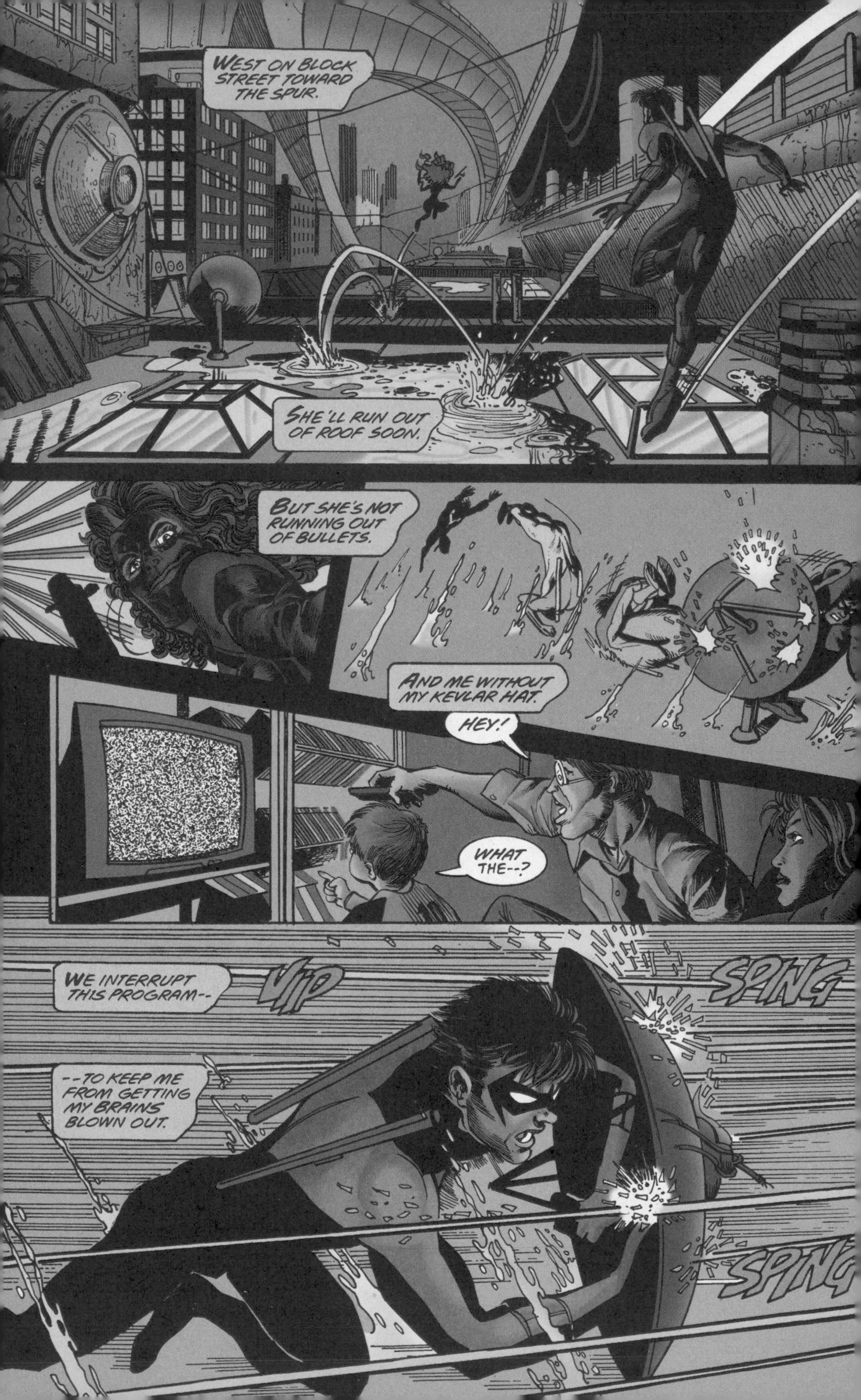
WEST ON BLOCK STREET TOWARD THE SPUR.
SHE'LL RUN OUT OF ROOF SOON.
BUT SHE'S NOT RUNNING OUT OF BULLETS.
AND ME WITHOUT MY KEVLAR HAT.
HEY!
WHAT THE--?
WE INTERRUPT THIS PROGRAM--
VIP
SPING
--TO KEEP ME FROM GETTING MY BRAINS BLOWN OUT.
SPING

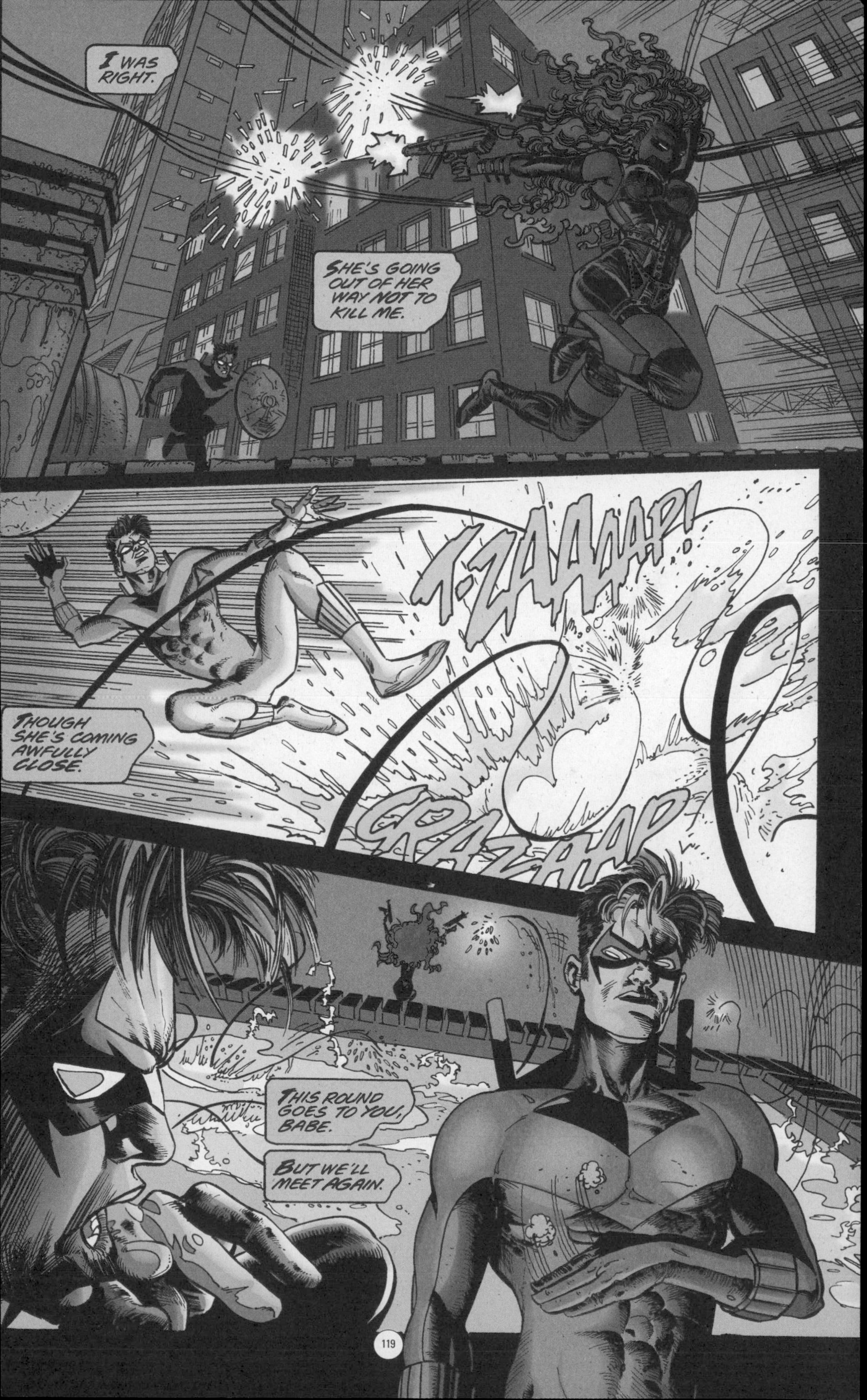

I WAS RIGHT.
SHE'S GOING OUT OF HER WAY NOT TO KILL ME.
T-ZAAAAAP!
THOUGH SHE'S COMING AWFULLY CLOSE.
GRAZAAAP
THIS ROUND GOES TO YOU, BABE.
BUT WE'LL MEET AGAIN.

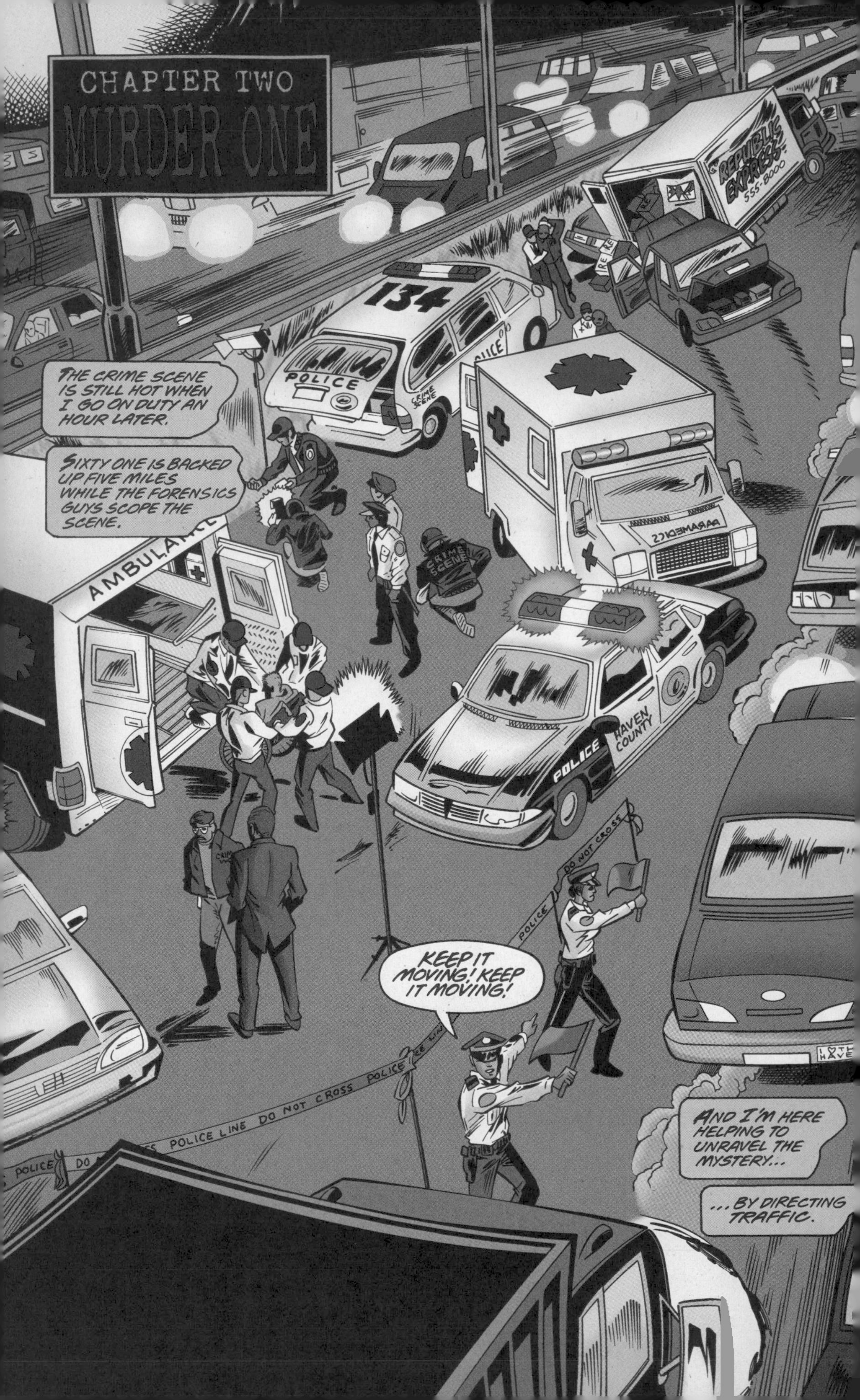
CHAPTER TWO
MURDER ONE
REPUBLIC EXPRESS
555-8000
134
POLICE
CRIME SCENE
THE CRIME SCENE IS STILL HOT WHEN I GO ON DUTY AN HOUR LATER.
SIXTY ONE IS BACKED UP FIVE MILES WHILE THE FORENSICS GUYS SCOPE THE SCENE.
AMBULANCE
PARAMEDICS
CRIME SCENE
POLICE
HAVEN COUNTY
DO NOT CROSS
KEEP IT MOVING! KEEP IT MOVING!
POLICE LINE DO NOT CROSS
AND I'M HERE HELPING TO UNRAVEL THE MYSTERY...
...BY DIRECTING TRAFFIC.

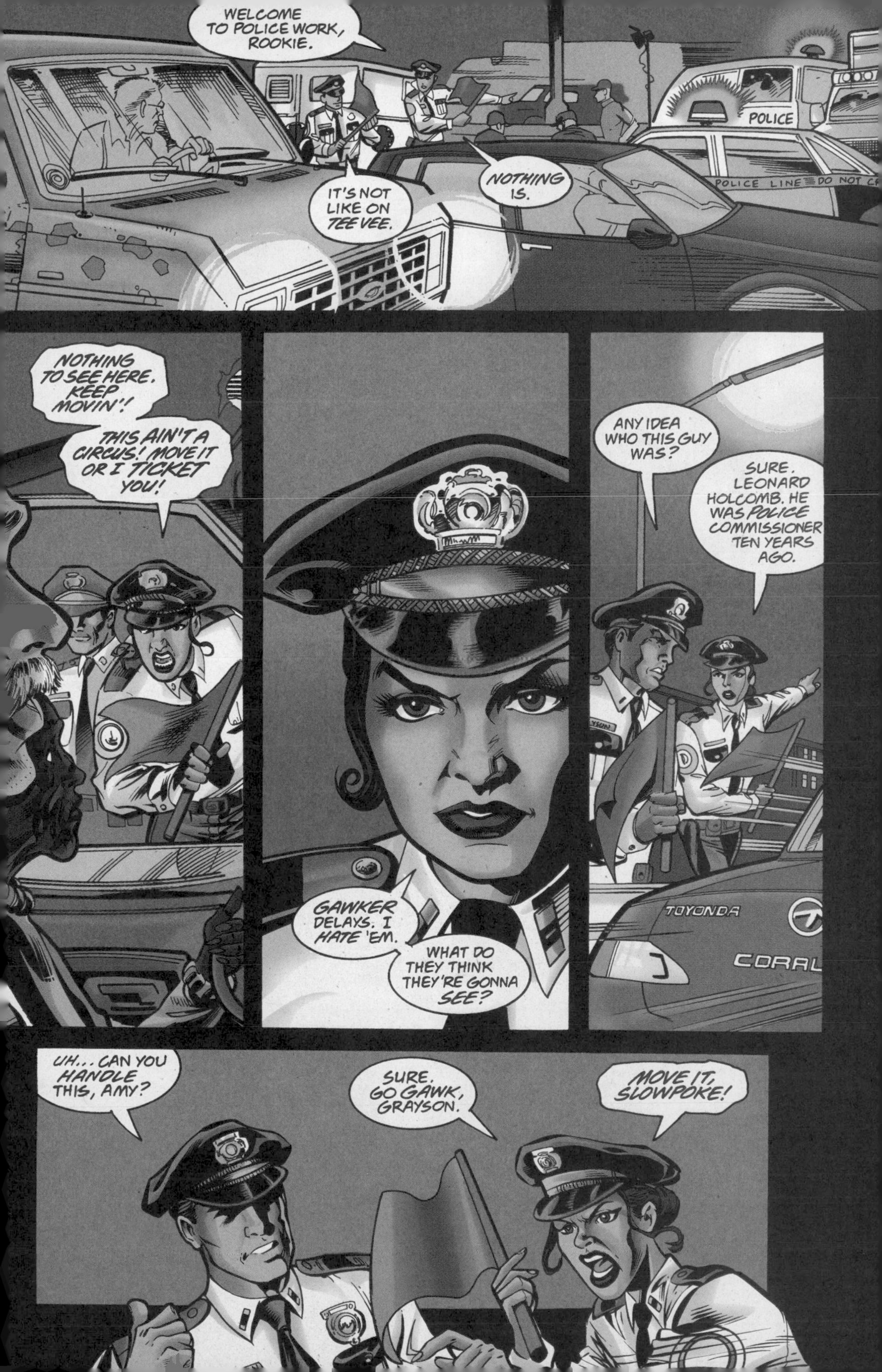

WELCOME TO POLICE WORK, ROOKIE.
IT'S NOT LIKE ON TEE VEE.
NOTHING IS.
POLICE
POLICE LINE DO NOT C
NOTHING TO SEE HERE. KEEP MOVIN'!
THIS AIN'T A CIRCUS! MOVE IT OR I TICKET YOU!
GAWKER DELAYS. I HATE 'EM.
WHAT DO THEY THINK THEY'RE GONNA SEE?
ANY IDEA WHO THIS GUY WAS?
SURE. LEONARD HOLCOMB. HE WAS POLICE COMMISSIONER TEN YEARS AGO.
TOYONDA
CORAL
UH... CAN YOU HANDLE THIS, AMY?
SURE. GO GAWK, GRAYSON.
MOVE IT, SLOWPOKE!

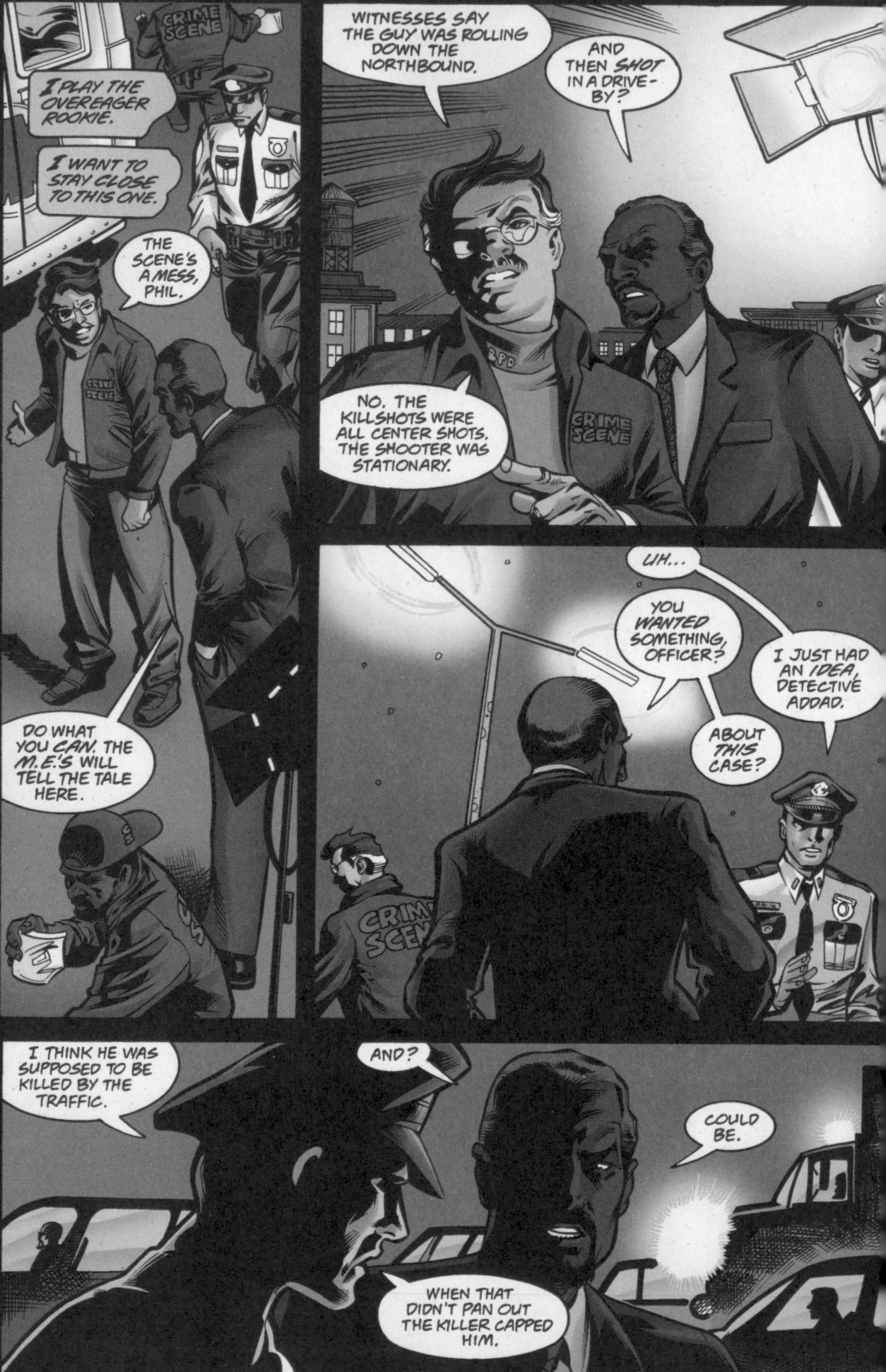

CRIME SCENE
I PLAY THE OVEREAGER ROOKIE.
I WANT TO STAY CLOSE TO THIS ONE.
THE SCENE'S A MESS, PHIL.
DO WHAT YOU CAN. THE M.E.'S WILL TELL THE TALE HERE.
WITNESSES SAY THE GUY WAS ROLLING DOWN THE NORTHBOUND.
AND THEN SHOT IN A DRIVE-BY?
NO. THE KILLSHOTS WERE ALL CENTER SHOTS. THE SHOOTER WAS STATIONARY.
CRIME SCENE
UH...
YOU WANTED SOMETHING, OFFICER?
I JUST HAD AN IDEA, DETECTIVE ADDAD.
ABOUT THIS CASE?
I THINK HE WAS SUPPOSED TO BE KILLED BY THE TRAFFIC.
AND?
COULD BE.
WHEN THAT DIDN'T PAN OUT THE KILLER CAPPED HIM.

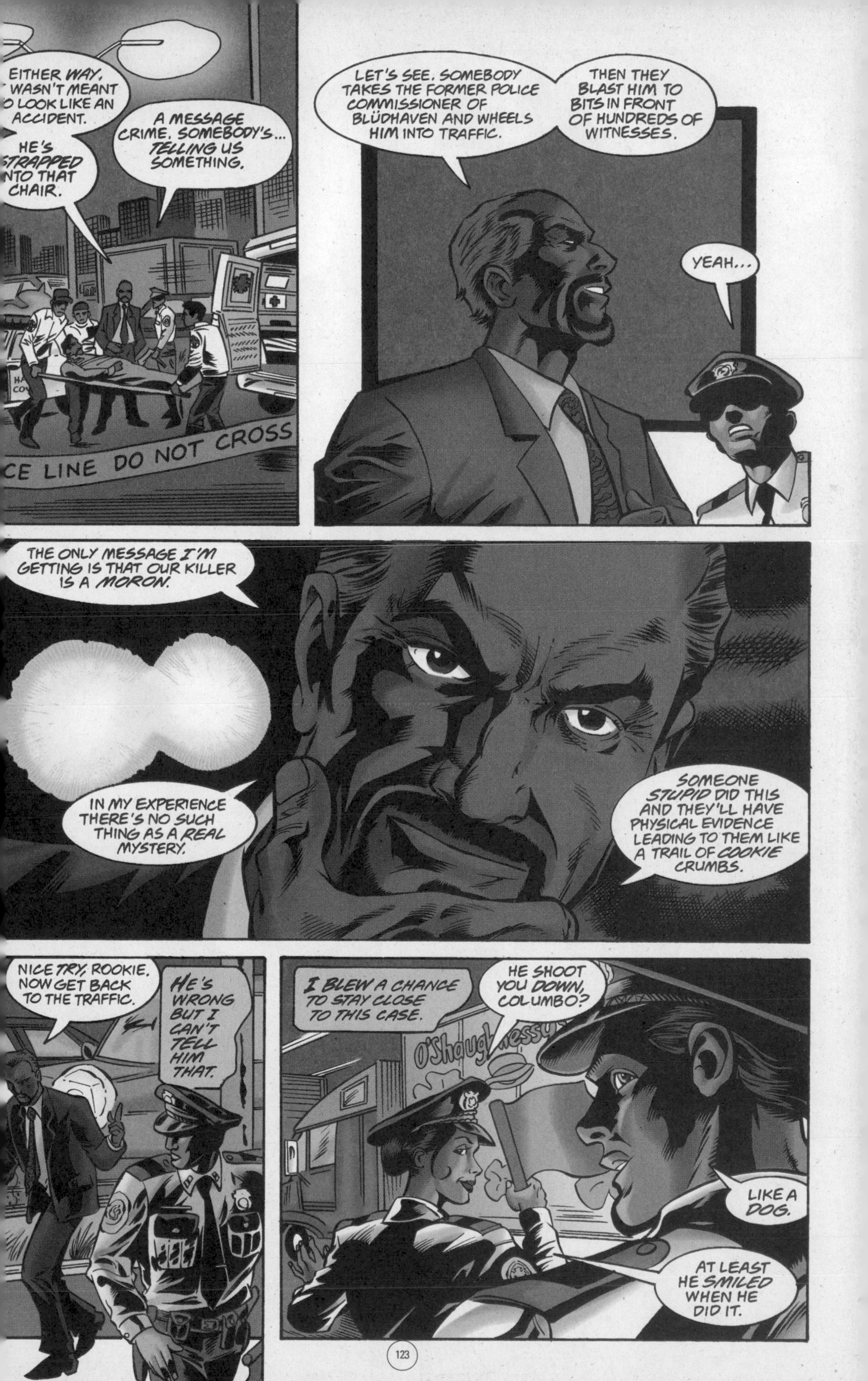
EITHER WAY, T WASN'T MEANT TO LOOK LIKE AN ACCIDENT.
HE'S STRAPPED INTO THAT CHAIR.
A MESSAGE CRIME. SOMEBODY'S... TELLING US SOMETHING.
CE LINE DO NOT CROSS
LET'S SEE. SOMEBODY TAKES THE FORMER POLICE COMMISSIONER OF BLÜDHAVEN AND WHEELS HIM INTO TRAFFIC.
THEN THEY BLAST HIM TO BITS IN FRONT OF HUNDREDS OF WITNESSES.
YEAH...
THE ONLY MESSAGE I'M GETTING IS THAT OUR KILLER IS A MORON.
IN MY EXPERIENCE THERE'S NO SUCH THING AS A REAL MYSTERY.
SOMEONE STUPID DID THIS AND THEY'LL HAVE PHYSICAL EVIDENCE LEADING TO THEM LIKE A TRAIL OF COOKIE CRUMBS.
NICE TRY, ROOKIE. NOW GET BACK TO THE TRAFFIC.
HE'S WRONG BUT I CAN'T TELL HIM THAT.
I BLEW A CHANCE TO STAY CLOSE TO THIS CASE.
HE SHOOT YOU DOWN, COLUMBO?
O'Shaughnessy's
LIKE A DOG.
AT LEAST HE SMILED WHEN HE DID IT.

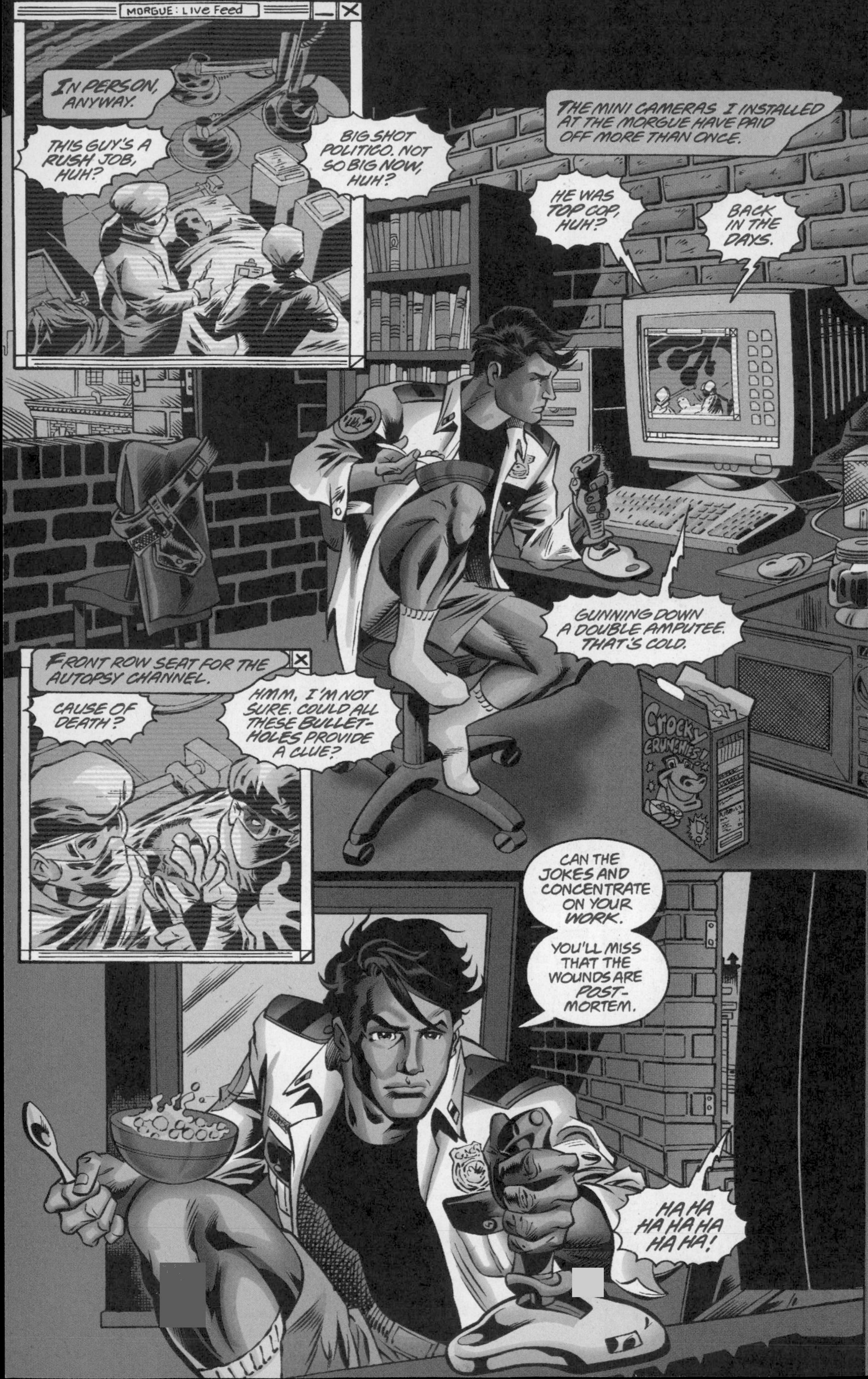
MORGUE: Live Feed
IN PERSON, ANYWAY.
THIS GUY'S A RUSH JOB, HUH?
BIG SHOT POLITICO. NOT SO BIG NOW, HUH?
THE MINI CAMERAS I INSTALLED AT THE MORGUE HAVE PAID OFF MORE THAN ONCE.
HE WAS TOP COP, HUH?
BACK IN THE DAYS.
GUNNING DOWN A DOUBLE AMPUTEE. THAT'S COLD.
FRONT ROW SEAT FOR THE AUTOPSY CHANNEL.
CAUSE OF DEATH?
HMM, I'M NOT SURE. COULD ALL THESE BULLET-HOLES PROVIDE A CLUE?
CAN THE JOKES AND CONCENTRATE ON YOUR WORK.
YOU'LL MISS THAT THE WOUNDS ARE POST-MORTEM.
HA HA HA HA HA HA HA!

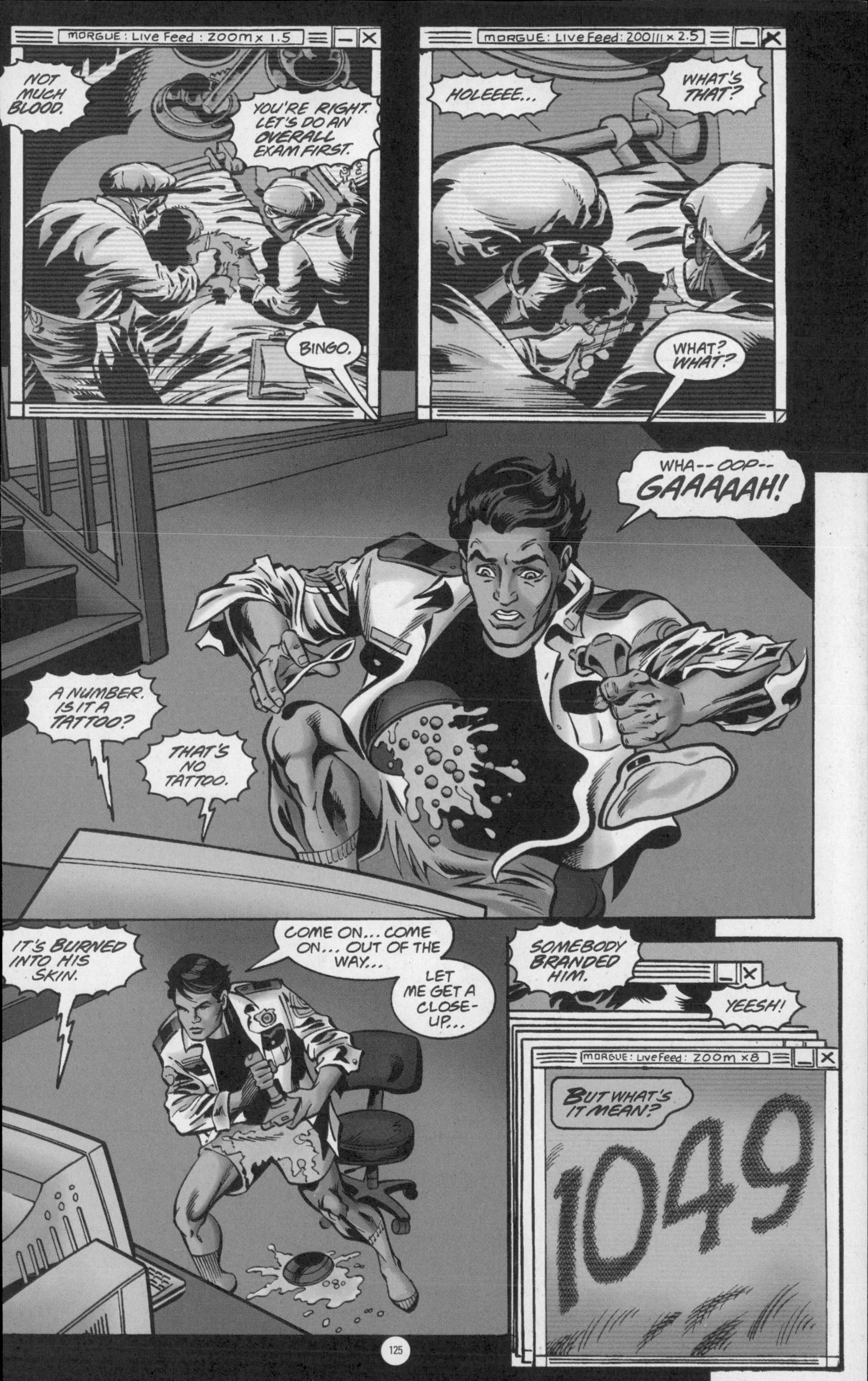
MORGUE : Live Feed : ZOOM x 1.5
NOT MUCH BLOOD.
YOU'RE RIGHT. LET'S DO AN OVERALL EXAM FIRST.
BINGO.
MORGUE : Live Feed : ZOOM x 2.5
HOLEEEE...
WHAT'S THAT?
WHAT? WHAT?
WHA-- OOP-- GAAAAAH!
A NUMBER. IS IT A TATTOO?
THAT'S NO TATTOO.
IT'S BURNED INTO HIS SKIN.
COME ON... COME ON... OUT OF THE WAY...
LET ME GET A CLOSE-UP...
SOMEBODY BRANDED HIM.
YEESH!
MORGUE : Live Feed : ZOOM x8
BUT WHAT'S IT MEAN?
1049

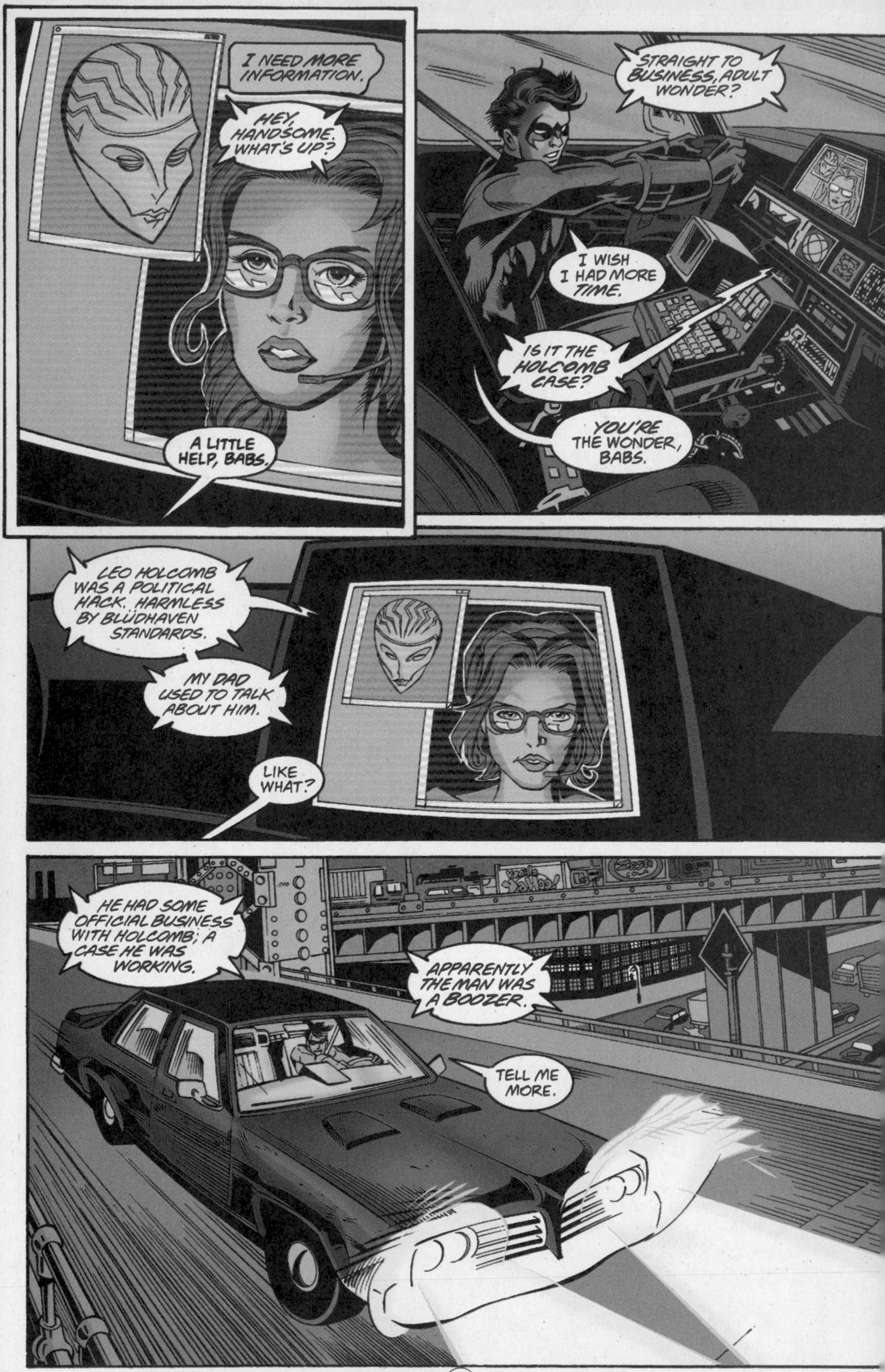

I NEED MORE INFORMATION.
HEY, HANDSOME. WHAT'S UP?
A LITTLE HELP, BABS.
STRAIGHT TO BUSINESS, ADULT WONDER?
I WISH I HAD MORE TIME.
IS IT THE HOLCOMB CASE?
YOU'RE THE WONDER, BABS.
LEO HOLCOMB WAS A POLITICAL HACK. HARMLESS BY BLÜDHAVEN STANDARDS.
MY DAD USED TO TALK ABOUT HIM.
LIKE WHAT?
HE HAD SOME OFFICIAL BUSINESS WITH HOLCOMB; A CASE HE WAS WORKING.
APPARENTLY THE MAN WAS A BOOZER.
TELL ME MORE.

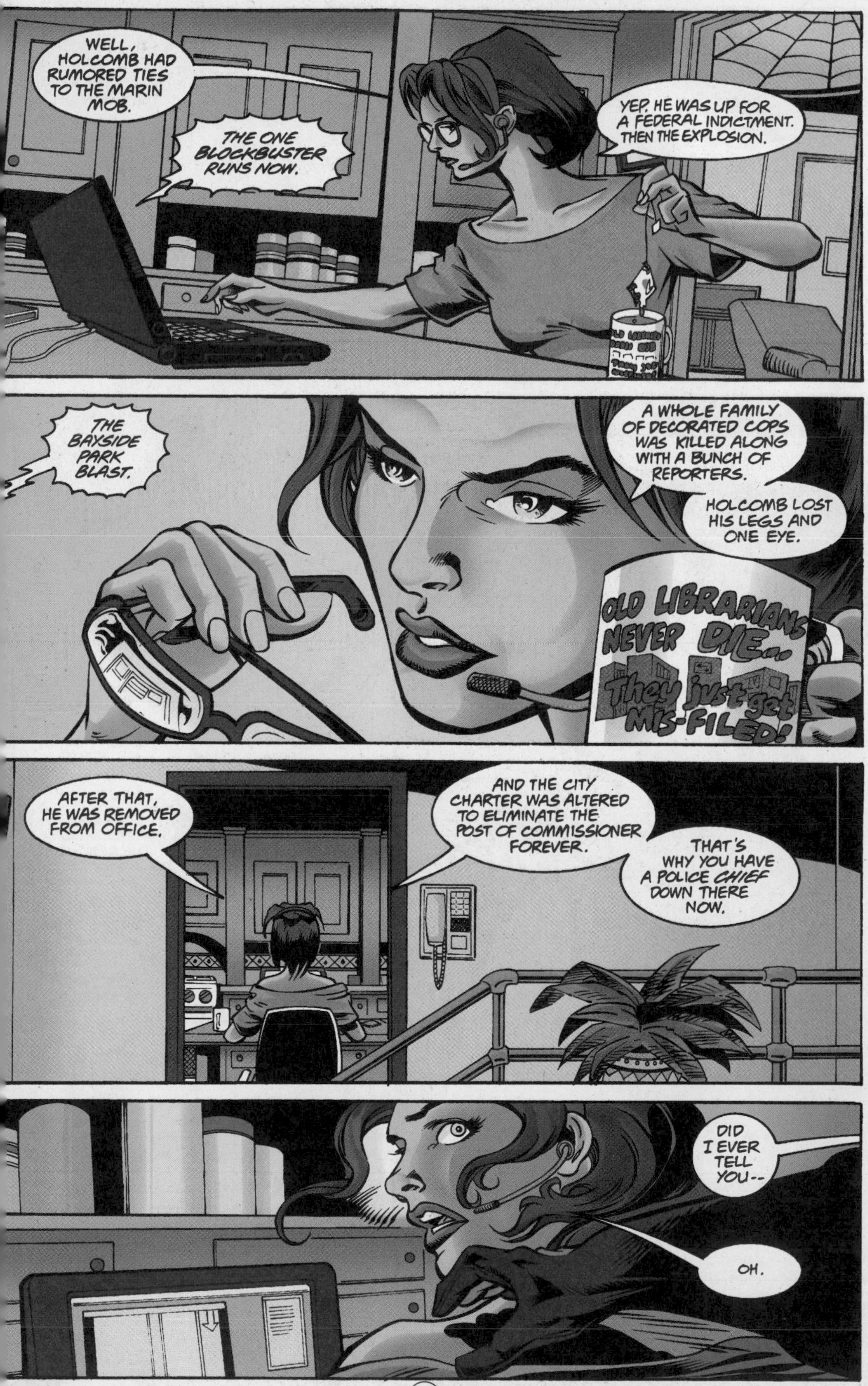
WELL, HOLCOMB HAD RUMORED TIES TO THE MARIN MOB.
THE ONE BLOCKBUSTER RUNS NOW.
YEP. HE WAS UP FOR A FEDERAL INDICTMENT. THEN THE EXPLOSION.
THE BAYSIDE PARK BLAST.
A WHOLE FAMILY OF DECORATED COPS WAS KILLED ALONG WITH A BUNCH OF REPORTERS.
HOLCOMB LOST HIS LEGS AND ONE EYE.
OLD LIBRARIANS NEVER DIE... They just get MIS-FILED!
AFTER THAT, HE WAS REMOVED FROM OFFICE.
AND THE CITY CHARTER WAS ALTERED TO ELIMINATE THE POST OF COMMISSIONER FOREVER.
THAT'S WHY YOU HAVE A POLICE CHIEF DOWN THERE NOW.
DID I EVER TELL YOU--
OH.

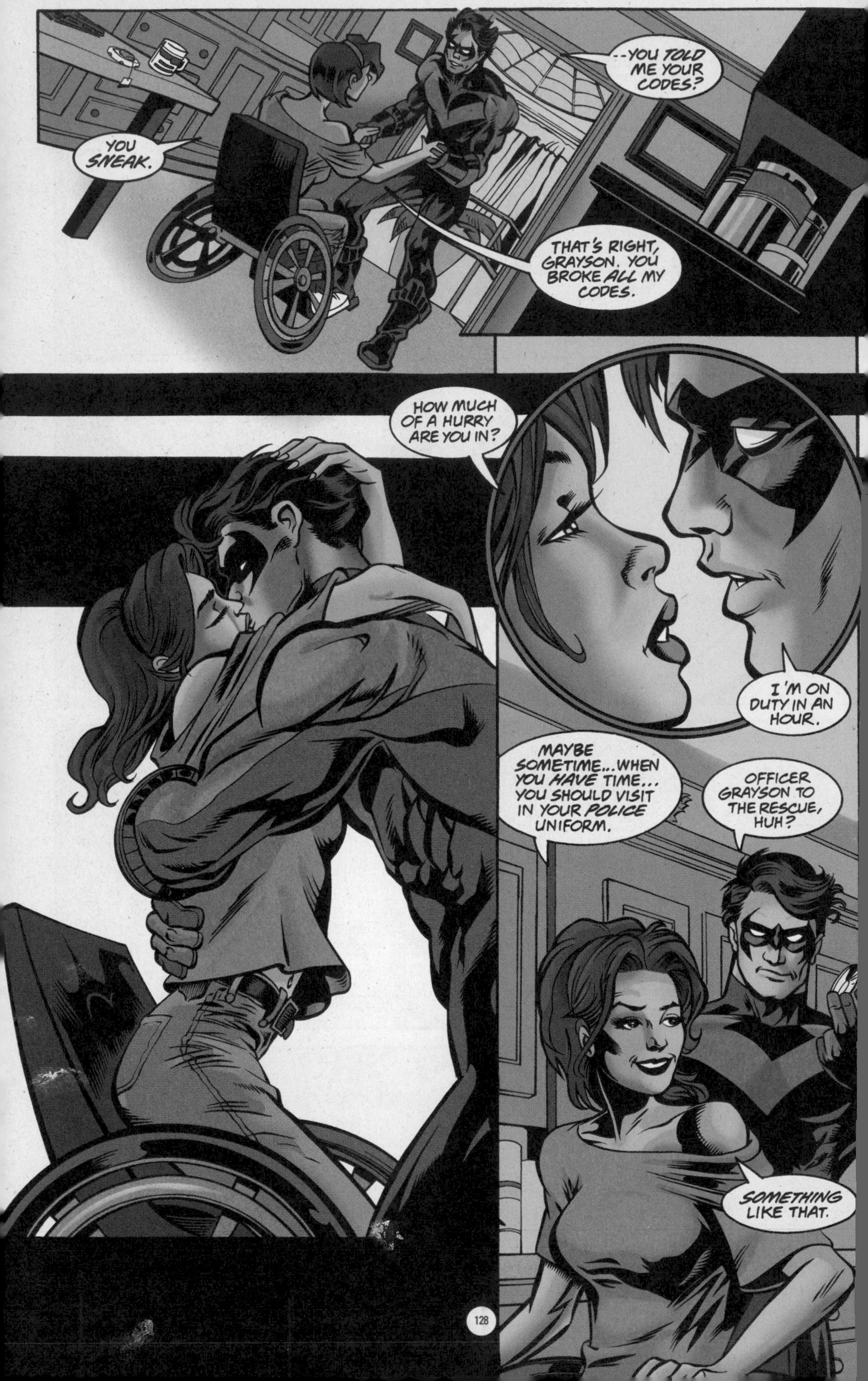
--YOU TOLD ME YOUR CODES?
YOU SNEAK.
THAT'S RIGHT, GRAYSON. YOU BROKE ALL MY CODES.
HOW MUCH OF A HURRY ARE YOU IN?
I'M ON DUTY IN AN HOUR.
MAYBE SOMETIME... WHEN YOU HAVE TIME... YOU SHOULD VISIT IN YOUR POLICE UNIFORM.
OFFICER GRAYSON TO THE RESCUE, HUH?
SOMETHING LIKE THAT.

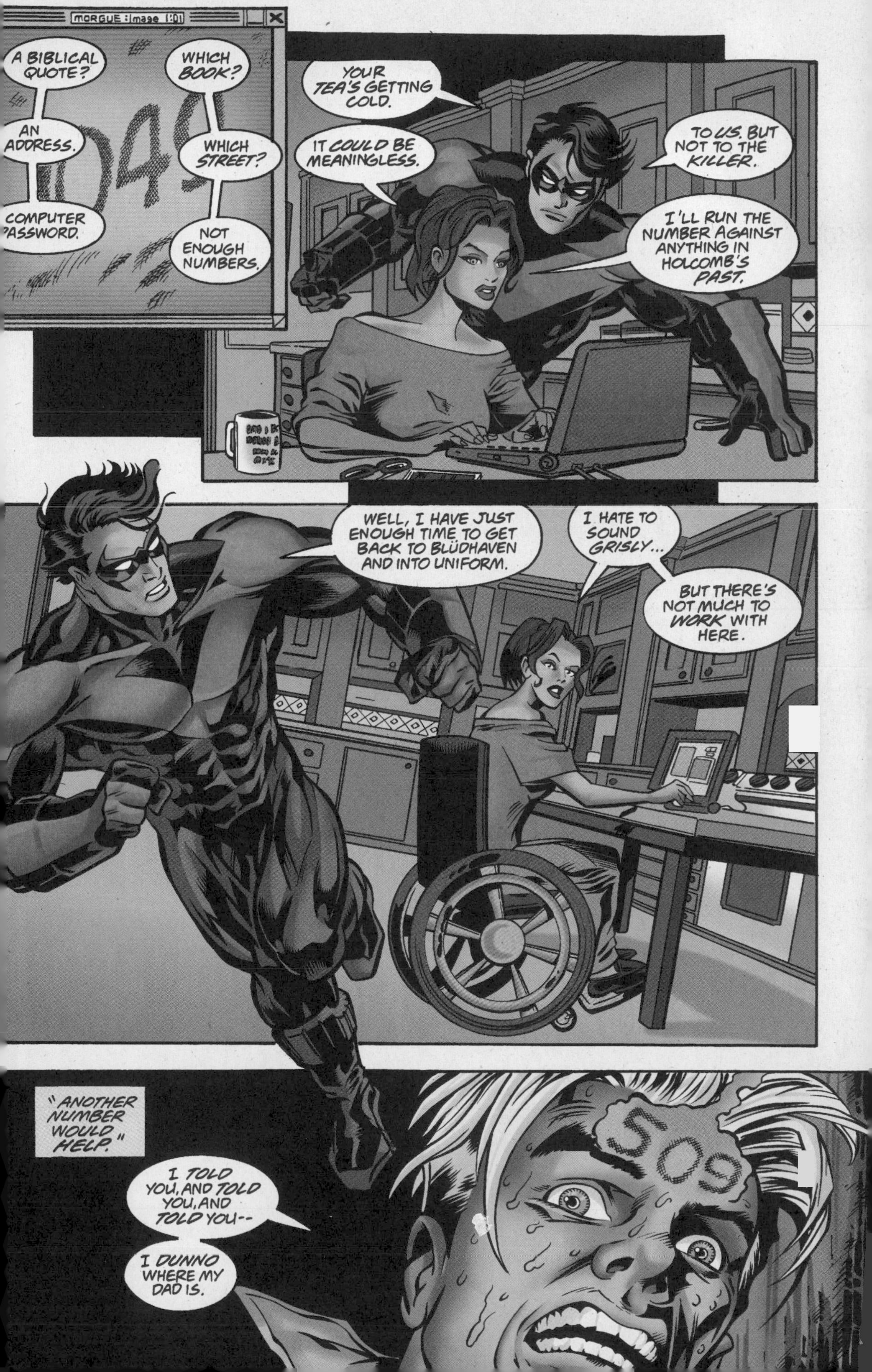
MORGUE : image 1:01
A BIBLICAL QUOTE?
WHICH BOOK?
AN ADDRESS.
WHICH STREET?
COMPUTER PASSWORD.
NOT ENOUGH NUMBERS.
YOUR TEA'S GETTING COLD.
IT COULD BE MEANINGLESS.
TO US. BUT NOT TO THE KILLER.
I'LL RUN THE NUMBER AGAINST ANYTHING IN HOLCOMB'S PAST.
WELL, I HAVE JUST ENOUGH TIME TO GET BACK TO BLÜDHAVEN AND INTO UNIFORM.
I HATE TO SOUND GRISLY...
BUT THERE'S NOT MUCH TO WORK WITH HERE.
"ANOTHER NUMBER WOULD HELP."
I TOLD YOU, AND TOLD YOU, AND TOLD YOU--
I DUNNO WHERE MY DAD IS.

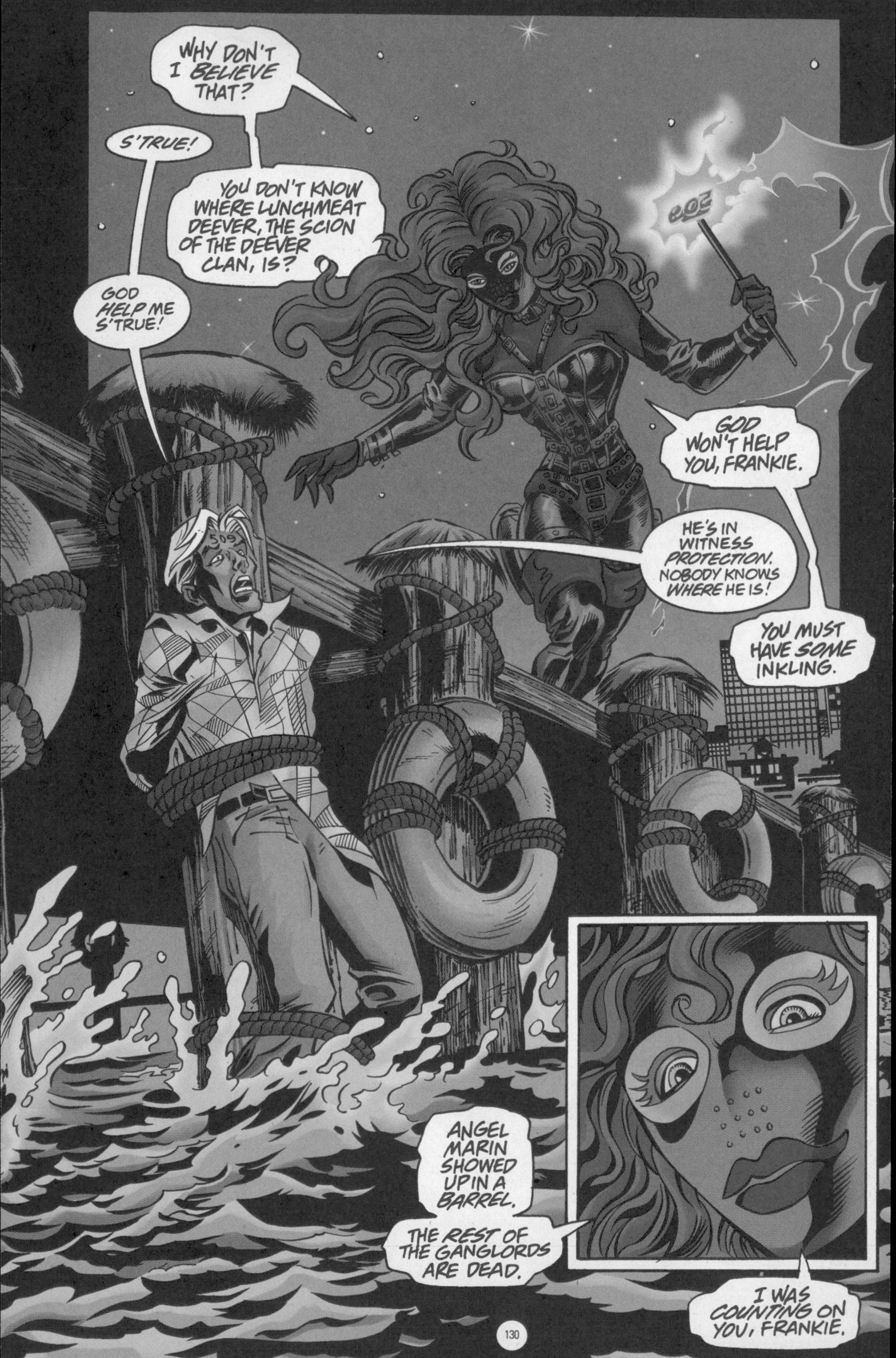
WHY DON'T I BELIEVE THAT?
S'TRUE!
YOU DON'T KNOW WHERE LUNCHMEAT DEEVER, THE SCION OF THE DEEVER CLAN, IS?
GOD HELP ME S'TRUE!
GOD WON'T HELP YOU, FRANKIE.
HE'S IN WITNESS PROTECTION. NOBODY KNOWS WHERE HE IS!
YOU MUST HAVE SOME INKLING.
ANGEL MARIN SHOWED UP IN A BARREL.
THE REST OF THE GANGLORDS ARE DEAD.
I WAS COUNTING ON YOU, FRANKIE.

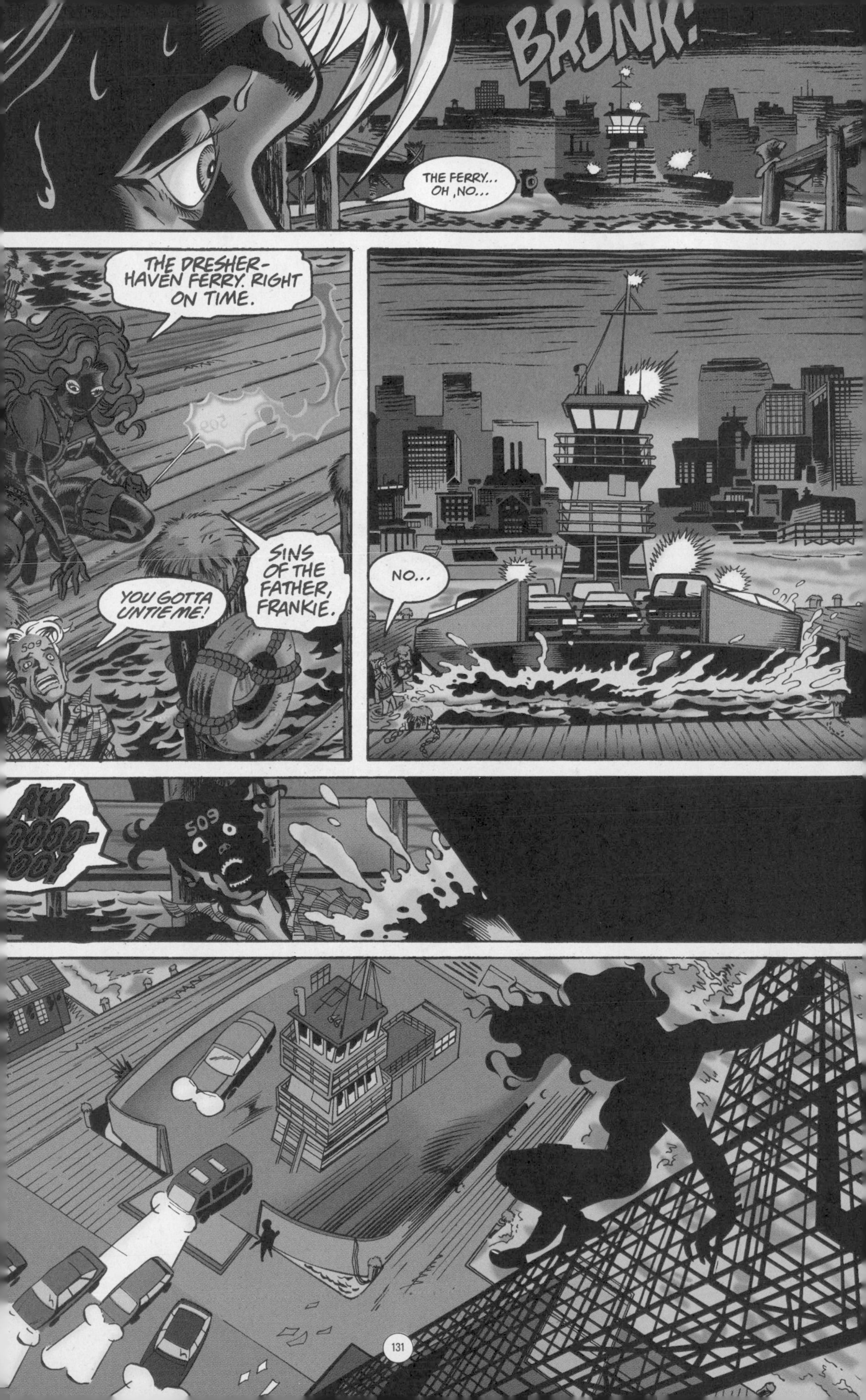
BRONK!
THE FERRY... OH, NO...
THE DRESHER-HAVEN FERRY. RIGHT ON TIME.
SINS OF THE FATHER, FRANKIE.
YOU GOTTA UNTIE ME!
NO...
AW OOOO-OOO!

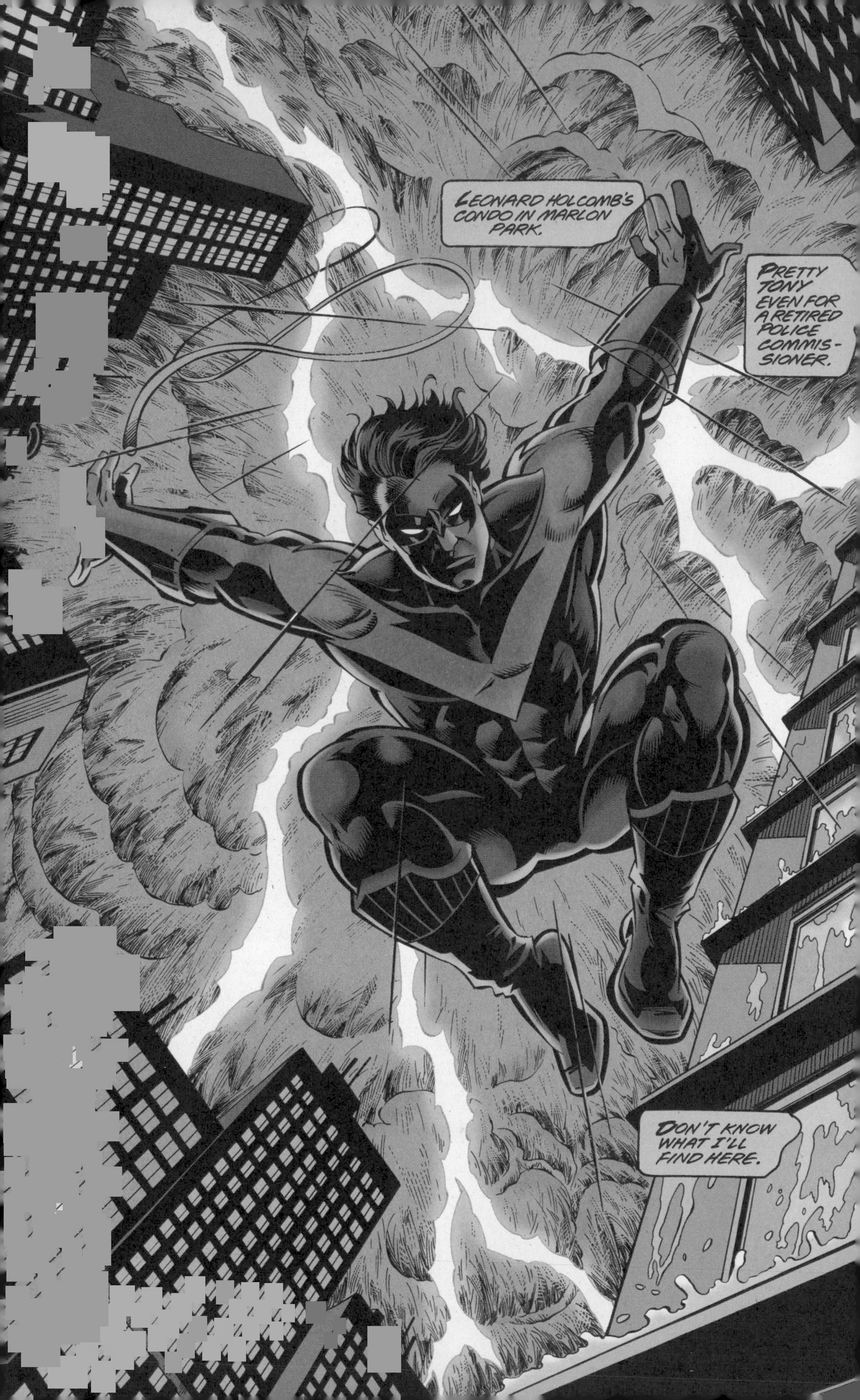
LEONARD HOLCOMB'S CONDO IN MARLON PARK.
PRETTY TONY EVEN FOR A RETIRED POLICE COMMIS-SIONER.
DON'T KNOW WHAT I'LL FIND HERE.

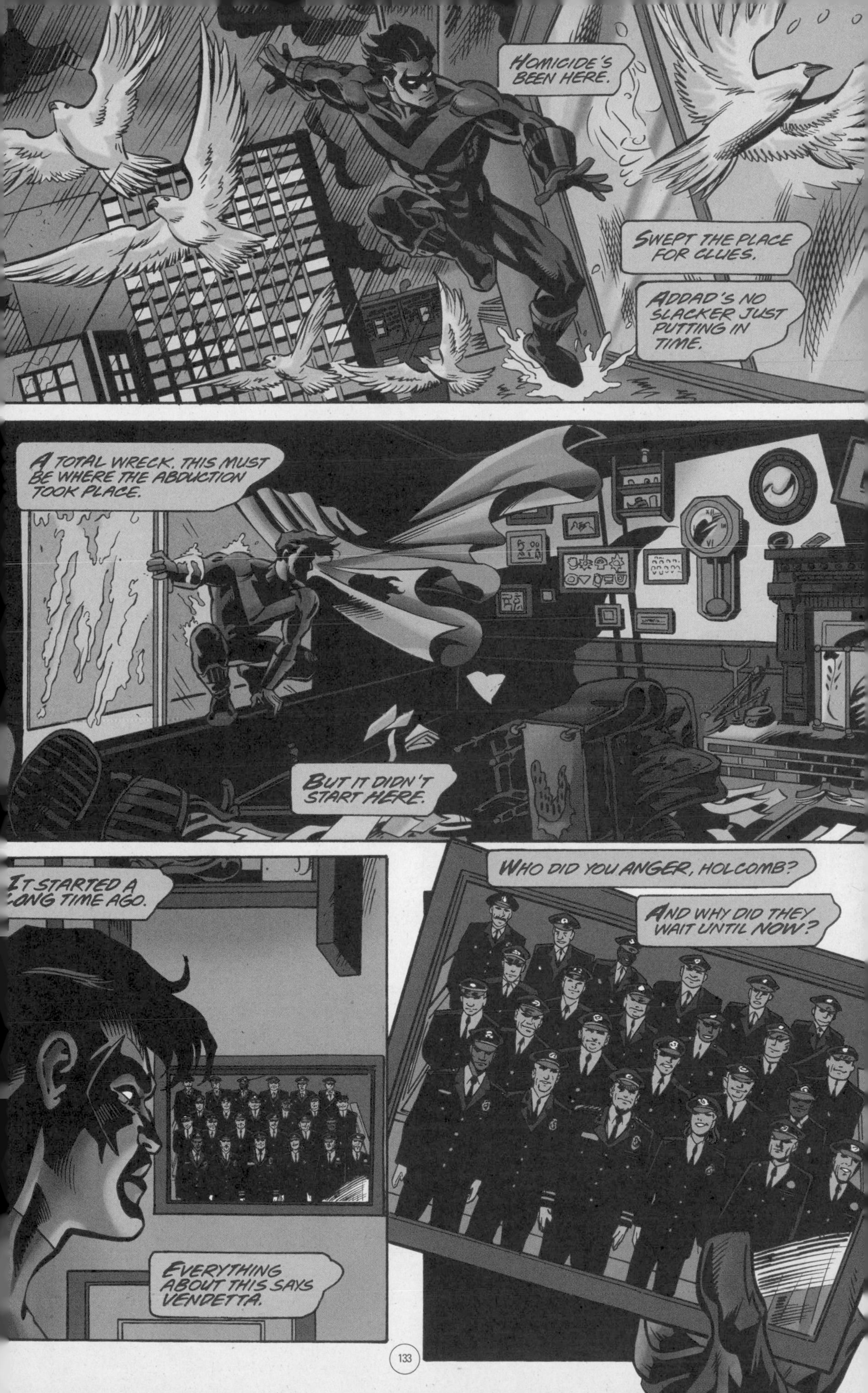
HOMICIDE'S BEEN HERE.
SWEPT THE PLACE FOR CLUES.
ADDAD'S NO SLACKER JUST PUTTING IN TIME.
A TOTAL WRECK. THIS MUST BE WHERE THE ABDUCTION TOOK PLACE.
BUT IT DIDN'T START HERE.
IT STARTED A LONG TIME AGO.
EVERYTHING ABOUT THIS SAYS VENDETTA.
WHO DID YOU ANGER, HOLCOMB?
AND WHY DID THEY WAIT UNTIL NOW?

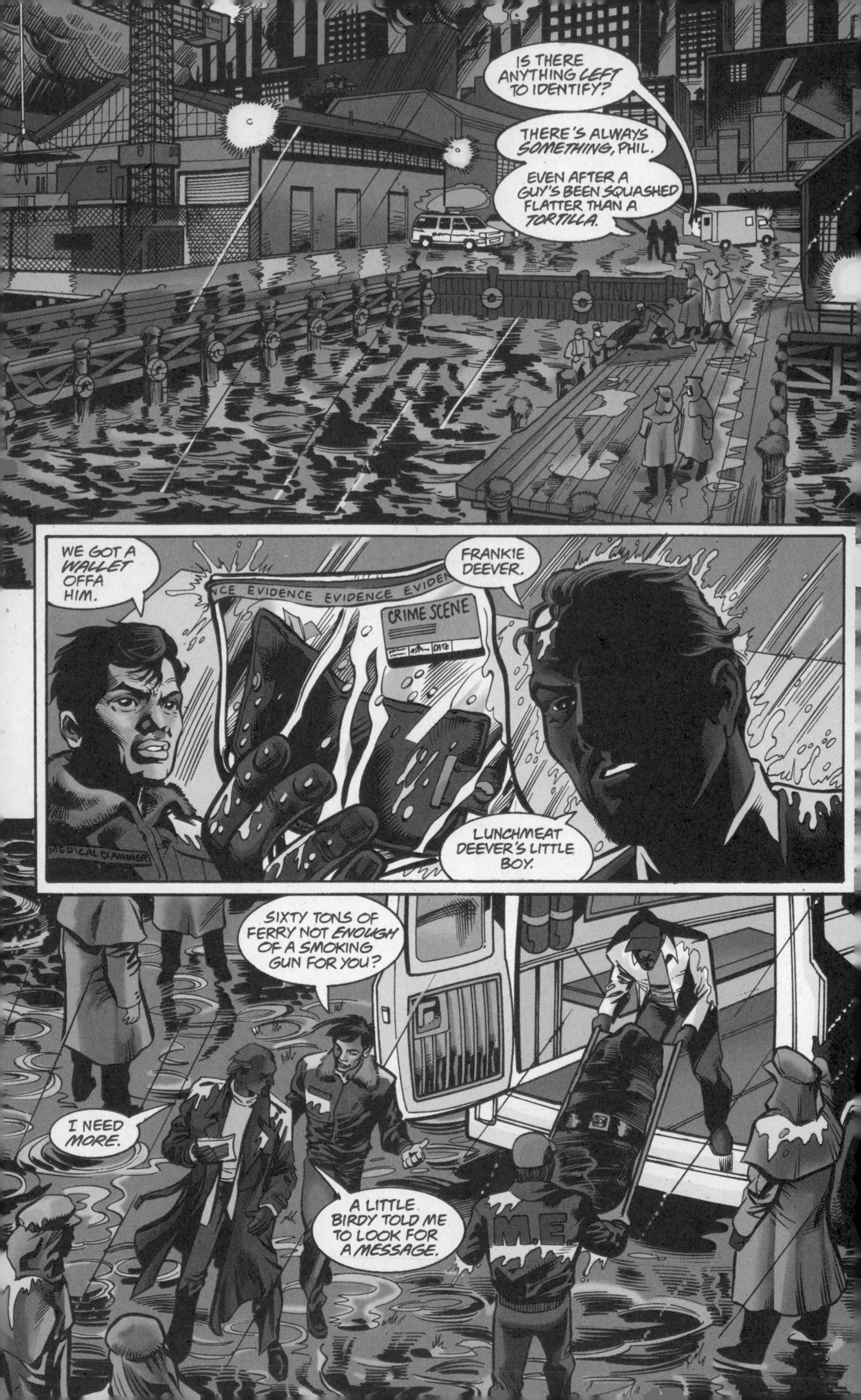
IS THERE ANYTHING LEFT TO IDENTIFY?
THERE'S ALWAYS SOMETHING, PHIL.
EVEN AFTER A GUY'S BEEN SQUASHED FLATTER THAN A TORTILLA.
WE GOT A WALLET OFFA HIM.
FRANKIE DEEVER.
EVIDENCE EVIDENCE EVIDENCE
CRIME SCENE
DATE
MEDICAL EXAMINER
LUNCHMEAT DEEVER'S LITTLE BOY.
SIXTY TONS OF FERRY NOT ENOUGH OF A SMOKING GUN FOR YOU?
I NEED MORE.
A LITTLE BIRDY TOLD ME TO LOOK FOR A MESSAGE.
M.E.

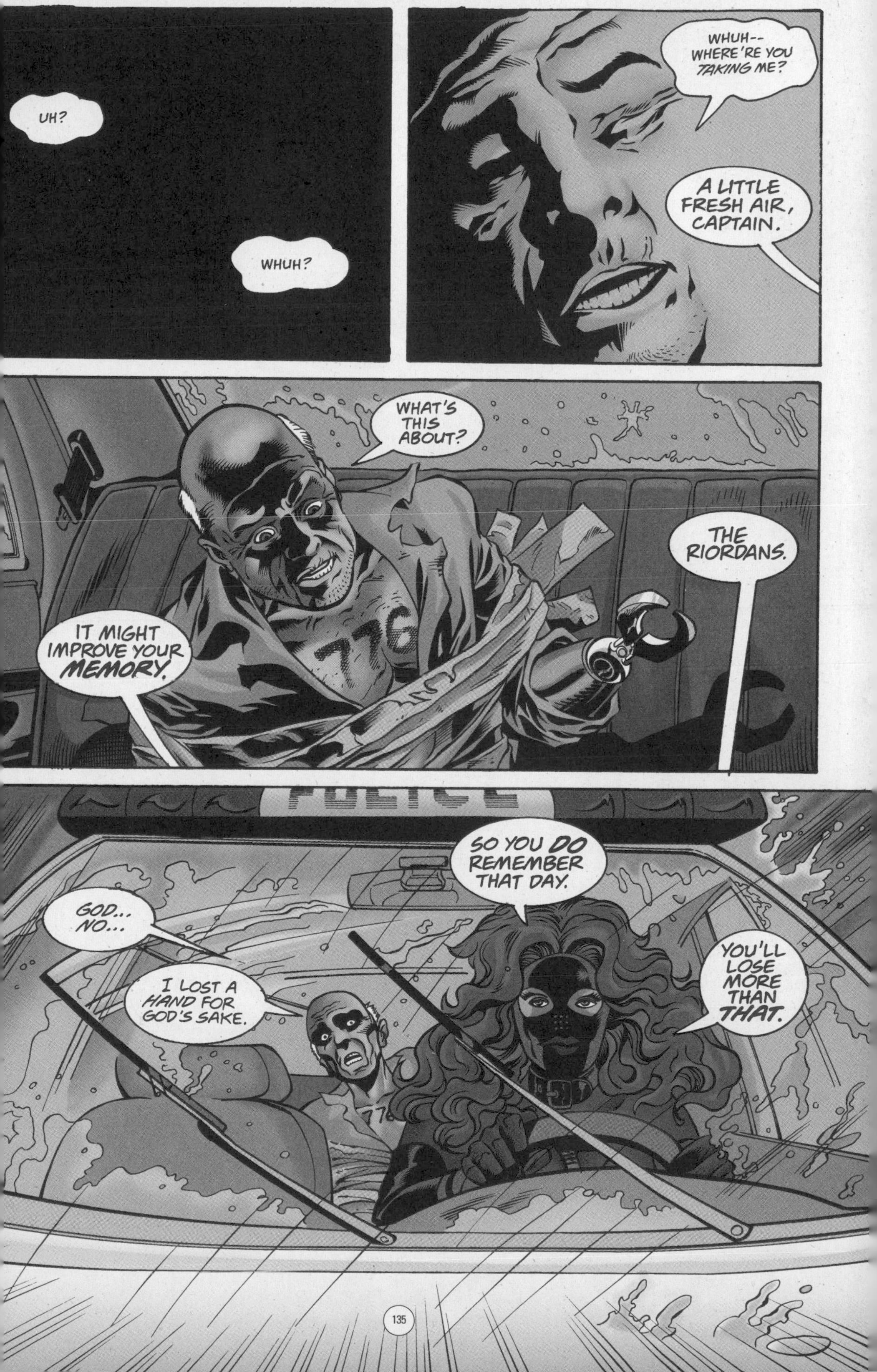
UH?
WHUH?
WHUH-- WHERE'RE YOU TAKING ME?
A LITTLE FRESH AIR, CAPTAIN.
WHAT'S THIS ABOUT?
THE RIORDANS.
IT MIGHT IMPROVE YOUR MEMORY.
SO YOU DO REMEMBER THAT DAY.
GOD... NO...
I LOST A HAND FOR GOD'S SAKE.
YOU'LL LOSE MORE THAN THAT.

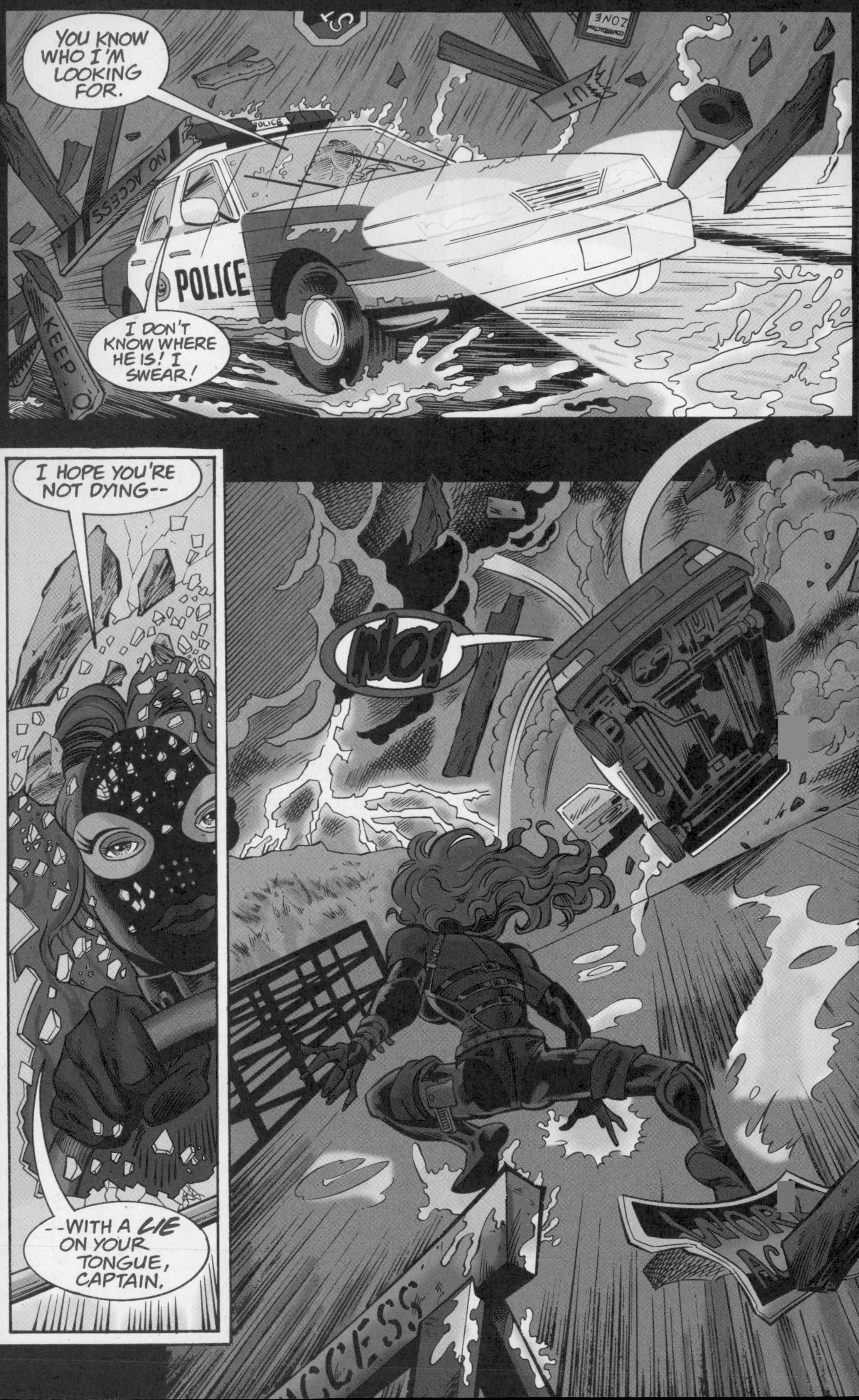
YOU KNOW WHO I'M LOOKING FOR.
I DON'T KNOW WHERE HE IS! I SWEAR!
I HOPE YOU'RE NOT DYING--
NO!
--WITH A LIE ON YOUR TONGUE, CAPTAIN.

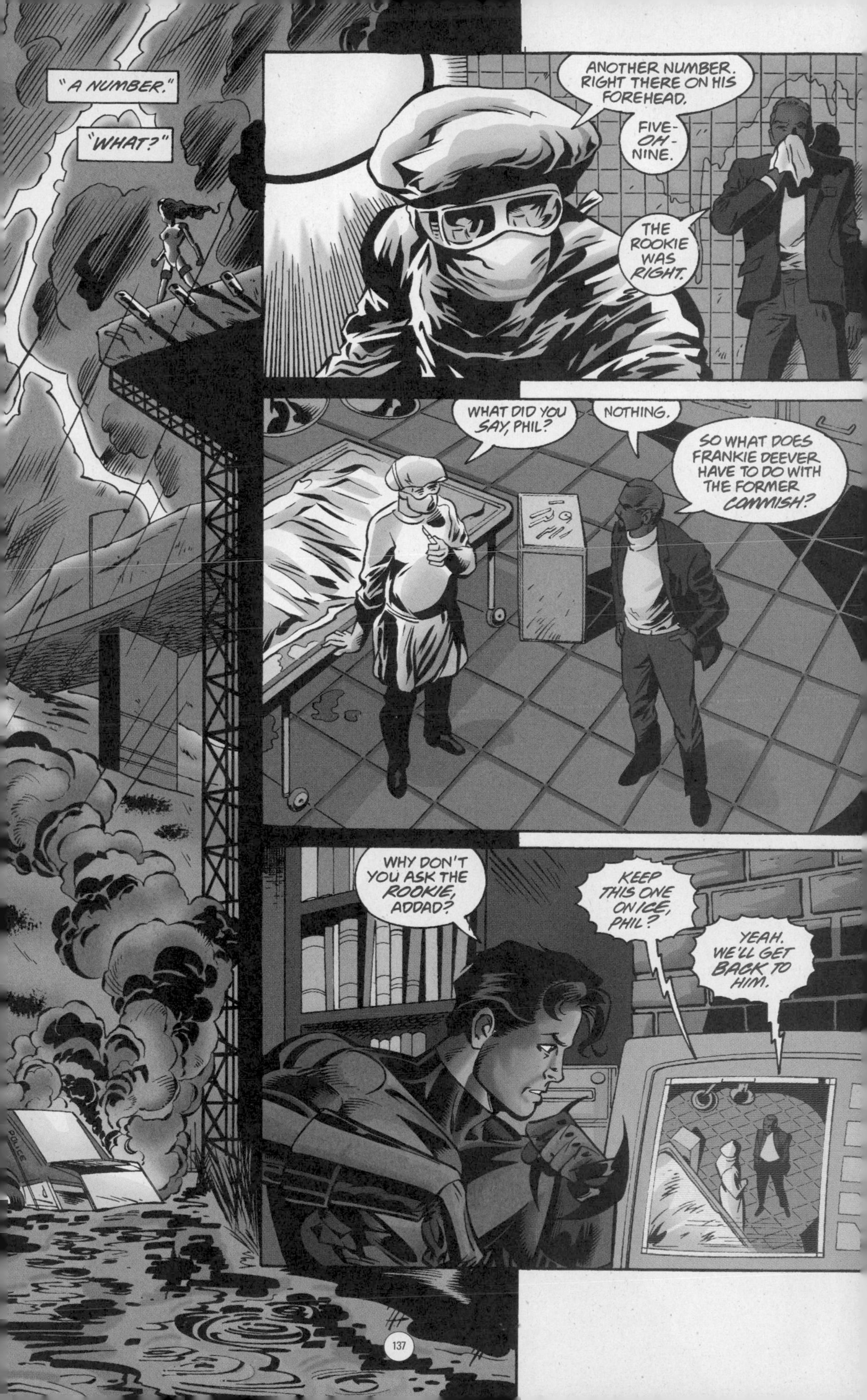
"A NUMBER."
"WHAT?"
ANOTHER NUMBER. RIGHT THERE ON HIS FOREHEAD.
FIVE-OH-NINE.
THE ROOKIE WAS RIGHT.
WHAT DID YOU SAY, PHIL?
NOTHING.
SO WHAT DOES FRANKIE DEEVER HAVE TO DO WITH THE FORMER COMMISH?
WHY DON'T YOU ASK THE ROOKIE, ADDAD?
KEEP THIS ONE ON ICE, PHIL?
YEAH. WE'LL GET BACK TO HIM.
POLICE

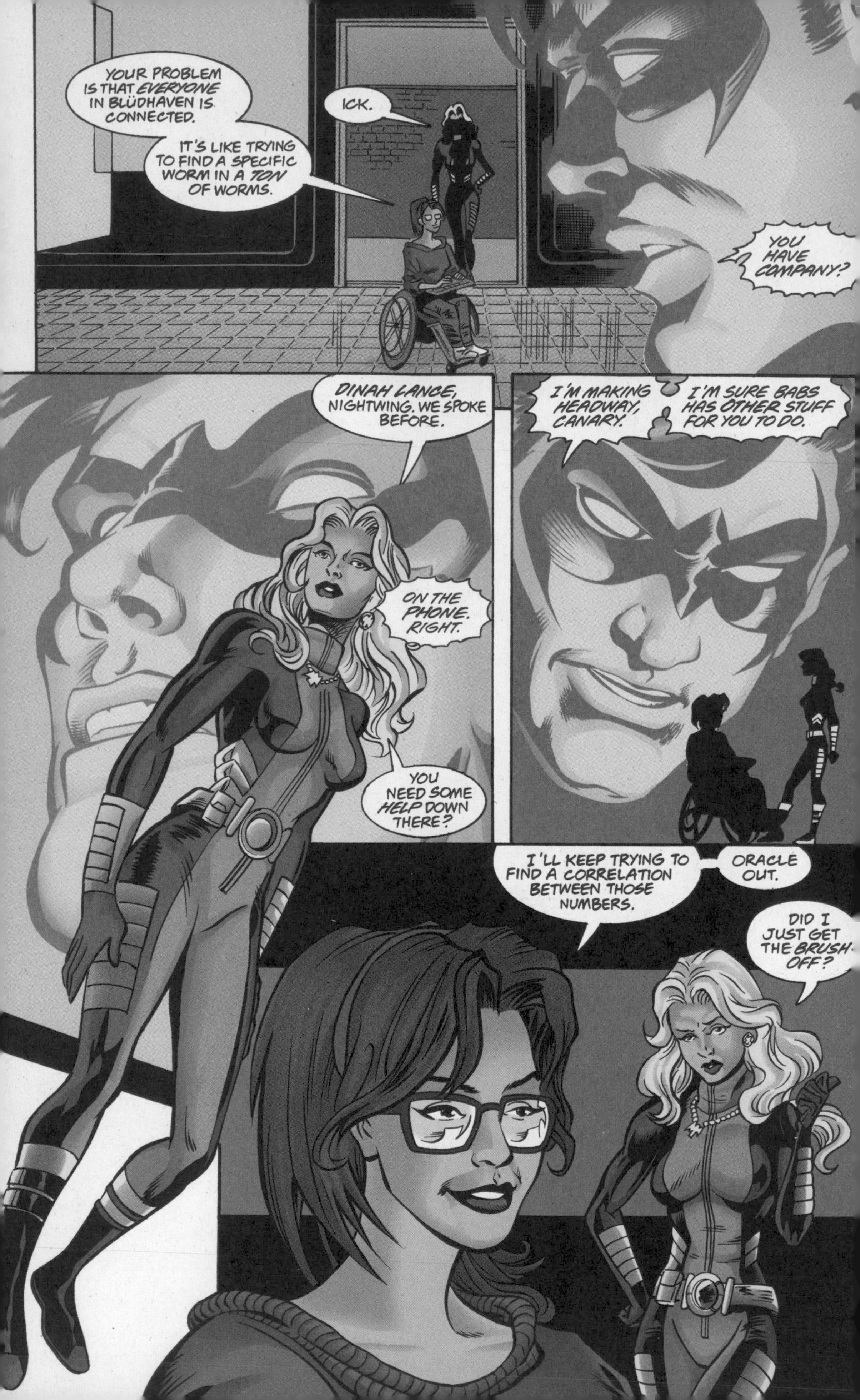
YOUR PROBLEM IS THAT EVERYONE IN BLÜDHAVEN IS CONNECTED.
IT'S LIKE TRYING TO FIND A SPECIFIC WORM IN A TON OF WORMS.
ICK.
YOU HAVE COMPANY?
DINAH LANCE, NIGHTWING. WE SPOKE BEFORE.
ON THE PHONE. RIGHT.
YOU NEED SOME HELP DOWN THERE?
I'M MAKING HEADWAY, CANARY.
I'M SURE BABS HAS OTHER STUFF FOR YOU TO DO.
I'LL KEEP TRYING TO FIND A CORRELATION BETWEEN THOSE NUMBERS.
ORACLE OUT.
DID I JUST GET THE BRUSH-OFF?

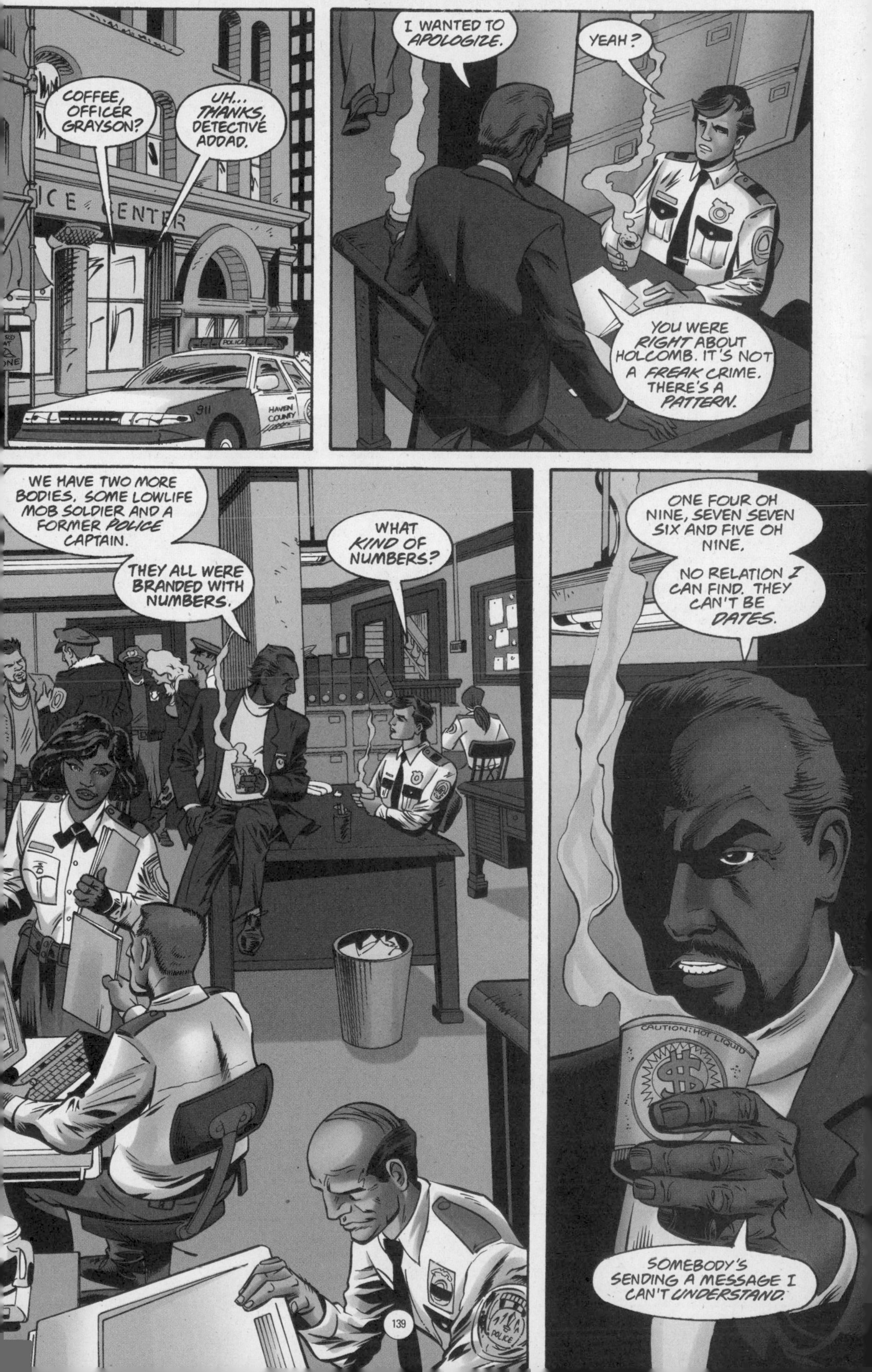

COFFEE, OFFICER GRAYSON?
UH... THANKS, DETECTIVE ADDAD.
ICE CENTER
POLICE
HAVEN COUNTY
911
I WANTED TO APOLOGIZE.
YEAH?
YOU WERE RIGHT ABOUT HOLCOMB. IT'S NOT A FREAK CRIME. THERE'S A PATTERN.
WE HAVE TWO MORE BODIES. SOME LOWLIFE MOB SOLDIER AND A FORMER POLICE CAPTAIN.
THEY ALL WERE BRANDED WITH NUMBERS.
WHAT KIND OF NUMBERS?
ONE FOUR OH NINE, SEVEN SEVEN SIX AND FIVE OH NINE.
NO RELATION I CAN FIND. THEY CAN'T BE DATES.
CAUTION: HOT LIQUID
SOMEBODY'S SENDING A MESSAGE I CAN'T UNDERSTAND.

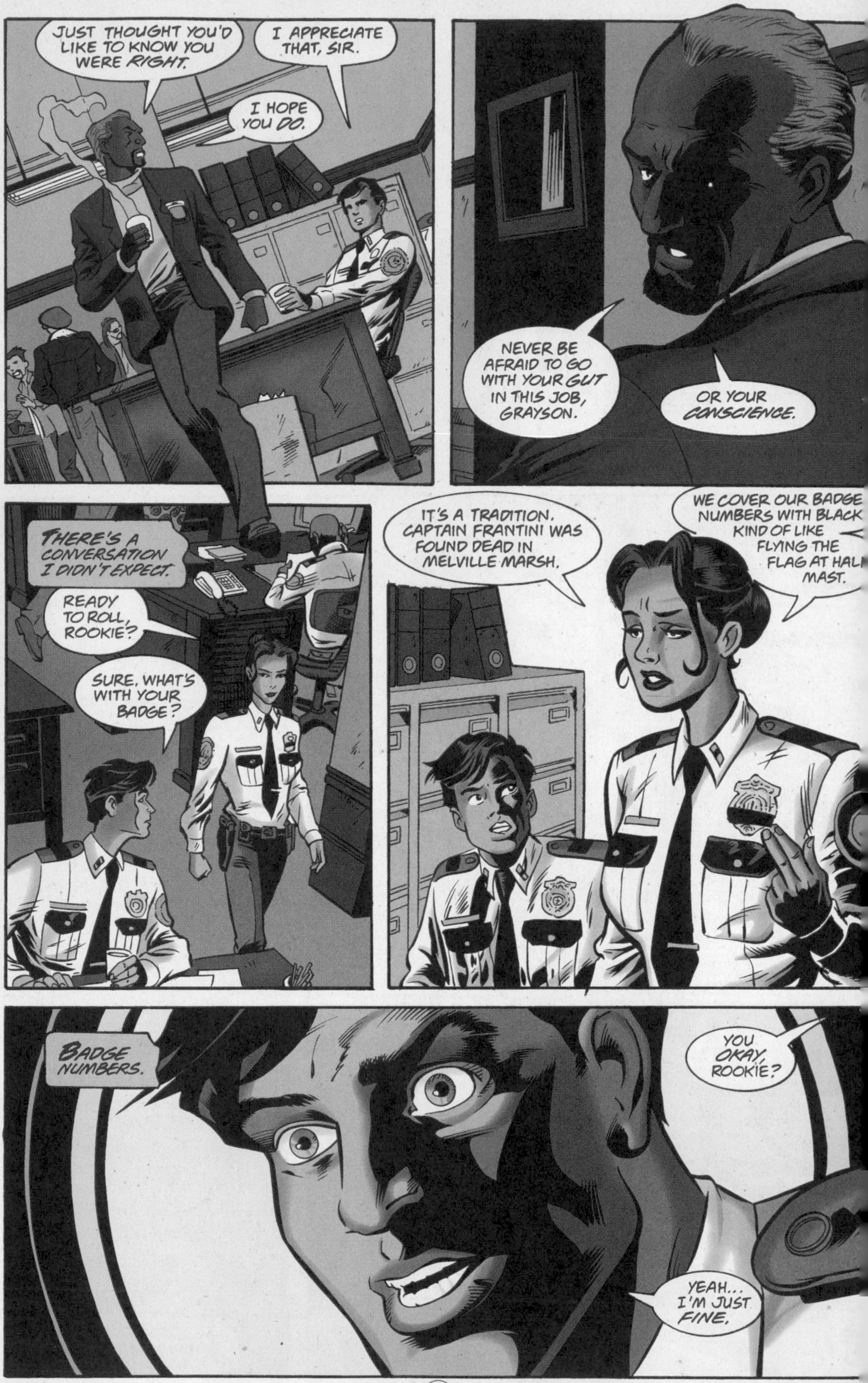
JUST THOUGHT YOU'D LIKE TO KNOW YOU WERE RIGHT.
I APPRECIATE THAT, SIR.
I HOPE YOU DO.
NEVER BE AFRAID TO GO WITH YOUR GUT IN THIS JOB, GRAYSON.
OR YOUR CONSCIENCE.
THERE'S A CONVERSATION I DIDN'T EXPECT.
READY TO ROLL, ROOKIE?
SURE. WHAT'S WITH YOUR BADGE?
IT'S A TRADITION. CAPTAIN FRANTINI WAS FOUND DEAD IN MELVILLE MARSH.
WE COVER OUR BADGE NUMBERS WITH BLACK KIND OF LIKE FLYING THE FLAG AT HAL MAST.
BADGE NUMBERS.
YOU OKAY, ROOKIE?
YEAH... I'M JUST FINE.

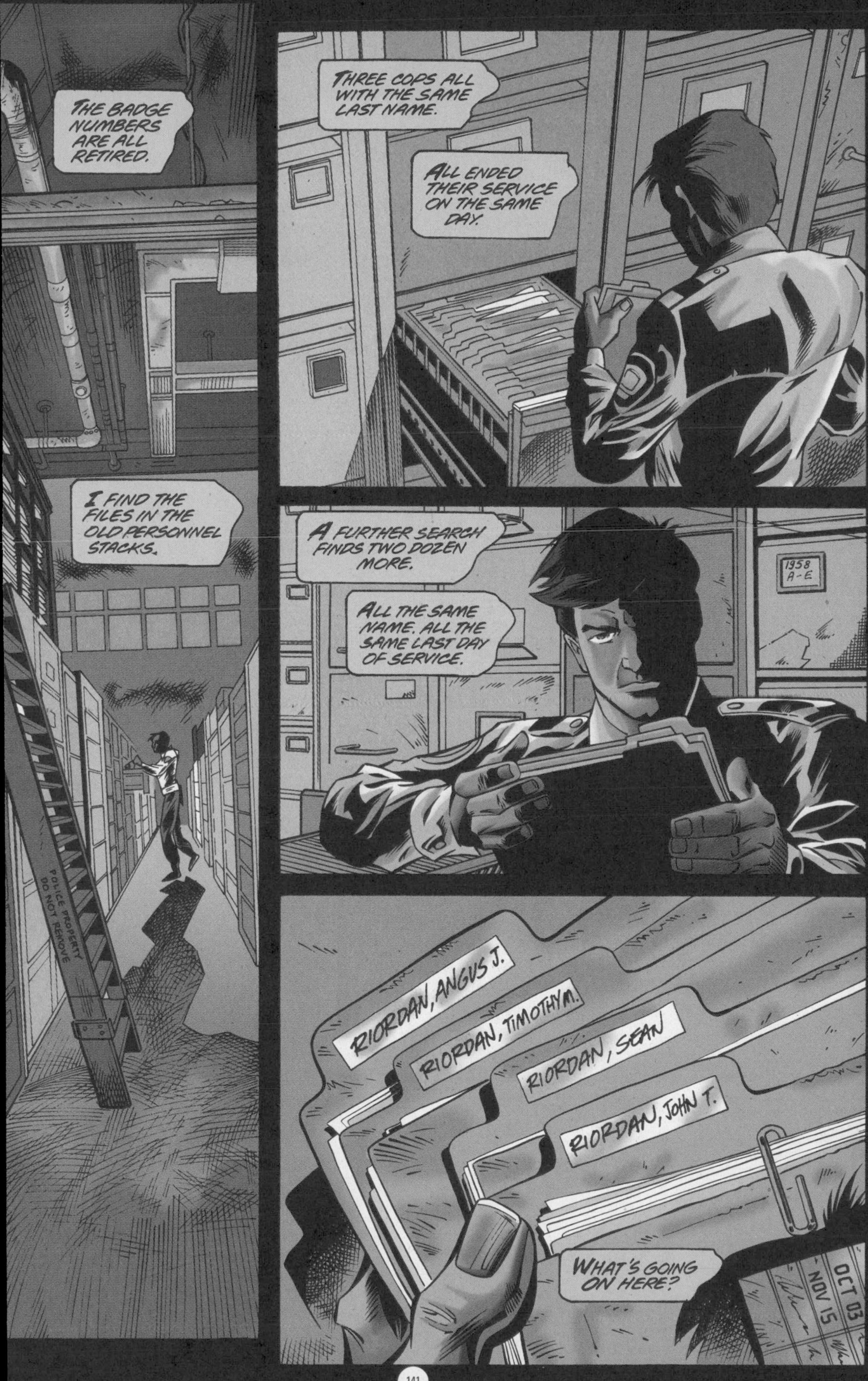

THE BADGE NUMBERS ARE ALL RETIRED.
I FIND THE FILES IN THE OLD PERSONNEL STACKS.
POLICE PROPERTY DO NOT REMOVE
THREE COPS ALL WITH THE SAME LAST NAME.
ALL ENDED THEIR SERVICE ON THE SAME DAY.
A FURTHER SEARCH FINDS TWO DOZEN MORE.
1958 A-E
ALL THE SAME NAME. ALL THE SAME LAST DAY OF SERVICE.
RIORDAN, ANGUS J.
RIORDAN, TIMOTHY M.
RIORDAN, SEAN
RIORDAN, JOHN T.
WHAT'S GOING ON HERE?
OCT 03
NOV 15

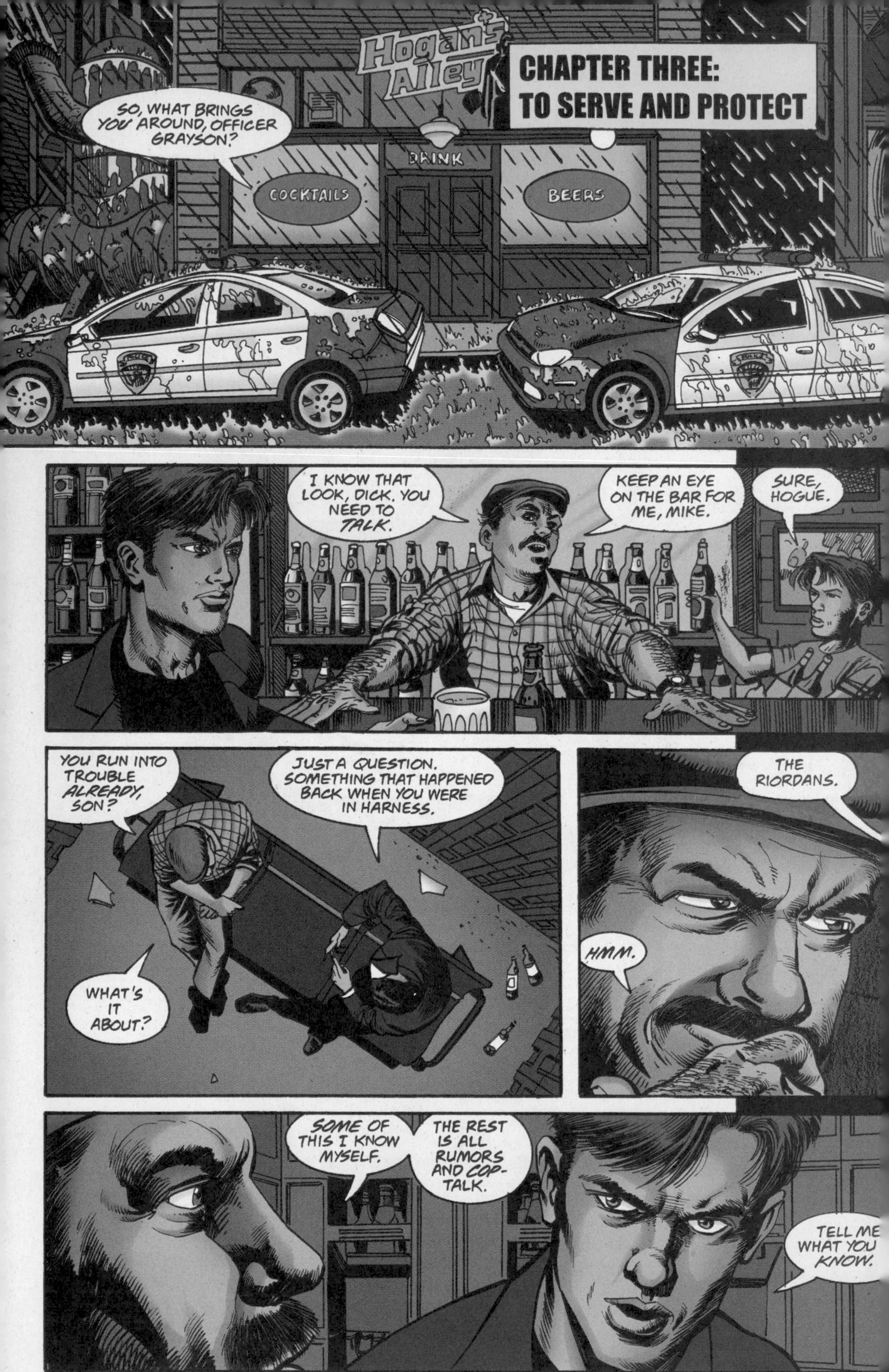
Hogan's Alley
CHAPTER THREE: TO SERVE AND PROTECT
SO, WHAT BRINGS YOU AROUND, OFFICER GRAYSON?
DRINK
COCKTAILS
BEERS
I KNOW THAT LOOK, DICK. YOU NEED TO TALK.
KEEP AN EYE ON THE BAR FOR ME, MIKE.
SURE, HOGUE.
YOU RUN INTO TROUBLE ALREADY, SON?
JUST A QUESTION. SOMETHING THAT HAPPENED BACK WHEN YOU WERE IN HARNESS.
WHAT'S IT ABOUT?
THE RIORDANS.
HMM.
SOME OF THIS I KNOW MYSELF.
THE REST IS ALL RUMORS AND COP-TALK.
TELL ME WHAT YOU KNOW.

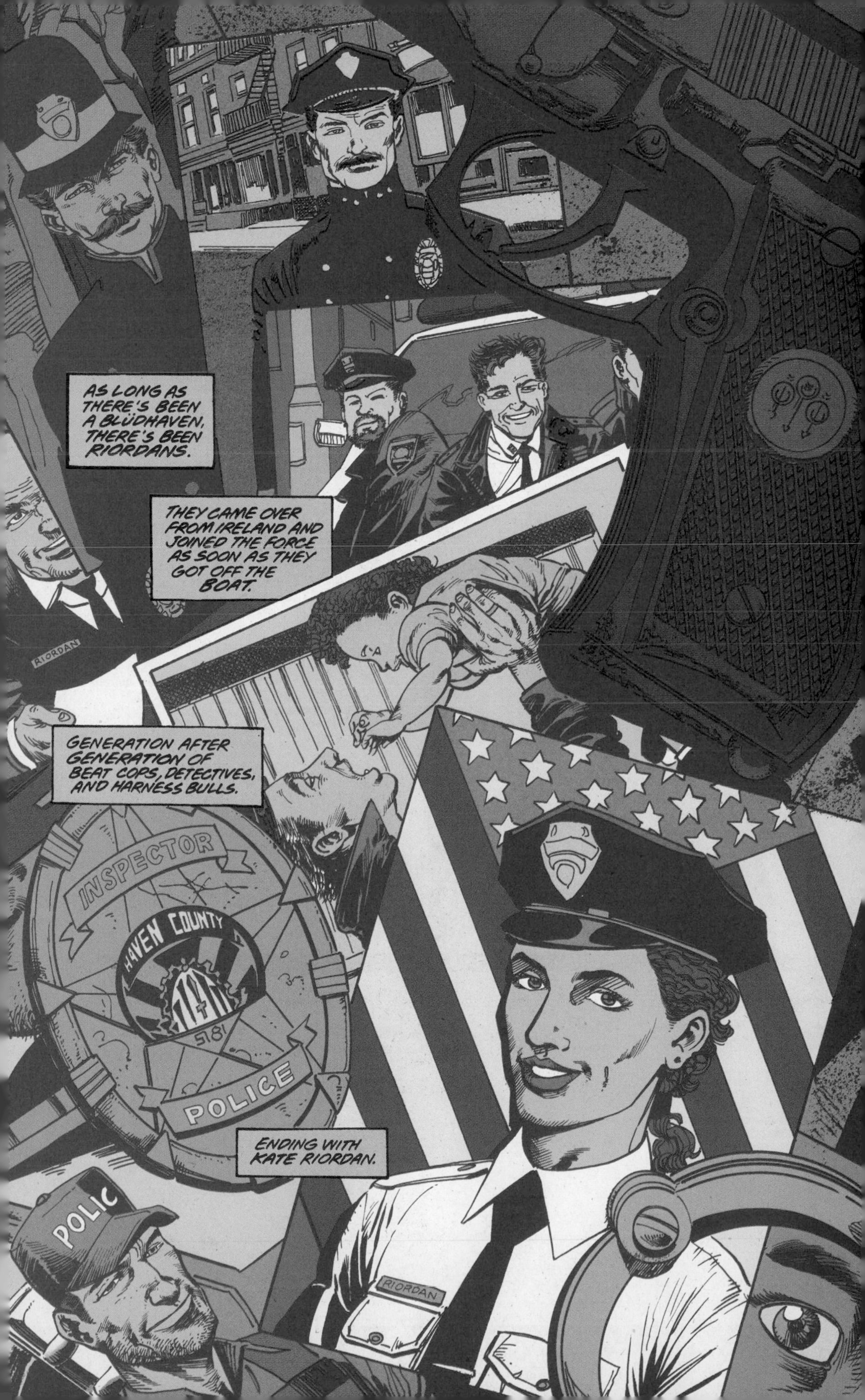
AS LONG AS THERE'S BEEN A BLÜDHAVEN, THERE'S BEEN RIORDANS.
THEY CAME OVER FROM IRELAND AND JOINED THE FORCE AS SOON AS THEY GOT OFF THE BOAT.
RIORDAN
GENERATION AFTER GENERATION OF BEAT COPS, DETECTIVES, AND HARNESS BULLS.
INSPECTOR
HAVEN COUNTY
5181
POLICE
ENDING WITH KATE RIORDAN.
POLIC
RIORDAN

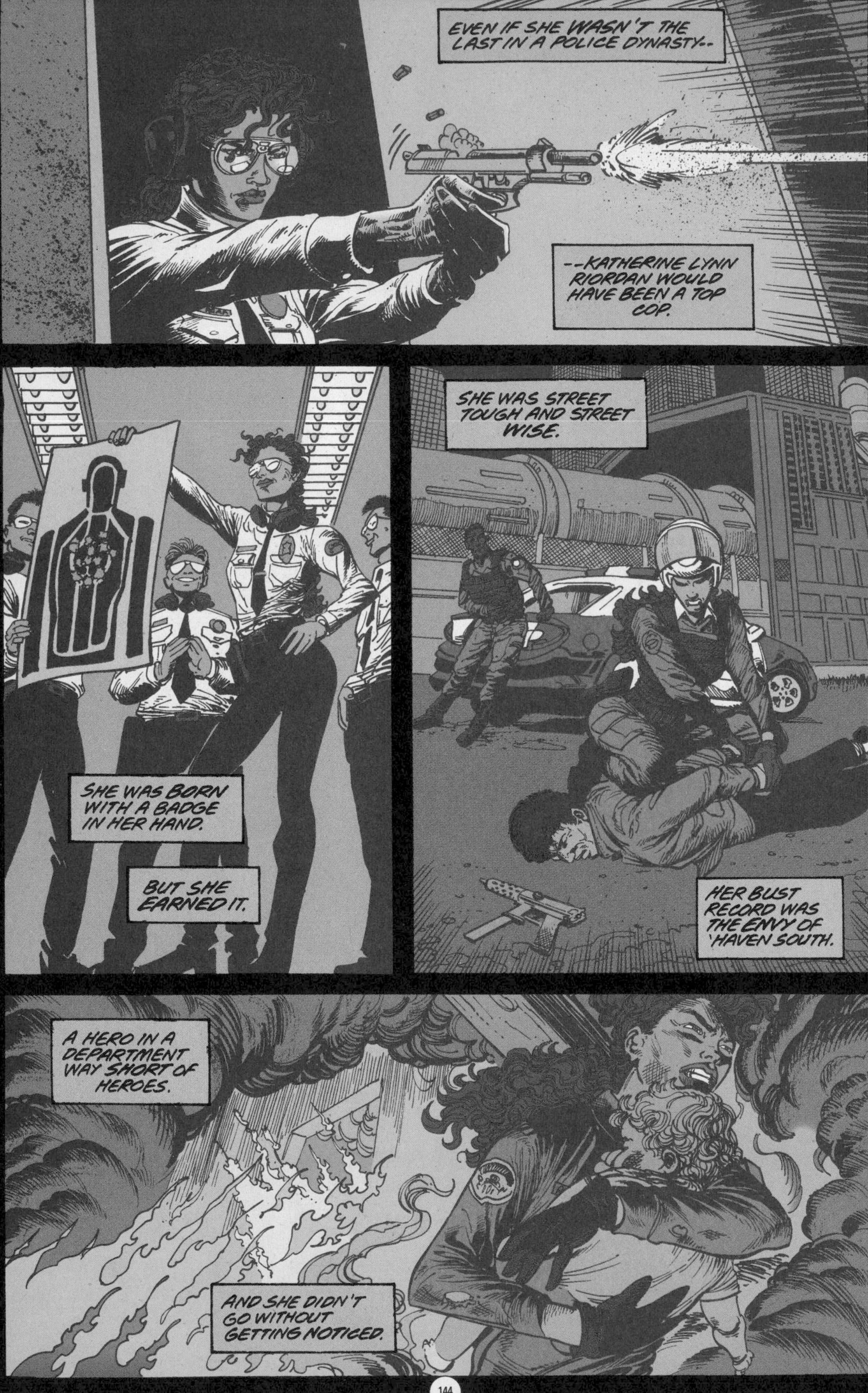
EVEN IF SHE WASN'T THE LAST IN A POLICE DYNASTY--
--KATHERINE LYNN RIORDAN WOULD HAVE BEEN A TOP COP.
SHE WAS BORN WITH A BADGE IN HER HAND.
BUT SHE EARNED IT.
SHE WAS STREET TOUGH AND STREET WISE.
HER BUST RECORD WAS THE ENVY OF 'HAVEN SOUTH.
A HERO IN A DEPARTMENT WAY SHORT OF HEROES.
AND SHE DIDN'T GO WITHOUT GETTING NOTICED.

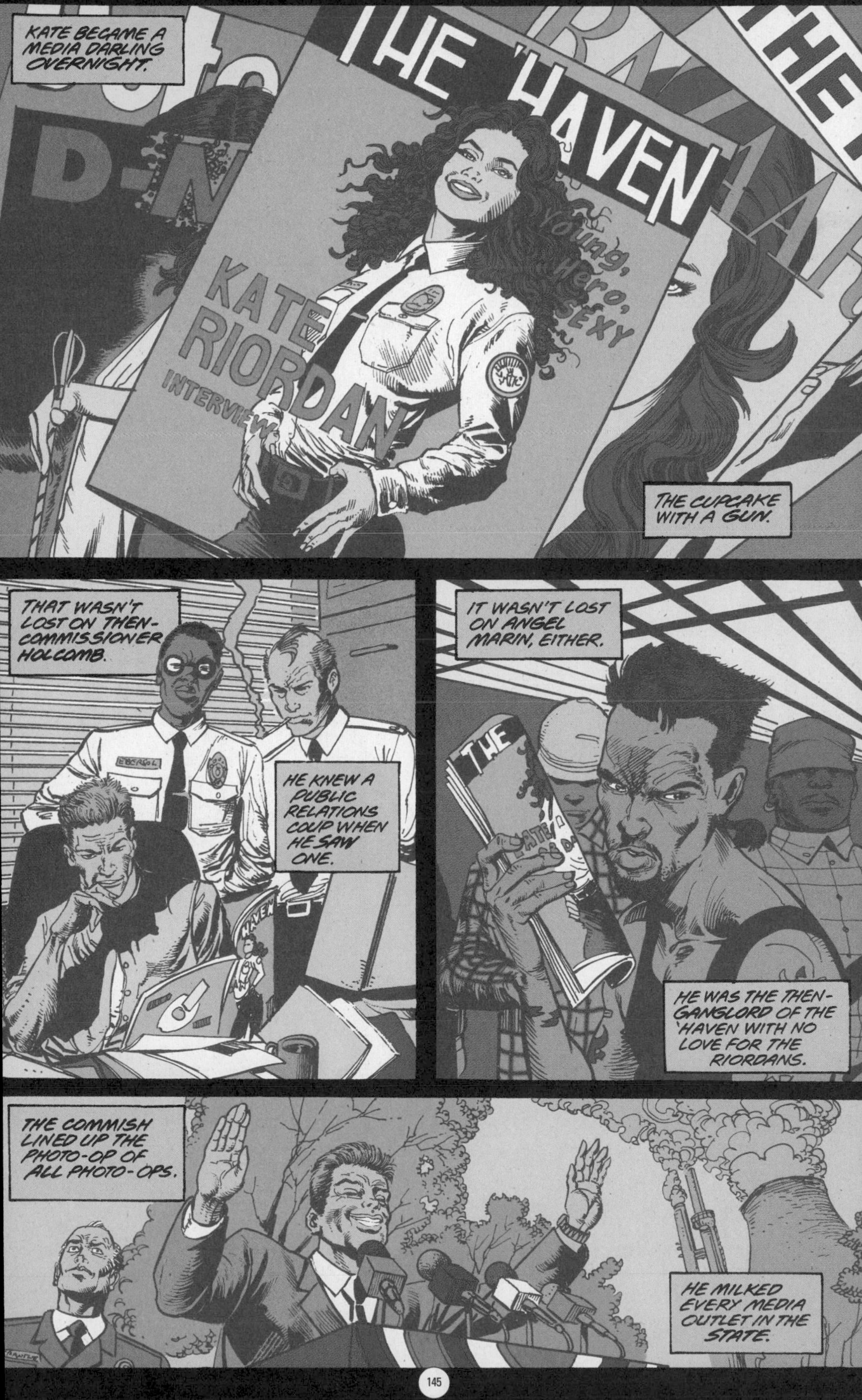
KATE BECAME A MEDIA DARLING OVERNIGHT.
THE HAVEN
KATE RIORDAN INTERVIEW
Young, hero, sexy
THE CUPCAKE WITH A GUN.
THAT WASN'T LOST ON THEN-COMMISSIONER HOLCOMB.
HE KNEW A PUBLIC RELATIONS COUP WHEN HE SAW ONE.
IT WASN'T LOST ON ANGEL MARIN, EITHER.
HE WAS THE THEN-GANGLORD OF THE 'HAVEN WITH NO LOVE FOR THE RIORDANS.
THE COMMISH LINED UP THE PHOTO-OP OF ALL PHOTO-OPS.
HE MILKED EVERY MEDIA OUTLET IN THE STATE.

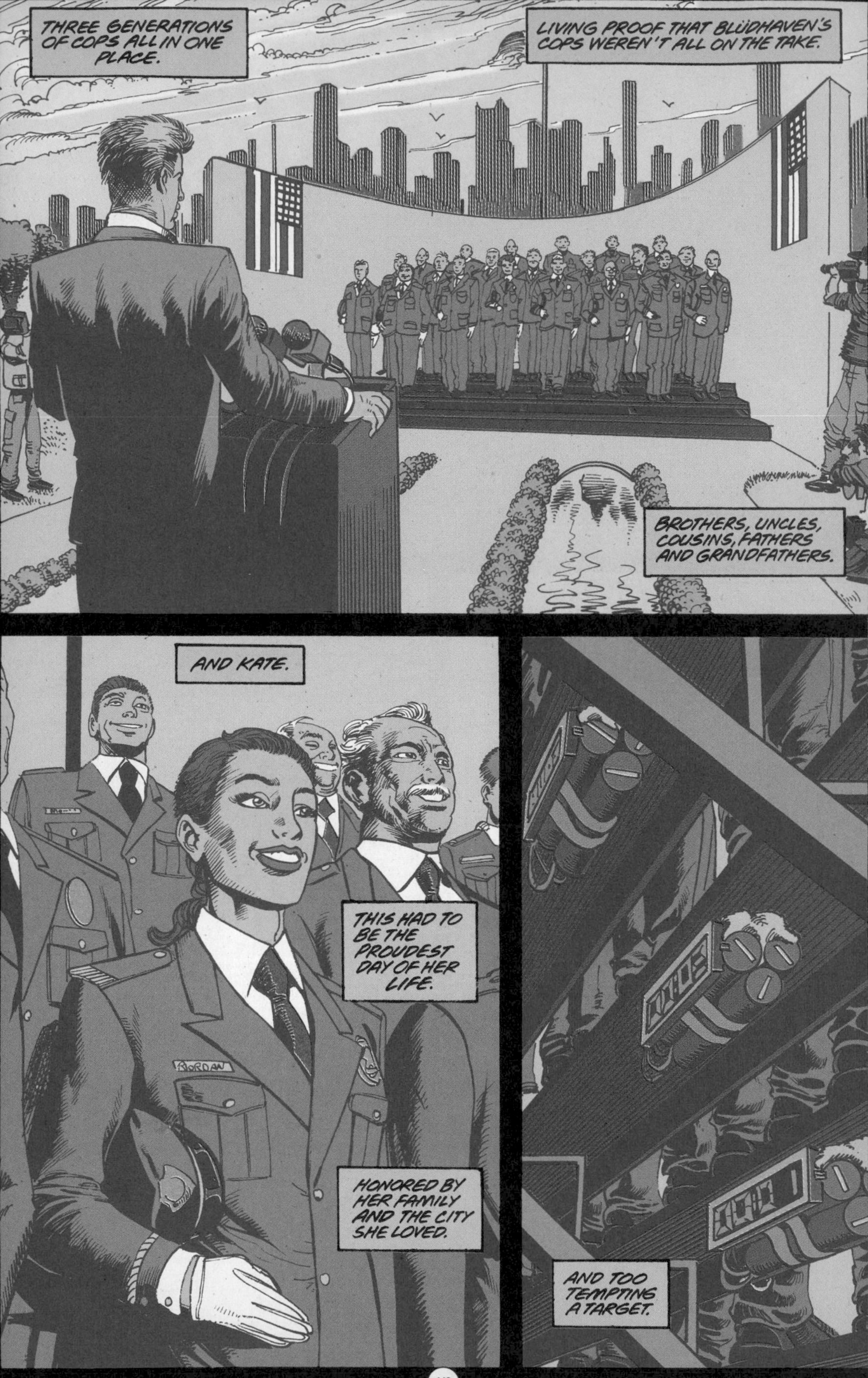

THREE GENERATIONS OF COPS ALL IN ONE PLACE.
LIVING PROOF THAT BLÜDHAVEN'S COPS WEREN'T ALL ON THE TAKE.
BROTHERS, UNCLES, COUSINS, FATHERS AND GRANDFATHERS.
AND KATE.
THIS HAD TO BE THE PROUDEST DAY OF HER LIFE.
HONORED BY HER FAMILY AND THE CITY SHE LOVED.
AND TOO TEMPTING A TARGET.

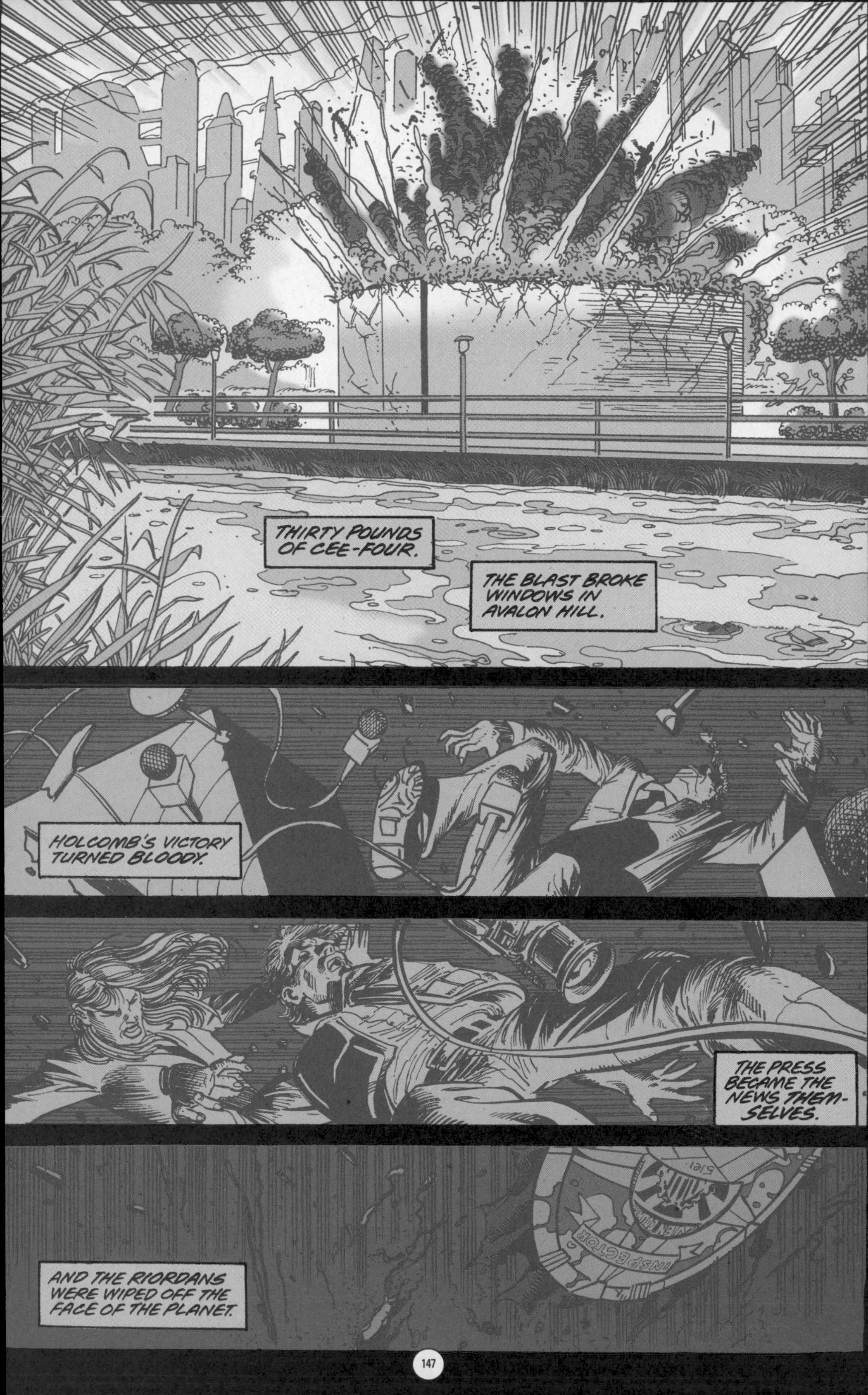
THIRTY POUNDS OF CEE-FOUR.
THE BLAST BROKE WINDOWS IN AVALON HILL.
HOLCOMB'S VICTORY TURNED BLOODY.
THE PRESS BECAME THE NEWS THEM-SELVES.
AND THE RIORDANS WERE WIPED OFF THE FACE OF THE PLANET.

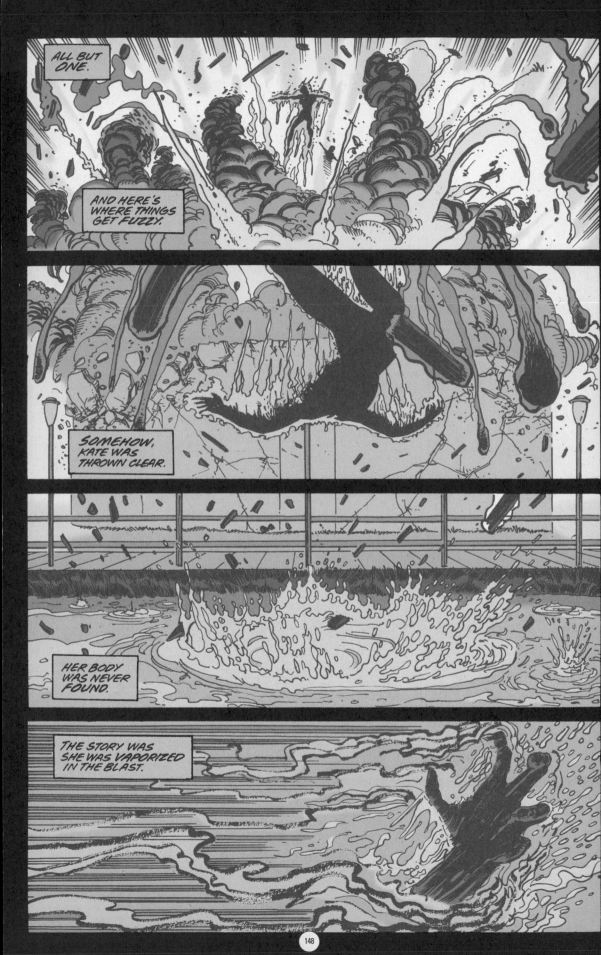

ALL BUT ONE.

AND HERE'S WHERE THINGS GET FUZZY.

SOMEHOW, KATE WAS THROWN CLEAR.

HER BODY WAS NEVER FOUND.

THE STORY WAS SHE WAS VAPORIZED IN THE BLAST.

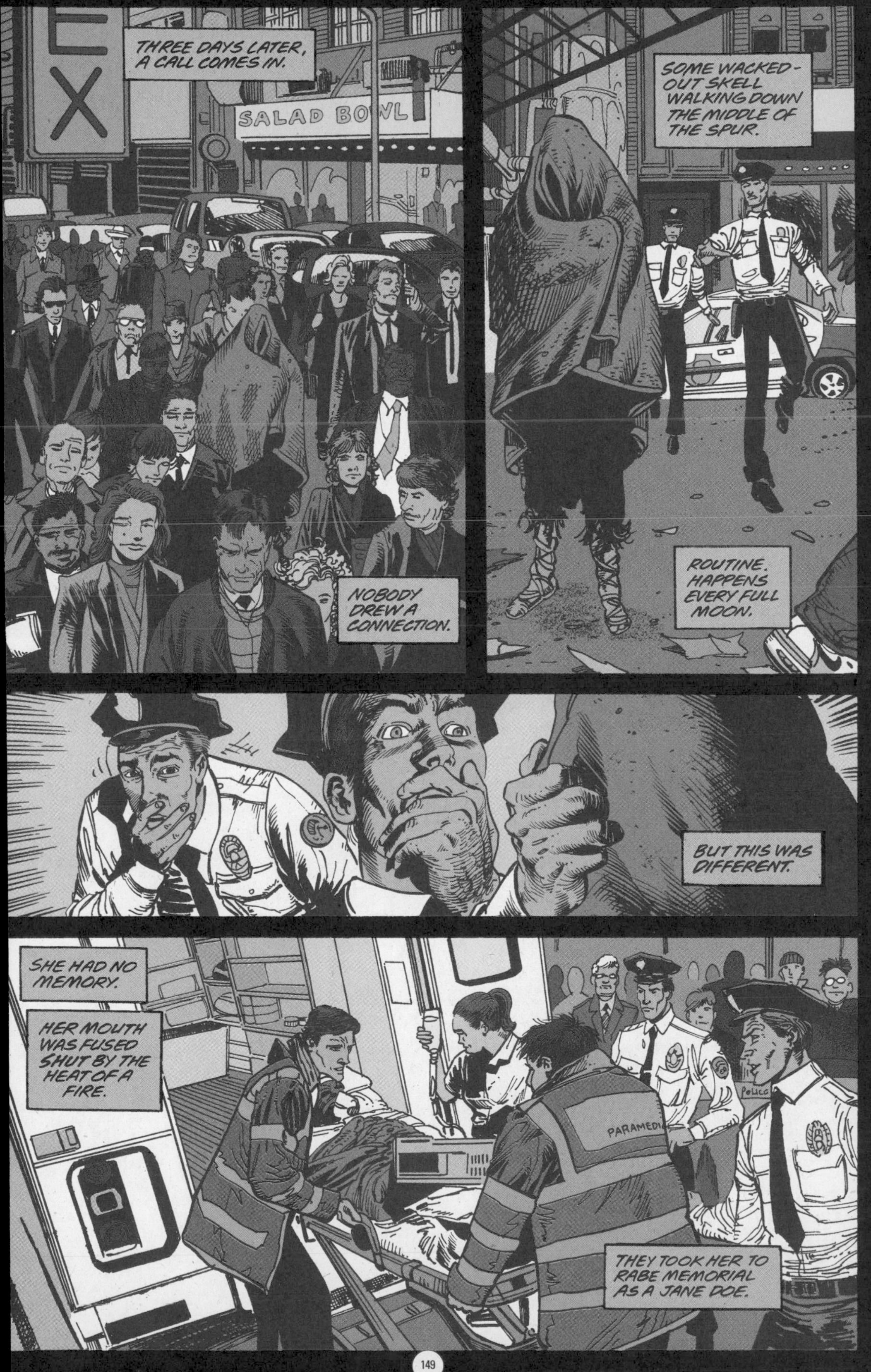
EX
THREE DAYS LATER, A CALL COMES IN.
SALAD BOWL
NOBODY DREW A CONNECTION.
SOME WACKED-OUT SKELL WALKING DOWN THE MIDDLE OF THE SPUR.
ROUTINE. HAPPENS EVERY FULL MOON.
BUT THIS WAS DIFFERENT.
SHE HAD NO MEMORY.
HER MOUTH WAS FUSED SHUT BY THE HEAT OF A FIRE.
PARAMEDI
POLICE
THEY TOOK HER TO RABE MEMORIAL AS A JANE DOE.

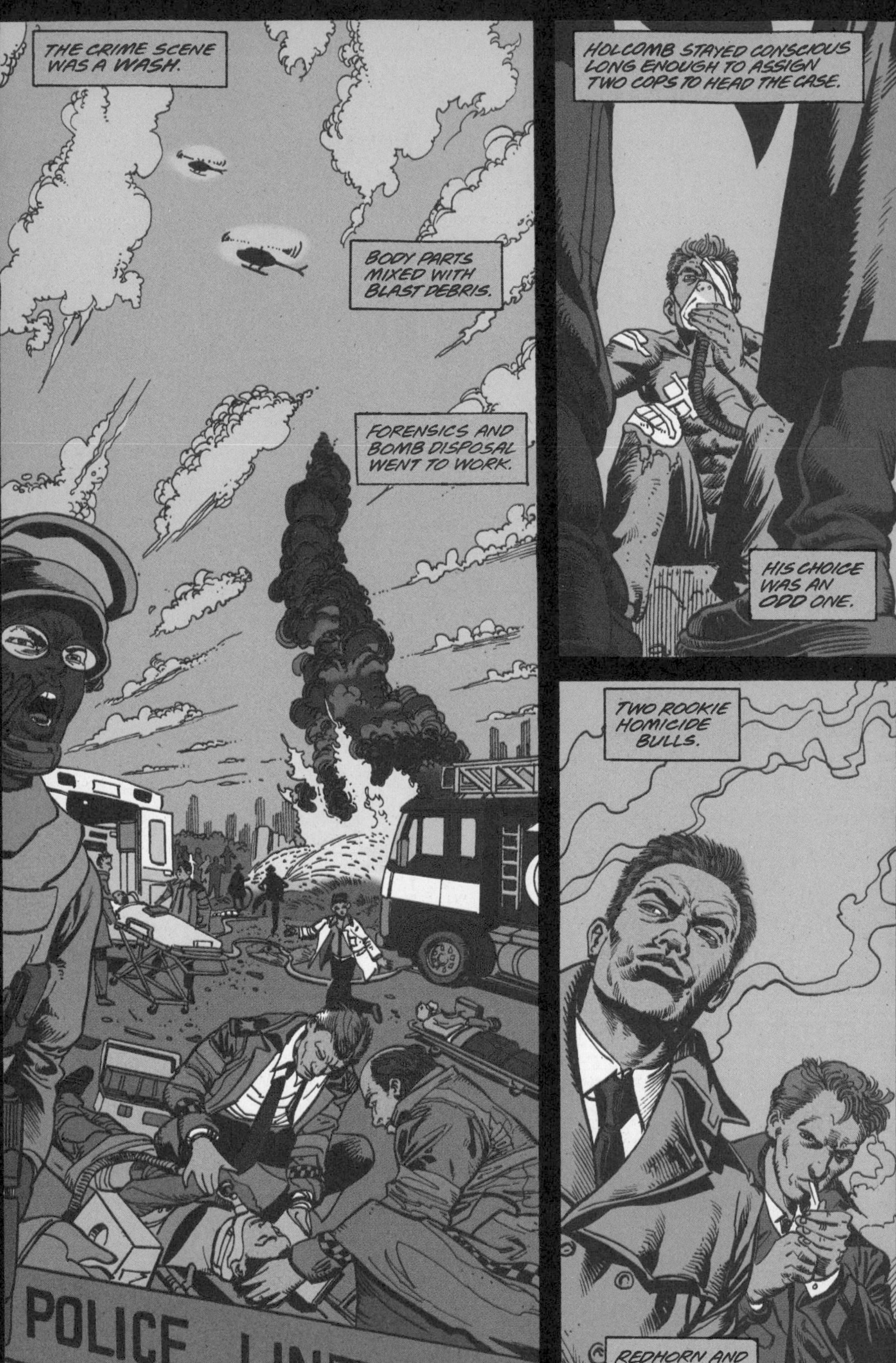
THE CRIME SCENE WAS A WASH.
BODY PARTS MIXED WITH BLAST DEBRIS.
FORENSICS AND BOMB DISPOSAL WENT TO WORK.
POLICE LINE DON
HOLCOMB STAYED CONSCIOUS LONG ENOUGH TO ASSIGN TWO COPS TO HEAD THE CASE.
HIS CHOICE WAS AN ODD ONE.
TWO ROOKIE HOMICIDE BULLS.
REDHORN AND SOAMES.

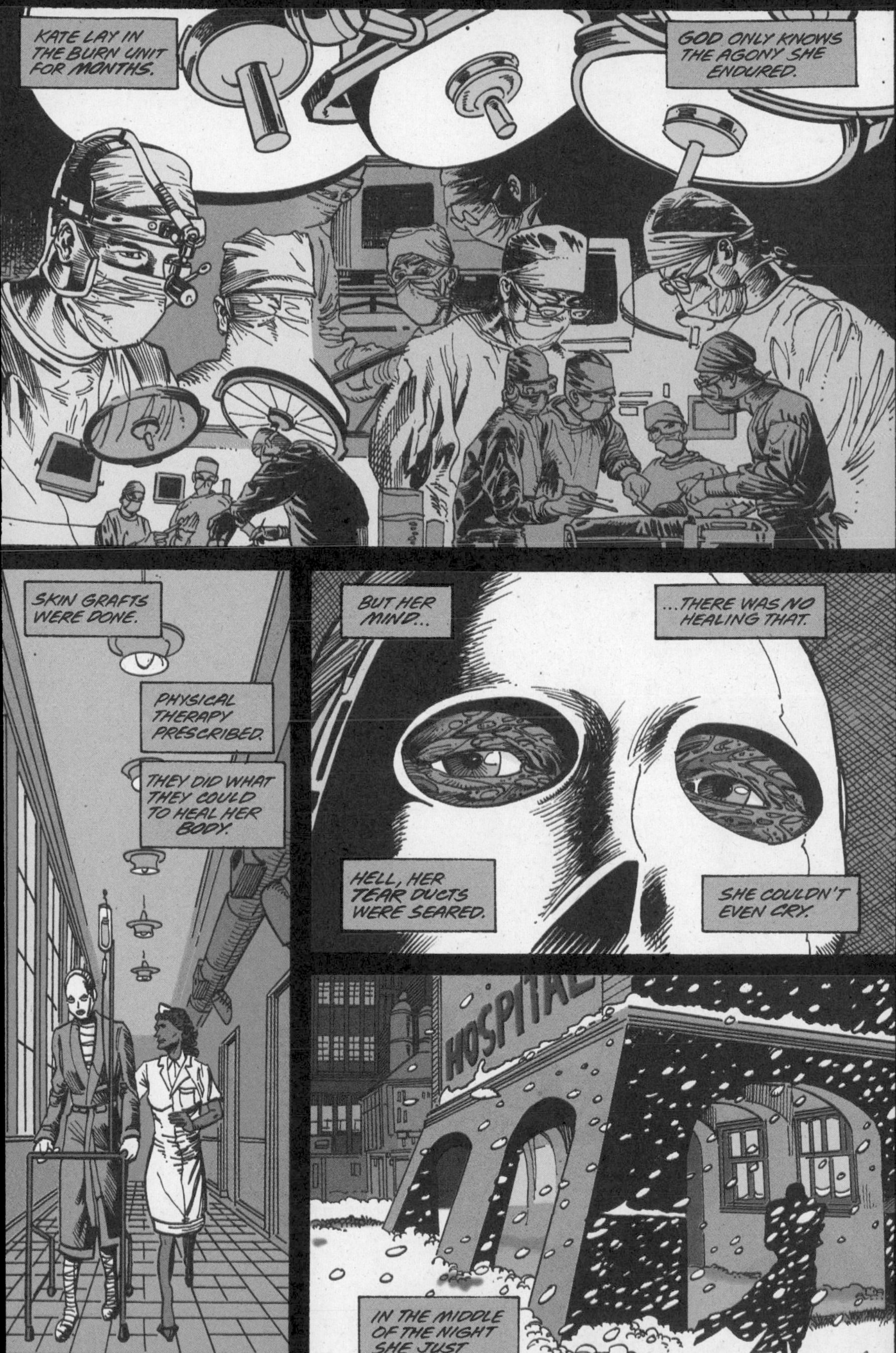
KATE LAY IN THE BURN UNIT FOR MONTHS.
GOD ONLY KNOWS THE AGONY SHE ENDURED.
SKIN GRAFTS WERE DONE.
PHYSICAL THERAPY PRESCRIBED.
THEY DID WHAT THEY COULD TO HEAL HER BODY.
BUT HER MIND...
...THERE WAS NO HEALING THAT.
HELL, HER TEAR DUCTS WERE SEARED.
SHE COULDN'T EVEN CRY.
HOSPITAL
IN THE MIDDLE OF THE NIGHT SHE JUST WALKED AWAY.

SOMEHOW THE SMALL AMOUNT OF PRINTS LEFT ON KATE'S HANDS WOUND UP IN FORENSICS.

RABE'S JANE DOE WAS A MATCH FOR KATE RIORDAN.

REDHORN AND SOAMES WERE TOO LATE.

BAD LUCK FOR THEM. GOOD LUCK FOR KATE.

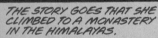

THE STORY GOES THAT SHE CLIMBED TO A MONASTERY IN THE HIMALAYAS.

OR THAT SHE WENT TO HAITI AND VISITED A VOODOO PRIEST.

OR THAT SHE VOLUNTEERED FOR EXPERIMENTS WITH REPTILE EMBRYOS AND RADIATION.

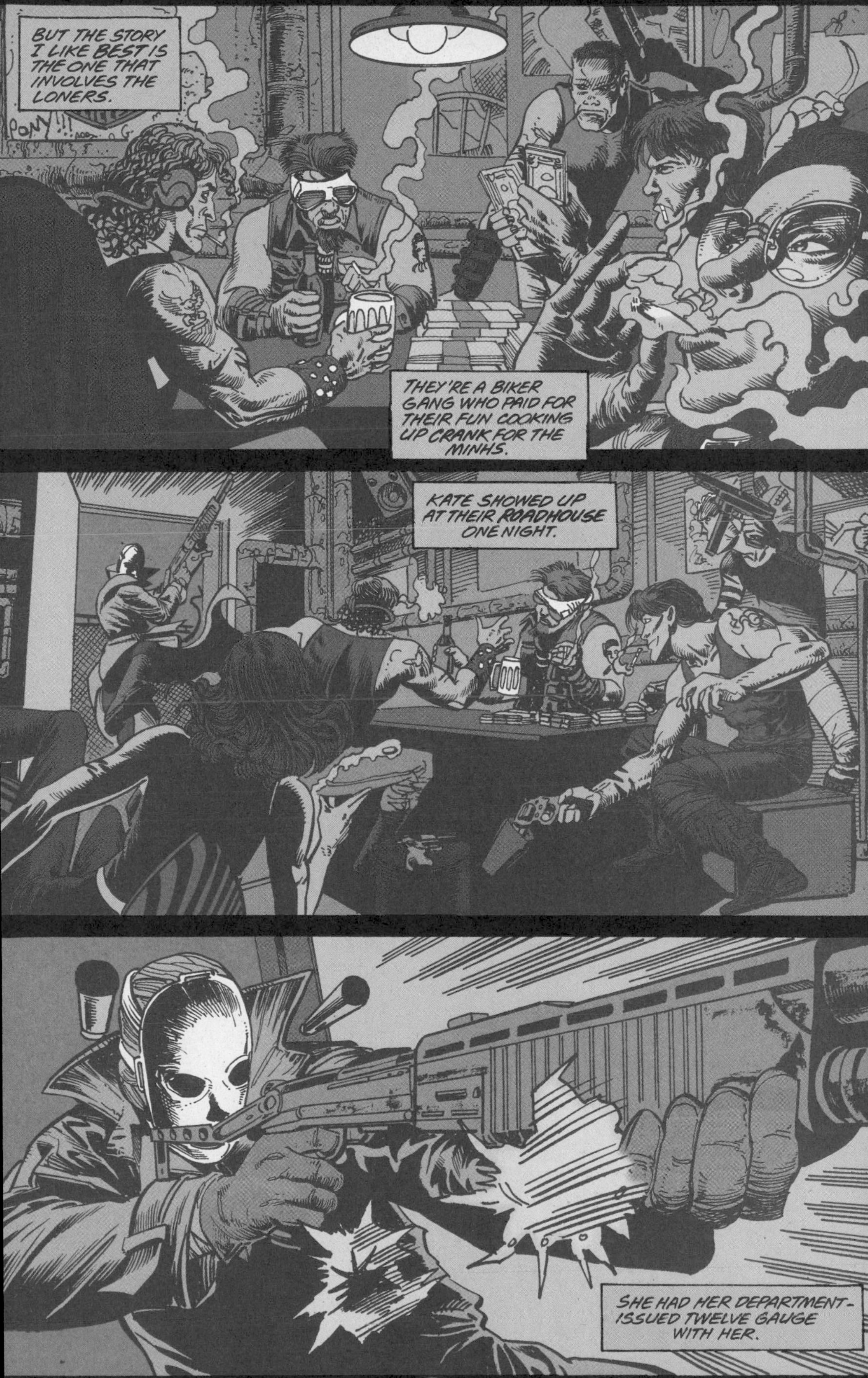
BUT THE STORY I LIKE BEST IS THE ONE THAT INVOLVES THE LONERS.
THEY'RE A BIKER GANG WHO PAID FOR THEIR FUN COOKING UP CRANK FOR THE MINHS.
KATE SHOWED UP AT THEIR ROADHOUSE ONE NIGHT.
SHE HAD HER DEPARTMENT-ISSUED TWELVE GAUGE WITH HER.

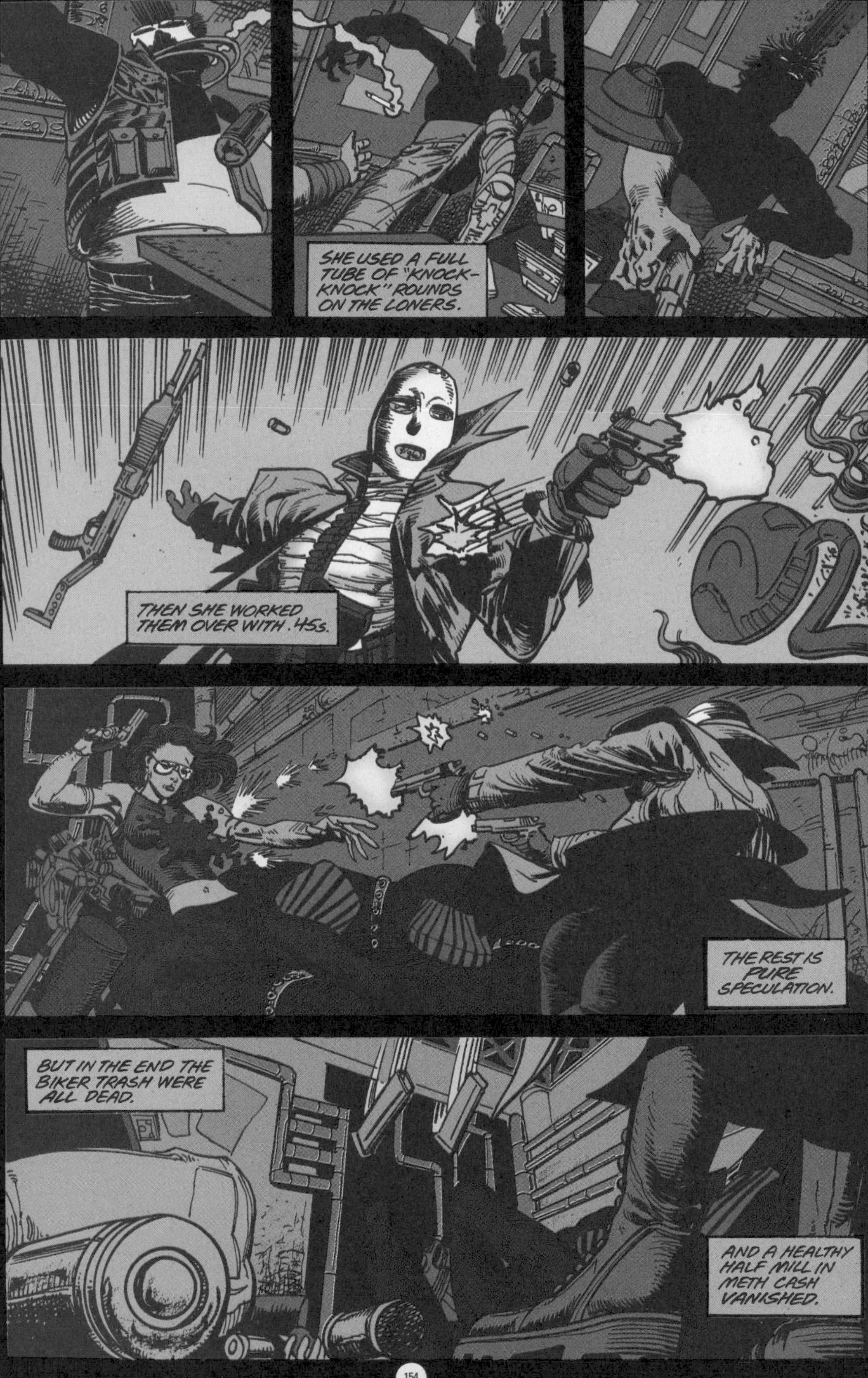
SHE USED A FULL TUBE OF "KNOCK-KNOCK" ROUNDS ON THE LONERS.
THEN SHE WORKED THEM OVER WITH .45s.
THE REST IS PURE SPECULATION.
BUT IN THE END THE BIKER TRASH WERE ALL DEAD.
AND A HEALTHY HALF MILL IN METH CASH VANISHED.

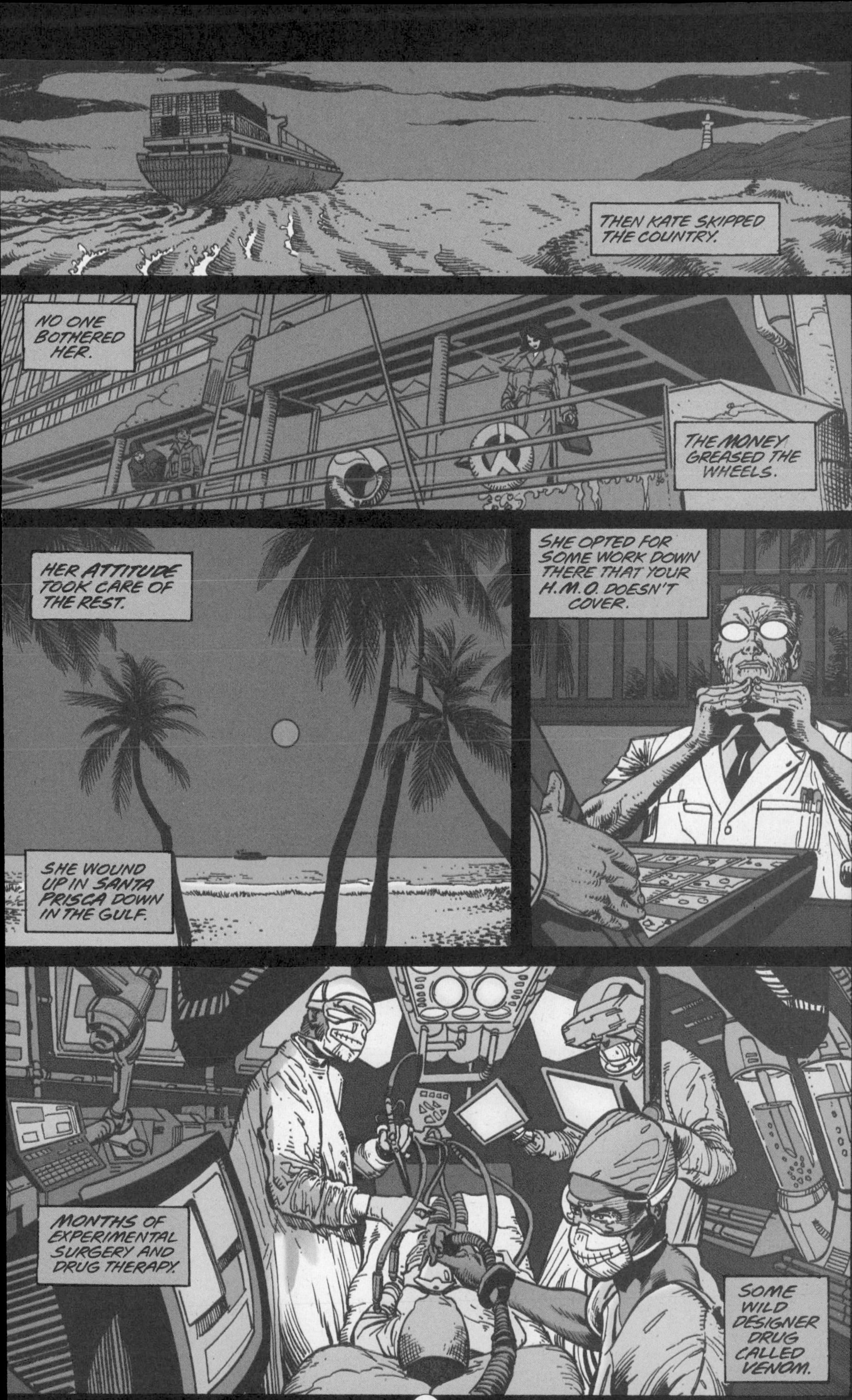
THEN KATE SKIPPED THE COUNTRY.
NO ONE BOTHERED HER.
THE MONEY GREASED THE WHEELS.
HER ATTITUDE TOOK CARE OF THE REST.
SHE WOUND UP IN SANTA PRISCA DOWN IN THE GULF.
SHE OPTED FOR SOME WORK DOWN THERE THAT YOUR H.M.O. DOESN'T COVER.
MONTHS OF EXPERIMENTAL SURGERY AND DRUG THERAPY.
SOME WILD DESIGNER DRUG CALLED VENOM.

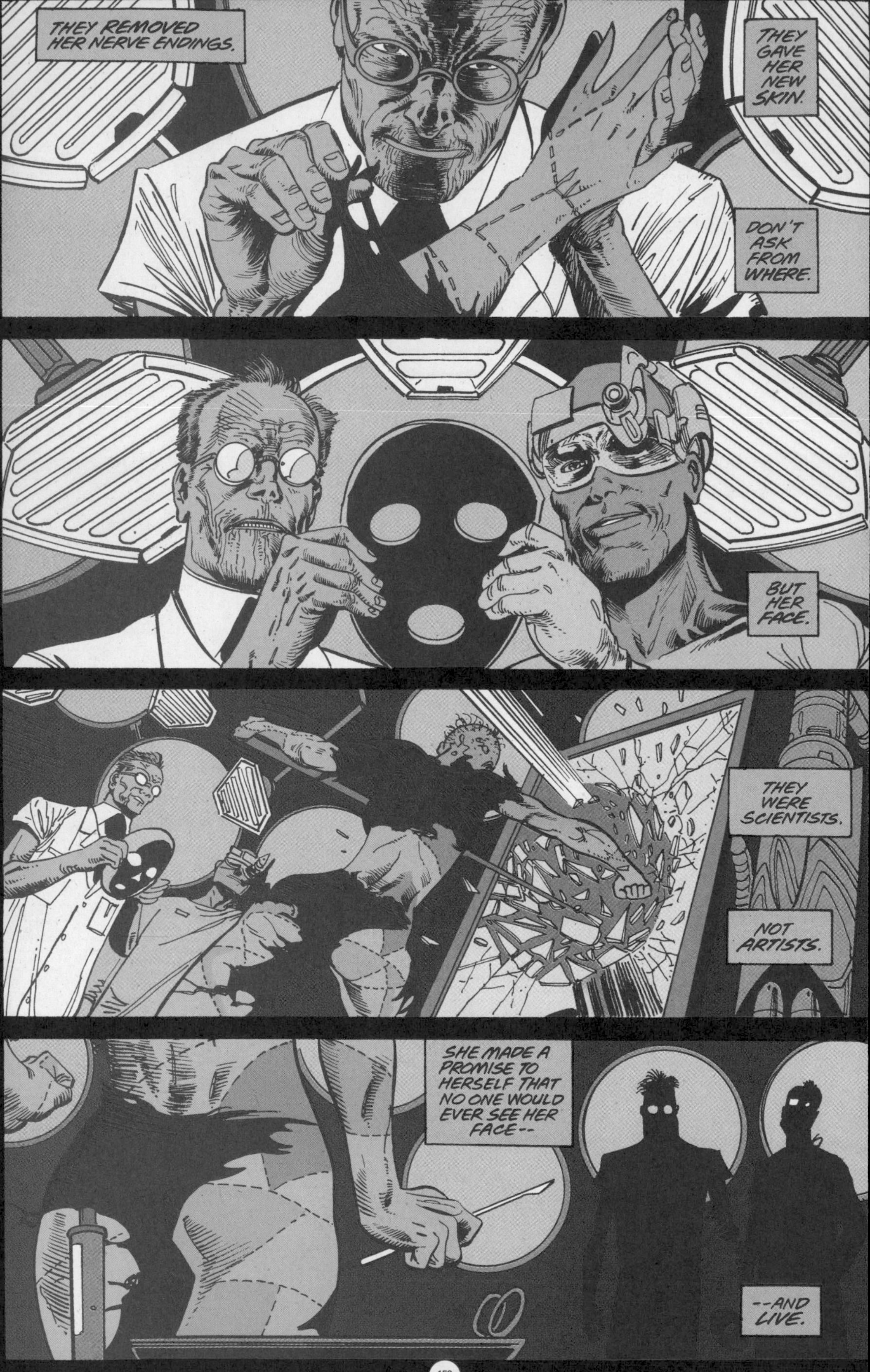
THEY REMOVED HER NERVE ENDINGS.
THEY GAVE HER NEW SKIN.
DON'T ASK FROM WHERE.
BUT HER FACE.
THEY WERE SCIENTISTS.
NOT ARTISTS.
SHE MADE A PROMISE TO HERSELF THAT NO ONE WOULD EVER SEE HER FACE--
--AND LIVE.

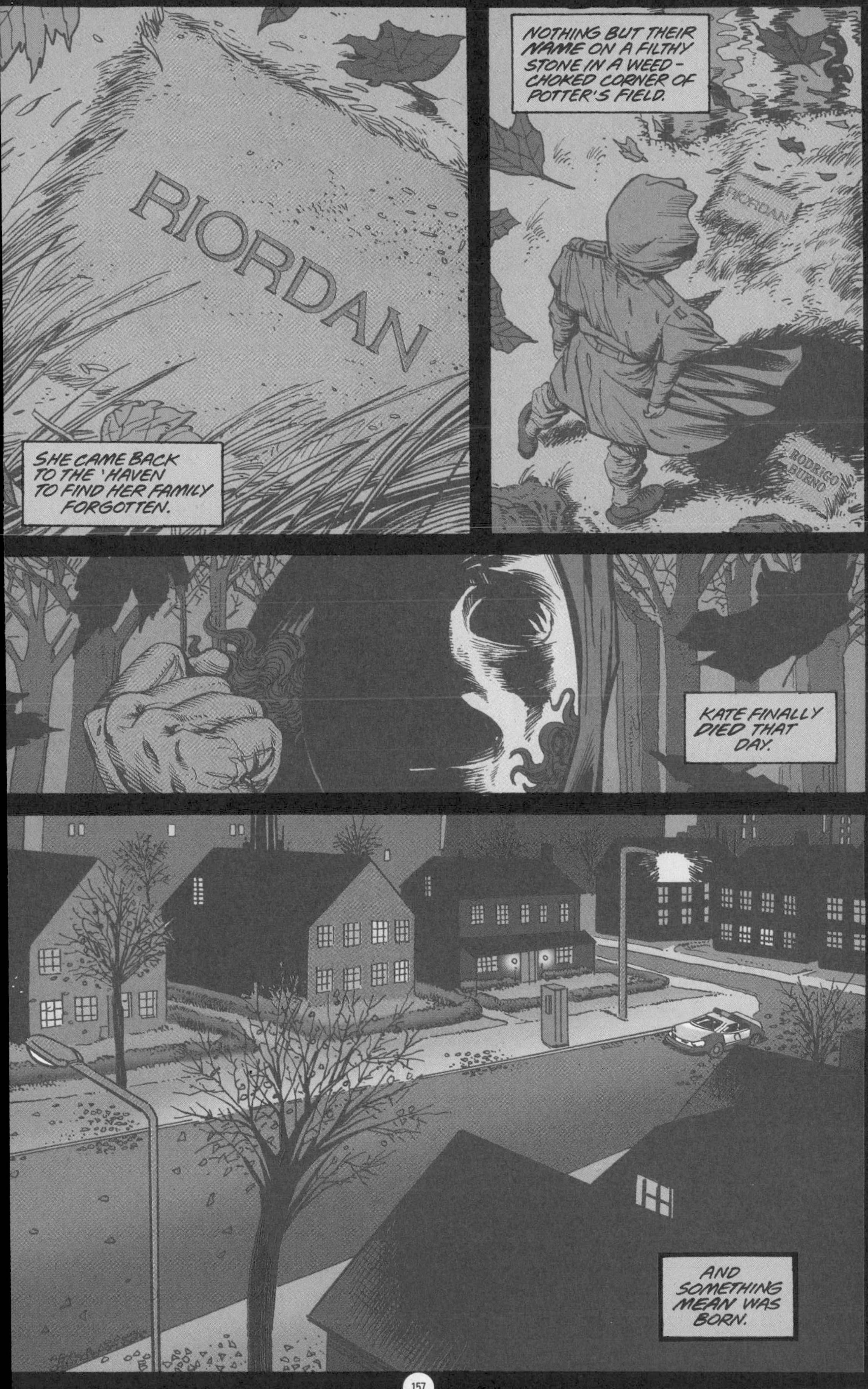
RIORDAN
SHE CAME BACK TO THE 'HAVEN TO FIND HER FAMILY FORGOTTEN.
NOTHING BUT THEIR NAME ON A FILTHY STONE IN A WEED-CHOKED CORNER OF POTTER'S FIELD.
RIORDAN
RODRIGO BUENO
KATE FINALLY DIED THAT DAY.
AND SOMETHING MEAN WAS BORN.

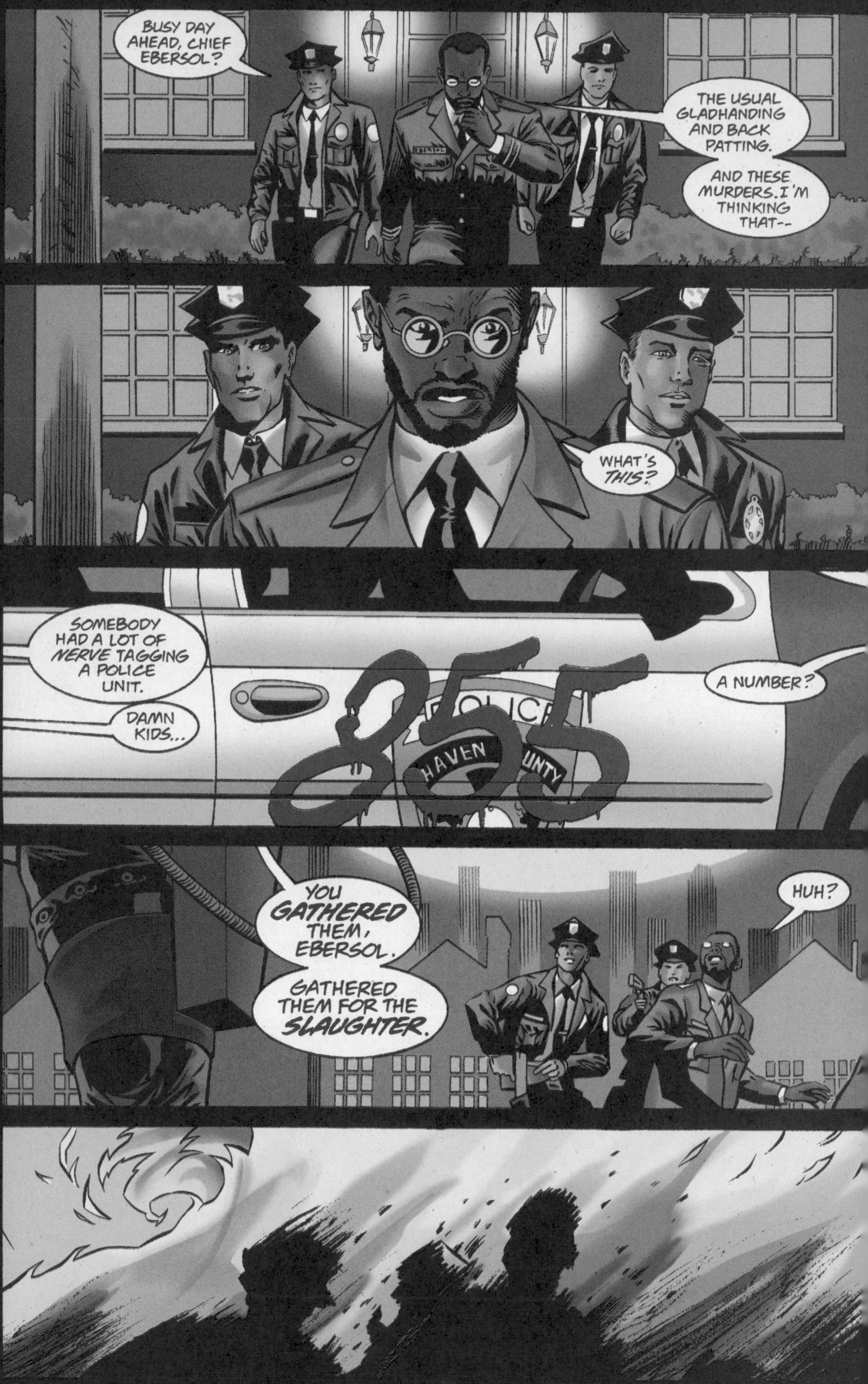
BUSY DAY AHEAD, CHIEF EBERSOL?
THE USUAL GLADHANDING AND BACK PATTING.
AND THESE MURDERS. I'M THINKING THAT--
WHAT'S *THIS*?
SOMEBODY HAD A LOT OF *NERVE* TAGGING A POLICE UNIT.
DAMN KIDS...
A NUMBER?
855
POLICE
HAVEN
UNTY
YOU **GATHERED** THEM, EBERSOL.
GATHERED THEM FOR THE ***SLAUGHTER***.
HUH?

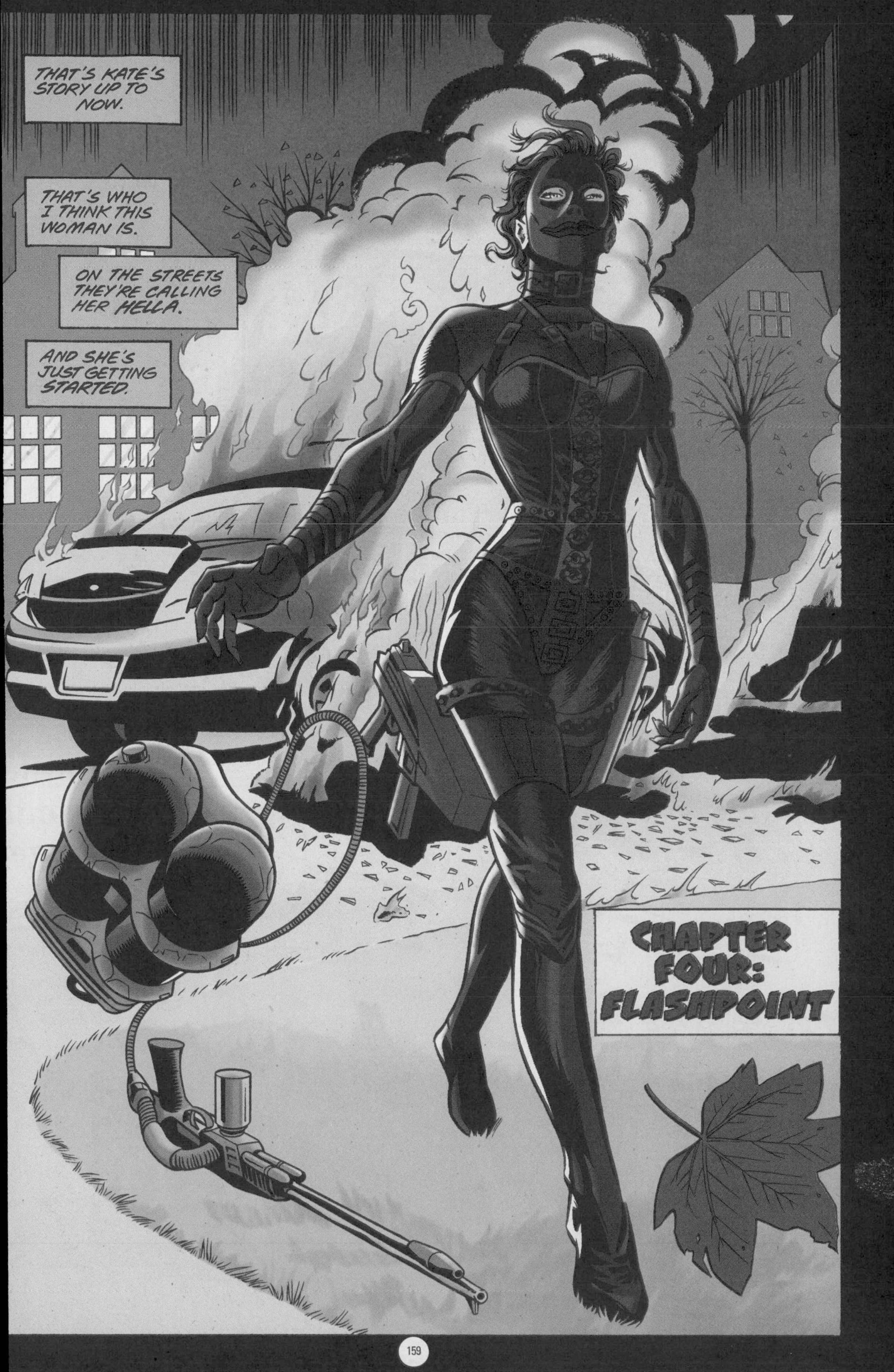
THAT'S KATE'S STORY UP TO NOW.
THAT'S WHO I THINK THIS WOMAN IS.
ON THE STREETS THEY'RE CALLING HER HELLA.
AND SHE'S JUST GETTING STARTED.
CHAPTER FOUR: FLASHPOINT

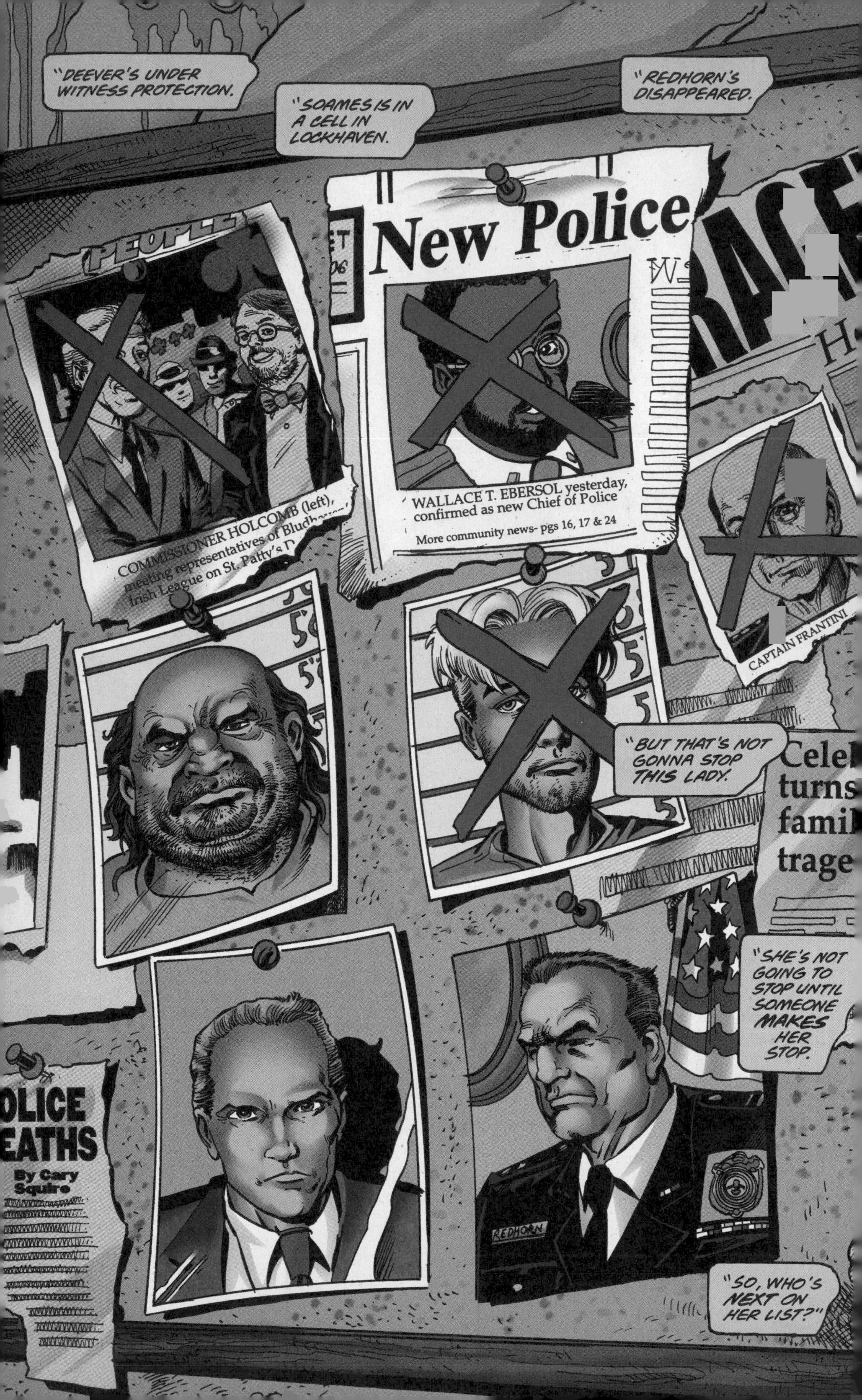
"DEEVER'S UNDER WITNESS PROTECTION.
"SOAMES IS IN A CELL IN LOCKHAVEN.
"REDHORN'S DISAPPEARED.
PEOPLE
New Police
COMMISSIONER HOLCOMB (left), meeting representatives of
Irish League on St. Patty's
WALLACE T. EBERSOL yesterday, confirmed as new Chief of Police
More community news- pgs 16, 17 & 24
CAPTAIN FRANTINI
"BUT THAT'S NOT GONNA STOP THIS LADY.
"SHE'S NOT GOING TO STOP UNTIL SOMEONE MAKES HER STOP.
By Cary Squire
REDHORN
"SO, WHO'S NEXT ON HER LIST?"

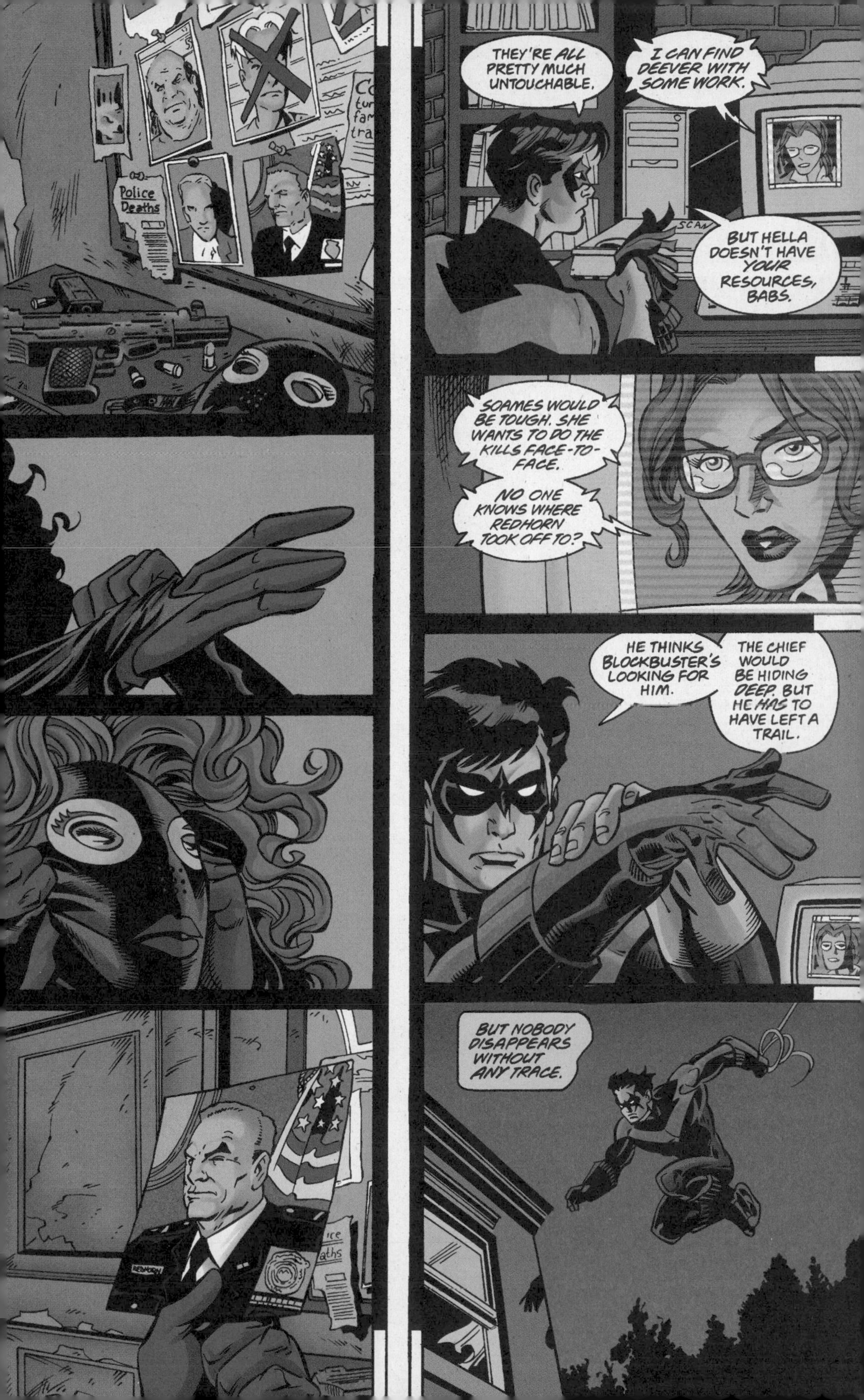
Police Deaths
THEY'RE *ALL* PRETTY MUCH UNTOUCHABLE.
I CAN FIND DEEVER WITH SOME WORK.
SCAN
BUT HELLA DOESN'T HAVE *YOUR* RESOURCES, BABS.
SOAMES WOULD BE TOUGH. SHE WANTS TO DO THE KILLS FACE-TO-FACE.
NO ONE KNOWS WHERE REDHORN TOOK OFF TO?
HE THINKS BLOCKBUSTER'S LOOKING FOR HIM.
THE CHIEF WOULD BE HIDING *DEEP*. BUT HE *HAS* TO HAVE LEFT A TRAIL.
REDHORN
BUT NOBODY DISAPPEARS WITHOUT ANY TRACE.

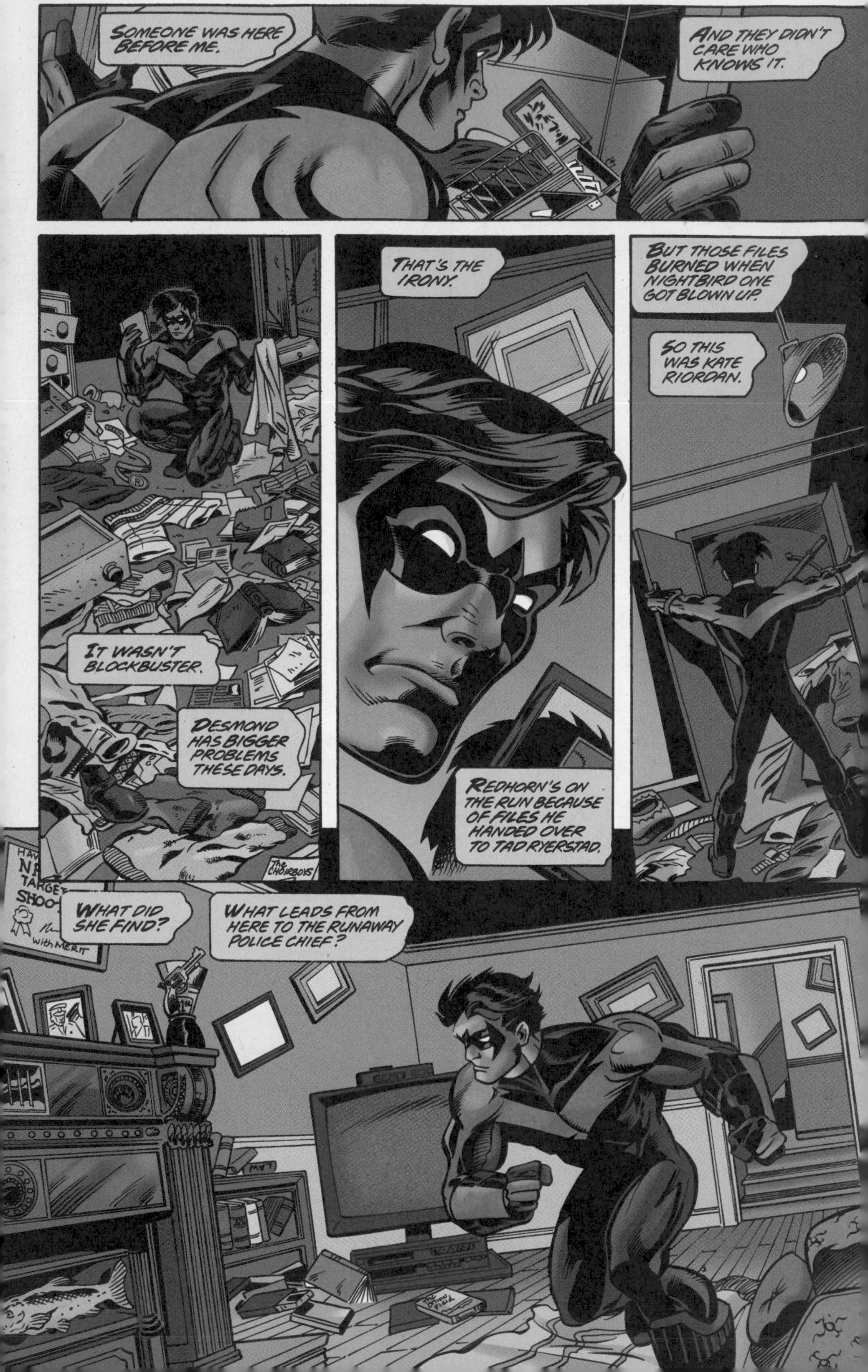
SOMEONE WAS HERE BEFORE ME.
AND THEY DIDN'T CARE WHO KNOWS IT.
IT WASN'T BLOCKBUSTER.
DESMOND HAS BIGGER PROBLEMS THESE DAYS.
THE CHOIRBOYS
THAT'S THE IRONY.
REDHORN'S ON THE RUN BECAUSE OF FILES HE HANDED OVER TO TAD RYERSTAD.
BUT THOSE FILES BURNED WHEN NIGHTBIRD ONE GOT BLOWN UP.
SO THIS WAS KATE RIORDAN.
WHAT DID SHE FIND?
WHAT LEADS FROM HERE TO THE RUNAWAY POLICE CHIEF?
with MERIT
LAW

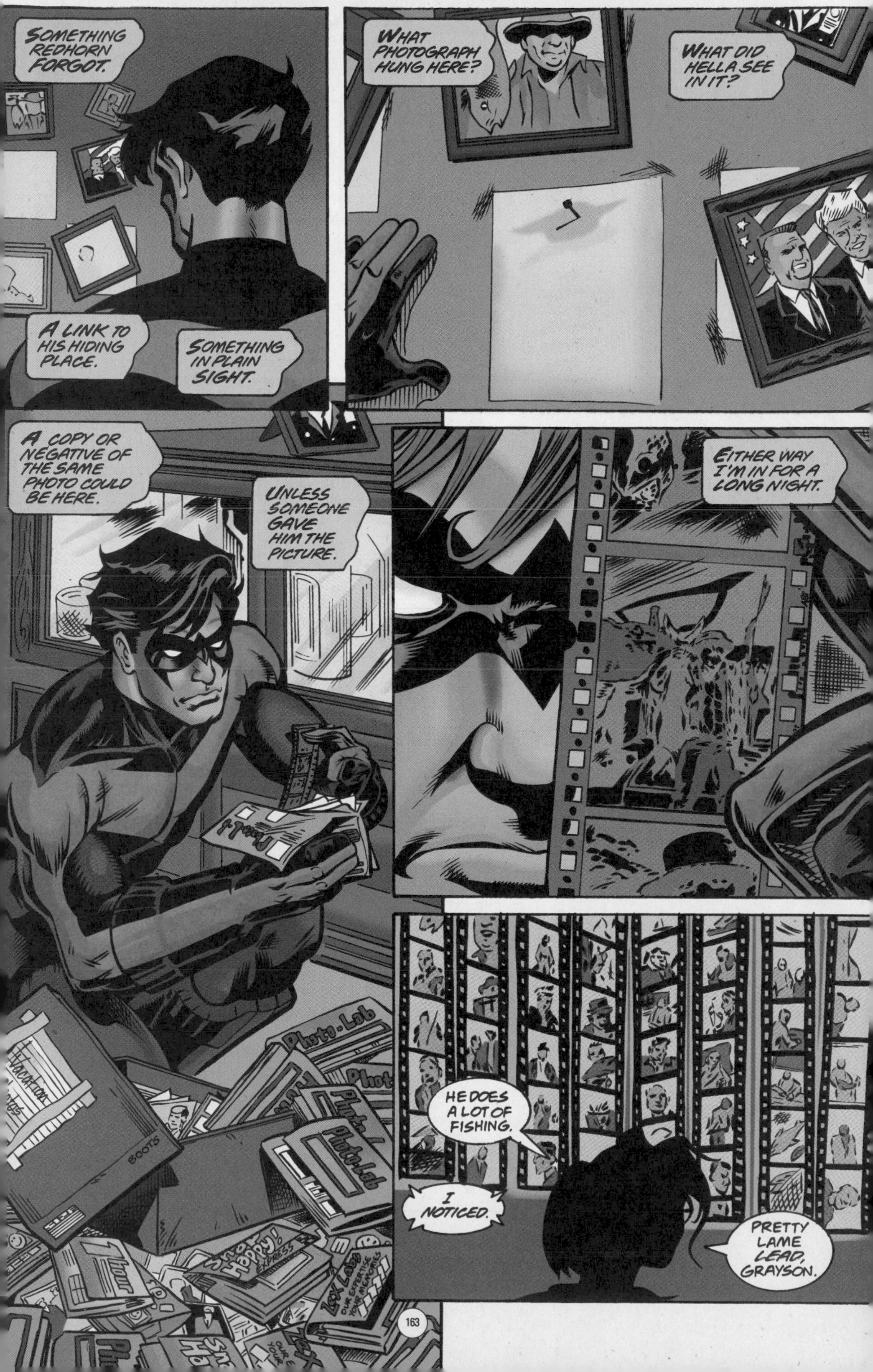
SOMETHING REDHORN FORGOT.
A LINK TO HIS HIDING PLACE.
SOMETHING IN PLAIN SIGHT.
WHAT PHOTOGRAPH HUNG HERE?
WHAT DID HELLA SEE IN IT?
A COPY OR NEGATIVE OF THE SAME PHOTO COULD BE HERE.
UNLESS SOMEONE GAVE HIM THE PICTURE.
EITHER WAY I'M IN FOR A LONG NIGHT.
HE DOES A LOT OF FISHING.
I NOTICED.
PRETTY LAME LEAD, GRAYSON.
Photo-Lab
BOOTS
1 Hour
Snap Happy! EXPRESS
Lex Labs OUR EXPERTISE YOUR MEMORIES

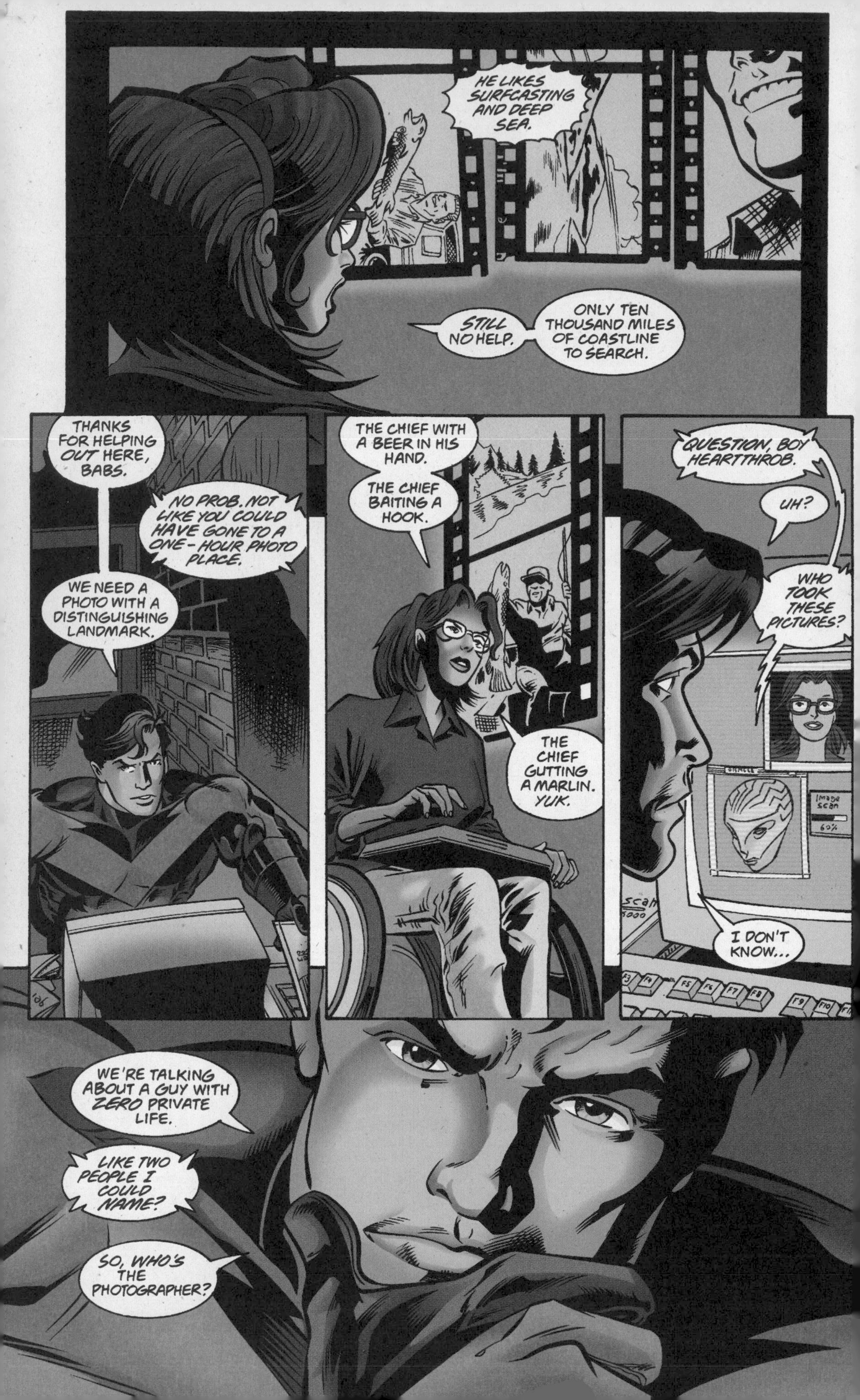
HE LIKES SURFCASTING AND DEEP SEA.
STILL NO HELP.
ONLY TEN THOUSAND MILES OF COASTLINE TO SEARCH.
THANKS FOR HELPING OUT HERE, BABS.
NO PROB. NOT LIKE YOU COULD HAVE GONE TO A ONE-HOUR PHOTO PLACE.
WE NEED A PHOTO WITH A DISTINGUISHING LANDMARK.
THE CHIEF WITH A BEER IN HIS HAND.
THE CHIEF BAITING A HOOK.
THE CHIEF GUTTING A MARLIN. YUK.
QUESTION, BOY HEARTTHROB.
UH?
WHO TOOK THESE PICTURES?
I DON'T KNOW...
WE'RE TALKING ABOUT A GUY WITH ZERO PRIVATE LIFE.
LIKE TWO PEOPLE I COULD NAME?
SO, WHO'S THE PHOTOGRAPHER?

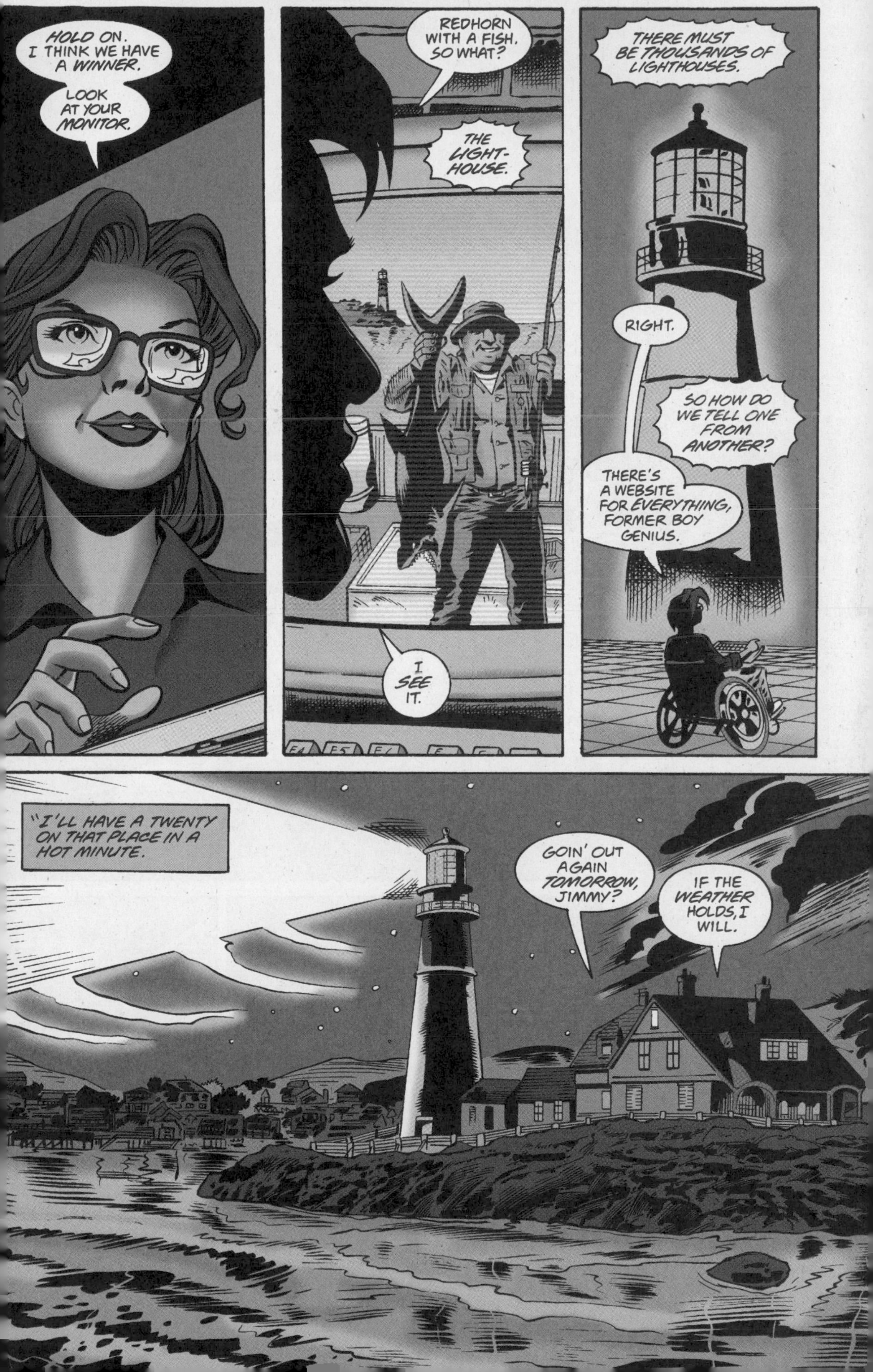
HOLD ON. I THINK WE HAVE A WINNER.
LOOK AT YOUR MONITOR.
REDHORN WITH A FISH. SO WHAT?
THE LIGHT-HOUSE.
I SEE IT.
THERE MUST BE THOUSANDS OF LIGHTHOUSES.
RIGHT.
SO HOW DO WE TELL ONE FROM ANOTHER?
THERE'S A WEBSITE FOR EVERYTHING, FORMER BOY GENIUS.
"I'LL HAVE A TWENTY ON THAT PLACE IN A HOT MINUTE.
GOIN' OUT AGAIN TOMORROW, JIMMY?
IF THE WEATHER HOLDS, I WILL.

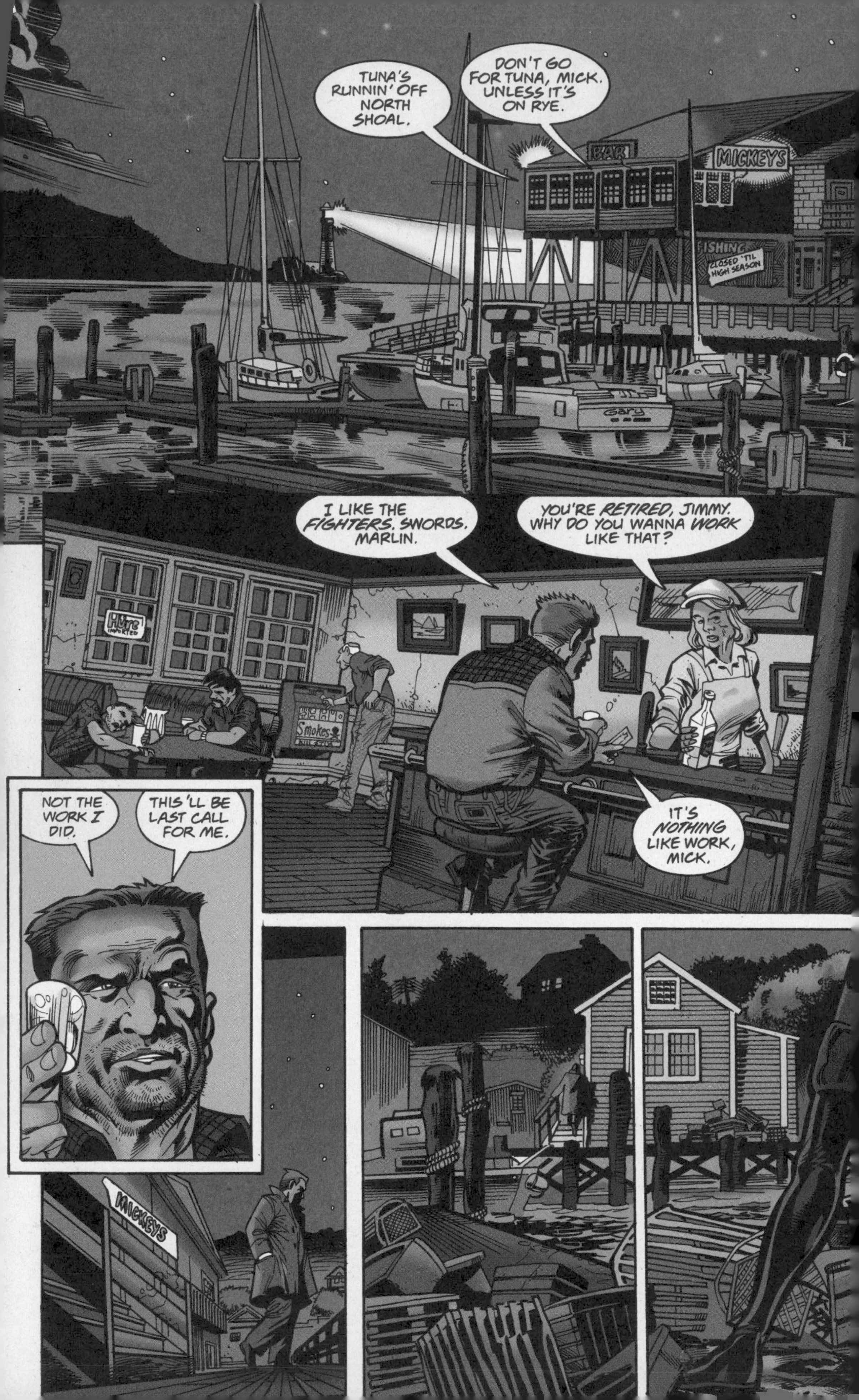
TUNA'S RUNNIN' OFF NORTH SHOAL.
DON'T GO FOR TUNA, MICK. UNLESS IT'S ON RYE.
BAR
MICKEYS
FISHING
CLOSED 'TIL HIGH SEASON
I LIKE THE FIGHTERS. SWORDS. MARLIN.
YOU'RE RETIRED, JIMMY. WHY DO YOU WANNA WORK LIKE THAT?
Smokes
IT'S NOTHING LIKE WORK, MICK.
NOT THE WORK I DID.
THIS'LL BE LAST CALL FOR ME.
MICKEYS

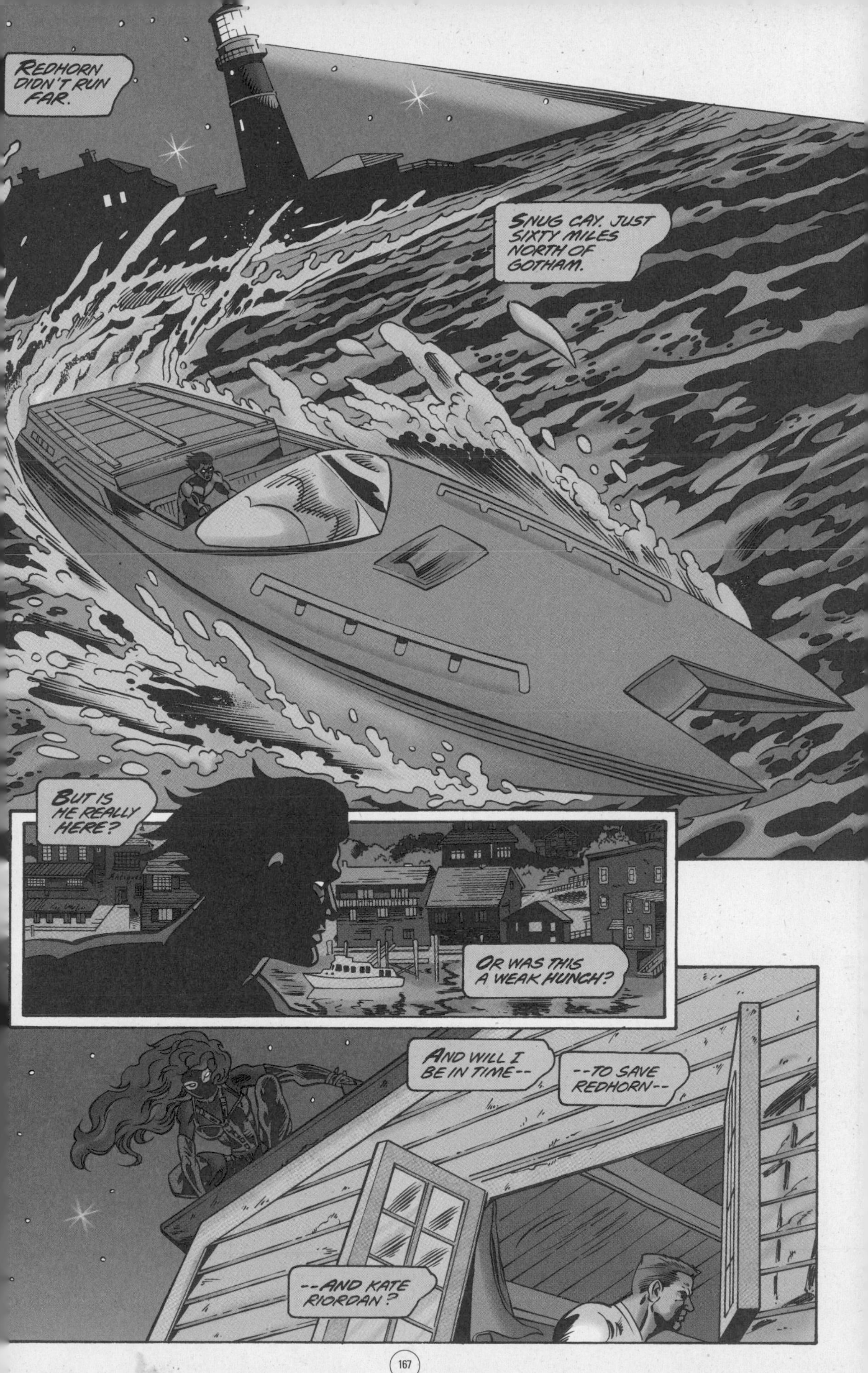
REDHORN DIDN'T RUN FAR.
SNUG CAY. JUST SIXTY MILES NORTH OF GOTHAM.
BUT IS HE REALLY HERE?
OR WAS THIS A WEAK HUNCH?
AND WILL I BE IN TIME--
--TO SAVE REDHORN--
--AND KATE RIORDAN?

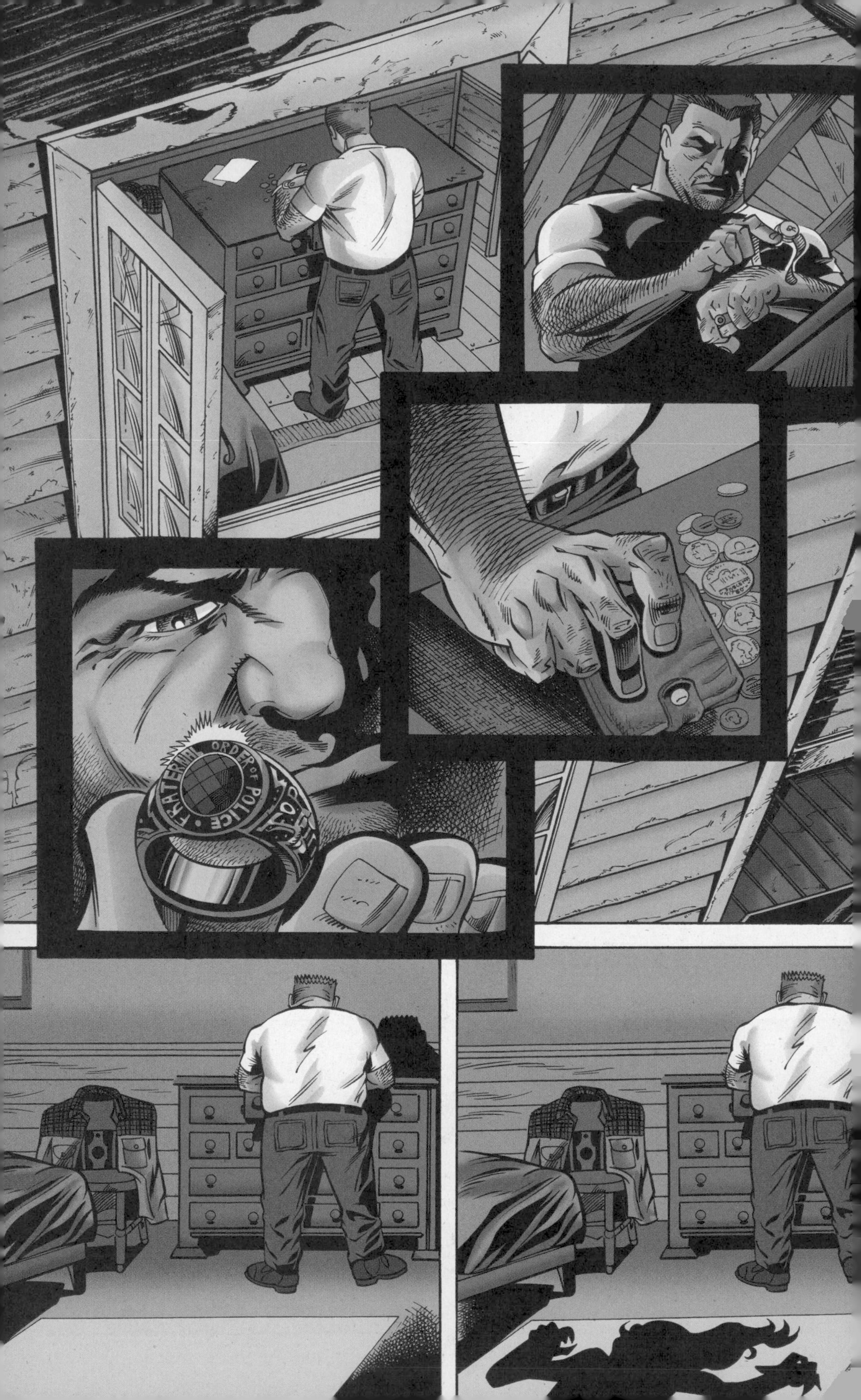
ORDER OF POLICE

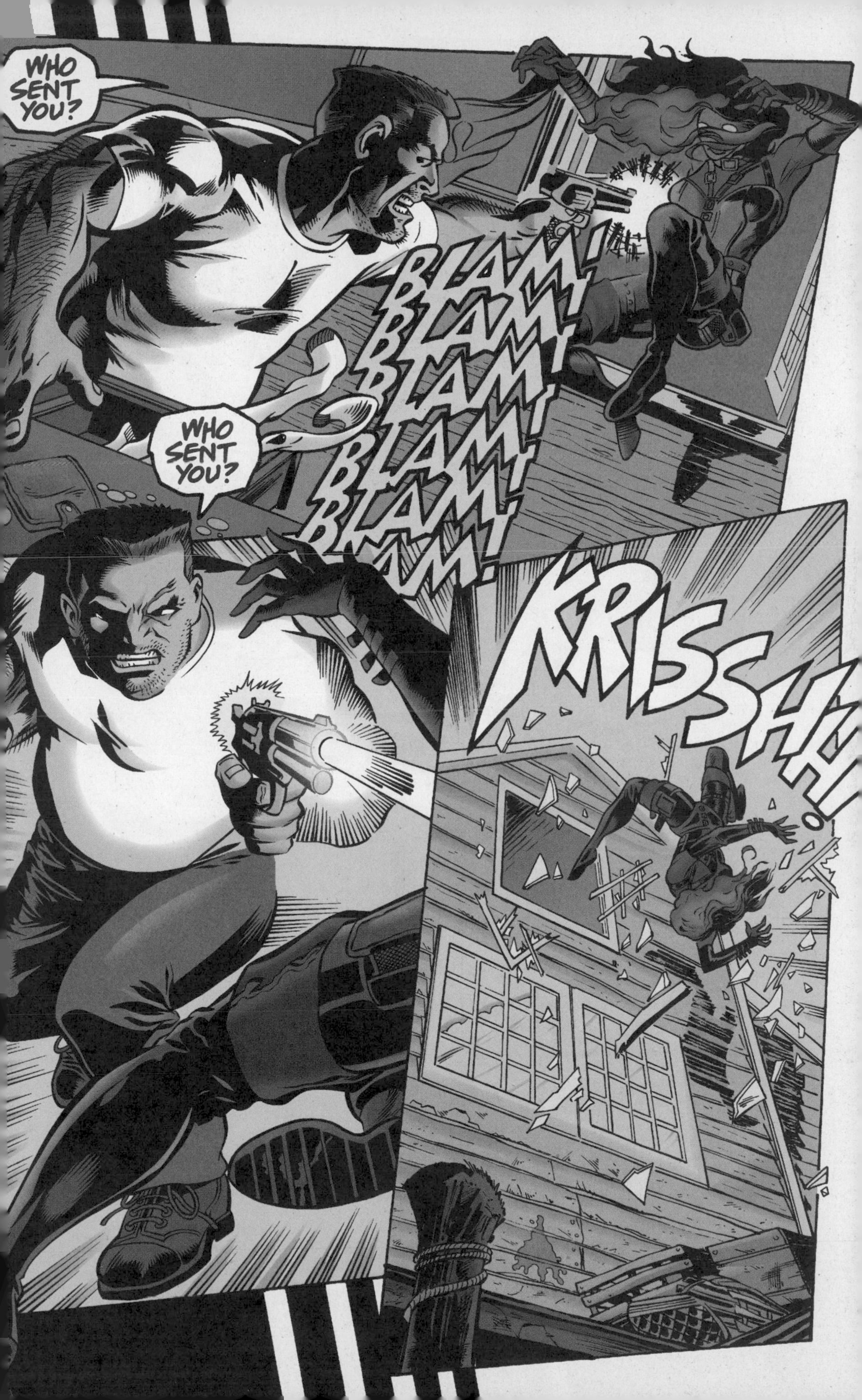
WHO SENT YOU?
WHO SENT YOU?
BLAM! BLAM! BLAM! BLAM! BLAM! BLAM!
KRISSSH!!

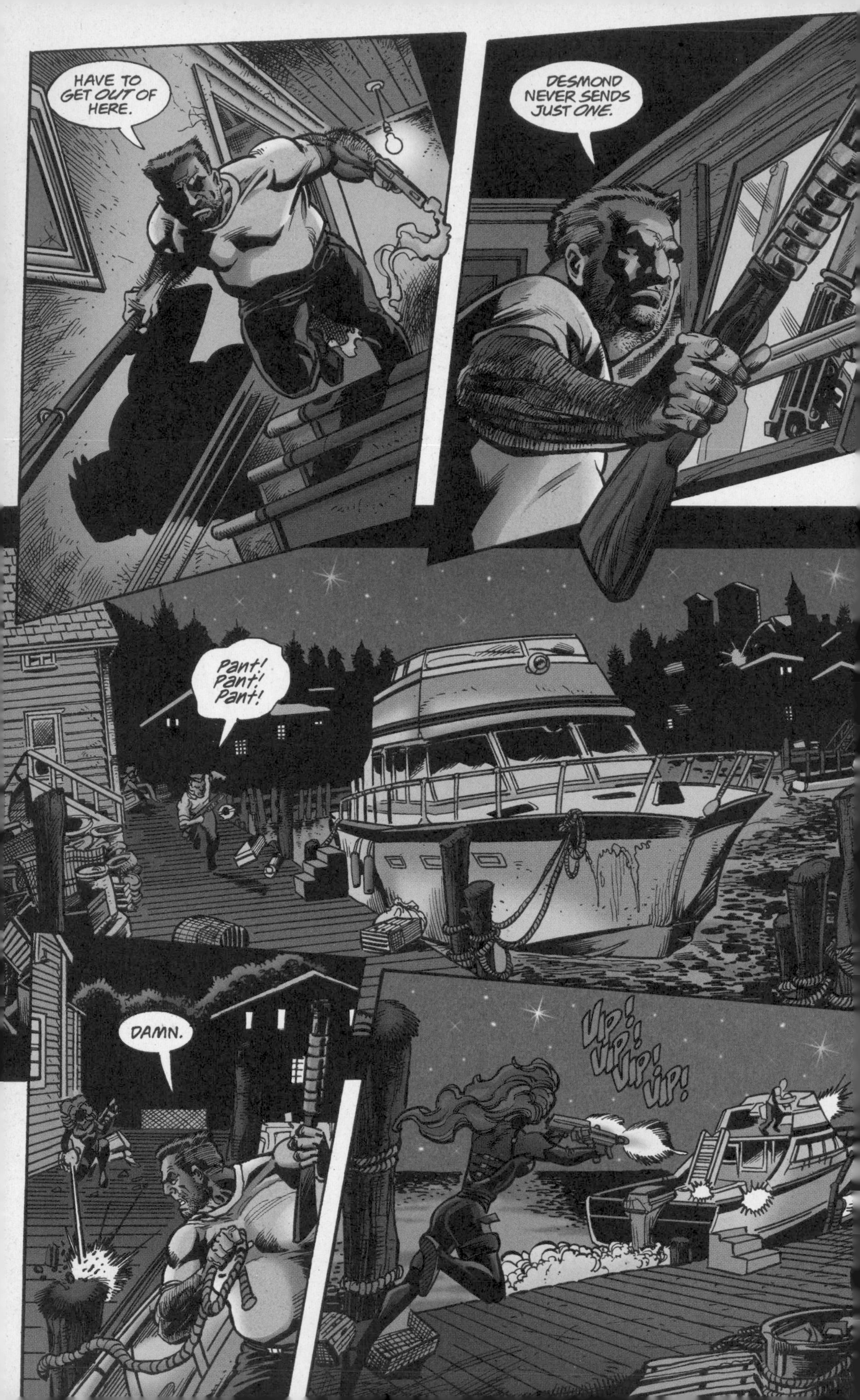
HAVE TO GET OUT OF HERE.
DESMOND NEVER SENDS JUST ONE.
Pant! Pant! Pant!
DAMN.
UP! UP! UP! UP!

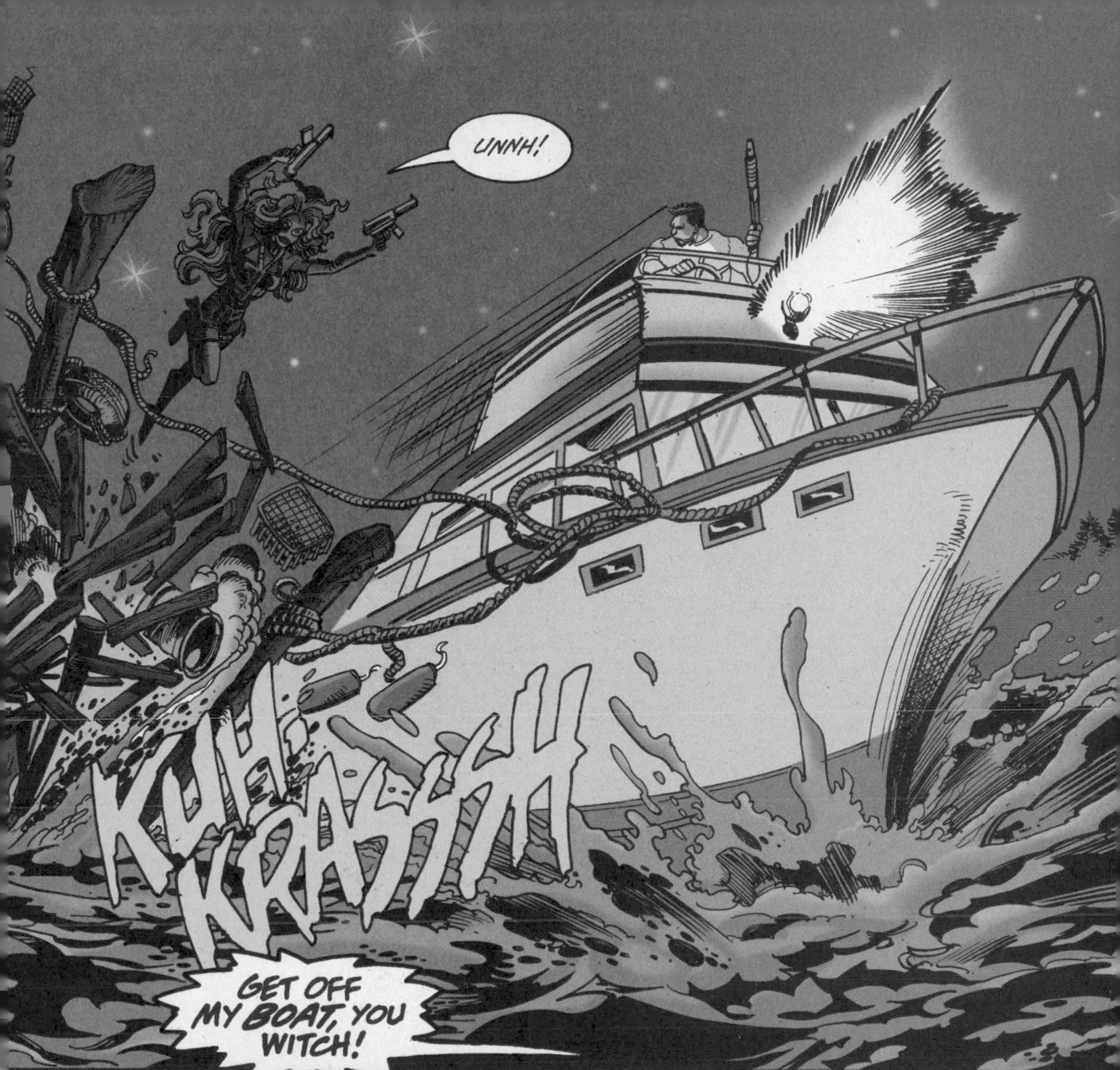
UNNH!
KUH-KRASSHH
GET OFF MY BOAT, YOU WITCH!

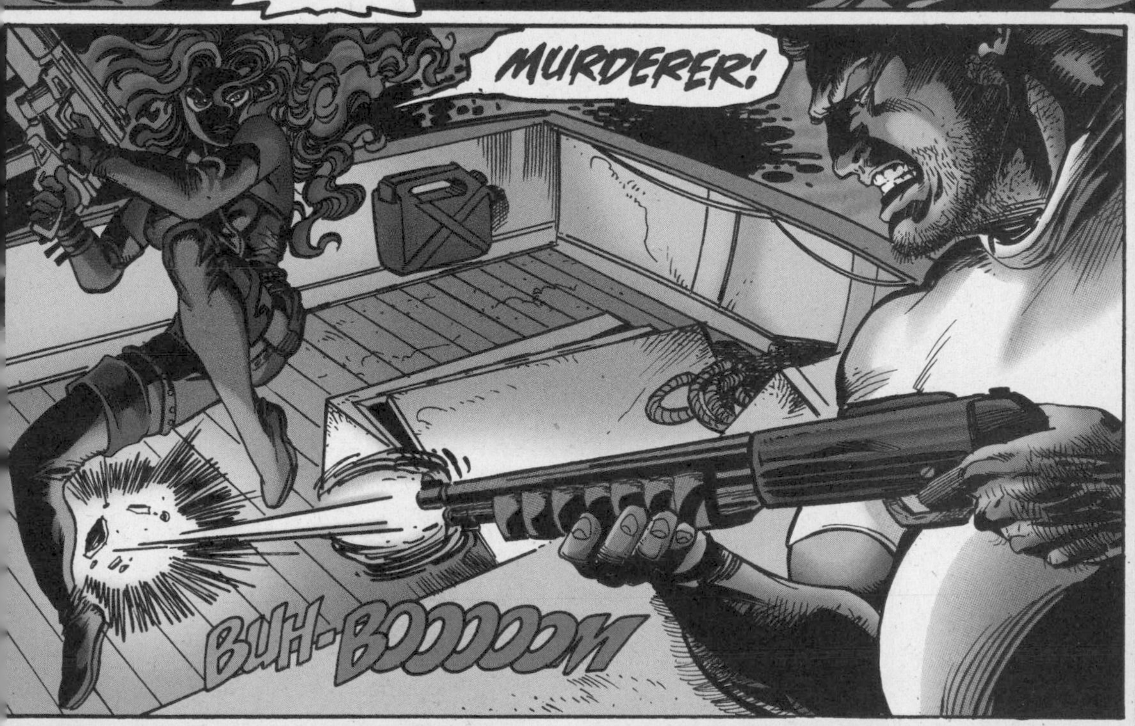
MURDERER!
BUH-BOOOOOOM

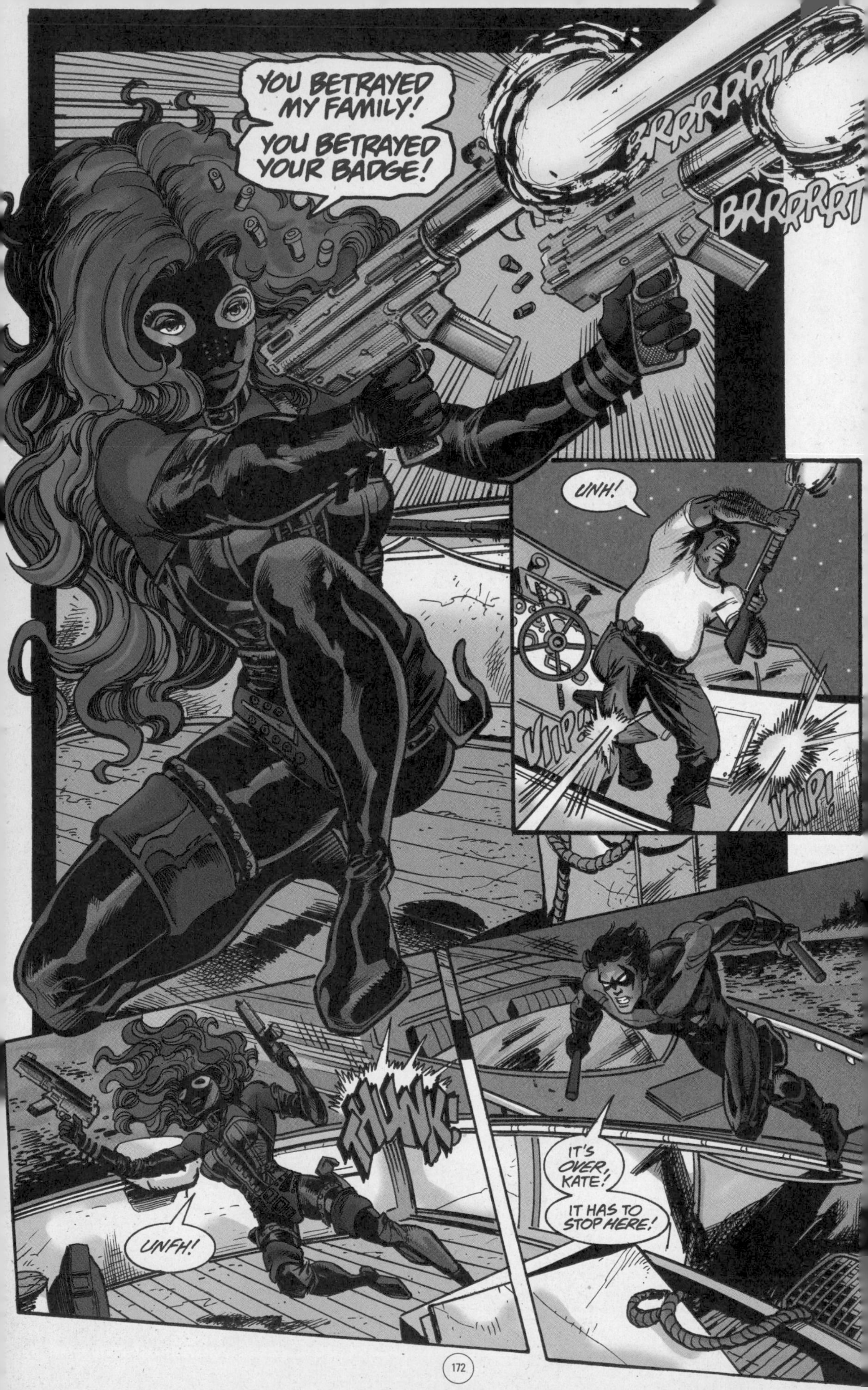
YOU BETRAYED MY FAMILY!
YOU BETRAYED YOUR BADGE!
BRRRRRT
BRRRRRT
UNH!
VIIP!
VIIP!
HUNK!
UNFH!
IT'S OVER, KATE!
IT HAS TO STOP HERE!

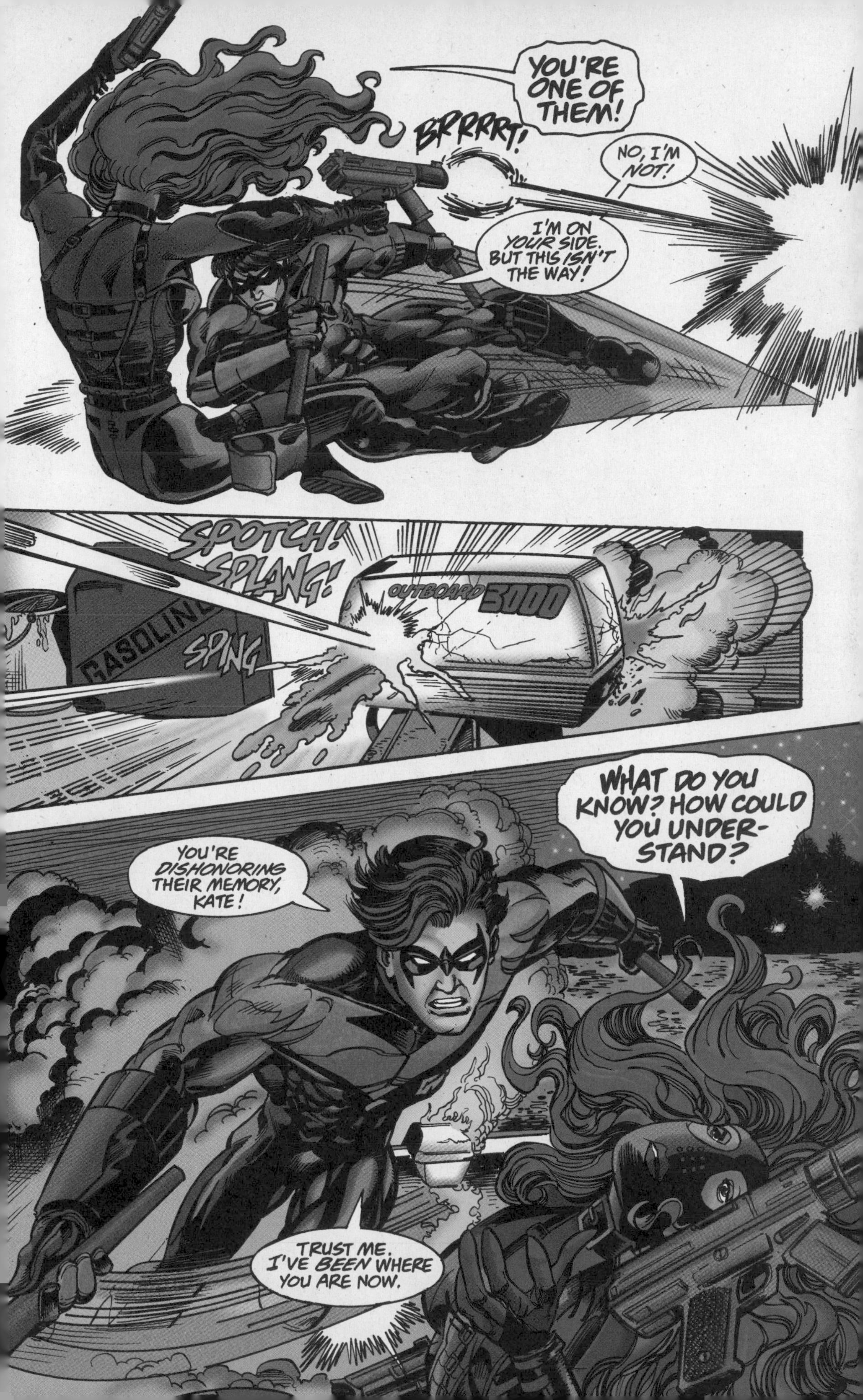
YOU'RE ONE OF THEM!
BRRRRT!
NO, I'M NOT!
I'M ON YOUR SIDE. BUT THIS ISN'T THE WAY!
SPOTCH!
SPLANG!
OUTBOARD 3000
GASOLINE
SPING
YOU'RE DISHONORING THEIR MEMORY, KATE!
WHAT DO YOU KNOW? HOW COULD YOU UNDER-STAND?
TRUST ME. I'VE BEEN WHERE YOU ARE NOW.

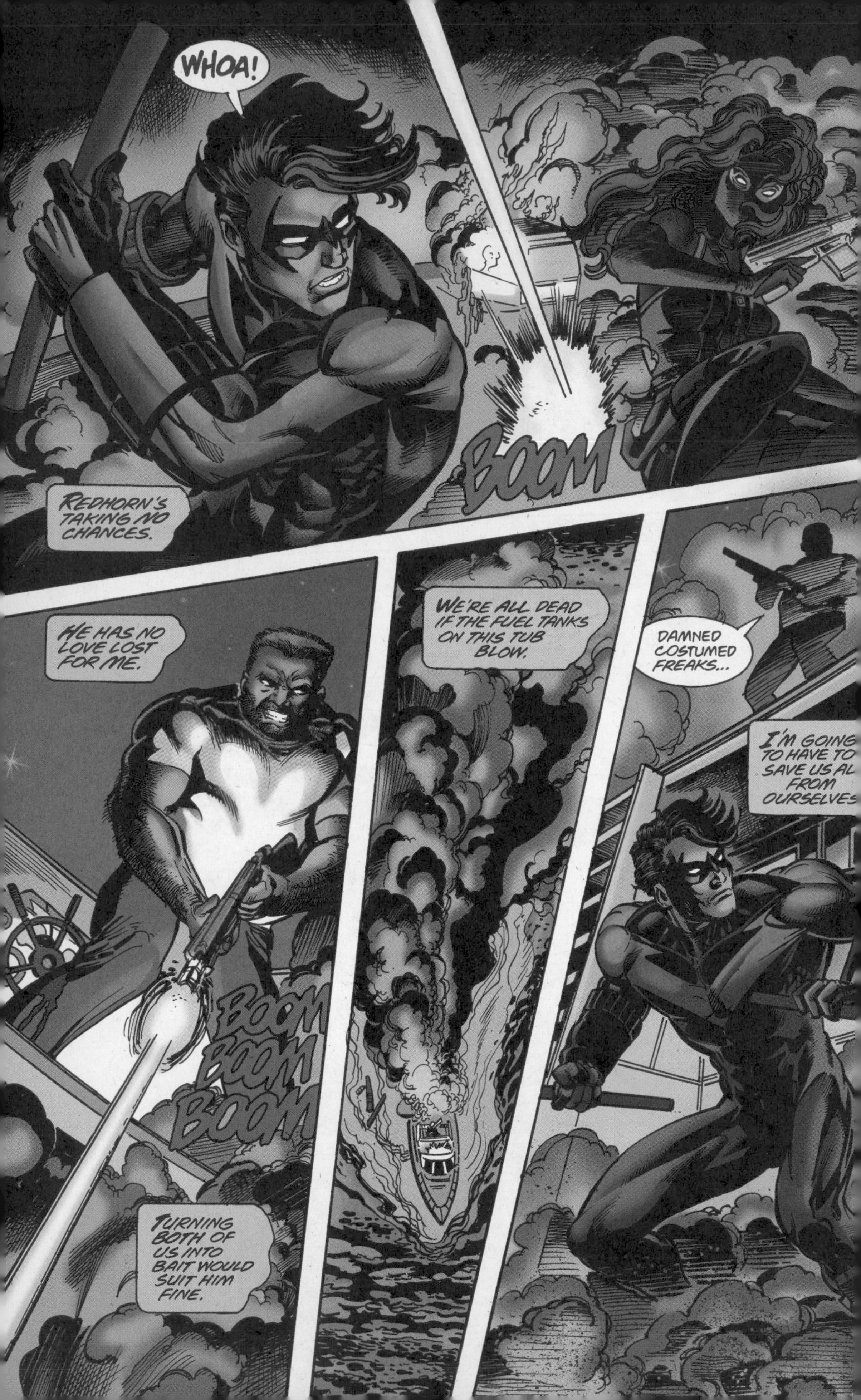

WHOA!
BOOM
REDHORN'S TAKING NO CHANCES.
HE HAS NO LOVE LOST FOR ME.
BOOM BOOM BOOM
TURNING BOTH OF US INTO BAIT WOULD SUIT HIM FINE.
WE'RE ALL DEAD IF THE FUEL TANKS ON THIS TUB BLOW.
DAMNED COSTUMED FREAKS...
I'M GOING TO HAVE TO SAVE US AL FROM OURSELVES

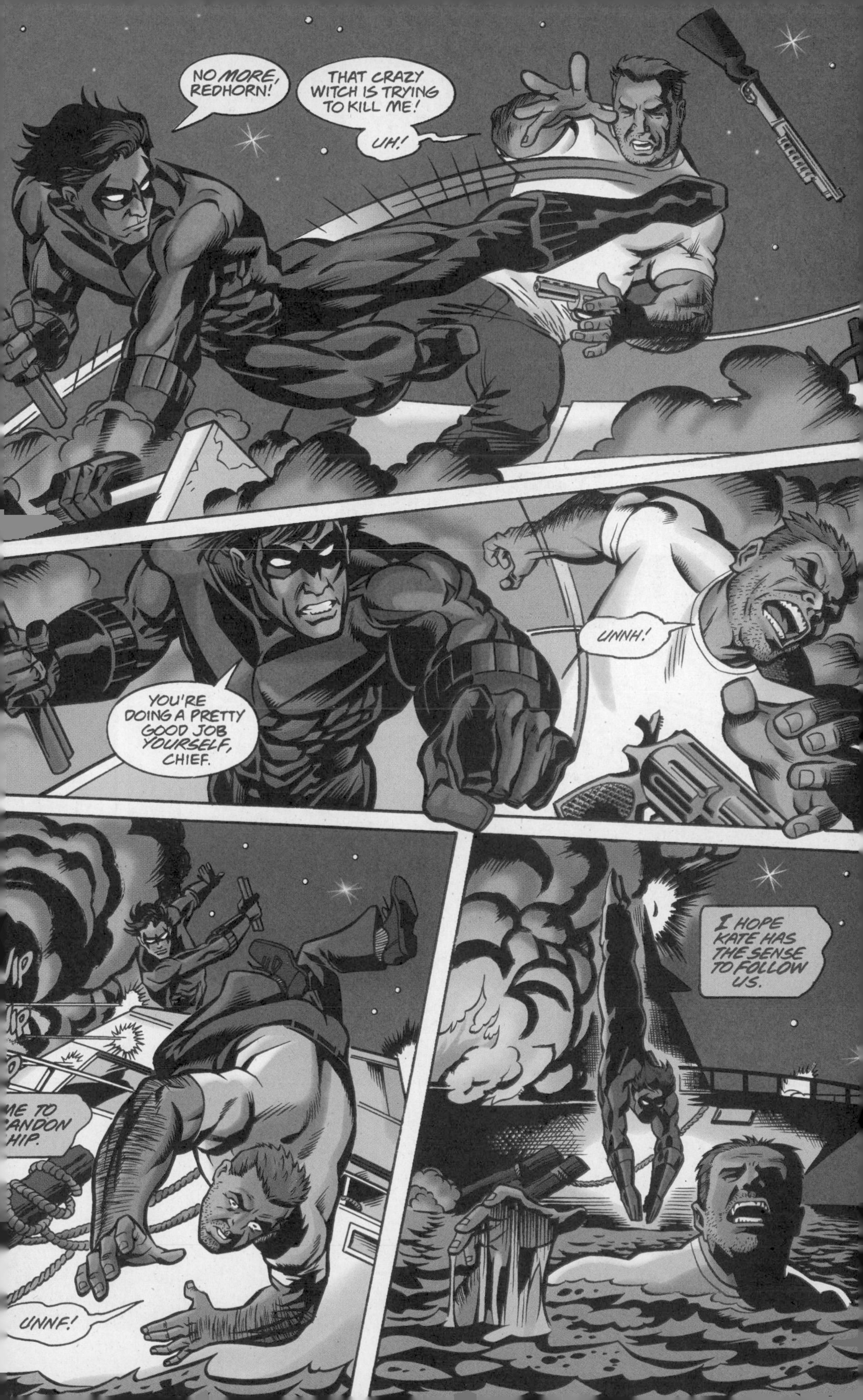
NO MORE, REDHORN!
THAT CRAZY WITCH IS TRYING TO KILL ME!
UH!
UNNH!
YOU'RE DOING A PRETTY GOOD JOB YOURSELF, CHIEF.
ME TO
ANDON
HIP.
UNNF!
I HOPE KATE HAS THE SENSE TO FOLLOW US.

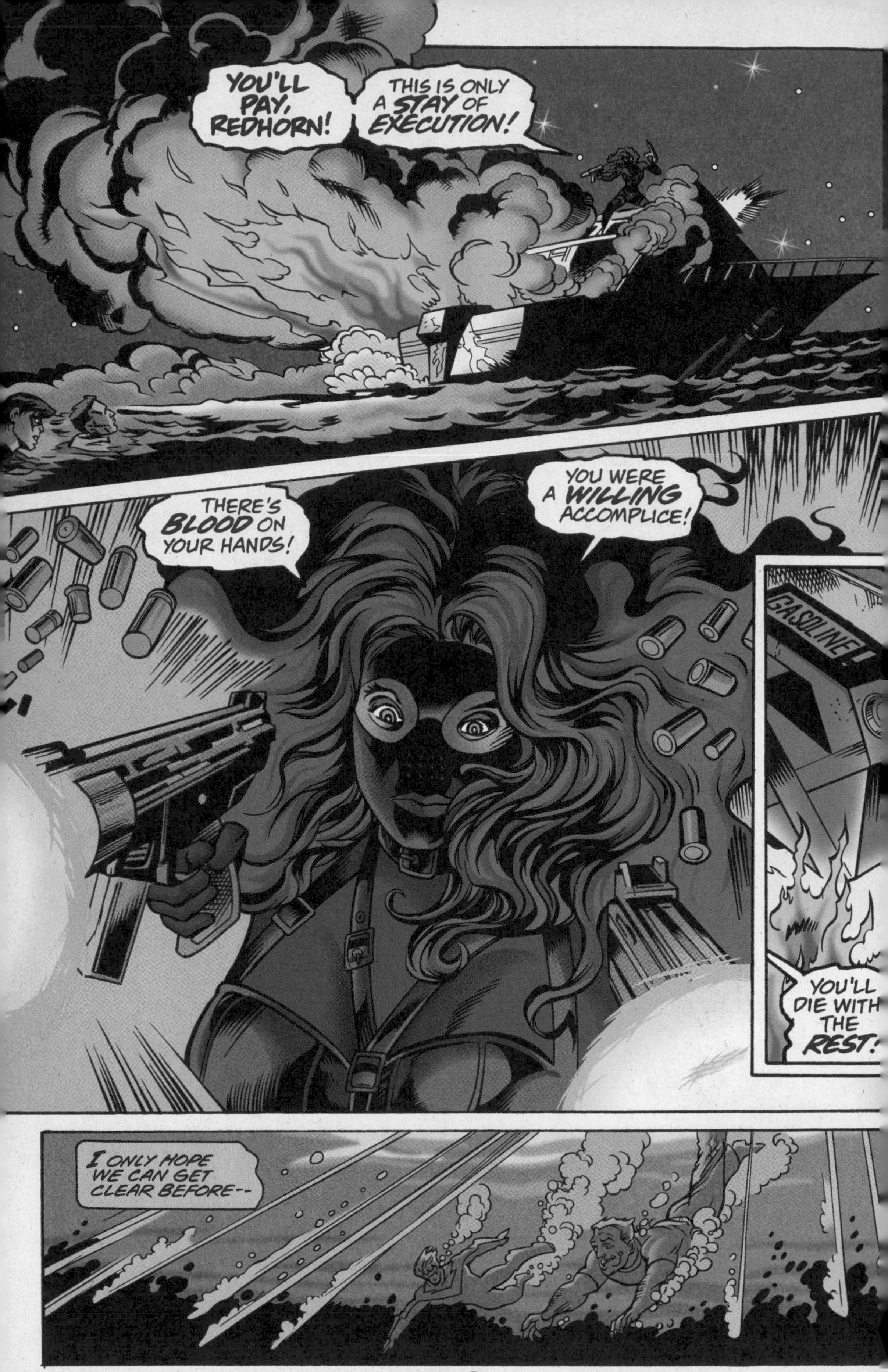
YOU'LL PAY, REDHORN!
THIS IS ONLY A STAY OF EXECUTION!
THERE'S BLOOD ON YOUR HANDS!
YOU WERE A WILLING ACCOMPLICE!
GASOLINE
YOU'LL DIE WITH THE REST!
I ONLY HOPE WE CAN GET CLEAR BEFORE--

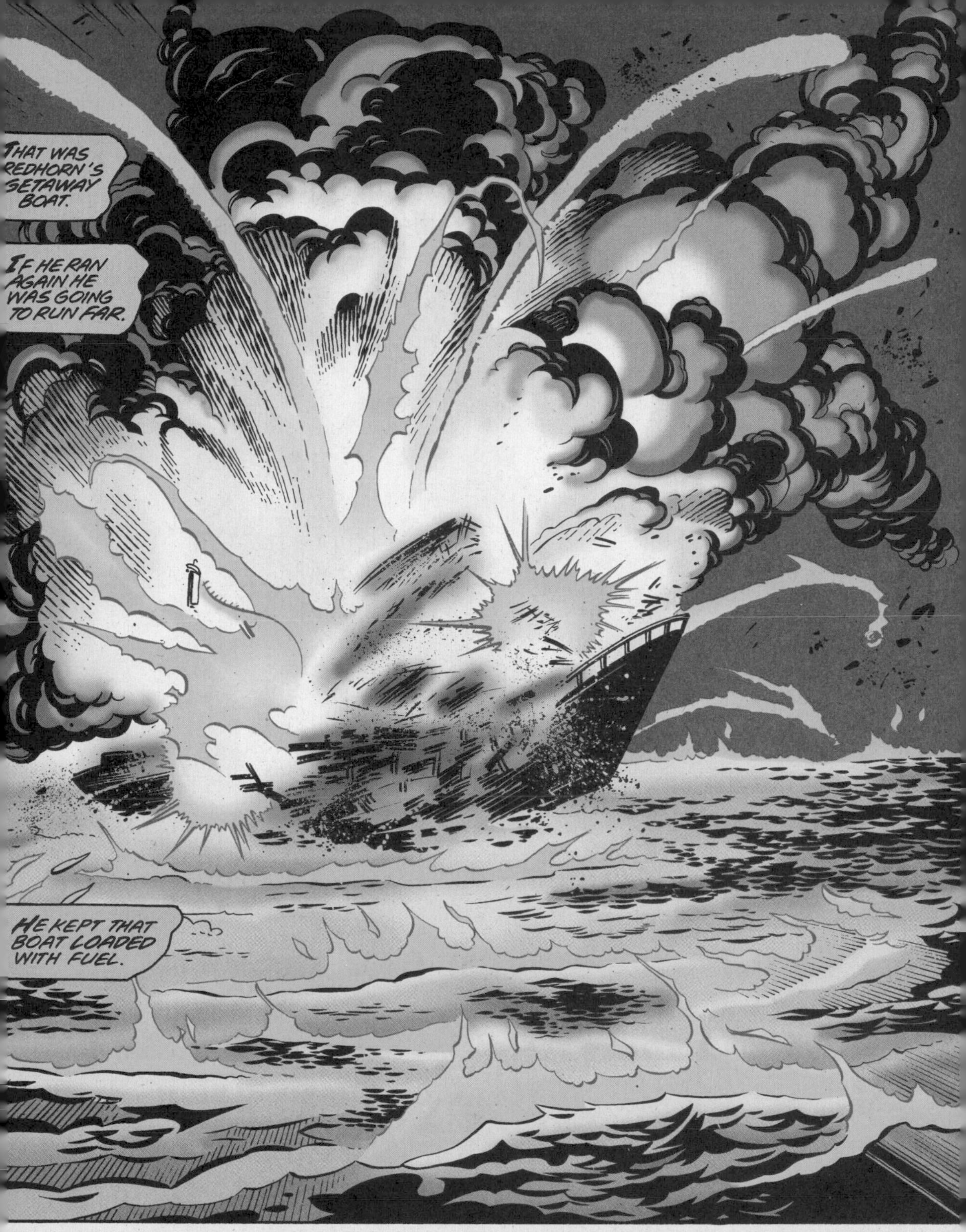
THAT WAS REDHORN'S GETAWAY BOAT.
IF HE RAN AGAIN HE WAS GOING TO RUN FAR.
HE KEPT THAT BOAT LOADED WITH FUEL.

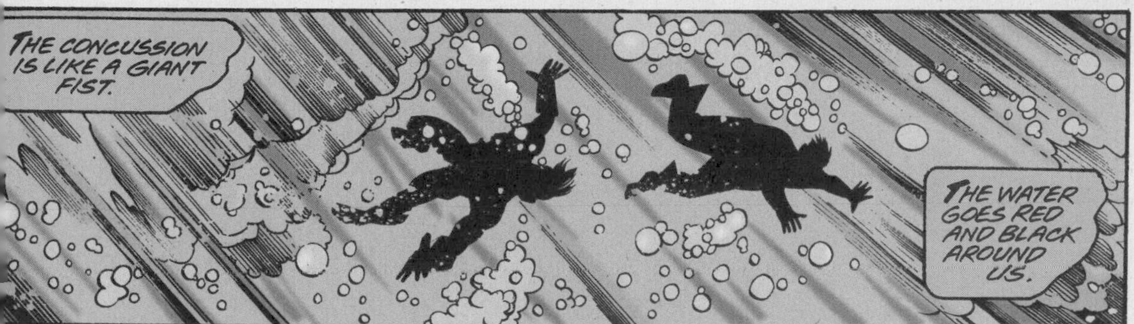
THE CONCUSSION IS LIKE A GIANT FIST.
THE WATER GOES RED AND BLACK AROUND US.

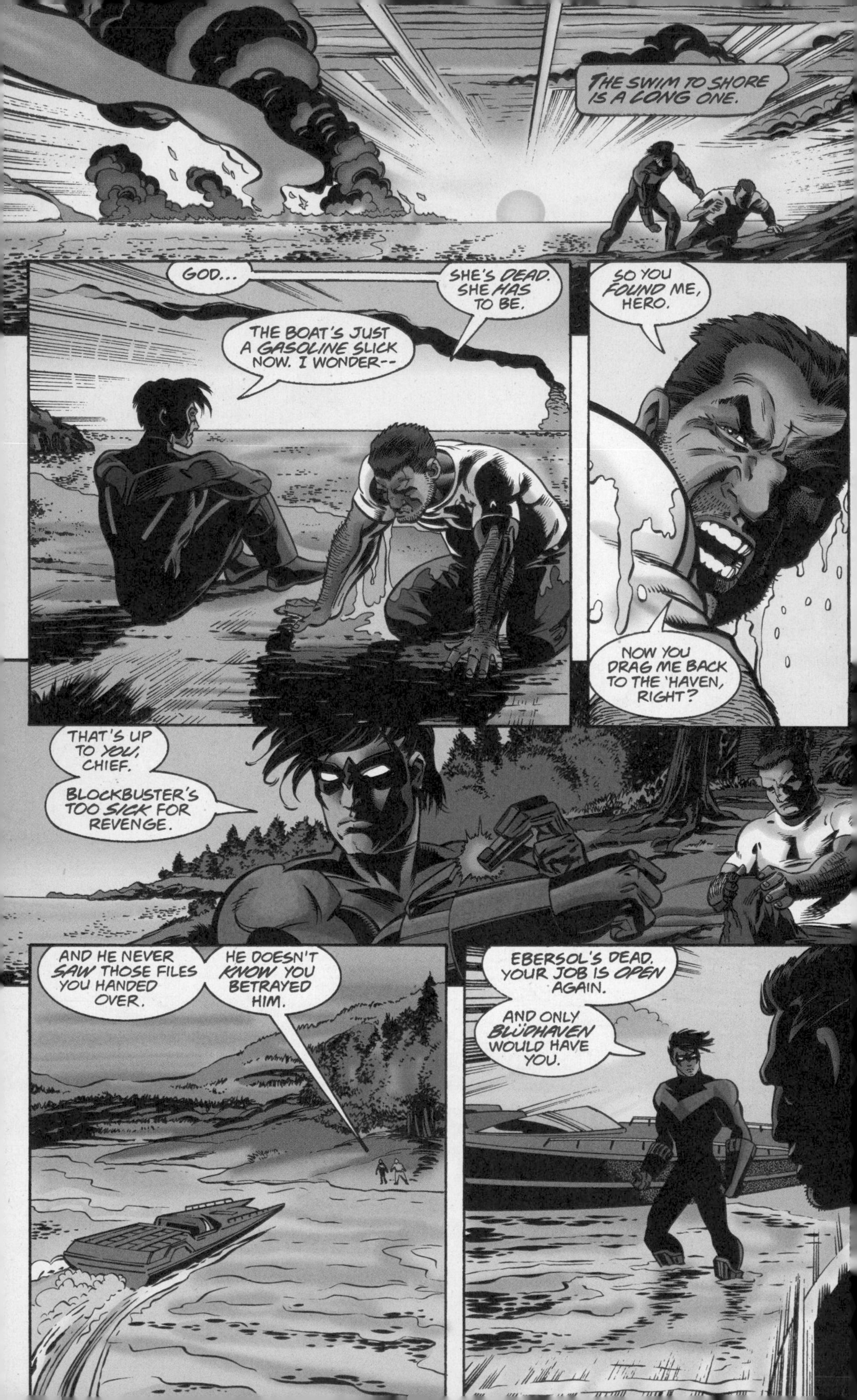
THE SWIM TO SHORE IS A LONG ONE.
GOD...
THE BOAT'S JUST A GASOLINE SLICK NOW. I WONDER--
SHE'S DEAD. SHE HAS TO BE.
SO YOU FOUND ME, HERO.
NOW YOU DRAG ME BACK TO THE 'HAVEN, RIGHT?
THAT'S UP TO YOU, CHIEF.
BLOCKBUSTER'S TOO SICK FOR REVENGE.
AND HE NEVER SAW THOSE FILES YOU HANDED OVER.
HE DOESN'T KNOW YOU BETRAYED HIM.
EBERSOL'S DEAD. YOUR JOB IS OPEN AGAIN.
AND ONLY BLÜDHAVEN WOULD HAVE YOU.

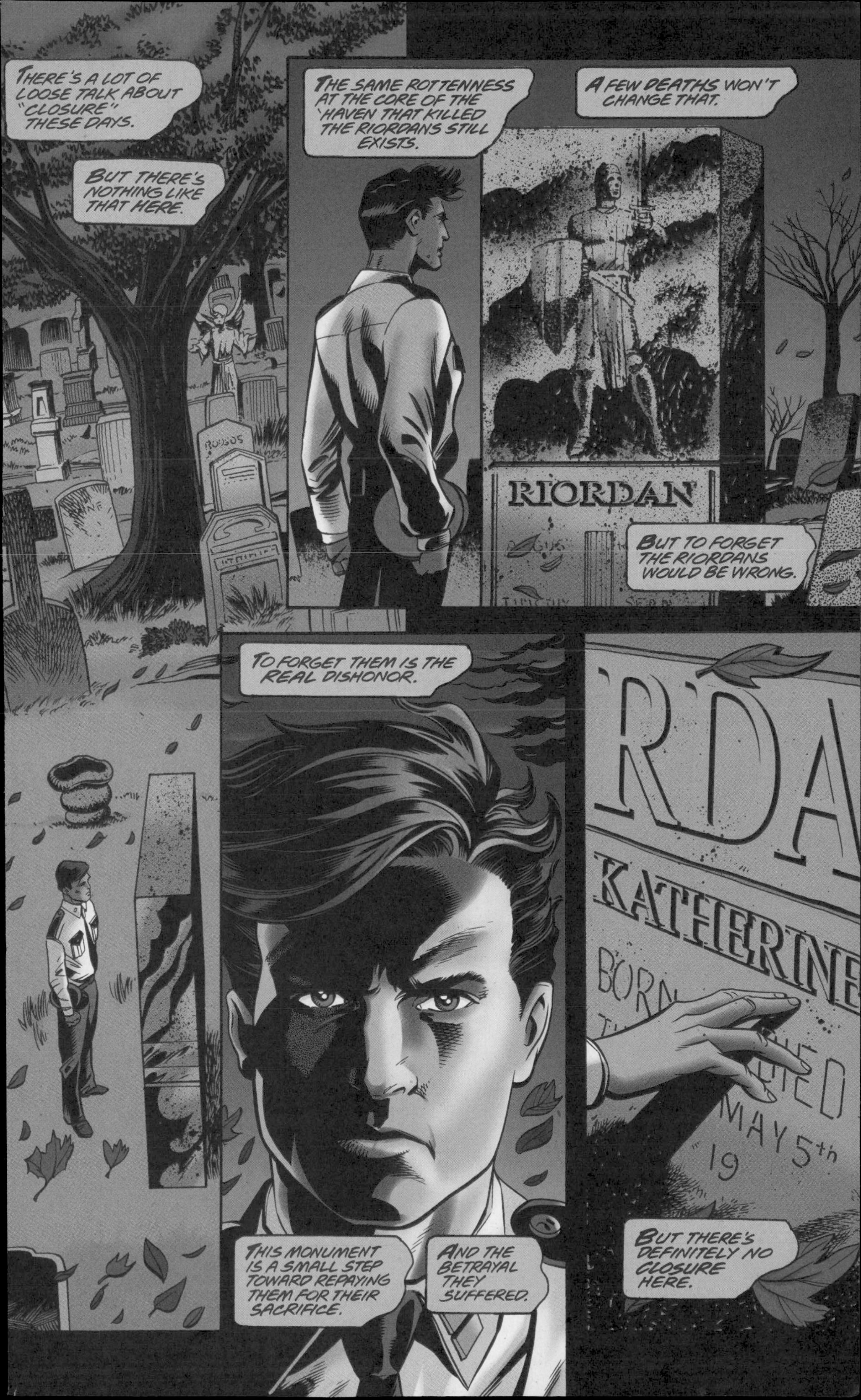
THERE'S A LOT OF LOOSE TALK ABOUT "CLOSURE" THESE DAYS.
BUT THERE'S NOTHING LIKE THAT HERE.
THE SAME ROTTENNESS AT THE CORE OF THE 'HAVEN THAT KILLED THE RIORDANS STILL EXISTS.
A FEW DEATHS WON'T CHANGE THAT.
RIORDAN
BUT TO FORGET THE RIORDANS WOULD BE WRONG.
TO FORGET THEM IS THE REAL DISHONOR.
THIS MONUMENT IS A SMALL STEP TOWARD REPAYING THEM FOR THEIR SACRIFICE.
AND THE BETRAYAL THEY SUFFERED.
RDA
KATHERINE
BORN
MAY 5th
19
BUT THERE'S DEFINITELY NO CLOSURE HERE.

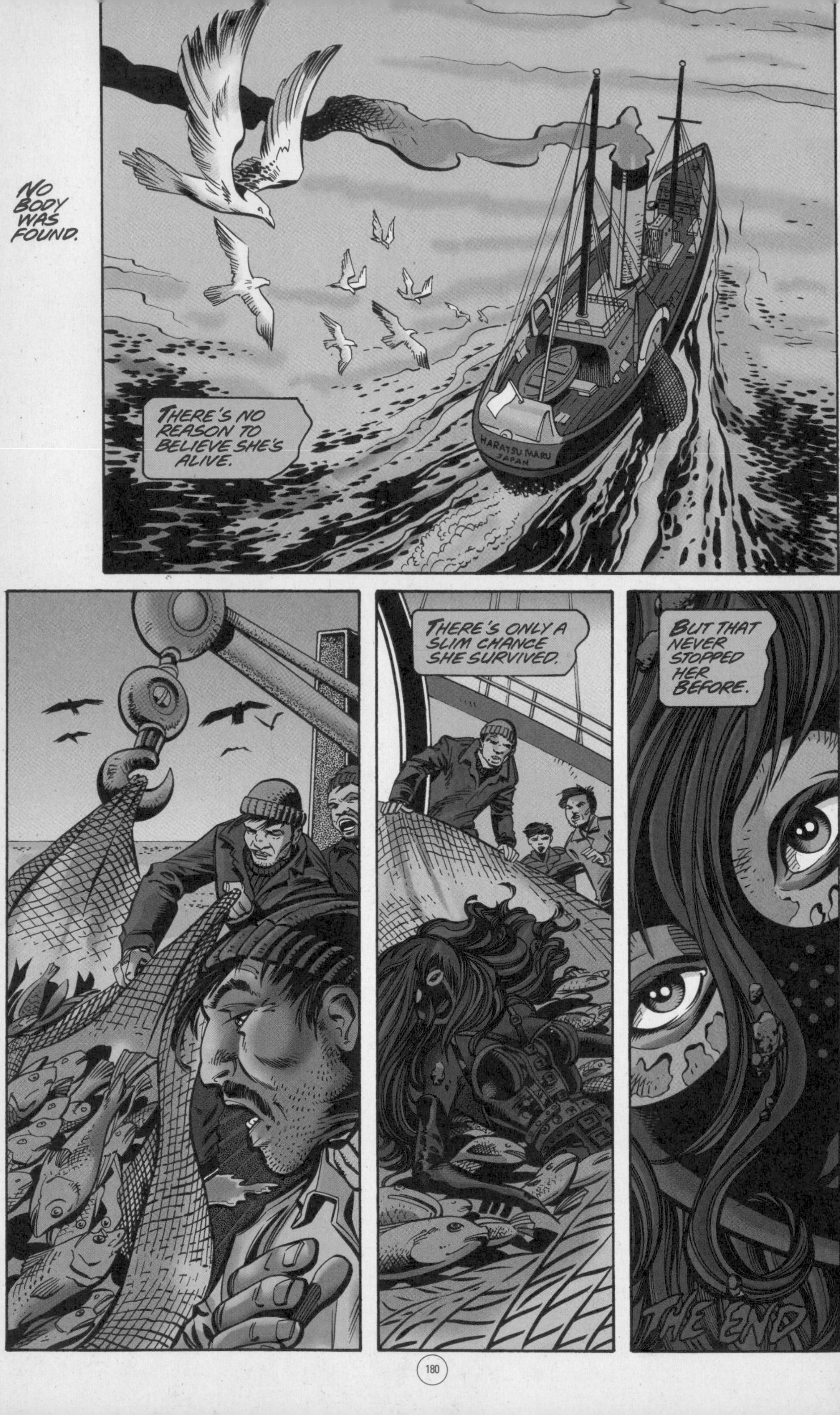
NO BODY WAS FOUND.
THERE'S NO REASON TO BELIEVE SHE'S ALIVE.
HARATSU MARU JAPAN
THERE'S ONLY A SLIM CHANCE SHE SURVIVED.
BUT THAT NEVER STOPPED HER BEFORE.
THE END

# NIGHTWING'S BLÜDHAVEN APARTMENT/HQ

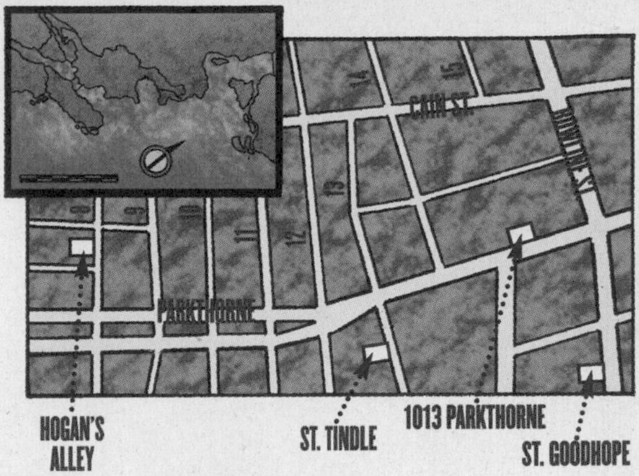
CAIN ST.
PARKTHORNE
HOGAN'S ALLEY
ST. TINDLE
1013 PARKTHORNE
ST. GOODHOPE

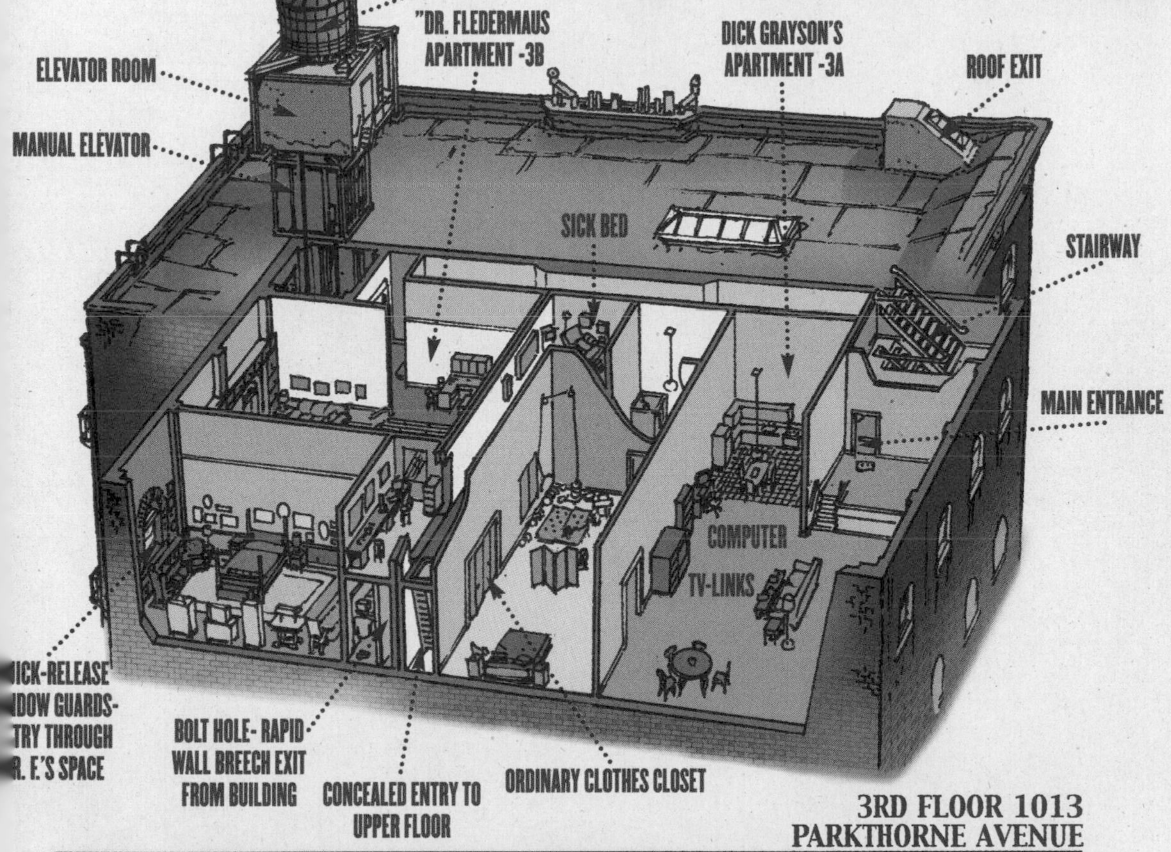
ROOF TANK
"DR. FLEDERMAUS APARTMENT -3B
DICK GRAYSON'S APARTMENT -3A
ROOF EXIT
ELEVATOR ROOM
MANUAL ELEVATOR
SICK BED
STAIRWAY
MAIN ENTRANCE
COMPUTER
TV-LINKS
ICK-RELEASE
NDOW GUARDS-
TRY THROUGH
R. F.'S SPACE
BOLT HOLE- RAPID WALL BREECH EXIT FROM BUILDING
CONCEALED ENTRY TO UPPER FLOOR
ORDINARY CLOTHES CLOSET

## 3RD FLOOR 1013 PARKTHORNE AVENUE

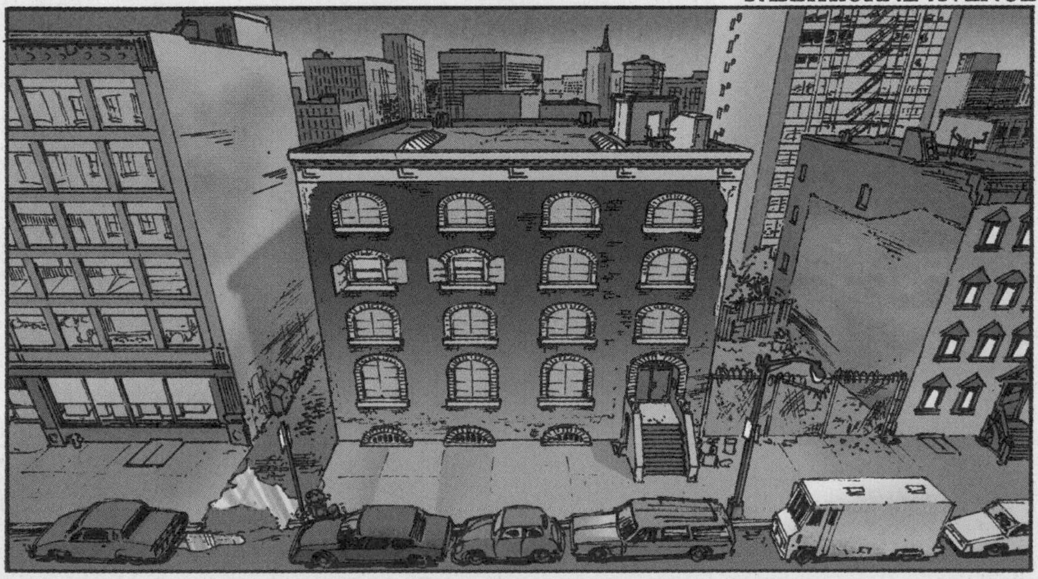

**Written and designed by Eliot Brown, color by Digital Chameleon**

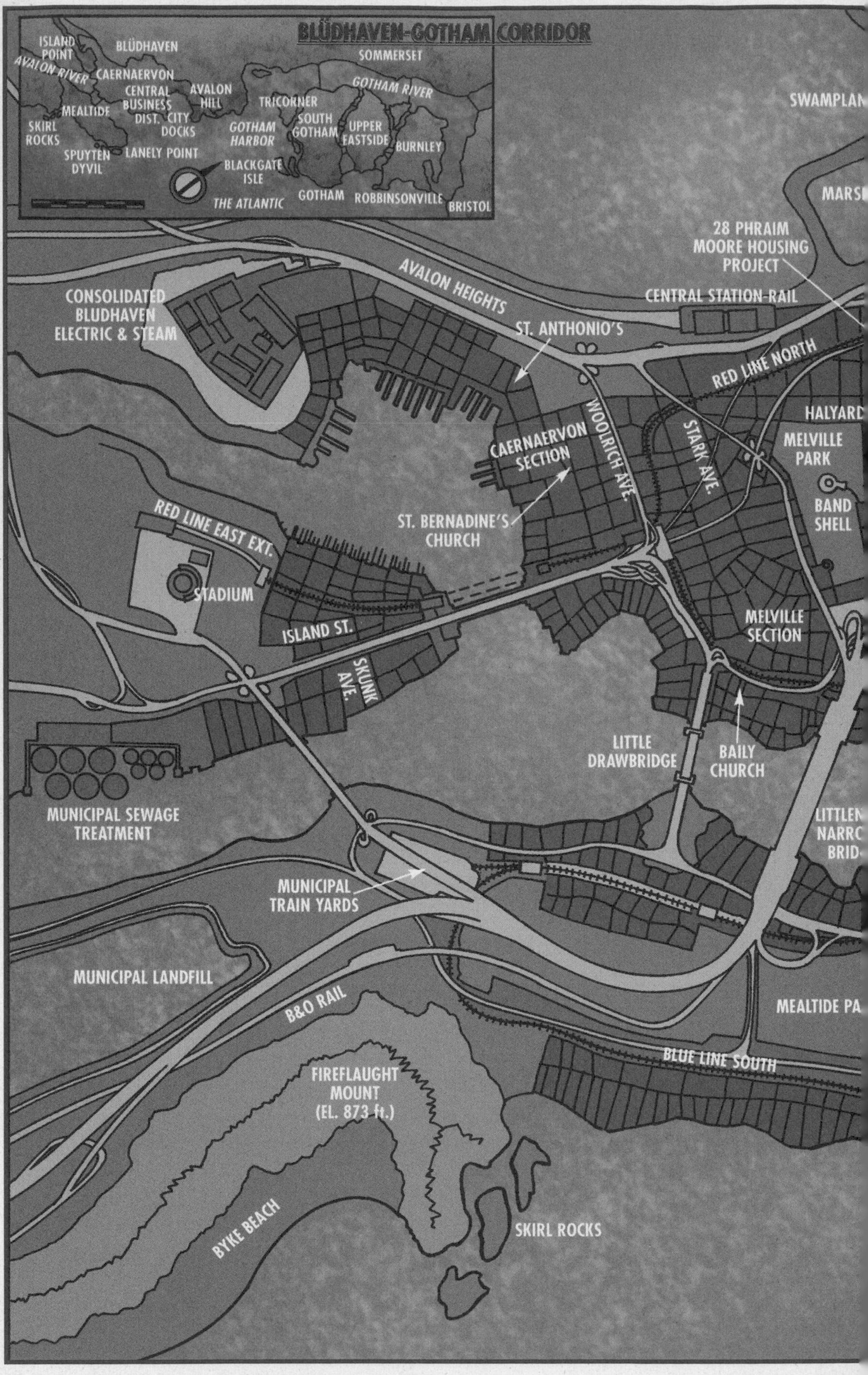
BLÜDHAVEN-GOTHAM CORRIDOR
ISLAND POINT
BLÜDHAVEN
SOMMERSET
AVALON RIVER
CAERNAERVON
CENTRAL BUSINESS DIST.
AVALON HILL
GOTHAM RIVER
TRICORNER
MEALTIDE
CITY DOCKS
SOUTH GOTHAM
UPPER EASTSIDE
SKIRL ROCKS
GOTHAM HARBOR
BURNLEY
SPUYTEN DYVIL
LANELY POINT
BLACKGATE ISLE
THE ATLANTIC
GOTHAM
ROBBINSONVILLE
BRISTOL
SWAMPLAN
MARS
28 PHRAIM MOORE HOUSING PROJECT
CONSOLIDATED BLUDHAVEN ELECTRIC & STEAM
AVALON HEIGHTS
CENTRAL STATION-RAIL
ST. ANTHONIO'S
RED LINE NORTH
HALYARD
WOOLRICH AVE.
STARK AVE.
CAERNAERVON SECTION
MELVILLE PARK
BAND SHELL
RED LINE EAST EXT.
ST. BERNADINE'S CHURCH
STADIUM
ISLAND ST.
MELVILLE SECTION
SKUNK AVE.
LITTLE DRAWBRIDGE
BAILY CHURCH
MUNICIPAL SEWAGE TREATMENT
LITTLEN NARRO BRID
MUNICIPAL TRAIN YARDS
MUNICIPAL LANDFILL
B&O RAIL
MEALTIDE PA
BLUE LINE SOUTH
FIREFLAUGHT MOUNT (EL. 873 ft.)
SKIRL ROCKS
BYKE BEACH

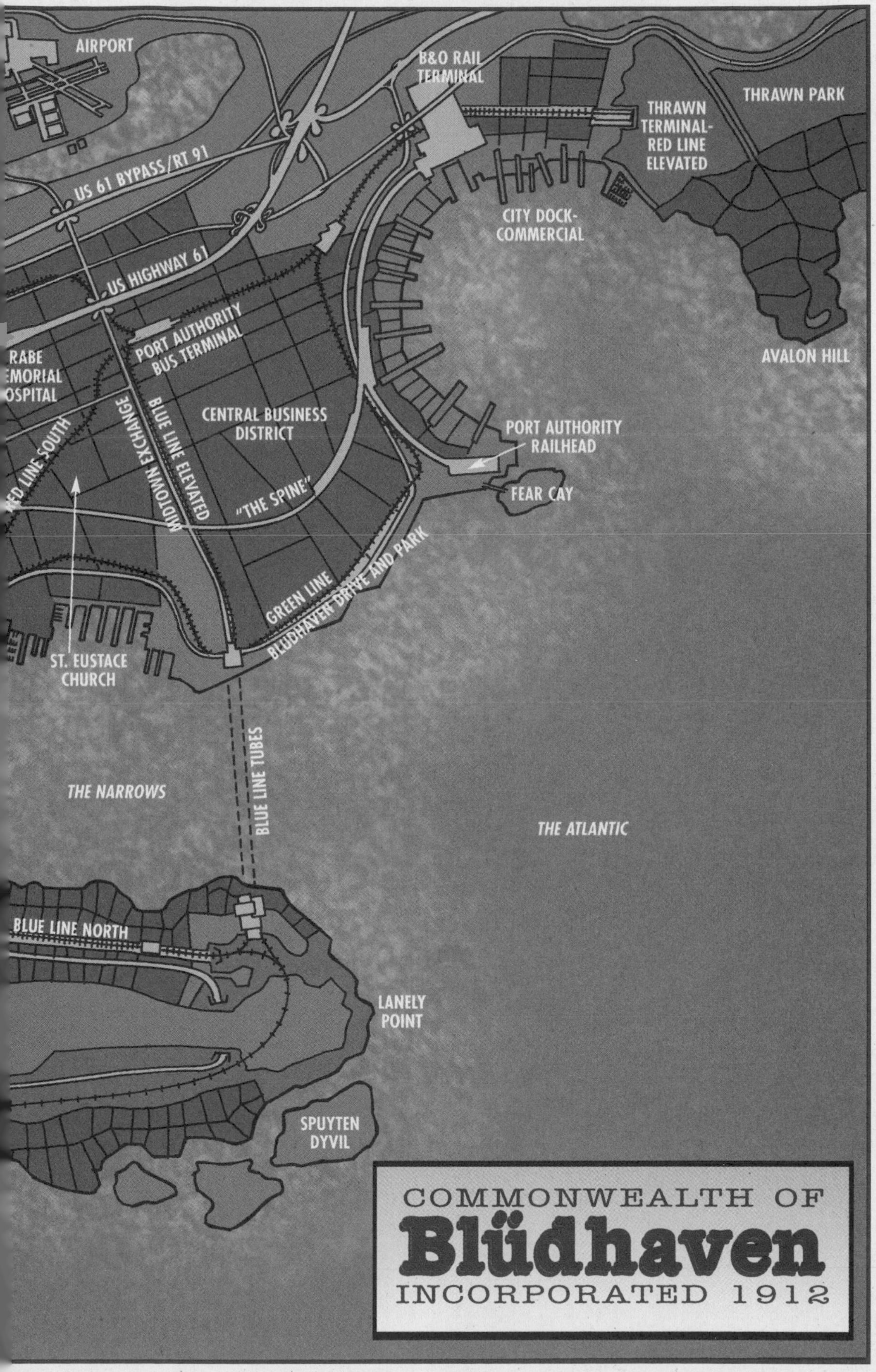
AIRPORT
B&O RAIL TERMINAL
THRAWN PARK
THRAWN TERMINAL-RED LINE ELEVATED
US 61 BYPASS/RT 91
CITY DOCK-COMMERCIAL
US HIGHWAY 61
PORT AUTHORITY BUS TERMINAL
RABE
EMORIAL
OSPITAL
AVALON HILL
CENTRAL BUSINESS DISTRICT
MIDTOWN EXCHANGE
BLUE LINE ELEVATED
ED LINE SOUTH
PORT AUTHORITY RAILHEAD
FEAR CAY
"THE SPINE"
GREEN LINE
BLUDHAVEN DRIVE AND PARK
ST. EUSTACE CHURCH
BLUE LINE TUBES
THE NARROWS
THE ATLANTIC
BLUE LINE NORTH
LANELY POINT
SPUYTEN DYVIL
COMMONWEALTH OF
Blüdhaven
INCORPORATED 1912

Written and designed by Eliot Brown, color by Digital Chameleon

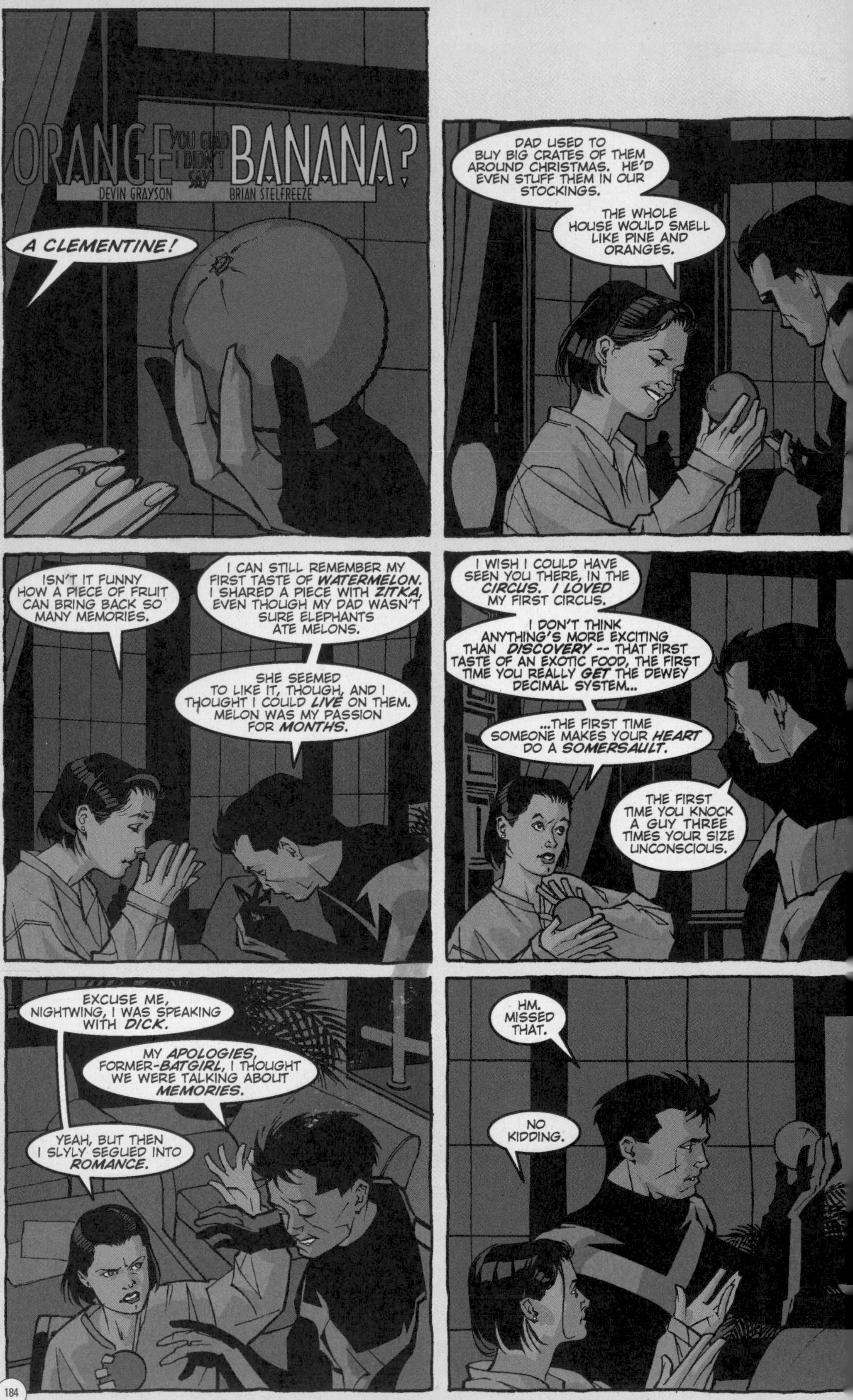
ORANGE YOU GLAD I DIDN'T SAY BANANA?
DEVIN GRAYSON
BRIAN STELFREEZE
A CLEMENTINE!
DAD USED TO BUY BIG CRATES OF THEM AROUND CHRISTMAS. HE'D EVEN STUFF THEM IN OUR STOCKINGS.
THE WHOLE HOUSE WOULD SMELL LIKE PINE AND ORANGES.
ISN'T IT FUNNY HOW A PIECE OF FRUIT CAN BRING BACK SO MANY MEMORIES.
I CAN STILL REMEMBER MY FIRST TASTE OF WATERMELON. I SHARED A PIECE WITH ZITKA, EVEN THOUGH MY DAD WASN'T SURE ELEPHANTS ATE MELONS.
SHE SEEMED TO LIKE IT, THOUGH, AND I THOUGHT I COULD LIVE ON THEM. MELON WAS MY PASSION FOR MONTHS.
I WISH I COULD HAVE SEEN YOU THERE, IN THE CIRCUS. I LOVED MY FIRST CIRCUS.
I DON'T THINK ANYTHING'S MORE EXCITING THAN DISCOVERY -- THAT FIRST TASTE OF AN EXOTIC FOOD, THE FIRST TIME YOU REALLY GET THE DEWEY DECIMAL SYSTEM...
...THE FIRST TIME SOMEONE MAKES YOUR HEART DO A SOMERSAULT.
THE FIRST TIME YOU KNOCK A GUY THREE TIMES YOUR SIZE UNCONSCIOUS.
EXCUSE ME, NIGHTWING, I WAS SPEAKING WITH DICK.
MY APOLOGIES, FORMER-BATGIRL, I THOUGHT WE WERE TALKING ABOUT MEMORIES.
YEAH, BUT THEN I SLYLY SEGUED INTO ROMANCE.
HM. MISSED THAT.
NO KIDDING.

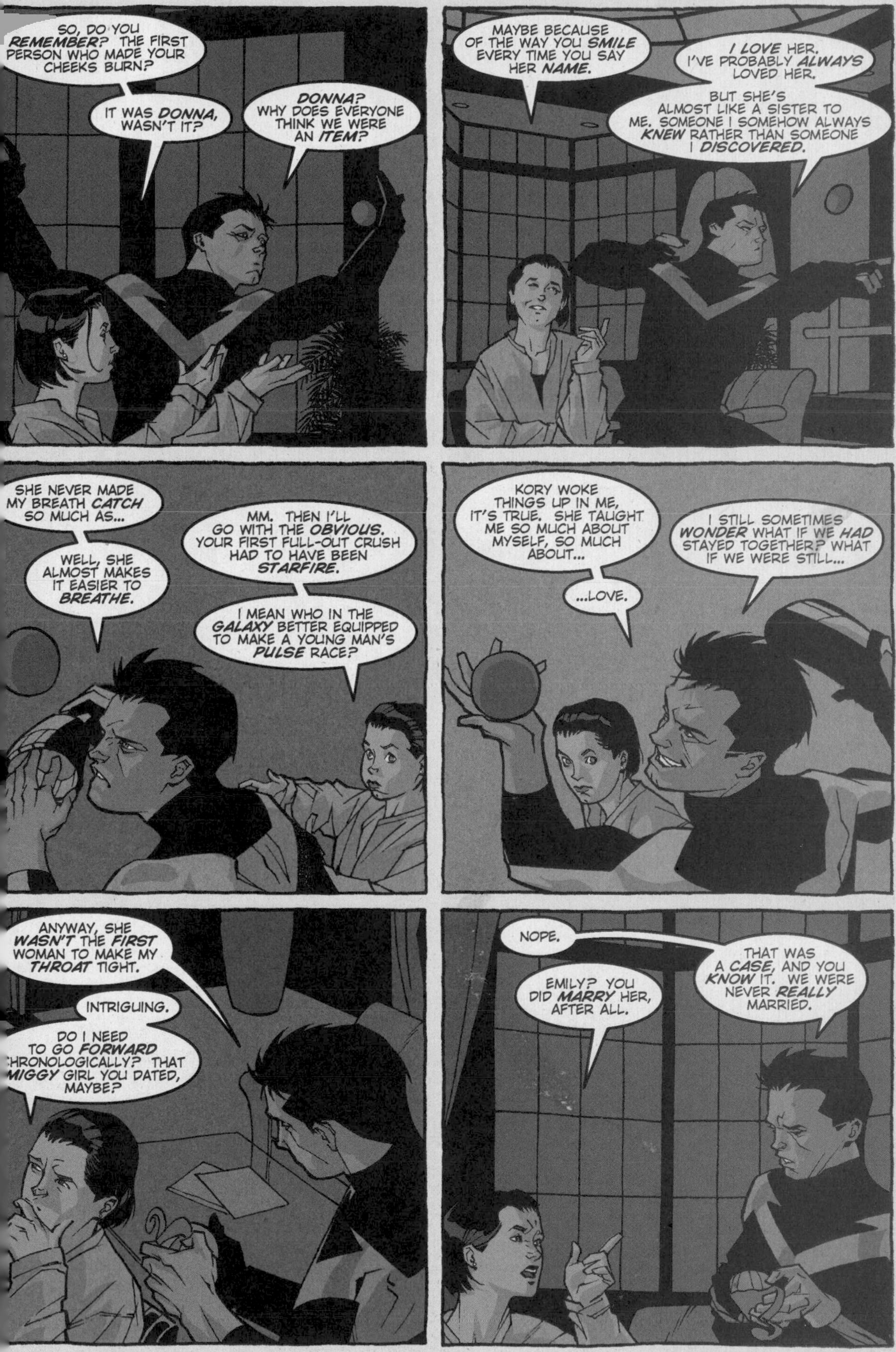
SO, DO YOU REMEMBER? THE FIRST PERSON WHO MADE YOUR CHEEKS BURN?
IT WAS DONNA, WASN'T IT?
DONNA? WHY DOES EVERYONE THINK WE WERE AN ITEM?
MAYBE BECAUSE OF THE WAY YOU SMILE EVERY TIME YOU SAY HER NAME.
I LOVE HER. I'VE PROBABLY ALWAYS LOVED HER.
BUT SHE'S ALMOST LIKE A SISTER TO ME. SOMEONE I SOMEHOW ALWAYS KNEW RATHER THAN SOMEONE I DISCOVERED.
SHE NEVER MADE MY BREATH CATCH SO MUCH AS...
WELL, SHE ALMOST MAKES IT EASIER TO BREATHE.
MM. THEN I'LL GO WITH THE OBVIOUS. YOUR FIRST FULL-OUT CRUSH HAD TO HAVE BEEN STARFIRE.
I MEAN WHO IN THE GALAXY BETTER EQUIPPED TO MAKE A YOUNG MAN'S PULSE RACE?
KORY WOKE THINGS UP IN ME, IT'S TRUE. SHE TAUGHT ME SO MUCH ABOUT MYSELF, SO MUCH ABOUT...
...LOVE.
I STILL SOMETIMES WONDER WHAT IF WE HAD STAYED TOGETHER? WHAT IF WE WERE STILL...
ANYWAY, SHE WASN'T THE FIRST WOMAN TO MAKE MY THROAT TIGHT.
INTRIGUING.
DO I NEED TO GO FORWARD CHRONOLOGICALLY? THAT MIGGY GIRL YOU DATED, MAYBE?
NOPE.
EMILY? YOU DID MARRY HER, AFTER ALL.
THAT WAS A CASE, AND YOU KNOW IT. WE WERE NEVER REALLY MARRIED.

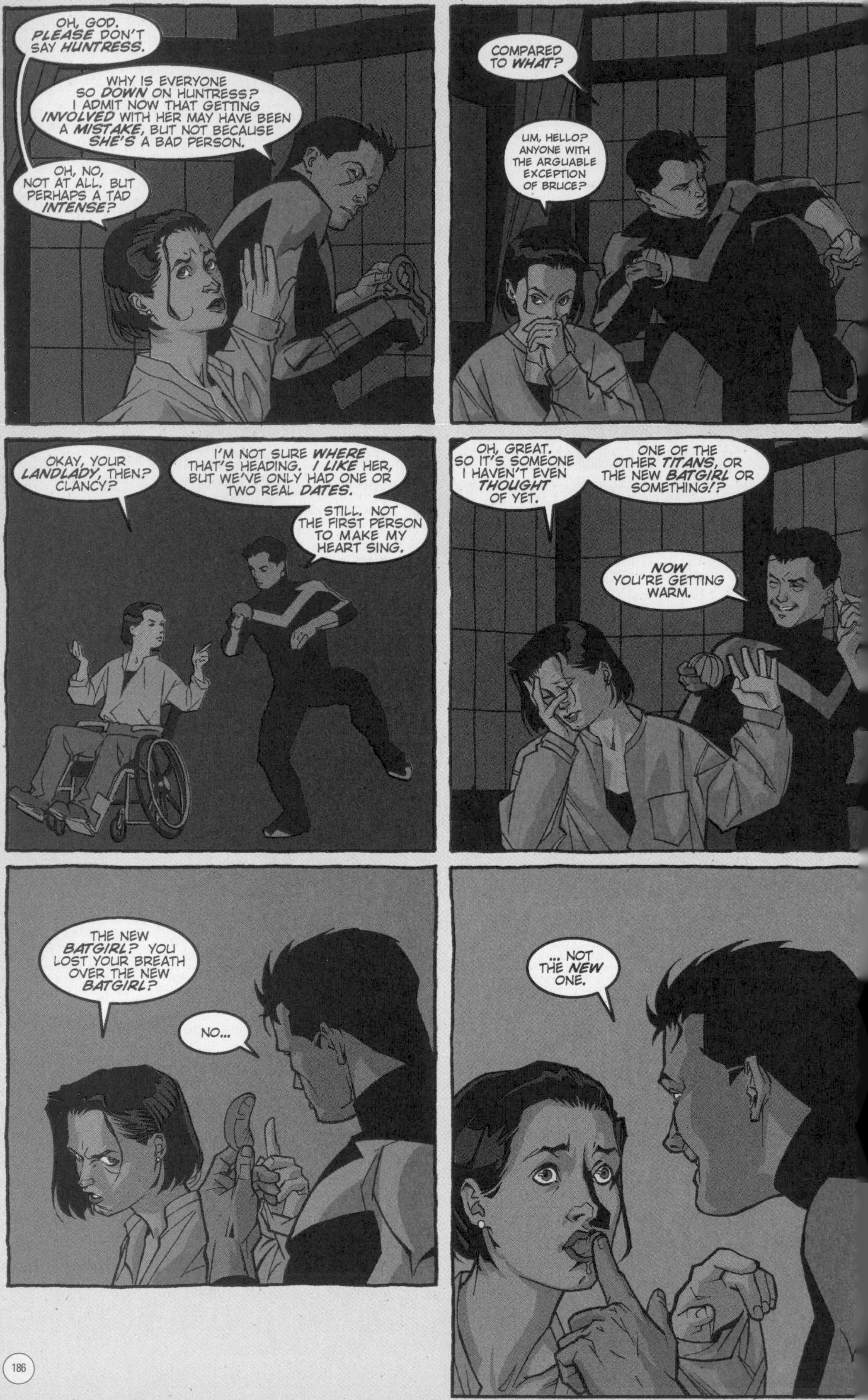

OH, GOD. PLEASE DON'T SAY HUNTRESS.
WHY IS EVERYONE SO DOWN ON HUNTRESS? I ADMIT NOW THAT GETTING INVOLVED WITH HER MAY HAVE BEEN A MISTAKE, BUT NOT BECAUSE SHE'S A BAD PERSON.
OH, NO, NOT AT ALL. BUT PERHAPS A TAD INTENSE?
COMPARED TO WHAT?
UM, HELLO? ANYONE WITH THE ARGUABLE EXCEPTION OF BRUCE?
OKAY, YOUR LANDLADY, THEN? CLANCY?
I'M NOT SURE WHERE THAT'S HEADING. I LIKE HER, BUT WE'VE ONLY HAD ONE OR TWO REAL DATES.
STILL. NOT THE FIRST PERSON TO MAKE MY HEART SING.
OH, GREAT. SO IT'S SOMEONE I HAVEN'T EVEN THOUGHT OF YET.
ONE OF THE OTHER TITANS, OR THE NEW BATGIRL OR SOMETHING!?
NOW YOU'RE GETTING WARM.
THE NEW BATGIRL? YOU LOST YOUR BREATH OVER THE NEW BATGIRL?
NO...
... NOT THE NEW ONE.

over by Mark Texeira

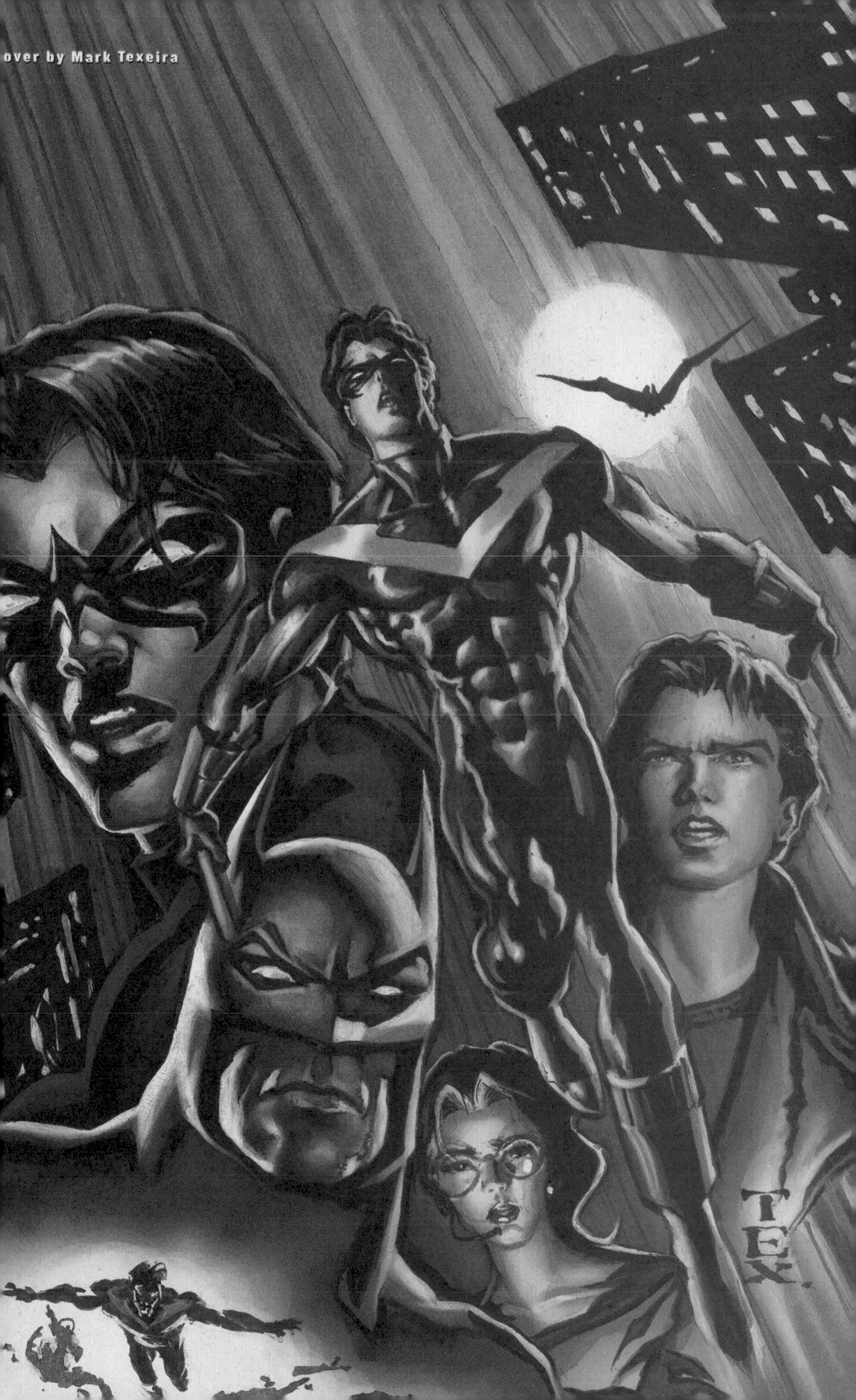
TEX.

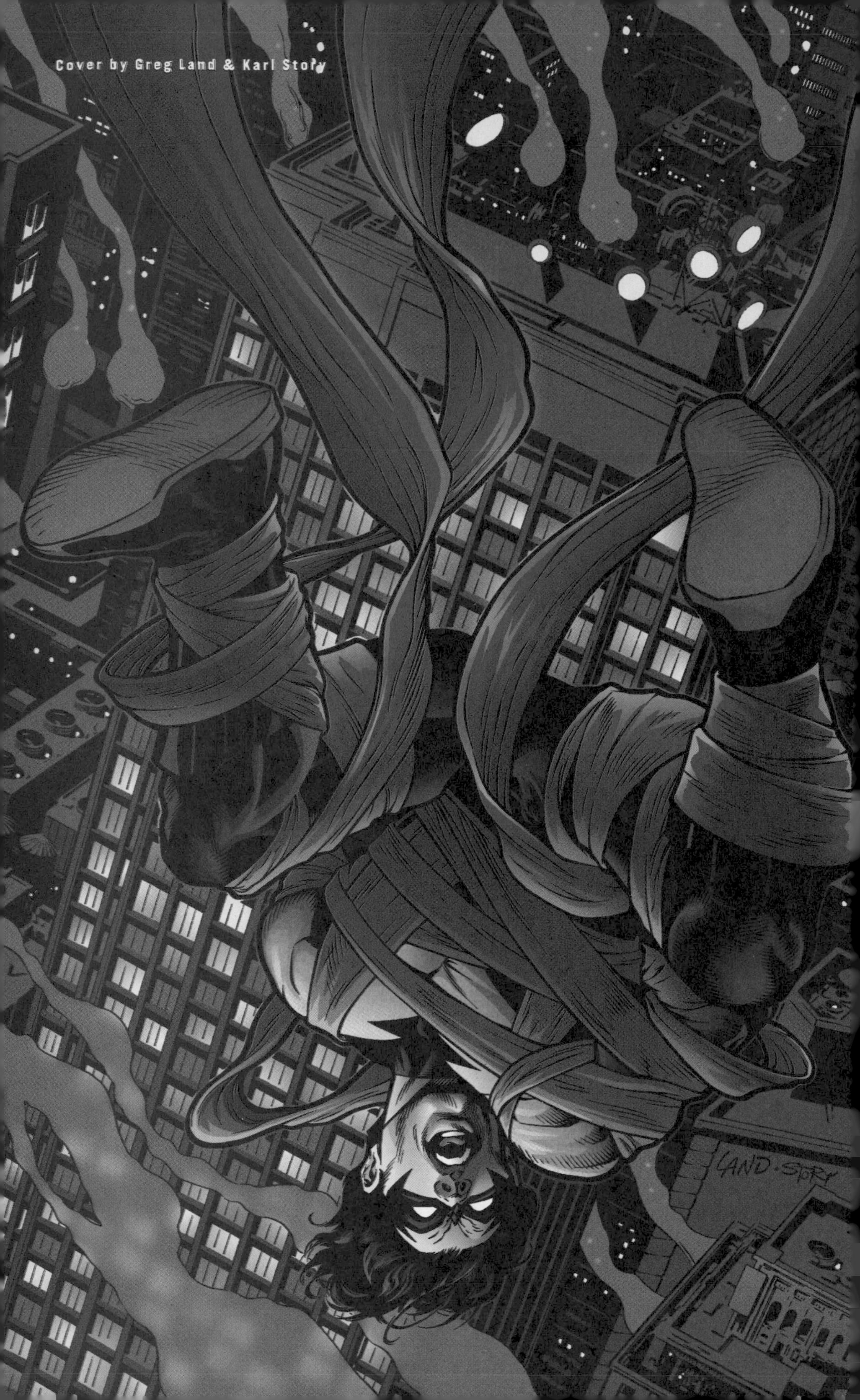
LAND·STORY

Cover by Greg Land & Karl Story

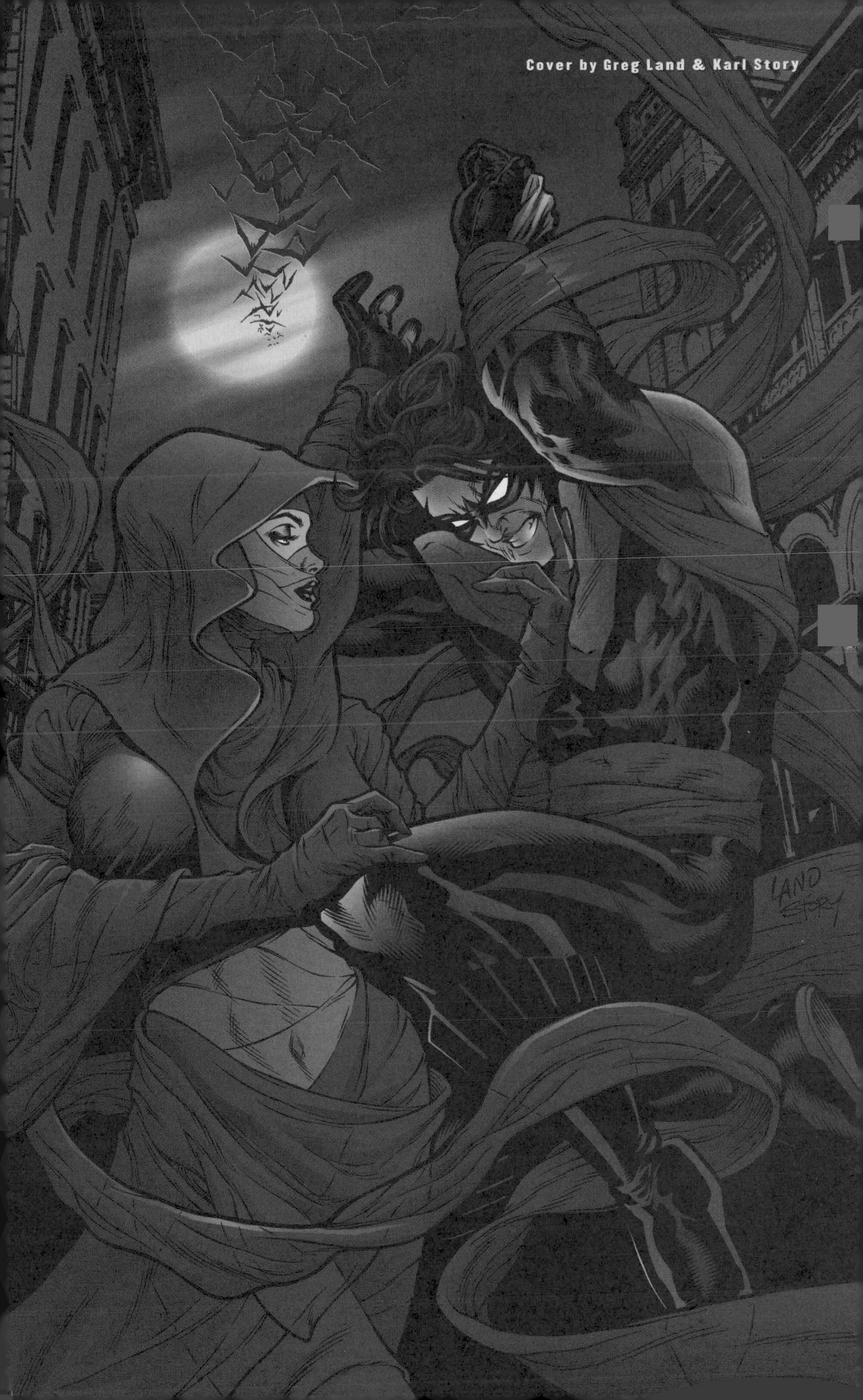
LAND
STORY

Cover by Greg Land & Karl Story

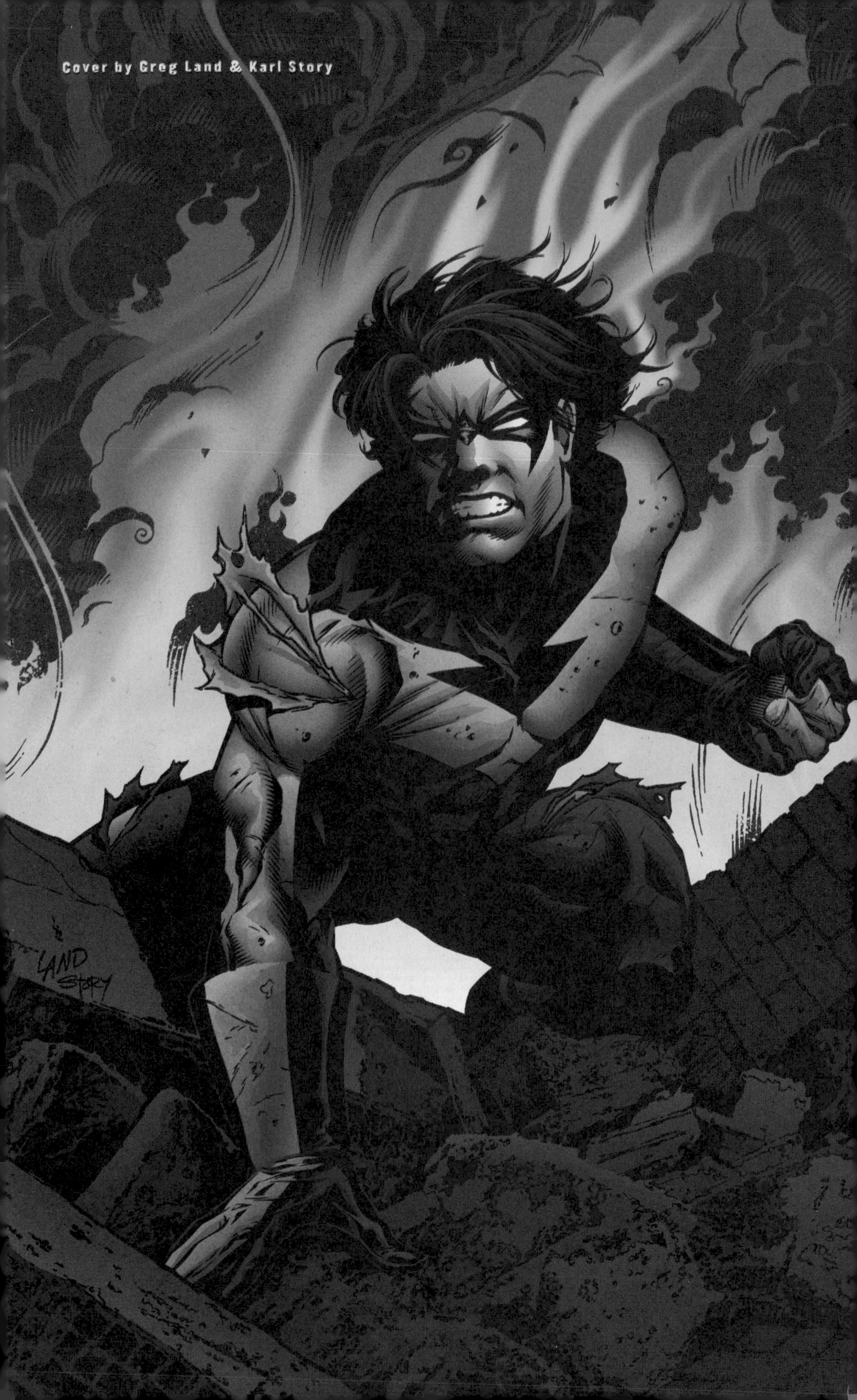
LAND
STORY
Cover by Greg Land & Karl Story

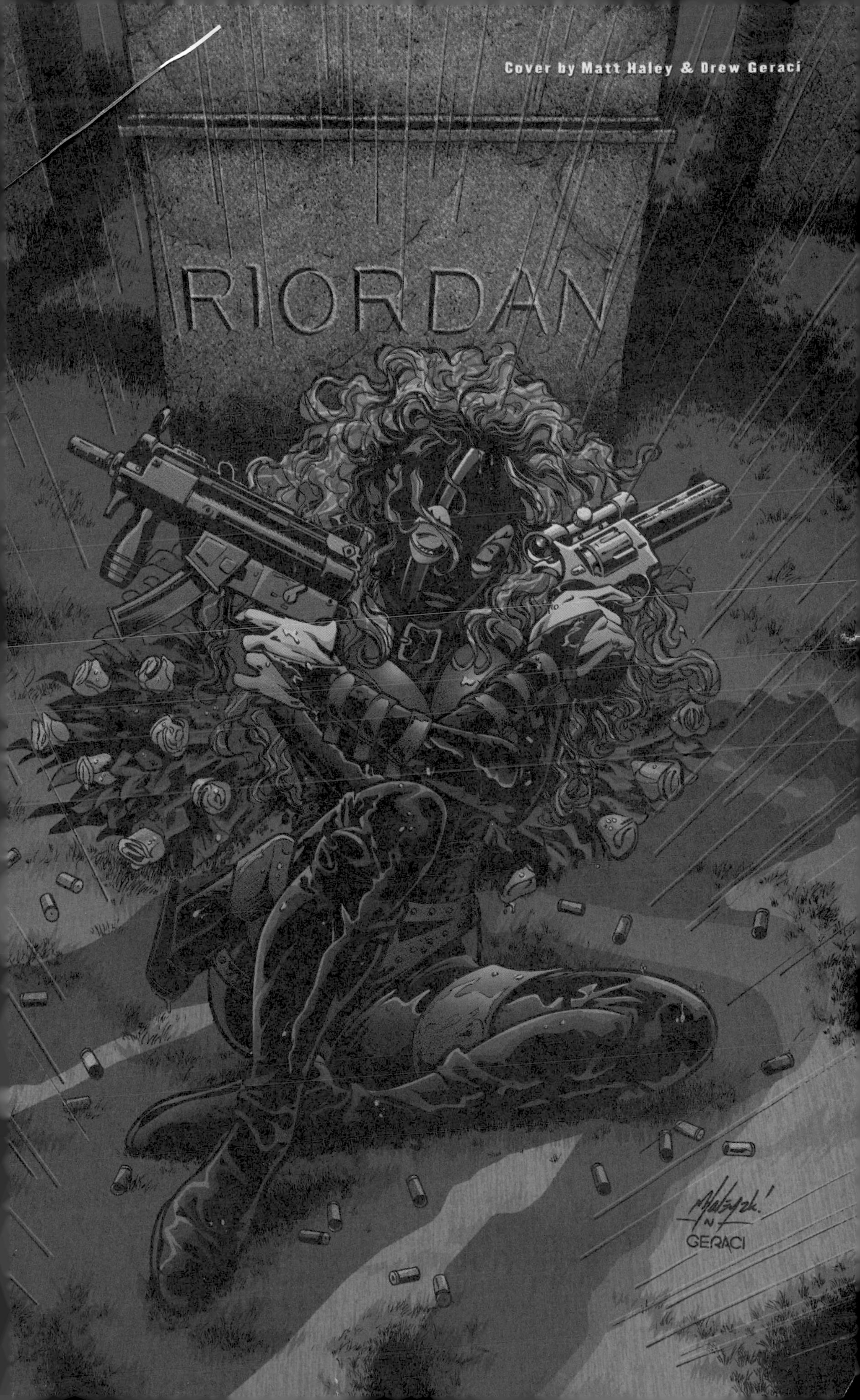
Cover by Matt Haley & Drew Geraci
RIORDAN
GERACI

# B A T M A N
## THE QUEST FOR JUSTICE CONTINUES IN THESE BOOKS FROM DC:

### FOR READERS OF ALL AGES

**THE BATMAN ADVENTURES**
K. Puckett/T. Templeton/
R. Burchett/various

**BATMAN BEYOND**
Hilary Bader/Rick Burchett/
various

**BATMAN: THE DARK KNIGHT ADVENTURES**
Kelley Puckett/Mike Parobeck/
Rick Burchett

**BATMAN: WAR ON CRIME**
Paul Dini/Alex Ross

### GRAPHIC NOVELS

**BATMAN: ARKHAM ASYLUM**
Suggested for mature readers
Grant Morrison/Dave McKean

**BATMAN: BLOODSTORM**
Doug Moench/Kelley Jones/
John Beatty

**BATMAN: THE CHALICE**
Chuck Dixon/John Van Fleet

**BATMAN: CRIMSON MIST**
Doug Moench/Kelley Jones/
John Beatty

**BATMAN/DRACULA: RED RAIN**
Doug Moench/Kelley Jones/
Malcolm Jones III

**BATMAN: FORTUNATE SON**
Gerard Jones/Gene Ha

**BATMAN: HARVEST BREED**
George Pratt

**BATMAN: THE KILLING JOKE**
Suggested for mature readers
Alan Moore/Brian Bolland/
John Higgins

**BATMAN: NIGHT CRIES**
Archie Goodwin/Scott Hampton

**BATMAN: NINE LIVES**
Dean Motter/Michael Lark

**BATMAN: SON OF THE DEMON**
Mike Barr/Jerry Bingham

**CATWOMAN:
SELINA'S BIG SCORE**
Darwyn Cooke

### COLLECTIONS

**BATMAN: A DEATH IN
THE FAMILY**
Jim Starlin/Jim Aparo/
Mike DeCarlo

**BATMAN: A LONELY PLACE
OF DYING**
Marv Wolfman/George Pérez/
various

**BATMAN BLACK AND WHITE
Vols. 1 & 2**
Various writers and artists

**BATMAN: BRUCE WAYNE —
MURDERER?**
Various writers and artists

**BATMAN: BRUCE WAYNE —
FUGITIVE Vol. 1**
Various writers and artists

**BATMAN: BRUCE WAYNE —
FUGITIVE Vol. 2**
Various writers and artists

**BATMAN: CATACLYSM**
Various writers and artists

**BATMAN: CHILD OF DREAMS**
Kia Asamiya

**BATMAN: DANGEROUS
DAMES & DEMONS**
Dini/Timm/various

**BATMAN: THE DARK KNIGHT
RETURNS**
Frank Miller/Klaus Janson/
Lynn Varley

**BATMAN: THE DARK KNIGHT
STRIKES AGAIN**
Frank Miller/Lynn Varley

**BATMAN: DARK KNIGHT
DYNASTY**
M. Barr/S. Hampton/G. Frank/
S. McDaniels/various

**BATMAN: DARK VICTORY**
Jeph Loeb/Tim Sale

**BATMAN: EVOLUTION**
Rucka/Martinbrough/Mitchell/
various

**BATMAN: GOTHIC**
Grant Morrison/Klaus Janson

**BATMAN: HAUNTED KNIGHT**
Jeph Loeb/Tim Sale

**BATMAN/HUNTRESS:
CRY FOR BLOOD**
Rucka/Burchett/T. Beatty

**BATMAN IN THE FIFTIES
BATMAN IN THE SIXTIES
BATMAN IN THE SEVENTIES**
Various writers and artists

**THE KNIGHTFALL Trilogy
BATMAN: KNIGHTFALL Part 1:
Broken Bat
BATMAN: KNIGHTFALL Part 2:
Who Rules the Night**

**BATMAN: KNIGHTFALL Part 3:
KnightsEnd**
Various writers and artists

**BATMAN: THE LONG HALLOWEEN**
Jeph Loeb/Tim Sale

**BATMAN: NO MAN'S LAND
Vols. 1 - 5**
Various writers and artists

**BATMAN: OFFICER DOWN**
Various writers and artists

**BATMAN: PRODIGAL**
Various writers and artists

**BATMAN: STRANGE
APPARITIONS**
S. Englehart/M. Rogers/
T. Austin/various

**BATMAN: SWORD OF AZRAEL**
Dennis O'Neil/Joe Quesada/
Kevin Nowlan

**BATMAN: TALES OF THE DEMON**
Dennis O'Neil/Neal Adams/
various

**BATMAN: VENOM**
Dennis O'Neil/Trevor Von Eeden/
various

**BATMAN VS. PREDATOR:
THE COLLECTED EDITION**
Dave Gibbons/Andy Kubert/
Adam Kubert

**BATMAN: YEAR ONE**
Frank Miller/David Mazzucchelli

**BATMAN: YEAR TWO —
FEAR THE REAPER**
Barr/Davis/McFarlane/various

**BATGIRL: A KNIGHT ALONE**
Puckett/D. Scott/Turnbull/
Campanella/various

**BATGIRL: SILENT RUNNING**
Puckett/Peterson/D. Scott/
Campanella

**BIRDS OF PREY**
Various writers and artists

**BIRDS OF PREY: OLD FRIENDS,
NEW ENEMIES**
Dixon/Land/Geraci/various

**CATWOMAN: THE DARK END
OF THE STREET**
Brubaker/Cooke/Allred

**THE GREATEST BATMAN
STORIES EVER TOLD Vol. 1**
Various writers and artists

**THE GREATEST JOKER
STORIES EVER TOLD**
Various writers and artists

**NIGHTWING: A KNIGHT
IN BLÜDHAVEN**
Dixon/McDaniel/Story

**NIGHTWING: ROUGH JUSTICE**
Dixon/McDaniel/Story

**NIGHTWING: LOVE AND
BULLETS**
Dixon/McDaniel/Story

**NIGHTWING: A DARKER
SHADE OF JUSTICE**
Dixon/McDaniel/Story

**NIGHTWING: THE HUNT
FOR ORACLE**
Dixon/Land/Guice/Zircher/various

**ROBIN: FLYING SOLO**
Dixon/Grummett/P. Jimenez/
various

**ROBIN: YEAR ONE**
Dixon/S. Beatty/Pulido/
Martin/Campanella

### ARCHIVE EDITIONS

**BATMAN ARCHIVES Vol. 1**
(DETECTIVE COMICS 27-50)
**BATMAN ARCHIVES Vol. 2**
(DETECTIVE COMICS 51-70)
**BATMAN ARCHIVES Vol. 3**
(DETECTIVE COMICS 71-86)
**BATMAN ARCHIVES Vol. 4**
(DETECTIVE COMICS 87-102)
**BATMAN ARCHIVES Vol. 5**
(DETECTIVE COMICS 103-119)
All by B. Kane/B. Finger/D. Sprang/
various

**BATMAN: THE DARK KNIGHT
ARCHIVES Vol. 1**
(BATMAN 1-4)
**BATMAN: THE DARK KNIGHT
ARCHIVES Vol. 2**
(BATMAN 5-8)
**BATMAN: THE DARK KNIGHT
ARCHIVES Vol. 3**
(BATMAN 9-12)
All by Bob Kane/Bill Finger/various

**BATMAN: THE DYNAMIC DUO
ARCHIVES Vol. 1**
(BATMAN 164-167,
DETECTIVE COMICS 327-333)
B. Kane/Giella/Finger/Broome/
Fox/various

**WORLD'S FINEST COMICS
ARCHIVES Vol. 1**
(SUPERMAN 76,
WORLD'S FINEST 71-85)
B. Finger/E. Hamilton/C. Swan/
Sprang/various

TO FIND MORE COLLECTED EDITIONS AND MONTHLY COMIC BOOKS FROM DC COMICS,
CALL 1-888-COMIC BOOK FOR THE NEAREST COMICS SHOP OR GO TO YOUR LOCAL BOOK STORE.

Visit us at www.dccomics.com